Gender and the Media

Gender and the Media

Rosalind Gill

polity

The right of Rosalind Gill to be identified as Author of this Work has been asserted in accordance with the UK Copyright, Designs and Patents Act 1988.

First published in 2007 by Polity Press
Reprinted 2007, 2008

Polity Press
65 Bridge Street
Cambridge CB2 1UR, UK.

Polity Press
350 Main Street
Malden, MA 02148, USA

ISBN-13: 978-07456-1273-7
ISBN-13: 978-07456-1915-6 (pb)

A catalogue record for this book is available from the British Library.

Typeset in 10.5 on 13pt Swift
by Servis Filmsetting Ltd, Manchester
Printed and bound in Great Britain by MPG Books Ltd, Bodmin, Cornwall

The publisher has used its best endeavours to ensure that the URLs for external websites referred to in this book are correct and active at the time of going to press. However, the publisher has no responsibility for the websites and can make no guarantee that a site will remain live or that the content is or will remain appropriate.

Every effort has been made to trace all copyright holders, but if any have been inadvertently overlooked the publishers will be pleased to include any necessary credits in any subsequent reprint or edition.

For further information on Polity, visit our website: www.polity.co.uk

Contents

Acknowledgements

This book has taken hundreds of years to write. Well, perhaps I exaggerate a tad, but it has certainly taken much longer than it should have done. In the manner of many first books it has been through drafts and re-drafts and radical rewritings in the pursuit of some illusory (or certainly elusive) perfection. Now that I've finished the final, imperfect version two feelings dominate: first there is puzzlement – is that *it*? Why on earth did it take me so *long*?; and secondly there is *relief* – relief that finally I will be able to respond to all those friendly and kindly meant inquiries about how the book is going with a conclusive 'it's done'. In short, I'll be able to go to parties again!

One of the consequences of taking so long to write a book is that the acknowledgements page reads a bit like a list of 'everyone who knows me'. First, I would like to thank all the people who have assisted me directly with research for this book – whether tracking down adverts, searching for newspaper articles, or sharing ideas about chick lit or lad mags. Special thanks to Elena Herdieckerhoff, Kamy Naficy, Karin Heisecke, Jennie Middleton, Rachel Lille, Samantha Reay, Jessica Pring Ellis, Matt Torney, Deborah Finding, Naureen Khan and Danielle Bikhazi for their invaluable contributions, both practical and intellectual.

Several people read all or parts of the manuscript in draft form and I would like to express my gratitude for their incisive and insightful comments. Special appreciation to the wonderful women in my writing group (Rachel Falmagne, Lesley Hoggart, Ann Phoenix, Bruna Seu and Merl Storr) who not only made constructive criticism such a positive experience, but also offered a different vision of academic labour and a pleasurable intellectual 'home' in the cafes and bars of Bloomsbury. Angela McRobbie read and commented on the entire manuscript and I'm grateful for her feedback and encouragement, as well as the example of her own work which I have found consistently thoughtful and inspiring. Sylvia Chant's sheer energy and *joie de vivre* has made her a pleasure to know and I'm grateful for her unstinting enthusiasm for this project, and for fitting in comments on chapters while flying between Costa Rica, Mexico, Gambia and the Philippines.

Thanks also to Sadie Wearing, Dee Amy-Chinn, Christina Scharff, Paul Stenner and Dimitris Papadopoulos for helpful comments on sections of this book.

In addition to those generous people who have read and commented on parts of the book, my acknowledgements would not be complete without an expression of gratitude to a number of other people who have helped, supported and inspired me in my academic career so far. Despite its insularity, intellectual work is always a collective project and it would be impossible to thank everyone who has sparked new ideas or provoked me to think differently. But I would like to mention the following people for particular appreciation: Michael Billig, Margaret Wetherell, Stuart Hall, Jonathan Potter, Steve Woolgar and Valerie Walkerdine. Thank you.

The LSE has been a stimulating environment in which to work, and I have benefited from its excellent library, as well as from the many outstanding international scholars who provide a feast of lectures and seminars every day of the week. I'm grateful to the exceptionally inter-esting and talented students who have taken my Masters course in Gender and Media – many of them media practitioners themselves, and all of them set to make a positive difference in the world. I've been fortunate to have wonderful colleagues in the LSE's Gender Institute, and in the Sociology department at Goldsmiths where I worked previ-ously. I would like to highlight Clare Hemmings, Diane Perrons, Karen Throsby, Elisabeth Kelan and Caroline Ramozonoglu for intellectual nourishment and supportive collegiality.

Polity Press has been fabulous, and I would like to thank Gill Motley and Andrea Drugan for being a real pleasure to work with, and for good-humouredly tolerating more delays than a British train service, as I went for the unofficial award of 'most postponed manuscript in the history of academic publishing'. Thanks also, Andrea, for embrac-ing the 'crazy' fridge idea – instead of having me committed!

Two other people deserve special mention for their absolutely crucial but invisible contributions to this project. Gabrielle Bikhazi's consistently wonderful, loving care for Katarina over the past three years has freed up many of the hours I've spent working on this book. Gaby – you are a very special person and I hope you know how appre-ciated you are. The other 'behind the scenes' support has come from Hazel Johnstone, departmental manager of the Gender Institute and organizer-extraordinaire. Thank you, Hazel, for help and kindnesses that are literally too numerous to mention.

Finally, I would like to thank my dear friends, my adopted 'family' in London (and Nottingham). To Andy Pratt, Bruna Seu, Wilma Mangabeira, Paulo Wrobel, Ann Phoenix, Chris Phipps, Sylvia Chant and Veronica Forwood: thank you for everything – your love of life, generosity of spirit, sense of humour, for being there during all the bad times as well as the good, and for all the wonderful conversations, delicious food and red wine we have shared – and will, I hope, continue to share.

This book is dedicated to my mother, Janet Gill, and to the memory of my father, Michael Gill. Their love, care, humanity and passion for social justice has been a shining light throughout my life. It is also dedicated to Thomas and Katarina, with love.

Introduction

THIS is a book about the representation of gender in the media in contemporary Western societies. It is written against the backdrop of phenomenally rapid change: changes in gender relations; transformations in media technologies, regulatory frameworks, content, ownership and control, and globalization; and theoretical 'revolutions' in the approaches used to make sense of gender representations. *Gender and the Media* aims to freeze the frame, press the pause button, or hit the refresh key to explore how the media today construct femininity, masculinity and gender relations, and to think about the kinds of theoretical concepts and cultural politics that might be needed to engage with these changes.

The book is born out of an interest in the extraordinary contradictoriness of constructions of gender in today's media: confident expressions of 'girl power' sit alongside reports of 'epidemic' levels of anorexia and body dysmorphia; graphic tabloid reports of rape are placed cheek by jowl with adverts for lap-dancing clubs and telephone sex lines; lad magazines declare the 'sex war' over, while reinstating beauty contests and championing new, ironic modes of sexism; and there are regular moral panics about the impact on men of the new, idealized male body imagery, while the re-sexualization of women's bodies in public space goes virtually unremarked upon. Everywhere, it seems, feminist ideas have become a kind of common sense, yet feminism has never been more bitterly repudiated.

Some commentators see in this evidence of a powerful backlash against feminism (Faludi 1992). Germaine Greer (1999), for instance, argues that today's popular culture is significantly less feminist than that of thirty years ago, and Imelda Whelehan suggests that we have entered an era of 'retro-sexism' in which representations of women, 'from the banal to the downright offensive' are being 'defensively reinvented against cultural changes in women's lives' (2000: 11). By contrast, others regard the media as increasingly influenced by feminism, or, indeed, as becoming feminist. David Gauntlett argues 'the traditional view of a woman as a housewife or low status worker has been kick-boxed out of the picture by the feisty, successful "girl power" icons' (2002: 247). The media, he argues, offer popular feminism which is like 'a radio-friendly remix of a multilayered song, with the most exciting bits sampled and some of the dense stuff left out' (2002: 252). Meanwhile, Angela McRobbie points to the 'enormous energy in the way in which sexual politics now bursts across our television screens . . . From Newsnight to Oprah . . . [F]emale independence has entered into contemporary common sense' (1999: 126).

It seems to me that both these arguments are true. On the one hand feminist ideas are increasingly taken for granted across a range of media and genres, vibrant girlzines spring up all over the world, and the Web is home to an enormous diversity of feminist ideas ranging from support over breast cancer to 'babes against the bomb'. But on the other, boring and predictable patterns of sexism persist – such as the continued invisibility of older women on television, or the depressingly narrow range of depictions of black women – and newer representational practices are often far from hopeful – for example, the rise of 'porno chic', the growth of unabashed 'laddism', and the vitriolic attacks in press and magazines on women who fail to live up to increasingly narrow normative requirements of feminine appearance. It is precisely the contradictoriness of contemporary representations of gender in the media that makes the field so difficult and challenging.

Added to this picture of paradox and complexity, there is another issue: like the media, gender relations and feminist ideas are themselves changing and in flux. There is no stable, unchanging feminist perspective from which to make a cool appraisal of contemporary gender in the media. Rather, feminist ideas are constantly transforming in response to different critiques, to new or previously excluded constituencies, to younger generations, to new theoretical ideas, and to the experience of various kinds of struggle. There is no single feminism, but instead many, diverse feminisms. If media representations of gender have changed, then so too have the feminist ideas used to understand and critique them. And, likewise, gender relations are constantly changing. Indeed, we are often told that Western democracies are experiencing nothing short of a 'genderquake', so profound are the current transformations.

Gender and the Media is an attempt to make sense of this picture of flux and transformation. The book has three main aims. First, it seeks to provide an analysis of the contemporary representations of gender in the media in Western societies, in all their messy contradictoriness. Its particular focus is upon how media constructions of gender have changed in recent years in response to feminist critiques and wider social transformations, and, to that end, it looks in detail at five types of media where different kinds of change can be seen very clearly: news, advertising, talk shows, magazines and contemporary screen and paperback romances. In relation to each it is concerned not only with the representation of women, but also with constructions of masculinity, and how contemporary gender relations are depicted. How should we make sense of the increasing presence of eroticized images of the male body across the media landscape? What are we to make of the shift from discourses of romance to those of sex and celebrity in young women's magazines? Are talk shows like *Oprah* and *Ricki* redrawing the boundaries between the public and the private? What impact, if any, has the increasing number of female journalists had on 'news'? What kinds of constructions of heterosexual relationships are to be found in 'chick lit' and 'lad lit' and how different are these from traditional romances? These are just some of the questions asked.

Secondly, this book is concerned with the theoretical tools available for analysing media representations. It aims to interrogate some of the key terms that have been used to study gender in media texts, since scholars and activists first engaged with media representations of gender. *Gender and the Media* both acknowledges its debt to the vibrant and heterogeneous feminist media scholarship since the 1970s, and also seeks to question the relevance of some central concepts to critique in today's mediated world. For example, how useful is the notion of 'objectification' in a mediascape in which far from being presented as passive objects women are increasingly depicted as active, desiring sexual subjects? What does it mean to talk about the 'feminization' of an area (e.g. news)? Are the notions of 'backlash', 'retro-sexism' and 'postfeminism' helpful for making sense of contemporary media representations? How should the pervasive irony and playfulness of today's media be understood?

Thirdly, *Gender and the Media* is interested in cultural politics. It seeks to raise questions about what forms of political or cultural intervention are appropriate and effective to challenge particular constructions of gender, in a postmodern age in which critiques are routinely reflexively incorporated into media products and in which much sexism comes in an ironic guise which rebuffs easy protest: 'that is not a sexist image', we are told, 'it is a hilarious, knowing send-up of an old-fashioned "dumb blonde" stereotypes'! Whilst an earlier generation of feminist media activists put stickers or daubed graffiti on advertising images deemed to insult or trivialize women, today, as often as not, advertisers already orientate to potential critique within the adverts themselves – whether from feminists or simply from media-savvy and 'sign fatigued' consumers, weary of the relentless bombardment by consumer images. How, in this context, might people concerned or angry about media representations of men or women, lesbians or gays, mount an effective political critique? What kind of feminist cultural politics is appropriate for the new media age? I cannot claim exhaustively to answer these questions here, but by providing an analysis of contemporary media representations and pointing to some of the new ways in which gender is figured I hope to draw attention to the ways in which older critical languages may fail to engage with gender in the media today, and to point to spaces where a new cultural politics might be developed.

These three themes – constructions of gender, the theoretical tools for analysing gender in the media, and feminist cultural politics – are what animate this book. Above all, the book deals with what is new and distinctive about representations of gender today compared with earlier eras, what concepts are needed for making sense of this, and what kinds of cultural intervention might constitute effective engagements in the contemporary media landscape.

The book opens with a review of the central themes and concerns of research about gender and the media. Chapter 1 charts different theoretical and political investments in feminist studies of media texts, and examines the turn to audience studies. Although this book is limited to examining constructions of gender in the media, and does not report on audience research, the notion that texts are polysemic and can be interpreted in multiple ways is central to the analyses presented here. The implications of the shift away from textual determinism or hypodermic conceptions of meaning cannot be overestimated. The chapter also discusses how feminist perspectives have changed as a consequence of critiques by black and Third World women, and the impact of post-structuralism and postmodernism. The final part of the chapter considers some of the central debates about the representation of gender in the media.

The second chapter is more methodological in focus and examines the key approaches that have been used to analyse gender in media texts, for example content analysis, semiotics and discourse analysis, discussing their strengths and weaknesses. It also introduces ideas from postmodernism, postcolonial studies and queer theory, as they have been used in media studies. Together the first two chapters form a foundation for the remainder of the book, which is concerned with looking in detail at five broad areas.

Chapter 3, Advertising and Postfeminism, both reviews earlier studies of gender in advertisements and provides a new analysis of how advertising is changing. Several themes of postfeminist advertising are discussed, including the prevalence of gender reversals and revenge ads, the development of images of empowered, (hetero) sexually active young women, and the growth of 'queer chic' in advertising.

Chapter 4 looks at news and gender. Set against the context of journalism's transformation from a public service to a market-led product, the chapter examines the rise of 'infotainment' or 'newszak' and considers the gender dimensions of this shift. What makes something newsworthy? How are women represented in the news? Is news being dumbed down? And what is meant by the 'feminization' of journalism? A detailed case study of the reporting of sexual violence provides an opportunity for evaluating the continuities as well as changes in news about gender.

Television talk shows are the subject of chapter 5. The chapter distinguishes between audience discussion programmes, the therapeutic genre and 'trash' or confrontation talk shows, and considers whether talk shows constitute a new 'public sphere' which today eclipses political institutions as a site of significant public debate. Notions of the talk show as the new 'confessional' are also discussed and the chapter examines whether talk shows might be empowering for marginalized groups by giving voice to people not usually heard on mainstream TV and allowing the articulation of anti-normative messages.

Chapter 6 focuses on magazines. It describes some of the shifts in recent years in magazines aimed at girls and women, in particular the adoption of a feminist register, the emphasis upon celebrity, and the promotion of the sexualized body as the key site of femininity. It also examines in detail the rise of the 'lad magazines' since the mid-1990s and asks how this should be understood – as a response to feminism, a reaction against 'de-sexualized' new man scripts or a distinctive new classed and racialized articulation of masculinity.

The last of the substantive chapters considers the genre of romance, which has shown remarkable resilience and staying power in the face of significant social structural shifts and ongoing transformations of intimacy. Focusing on *Bridget Jones's Diary* and the rise of 'chick lit' the chapter examines constructions of gender, 'race' and sexuality and asks in what ways contemporary popular depictions of heterosexual love are different from earlier romances. These texts are interesting because they are structured both by conventional formulas and by an engagement with feminism. Do they offer new versions of heterosexual partnerships? How different are their constructions of femininity and masculinity compared with Harlequin or Mills & Boon novels? Why and in what way have singleness and the body become such preoccupations? The chapter concludes with a discussion of two popular TV shows – *Ally McBeal* and *Sex and the City* – to put forward an argument about a new postfeminist sensibility.

This argument is developed in the conclusion, which draws together the strands of the book and attempts to provide an assessment of some of the ways in which the representation of gender in the media is changing – partly in response to feminism. The concluding chapter also returns to questions about cultural politics, and, in the light of the arguments provided in the book, asks what kinds of intervention are needed today to engage with and challenge representations of gender in the media in order to produce gender relations that are more equal, open, generous and hopeful.

1

Gender and the Media

Introduction: Representations Matter

WE live in a world that is stratified along lines of gender, race, ethnicity, class, age, disability, sexuality and location, and in which the privileges, disadvantages and exclusions associated with such categories are unevenly distributed. We also live in a world which is increasingly saturated by media and information and communication technologies. In many respects, the last four decades of research in feminist media studies has been an attempt to explore the relationship between these two facts.

Starting from the proposition that representations matter, feminist analyses of the media have been animated by the desire to understand how images and cultural constructions are connected to patterns of inequality, domination and oppression. Sometimes this has involved examining representations and textual practices in some detail. Sometimes it has emphasized the active, creative negotiations that audiences make with texts. Sometimes the pleasures offered by the media have been foregrounded, and at other times their ideological impact has been stressed. Occasionally, researchers have gone 'behind-the-scenes' to look at the production of particular media, or at the political economy of media industries which means that some media products are made, while others are not even dreamed. Taken together this research has produced a field that is vibrant, exciting and diverse. It is a field that strives to be both theoretically engaged and empirically driven, and which produces rigorous analyses in the context of ethical and political commitments to creating a more just world.

The study of gender and media is extraordinarily heterogeneous. Researchers may agree that cultural representations constitute an important site for examination and struggle, but on all else they disagree. The field is thus characterized by a plurality of different approaches and perspectives: different methodologies, different theoretical perspectives, different epistemological commitments, different understandings of power, different conceptualizations of the relationship between representations and 'reality', and different understandings of how media images relate to individuals' sense of identity and subjectivity. A feeling for the differences and debates should emerge throughout this book, and the diversity of different approaches is dealt with in detail in chapter 2. In this chapter I want to offer an overview of the field, looking at some of its central themes and preoccupations and examining how and why the study of gender and the media has changed. Of course, this review is a partial and interested one, and its focus is upon laying the foundations to think about how representations have changed since the early studies of gender and media in the 1960s and 1970s, how the available critical vocabularies have been transformed, and what kind of feminist cultural critique is now possible.

The chapter is divided into five parts. In the first part I will look at the assumptions that underpinned early feminist studies of the representation of women in the media and will highlight a number of key features of this work, including its connection to and embeddedness in feminist activist communities and its sense of certainty and confidence about both the meaning of images and the possibility of change. This section will then go on to consider the impact of more complex theories of meaning coming from post-structuralist theory, psychoanalysis and deconstruction, and will also examine the 'turn to pleasure'.

The second section of the chapter is concerned with the development of audience studies, as a reaction against problematic notions of textual determinism which posited the viewer/reader/hearer as entirely passive. Three types of audience research are considered: focused on interpretations, pleasures, and the use of media as (domestic) communication technologies. This section also raises dilemmas about the role of the feminist cultural critic: should she be claiming respect for women's pleasures or criticizing gender ideologies; celebrating women's choices or formulating alternative representational strategies? What is the relationship of the feminist intellectual to women as a group?

Section three turns to feminism itself and argues that this too has transformed over the past decades in response to black women's critiques, to post-structuralist theory, to the growth of interest in masculinity and the arrival of queer theory on the intellectual scene.

The fourth section is concerned with feminist cultural politics and activism and explores the diverse ways in which feminist analyses of media representations have been translated into demands for change.

Finally, section five, the conclusion of the chapter, raises questions about the efficacy of contemporary critical vocabularies for both analysing and contesting media representations, briefly discussing different views of irony, objectification and the incorporation or commodification of feminist ideas, all of which are taken up and discussed in more detail later in the book. Overall, the chapter seeks to highlight the differences and debates within the study of gender and the media and to give a sense of the ongoing transformations in this field as critical, theoretical and political perspectives change alongside profound changes in the media themselves.

Representations of Women in the Media

The 1970s and all that

Those involved in the tide of feminist creativity, thinking and activism that swept the Western world in the late 1960s and 1970s faced a challenge that earlier women's movements had not known: a world dominated by media. Unlike their mothers and grandmothers, second-wave feminists were bombarded daily by representations of womanhood and gender relations in news and magazines, on radio and TV, in film and on billboards. Not surprisingly, then, the media became a major focus of feminist research, critique and intervention.

Early feminist media critique came from a number of different sources. Women working or studying in universities within the newly emerging disciplines of cultural studies or communication studies became increasingly aware of the 'blind spot' that characterized these fields in relation to gender. Whilst research from the 1960s and 1970s had a significant interest in the ideological nature of media (particularly news), it was largely defined in a way that excluded questions about the portrayal of women. It focused instead on topics such as the reporting of demonstrations and industrial disputes. The issues of class and class conflict were paramount – reflecting the early influence of Marxism – and research rarely engaged with gender, race or sexuality (CCCS Women's group 1978). Women in universities found that they were up against the 'male as norm' problem, in which women were frequently entirely invisible, and men were taken to stand for the whole human population.

A second strand of critique came from women who worked within journalism or broadcasting and were concerned about the lack of opportunities for women working within the media. They argued that the lack of interesting fictional roles, the absence of female newsreaders, and the poor representation of women within senior media positions had a profound impact upon how women were seen in society as a whole. Organizations such as Women in Media and the Equality Working Party of the National Union of Journalists in the UK played a key part in promoting awareness of issues about the representation of women and campaigning for change.

Meanwhile, outside both the academy and media industries, other groups of women were angry about what they saw as the narrow range of patronizing or demeaning stereotypes through which women were represented. A number of feminist groups were established in Europe, Australia and the USA (and elsewhere) whose aim was to monitor the way that women were portrayed, to campaign against sexist advertisements, and to challenge 'degrading' presentations of women, such as televisual events like the Miss World competition.

One of the things that is striking about this moment was the degree of congruence and overlap between the agendas of academics, media workers and activists. Indeed, one of the earliest and most famous studies of the representation of women in advertising in the USA was conducted by the National Organization of Women (NOW) and published in the *New York Times Magazine* (Hennessee 1972). It relied on 'ordinary women' from all over the USA analysing and coding television adverts. The study analysed more than 1,200 commercials over an eighteen-month period. It found that more than one-third of adverts showed women as domestic agents who were dependent upon men, and nearly half portrayed women as 'household functionaries'. The study also reported many examples of women being depicted as 'decorative objects' and portrayed as 'unintelligent'.

Many other studies from this era were conducted using a similar content analytic strategy. Essentially content analysis involves counting the number of instances of particular kinds of portrayal – such as the number of women relative to men, or the number of times women in adverts or dramas are shown in the kitchen or bedroom – to produce quantitative statistical data (see chapter 2 for more discussion). The advantages of this approach are that it is quick, cheap and produces high-status quantitative results. As the NOW study demonstrated, it can also be done by anyone after a minimum of training, and produces data that are hard-hitting and useful for campaigning purposes.

Not all gender and media research in the 1970s relied upon content analysis, however. Some researchers were extremely critical of the limitations of this form of analysis – attacking it for its problematic 'realist' assumptions, a preoccupation with only the manifest content of representations, and a focus on single images – usually well-worn stereotypes – rather than broader structures of meaning (Cowie 1978; Gledhill 1978; Baehr 1980; Jaddou and Williams 1981). In Europe, two other traditions of work developed in the 1970s – semiotic analysis and ideological analysis. This research did not rely for its force upon contrasts between representations and 'reality' but instead was concerned with how texts operate to produce meanings which reproduce dominant ideologies of gender (e.g. McRobbie 1977; Williamson 1978; Winship 1978).

Looking back from the vantage point of the twenty-first century, all this work is notable not only for building the foundations of feminist media studies, but also for the extraordinary (by today's academic standards) *confidence* of the analyses produced. Reviewing a decade of studies in 1978, Gaye Tuchman (1978) unequivocally entitled her article 'the symbolic annihilation of women in the mass media', and wrote of how women were being destroyed by a combination of 'absence', 'trivialization' and 'condemnation'. Such clear evaluations were not unique and were accompanied by similarly robust calls to action – whether these were voiced as demands for more women in the industry, campaigns for 'positive images' or 'guerrilla interventions' into billboard advertisements. Writing about this period of research on gender and the media, Angela McRobbie (1999) has characterized it as one of 'angry repudiation'.

Beyond transmission: instabilities of meaning

By the late 1980s 'angry repudiation' had largely given way to something more equivocal and complex. As Myra Macdonald (1995) has noted, one of the reasons for this is that media content changed dramatically over this period. The notion that the media offered a relatively stable template of femininity to which to aspire gave way to a much more plural and fragmented set of signifiers of gender. There was a new playfulness in media representations, a borrowing of codes between different genres, and a growing awareness and interest in processes of image construction, as evidenced in the increasing number of programmes which featured humourous outtakes from films, home video compilations, and behind-the-scenes programmes about the making of films, adverts and TV series. Overall, media output was shaped by producers and consumers who were increasingly 'media-savvy' and familiar with the terms of cultural critique, including feminism (Goldman 1992).

Paralleling this change in media content was a profound shift in the theoretical languages available to media scholars. Liesbet Van Zoonen (1994) has argued that despite the significant differences between content analysis, semiotics and ideological analysis, these positions all relied upon a *transmission model* of the media: a view that the media are agents of social control conveying stereotypical and ideological values about women and femininity. This view was challenged and disrupted by the arrival of post-structuralism onto the intellectual scene: a collection of ideas loosely associated with the writings of Derrida, Foucault and Lacan. There is not space to explore these thinkers' ideas in any detail here (but see chapter 2 for a longer discussion). Their impact on feminist media studies was felt largely in three ways.

First, this body of writing gave weight to the critique of realism that was already underway within feminist media studies. Indictment of media content for its bias or distortion relied on the notion of an unproblematic distinction between 'representations' and 'reality' that – in post-structuralist terms – is unsustainable: being premised on a notion of some pure, unmediated access to reality. In practice, as Charlotte Brunsdon (1987) has argued, calls for more realistic representations of gender are usually calls for one's own version of reality to be depicted. Moreover, 'more feminist' images might be perceived as thin and propagandist by many audiences because they do not have the familiarity or easy-recognizability of other more stereotypical representations. Rather than calling for a hall of mirrors in the media, calls for realism might best be reformulated as attempts to create greater diversity in representations of women – in a context in which most women who appear in the media are young, white, able-bodied, middle-class, apparently heterosexual and conventionally attractive (Macdonald 1995).

In place of the view of the media as reflecting reality, research drawing on post-structuralist frameworks argued that the media were involved in constructing reality. Quite literally they produced and constituted understandings, subjectivities and versions of the world. This insight extended to gender: rather than there being a pre-existing reality to the meaning of the categories masculine and feminine, the media were involved in actively producing gender. In the words of Theresa de Lauretis (1989), cinema, television, magazines are 'technologies of gender' (as well as of 'race', class, and other differences): the representation of gender *is* its construction. (A discussion of how Judith Butler's work extended this notion is found in chapter 2.)

This constructionist argument connects to a second impact of post-structuralism on feminist media studies: namely a developing interest in identity, subjectivity and desire. This represented a break with the traditional notion of the unified rational subject, and suggested that subjectivity was split, fragmented and contradictory. Femininity and masculinity were thus conceived of as shifting and subject to change; ongoing discursive constructions rather than fixed positions. In film studies and analyses of visual culture this led to developing interest in how texts positioned spectators. In the less psychoanalytically influenced world of media studies it was felt more powerfully as a 'turn to discourse' and an interest in the discursive construction of gender and sexuality. (Queer theory is discussed in chapter 2.)

Thirdly, post-structuralist ideas destabilized conventional notions of meaning. Building on the semiotic idea of chains of signification,

Derrida's work pointed to the ways that meaning could resist fixity and could be endlessly deferred. In post-structuralist theory meaning is never single, univocal or total, but rather is fluid, ambiguous and contradictory: a site of ongoing conflict and contestation. One of the issues this raised for studies of gender in the media was how, then, to identify representations as sexist or progressive. Was their meaning completely open? This remains a central tension in the field with ongoing debates about how particular images should be read. As notions of irony, parody and pastiche abound, such dilemmas have become even more complex: in the last few years, images that for some commentators represent crude and offensive stereotypes have been reclaimed as ironic, playful or even subversive comments or send-ups.

Finally post-structuralism called into question the 'innocence' of feminism, asking it to acknowledge its 'will to power', a point that had particular resonances with black women's critique of the ways that the feminist knowledge could be used to support attacks on the black population, for example in racist immigration policies (see later in this chapter). One can think also of how feminist-sounding ideas about women's oppression under the Taliban regime in Afghanistan were used by the Bush administration to justify bombing that country.

Media pleasures

If the language for critical evaluation of texts changed in the late 1980s, then feminist media studies was also transformed by what we might call the 'turn to pleasure'. This had a number of determinants. At a general level it grew out of the collapse in the notion of a straightforward, unproblematic distinction between high and popular culture that is associated with postmodernism and with the increasing institutional respectability of media and cultural studies (Jameson 1984; Foster 1985; Featherstone 1991). This challenged traditional notions of aesthetic value and argued that it was as meaningful to study Bob Dylan as John Keats, as one famous discussion put it (Hare 1992). It was connected with radical critiques of the artistic and literary 'canon' and with a desire to democratize what was seen by some as a white, male, elitist notion of 'culture'.

Another set of influences on the turn to pleasure came from the growing anger amongst feminist writers that media forms enjoyed by women were ignored, or condemned as trivial and uninteresting. This was not just a matter of academics ignoring popular culture; a specifically gendered dynamic was in play: it was understood as the dismissal of women's culture. Writing about her decision to study soap operas, for example, Christine Geraghty (1991) argued that programmes enjoyed by so many women should not be ignored and were worthy of attention simply because they offered so much pleasure to female audiences. The lack of attention to what were sometimes (problematically) known as 'women's genres' was regarded as part of a more general double standard which always worked to ignore or disparage women's interests: the time had come to 'rescue' these and accord them some proper attention and respect.

Alongside these factors there was also increasing frustration at the straitjacketing effect of critical readings of texts and what was perceived by some as the tedious monotony of their depressing findings about sexism in the media. For some writers, the reduction of studies of the media to studies of the working of gender ideologies constituted too restricted and impoverished an understanding. It did not even begin to address the multiple, contradictory and pleasurable ways in which media played a part in people's lives (Brown 1990). For others, a focus on pleasure was needed not to counterbalance the focus on ideology, but to deepen understandings of it: without knowing how texts address profound unmet desires or offer pleasures, a full understanding of the workings of ideology in the media was not deemed possible (Modleski 1982; Radway 1984).

The move was also given impetus by the 'guilty prefaces phenomenon'. This was the tendency of feminist critics to start their books or articles by professing of their (often secret) enjoyment of the texts under consideration (e.g. glossy magazines or soap operas) before proceeding with an ideological deconstruction in which pleasure would never be mentioned again (Winship 1987). As Jean Grimshaw put it, 'it is perfectly possible to agree in one's head that certain images of women might be reactionary or damaging or oppressive while remaining committed to them in emotion or desire' (1999: 99).

One of the earliest and most significant attempts to take pleasure seriously is to be found in Tania Modleski's (1982) *Loving with a Vengeance*, which analysed soap operas, Gothic novels and Harlequin romances. Positioned partly as a critique of earlier feminist writing on romance which dismissed it variously as a seductive trap to make male domination more palatable, a distraction (from women's struggle for equality) or a kind of false consciousness, Modleski used psychoanalytic theory to attempt to theorize the kinds of pleasure offered to women by these forms. Talking about popular romances, Modleski argued that they are not simply escapist fantasies designed to dope women but fictions that engage in complex and contradictory ways with real problems – offering temporary, magical, fantasy or symbolic solutions (see chapter 7 for detailed discussion).

Modleski's book was a *tour de force* which had a dramatic impact on the entire way romance was understood. Nevertheless it is worth pointing out that her thesis about the pleasures of soaps and other fictions was based entirely on her own textual reading and did not include any form of research with audiences or readers. This became the pattern for the wave of work that followed on soaps, dramas, quiz shows and music videos (Fiske 1987, 1990; Brown 1990; Geraghty 1991). Essentially, the turn to pleasure was a shift from reading texts for the purpose of uncovering gendered ideologies to reading them to speculate about gendered pleasures.

The shift was valuable in opening up more complex and nuanced understandings of texts and in widening scholarly engagement with the media in ways that went beyond simple critique. Some writing, like Modleski's, emphasized the significance of fantasy and desire in understanding how people related to media texts, and opened up new ways of thinking about identification/dis-identification (see also Blackman and Walkerdine 1996; Walkerdine 1997). Similarly the emphasis upon understanding pleasure contributed to fresh thinking about realism, and the pluralizing of the term to include the importance of emotional realism (Brunsdon 2000).

Too often, however, research on media pleasures remained trapped within an old notion of textual determinism. The pleasures were to be found encoded in the text, waiting to be discovered.

Another problem with this turn was its reliance on essentialist notions of gender. This operated at a number of levels: in assumptions about what constitute 'women's genres'; in the unexamined use of phrases such as 'women's culture', 'women's language' and 'feminine discourse'; in the lack of sensitivity to differences *between* women; and in the use of analytic concepts that rely on an assumed common gender sensibility – sometimes constructed in the most crude way, such as attributing women's liking for soap operas to similarities with their experience of orgasm (multiple, rather than involving one single climax) or, more socially, to their fit with the rhythms of domestic routines (Fiske 1987).

Perhaps paradoxically, a further tension in the literature on media pleasures is its desire to stay related to critique. Despite criticizing the impoverishing effects of feminist media studies' preoccupation with deconstructing pernicious gender discourses and ideologies, it seems that some writers wanted to maintain this focus *through* their analysis of textual pleasures. This led to rather an odd assumption in some research: namely the notion that the pleasures women derive from media are the outcome of the opportunities they offer for (psychic/political) resistance. Here is Mary Ellen Brown writing about her own perspective of feminist culturalist TV criticism or 'resistance theory': 'Resistance theory comprises a body of work which addresses the issue of how ordinary people and sub cultural groups can resist hegemonic or dominant pressures and consequently obtain pleasure' (Brown 1990: 12).

The key word in this quotation is 'consequently' – since it suggests that pleasure is intimately tied to, indeed consequent upon, resistance to hegemonic or dominant culture. This seems to me a strange assumption, yet it is present in much of this writing. I know from my own media use that sometimes pleasure is related to identifying with strong, empowered, critical characters, but just as often it is ideologically neutral (or difficult to pin down) or even relies on a collusion with dominant representations, for example the sensual pleasures of engaging with a women's magazine, with its smooth glossy pages, its scent of perfumes, and its feast of representations of beautiful women in sumptuous clothes and settings. To turn around Jean Grimshaw's insightful quote (see p. 14), it is perfectly possible to derive significant pleasure from representations that politically one may wish to critique!

Brown's position of simply eliding pleasure and resistance avoids all the difficult questions about complicity in subordination, and more broadly about the complex relationship between cultural representations and individual subjectivities, fantasies and desires. Turning the tables to take a look at one of the most dominant 'men's genres' – pornography – quickly shows the problems with this argument, for it would be difficult to sustain the notion that enjoyment of pornography was an act of resistance against hegemonic gender relations! It indicates yet another form of the essentialism prevalent in this body of work: a notion of the female subject as somehow essentially radical or resistant.

Writing more than twenty years ago Judith Williamson produced an excoriating critique of what she called 'pointless populism' in feminist media studies' preoccupation with pleasure: 'It used to be an act of daring on the left to claim enjoyment of *Dallas*, disco dancing or any other piece of mass popular culture. Now it seems to require equal daring to suggest that such activities, while certainly enjoyable, are not radical' (Williamson 1986b: 14). Similarly, Modleski, though one of the first to devote attention to pleasure, subsequently wrote with concern about what she perceived as an uncritical celebration of it:

> It seemed important at one historical moment to emphasize the way 'the people' resist mass culture's manipulation. Today, we are in danger of forgetting the crucial fact that like the rest of the world even the cultural analyst may sometimes be a 'cultural dupe' – which is, after all, only an ugly way of saying that we exist inside ideology, that we are all victims, down to the very depths of our psyches, of political and cultural domination. (Modleski 1991: 45)

Audience Studies

One of the limitations of textual analysis, as I have noted already, is that it tells us very little about how audiences might actually consume and make sense of different media products. The early research within media studies is often accused of 'textual determinism', that is, of implying that audiences are simply passive dupes who uncritically absorbed the messages sent to them in particular broadcasts or articles. This is closely related to criticisms of the 'hypodermic model' of effects research which dominated early communication studies in the 1940s and 1950s. There is not space here to review the effects paradigms and the uses and gratifications approach which followed it. Instead the focus is on audience studies as it developed from the 1980s onwards, profoundly influenced by feminist understandings. I will focus upon three different moments of recent audience studies: the encoding/decoding moment; the focus on audience pleasures; and the shift to studying information and communication technologies in the context of everyday life.

Encoding/decoding/interpretation

The first type of audience research drew on the encoding/decoding model developed by Stuart Hall (1973). This had three premises: first, that the same event can be encoded (represented) in more than one way; secondly, the message always contains more than one potential meaning besides the preferred encoded one; and thirdly, messages therefore have the potential to be read in different ways. Using these insights Charlotte Brunsdon and David Morley produced a landmark study of audience reception in 1980. The programme under analysis was a current affairs television magazine show called *Nationwide* that was aired in Britain throughout the 1970s, directly following the early evening news. In the first volume of their report they analysed the codes of the programme in some detail, using a range of critical analytical tools, broadly influenced by Marxism and semiotics (Brunsdon and Morley 1978). It was the second report, published by the BFI in 1980, that really broke new ground. It reported on their attempts to map and classify different people's responses to the programme. Rather than simply looking at the myriad different interpretations people made, Morley wanted to see the patterning of different responses. Drawing on Frank Parkin's (1972) work on how people inhabit different classed meaning systems, he proposed three broad types of audience position. He suggested that someone might take the meaning fully within the interpretive framework proposed and preferred by the programme – this would then be a dominant reading.

Alternatively, they might make a negotiated reading which modified the preferred reading slightly but without rejecting its entire terms. Or thirdly they might bring an alternative frame of reference to bear and read the encoded message in an oppositional way.

What Morley sought to do was to identify and code these different modes of interpretation and to investigate whether they were related to different kinds of structural location and cultural competencies. Class was a primary interest and he expected decodings systematically to co-vary with class position. However he was also interested in the way that different kinds of social/cultural memberships and competencies affected readings – and to this end interviewed schoolchildren, managers, trade union members and so on.

It is difficult to overestimate the significance of this study. Not only did it become a founding text of the 'new' audience studies, but it went beyond statements about texts being polysemic and audiences being active to actually investigate the patterned nature of different interpretations. It was interested in difference, especially in class, and its relationship to the cultural resources deployed in understanding a media text.

The influence of this work can be seen in much feminist media studies. Andrea Press's (1990; 1991) work in particular has been notable for taking seriously class differences in readings of the 1980s show *Dynasty*, and, more recently, in responses to media coverage of abortion (Press and Cole 1999). Elizabeth Frazer's (1987) work on teenage girls reading *Jackie* magazine was an early example of attempts to take seriously unevenly divided classed resources for sense making, and Dawn Currie's (1999) work on teenage magazine readers also bears the influence of this work. In recent years there have also been more studies which have looked at the impact of 'race' and ethnicity in mediating audiences' responses to programmes like the *Cosby Show* and other sitcoms.

Audience pleasures

A second type of audience research has been more concerned with fictional forms and understanding women's pleasures. Janice Radway's (1984) groundbreaking book *Reading the Romance* combined textual analysis of Harlequin novels with an interview-based ethnographic study of committed romance readers, and a detailed examination of publishing and bookselling as economic enterprises. Her work has sometimes been regarded as an exemplary example of media/cultural analysis in its attempt to grapple with different 'moments' of the cultural process – production, distribution, text and audience – in a way that allows romantic fiction to be understood as simultaneously an economic, cultural, ideological and pleasurable phenomenon.

Radway's audience analysis focused on a group of avid romance readers whom she calls the 'Smithton women', all of whom used the services of 'Dot' to advise them on which romance novels to purchase. Using a combination of semi-structured interviews, group discussions and observation, Radway attempted to uncover the meanings the women gave to their romance reading. She found that far from being unintelligent dopes the women were sophisticated readers of romance, able to make subtle differentiations within the genre and to pick up on small nuances and cues from the cover pictures and blurbs in order to determine whether books would meet their particular tastes and needs.

Radway's work is ambivalently positioned in relation to romantic fiction. On the one hand she is critical of Harlequin novels, arguing that they are profoundly conservative, posing some of the problems of life in a patriarchal society only to resolve them through an idealized depiction of heterosexual love. On the other hand she understands women's use of these novels as – in part – oppositional. Like Modleski she finds that one of the pleasures of romance reading is wish-fulfilment in which, in 'escaping' into the heroine's life, readers vicariously experience what it is to be really loved and nurtured in the way they crave.

The act of reading can also be understood as 'combative' and 'compensatory'; a way of carving out some time or space for themselves:

> In picking up a book . . . they refuse temporarily their family's otherwise constant demands that they tend to the wants of others even as they act deliberately to do something for their own private pleasure . . . Romance reading addresses needs created in them but not met by patriarchal institutions and engendering practices. (Radway 1984: 211)

Contradictory subjects: the feminist cultural critic

Radway's work has become the focus of a number of important debates in media and cultural studies. These are concerned with what feminist cultural criticism should involve (e.g. critique, celebration or affirmation, respect, etc.) and the nature of the relationship between the cultural critic and her respondents. Ien Ang (1996) has criticized Radway's work because of the relationship she establishes between herself as critic and the women she studies, and because of her attempts (as Ang sees it) to constantly re-invoke feminist authority.

Ang (1996) argues that Radway does not sufficiently reflect upon or problematize her relationship with the Smithton women, and that she draws far too stark and hierarchical a distinction between herself (a feminist and not a romance reader) and her respondents (romance readers but not feminists). Part of the problem, Ang argues, is that Radway starts from the premise that something *is wrong*, that is, that romance reading is a problematic activity that needs to be explained and resolved. This assumption informs the whole project so that even though the reading of romances is thought to contain some oppositional features, ultimately it is regarded as working to reconcile women to their subordination in heterosexual relationships. Indeed, Radway argues that romance reading may actually absorb some of women's critiques of patriarchal heterosexuality which might otherwise have been formulated as demands for 'real' change.

Ang (1996) contends that Radway is working with a thinly veiled political moralism – a vanguardism which seeks to make 'them' (romance readers) more like 'us' (feminists), and implicitly regards feminists accounts as superior. As well as contesting whether this is necessarily true (*would* feminism actually make these women happier?), Ang argues that Radway fails to take pleasure seriously in its own right because it is always read in terms of its ideological functions.

By contrast, Ang's (1985; 1990: 86) own research on audiences for *Dallas* refuses to make any judgements about the political effects of the fans' identifications. She argues that the position ascribed to the melodramatic heroine Sue Ellen is one of 'masochism and powerlessness: a self-destructive mode of femininity which in social and political terms must be seen as regressive and unproductive'. But rather than condemning this identification, she argues that it is possible to observe the gratification it offers to the women (and some men) involved, for example pleasures of abandonment, and so that self (re-) construction is not needed. She emphasizes that these are fantasy identifications with a fictional character and argues that it is simply not possible to say in the abstract whether these feelings might have an empowering or paralysing effect upon the subject experiencing them. This would require analysis of the context of fantasizing.

The debate between Radway and Ang goes beyond the issue of how particular texts and interpretations should be read, to the heart of questions about what feminist media studies should be or should do, and the nature of the relationship between the feminist critic and women.

In an insightful article Charlotte Brunsdon (Brunsdon 1993; see also 2005) argued that between the 1960s and 1990s there were important shifts in the way that feminists positioned themselves and have been positioned. Early feminist media critique, she argues, was written by women who were outside the academy or any other institutional setting, and was written for other women activists. More recently feminism has taken a place in the academy and a new contradictory subject has been formed: the feminist intellectual with a more ambiguous relationship to 'women'. Brunsdon identifies three different modes. In the *transparent mode*, the feminist saw herself as synonymous with and having a completely transparent relationship to other women. This was found particularly at the beginning of the second wave of the women's liberation movement. The *hegemonic mode* – by far the most dominant position – is one in which the feminist critic seeks to change/raise women's consciousness and transform feminine identifications into feminist ones. It is often contradictory, involving both the repudiation and defence of traditional femininity. Radway's work would be situated here. Finally, Brunsdon talks about the *fragmented mode*, influenced by postmodernism and seeking to highlight the fact that men and women as categories are produced by discourse, including feminist discourse. This approach seeks to radically denaturalize essential categories and assumed relations. The politics espoused is one of articulation and contingency. Brunsdon comments that if women were 'other' to the hegemonic approach, then everyone – including the writer herself – is 'other' to this approach, leading to autobiographical and reflexive accounts (Ien Ang's work is the best example).

Perhaps a fourth mode should be added to this typology: a postfeminist orientation. In this the writer takes up the position of feminist critic in order to critique not the media but previous (usually older) feminists for their 'horrible' dismissal of particular pieces of media culture. Charlotte Brunsdon (2005) has described 'an Ur feminist article':

> What does this article do? It explores a TV programme or film that has a central female character – or characters – and that is usually addressed to a feminine audience within the vocabulary and concerns of feminism. This usually involves setting up what is proposed as an 'obvious' feminist reading of the text in which the text itself – and the heroine – fails some sort of test. The heroine is not independent enough, she cares too much about shoes, she is always confined to the domestic sphere, she is always worrying about her looks, or she just wants to find a man and settle down. The author then mobilises her own engagement with the text, her fondness for the treatment of the dreams and dilemmas of the heroine, to interrogate the harsh dismissal of this popular text on 'feminist' grounds. The author thus reveals the complex and contradictory ways in which the text – and the heroine – negotiate the perilous path of living as a woman in a patriarchal world. The heroine of this genre is both the author and her textual surrogate, while her adversaries are both textual (vampires, lawyers, exhusbands) and extra textual – censorious feminists who will not let her like the story and its iconography, that is, the accoutrements of femininity. (Brunsdon 2005: 113)

A possible example of this kind of orientation is found in the opening page of Joke Hermes' book *Reading Women's Magazines*:

> I have always felt strongly that the feminist struggle should be aimed at claiming respect. It is probably for that reason that I have never felt very comfortable with the majority of feminist work that has been done on women's magazines . . . [T]he media in this type of discourse are seen as Janus-faced monster: agent of change and progress, but also the devil in disguise, agent of alienation, anomie and despair in the powerfully seductive guise of provider of entertainment and excitement . . . The worry and concern in older feminist criticism leads to a highly unequal relationship between the feminist author and 'ordinary women'. The feminist media critic is prophet and exorcist . . . Feminists . . . speak on behalf of others who are, implicitly, thought to be unable to see for themselves how bad such media texts as women's magazines are. They need to be enlightened; they need good feminist texts in order to be saved from their false consciousness. (Hermes 1995)

The generational dis-identification that Brunsdon discusses is clearly visible here, echoing the mother–daughter difficulties of a previous generation's rejection of the housewife (Brunsdon 2000), but here it is feminism itself who is 'the bad guy'. Divisions across age and gender are obviously significant, but so too are different genres of criticism: what is at issue here is nothing less than the question of what the role of the feminist cultural critic should be. Should she be, as Hermes argues, claiming respect for women's pleasures which have previously been treated dismissively, or be involved in ideological critique? What other roles might she play? Celebrating women's choices? Looking for strands of resistance and subversion in contemporary culture? Formulating alternative representational strategies? As feminist media studies comes of age and becomes more diverse these debates are more pertinent than ever – as the 'obviousness' of what it means to do feminist intellectual work breaks down.

Media as (domestic) communications technologies

Before concluding this section I want to return now to the third 'moment' of audience research, which focuses less on the interpretations or the pleasures of single media texts than on media use as an activity. This work, which developed from the 1980s onwards, has a number of shared features: a commitment to ethnographic methods, borrowed from anthropology, that is, to observing people and talking to them in their own settings; an interest in the media as domestic technologies; and a focus on the practices of media use in everyday life (e.g. studying radio listening, TV viewing or the use of the VCR) (Bausinger 1984; Morley 1986; Gray 1987, 1992; Silverstone and Hirsch 1992).

This body of work is notable for its strong emphasis upon gender, as one of the central organizing principles of everyday life. It is rooted in an acknowledgement that the space of the home, of domestic life, has historically had very different meanings for women and men. Whilst for men it may be experienced as an unambiguous space of leisure, pleasure and relaxation, for many women – even women who work outside the home – it is a site of repeated domestic labour, as well as having other meanings.

Morley's (1986) study of 'family television' argued that gender affected almost everything about individuals' relationship to TV: programme preferences, viewing choices, the amount of television watched, styles of viewing, and so on. Generally decisions about what to watch were made by men in the household, who would have the TV's remote control next to them on the arm of the chair, 'a visible symbol of condensed power relations'. Ann Gray's (1992) research reported the same finding, but also, interestingly, noted that many women *chose* not to learn how to program the VCR, lest it become yet another job for which they became responsible within the household. She describes this as 'calculated ignorance': it was a deliberate and strategic act of resistance on their part, even though it might be understood by their husbands and by others as simply an indication that 'women are useless with technology'.

Both studies found that women and men expressed preferences for different types of programmes, with men favouring news, factual programmes, 'realistic' dramas and sports programmes, whilst women preferred fiction, soaps and romances. Women's and men's styles of watching television also differed, with men watching quietly and attentively while women tended to use viewing as an accompaniment to other activities, often domestic duties like ironing or knitting, or talking to children. Women's viewing was more 'distracted', then, because of their position within the family structure and the expectations and time-demands placed upon them. But it was also related to the guilt which Morley and Gray both discovered most women felt about their own pleasures: 'They are, on the whole, prepared to concede that the drama and soap operas they like are "silly" or "badly acted" or inconsequential. They accept the terms of a masculine hegemony which defines their preferences as having a low status' (Morley 1992: 160). Given this, it is perhaps not surprising that for many women watching television only became a pleasurable activity when it was experienced away from their family – for example watching the omnibus edition of a soap while the rest of the family were asleep on a Sunday morning, or watching videos with other women friends. In both instances, however, a feeling of guilt often accompanied taking any time whatsoever for themselves.

The ethnographic turn represented by this research has been extremely valuable in locating media use in the contexts of daily life. Indeed, studies are often riveting accounts of people's lives, providing rich details about their use of time, space, the relationships between men and women and parents and children. The work has enriched our understanding of media consumption, by locating it right back where it takes place: in the home, in the workplace, and (increasingly as mobile technologies developed) during travel. Recent research has looked at the use of home computers, the Walkman, the iPod and the mobile phone (Du Gay 1997; Bull 2000; Bull and Back 2003; Brown, Green et al. 2005; Hamill and Lasen 2005).

There are significant overlaps between this work and a longer trajectory of research on gender and technology, some of which has explored the relationship between the design, manufacture, marketing, consumption and the use of domestic technologies such as the microwave or the telephone – charting the ways that technologies are reconfigured at each stage (Wajcman 1991; Rakow 1992; Cockburn and Ormrod 1993; Grint and Gill 1995). There has been less work within media studies on the production end of the chain, with notable exceptions such as Shaun Moores' (1988) fascinating study of the entry of radio into the home, the domestic adjustments that had to be made to accommodate 'the box on the dresser', and the assumptions about who would listen and what kind of activity listening should be, that went into both the design of sets and to early programming.

One limitation of this research is that it has largely taken as its focus white heterosexual nuclear families. There is not yet enough research which looks at different household forms, differentiated by class, 'race', ethnicity, sexuality or status. Little is known about how single people, lesbians and gay men, heterosexual couples without children use and consume media, for example, or about media practices of the diverse non-white communities that make up about one third of the population in many European cities. Marie Gillespie's (1995) groundbreaking study of the role of television in the lives of young Punjabi Londoners and Roza Tsagarousianou's (2001) study of diasporic media among the London Greek community are important signs of a growing interest in redressing this.

One of the dilemmas raised by this type of research concerns what status should be attributed to people's reports of their media use. Many studies have found extremely stereotypical accounts being offered by women and men of their television and radio preferences. How are these to be understood? Should they be taken at face value, read as honest, straightforward accounts of how people actually feel and what they actually do? Or should they perhaps be treated with more caution or scepticism? Reflecting upon the almost caricatured nature of the responses about programme preferences that David Morley received, he speculated retrospectively (Morley 1992) as to whether these were the consequence of interviewing families together, putting them in a situation where they felt they had to conform to gendered social expectations. This may indeed be the case. But the kinds of post-structuralist insight discussed earlier in this chapter may suggest something more significant is going on here: maybe media use is actually part of the practice of *doing gender*? That is, for a man to say that he prefers news and current affairs programmes and that he never watches soap operas may be part of the enactment of hegemonic masculinity. Sherry Turkle's (1984) work on the use of computers supports such an interpretation, showing that using the computer was understood as part of the performance of a particular gendered identity. At the very least, constructionist theories of language and meaning would suggest that people's accounts should be treated not as one-way mirrors to reality, but as complex, occasioned constructions.

This book does not examine audience interpretations, pleasures or uses of media but focuses instead on media texts. Nevertheless, it is premised on the notion that audience studies is crucially important to feminist media research, in emphasizing the polysemic nature of media texts and the complex ways in which they are consumed. In this section I have tried to convey some of the richness and complexity of this field, whilst also highlighting some of the dilemmas audience research raises – dilemmas about pleasure, identification, interpretation, the role of the critic and the ways to read audiences' accounts. These insights and dilemmas should be borne in mind throughout the reading of this book – the brake, the caveat, and the challenge to the textual analyses presented here.

Changing Feminisms

So far this chapter has focused upon the changing ways in which scholars of gender and the media have analysed media texts, and on studying how audiences use, enjoy and interpret media products. I have emphasized the ongoing transformations and debates within both arenas. In this section I will turn to a third area of change – change within feminism itself.

In this book I use the term feminism to signal a concern with enduring gender inequalities and injustices, amongst a matrix of other forms of oppression relating to 'race', ethnicity, class, age, sexuality, disability and health status. Such a definition is not unproblematic and, in historical terms, is relatively new. Throughout the period of the 1960s, 1970s and 1980s, books and articles about feminism would

habitually identify three different types of feminism: liberal feminism, radical feminism and socialist feminism. Broadly speaking
liberal feminists regarded women's lives as distorted by gender stereotyping and by restrictive roles which needed to be combated by legislation and by programmes and initiatives to help women 'catch up'
and move into domains previously dominated by men, such as engi-
neering and computing. As Sylvia Walby puts it, liberal feminists see
gender not as a social structure but as 'the summation of numerous
small-scale deprivations' (Walby 1990: 4). By contrast radical feminism
is often presented as rather less hopeful about a reform of gender relations. From this perspective, women and men are fundamentally
different (a fact largely attributable to women's reproductive capacities) and women's power, women's culture and women's pleasure are
regarded as having been systematically controlled and dominated by
men, operating through patriarchal institutions like medicine and
militarism. The socialist feminist position rejected both the essentialism of radical feminism and the superficiality of liberal feminism, and
instead made links between the class-based forms of capitalist
societies and women's subordination.

However, by the late 1980s such a threefold definition had become
unsustainable as an account of feminism, and here I want briefly to
explore why – looking at the impact of black feminist writing and
then, more briefly, at post-structuralist and postmodernist theory, the
rise of masculinity studies, and queer theory.

Black women: shaping feminist theory

Feminist work over the last two decades has had to reshape itself and
has done so largely by engaging with new ideas about identity, location and difference and by increasingly paying attention to the history
and politics of postcoloniality and imperialism (Soothill and Walby
1991; Bhavnani 2001). The urgency of the task was driven by vocal
critique of feminism's exclusions by black and Third World women
(Carby 1982; hooks 1982; Amos and Parmar 1984; hooks 1984; Lorde
1984; Ong 1988; Hill Collins 1989; Yuval-Davies 1989; Hill Collins 1991;
Minh-ha 1991; Mohanty 1988; Sandoval 1991; Dent, Wallace et al. 1992;
Bhavnani and Phoenix 1994; Brah 1996; Young 1996; Mirza 1997; Wing
1997; Anzaldúa 1999; Ang 2001). The general contours of the critique
were as follows.

Second-wave feminism was indicted first for its false universalism.
The charge against it – paradoxically – was similar to a criticism it
made of male-dominated knowledge: namely that it started from the
experience of a group of privileged, First World, middle-class, white
women and proceeded as if their experience of womanhood were

universally shared. In 1984 bell hooks produced a damning critique of one of the 'canonical' texts of the second wave: Betty Friedan's (1963) book about 'the problem with no name'. As hooks pointed out, this problem actually refers to the plight of a very select group of college-educated, upper middle-class, married white women: housewives bored with leisure, home and children, who wanted more out of life. Not only did Friedan claim that this was a universal plight affecting all American women, hooks argues, but she also made an extraordinarily offensive comparison between the psychological effects on white housewives of their domestic isolation and the experience of prisoners in Nazi concentration camps.

Secondly, feminism was criticized for entirely ignoring the differences in the histories and experiences of black and white women. One area where this was clear was in feminist thinking about the family. Whilst the nuclear family was regarded by a number of white feminists as the cornerstone of women's oppression, for many black women in Europe and the USA it represented a refuge from and bulwark against a racist society. As Hazel Carby put it: 'We do not wish to deny that the family can be a source of oppression for us, but we also wish to examine how the black family has functioned as a prime source of resistance to oppression' (Carby 1982: 47).

Another area where black feminists have pointed to the failure of white feminism to address their concerns is in relation to sexual and reproductive rights. As Caroline Ramazanoglu (1989) argued, many black women were alienated from feminist campaigns about abortion, seeing them as having little to do with them. Indeed, rather than getting access to abortion rights, many black women wanted the right *not* to have abortions and forced sterilizations imposed on them against their will as part of racist population policies. As the frequent 'guinea pigs' for trials of new forms of contraception such as Depo Provera and Norplant, abortion rights came relatively low down on many black women's list of feminist priorities. More broadly, it was argued that white feminism displayed a profound ignorance of the ways in which 'race' as well as gender structures are experienced.

If these criticisms concerned the absences and exclusions of white feminist thought – the invisibility of women of colour, the exclusion of their histories of struggle from white accounts of feminism (hooks 1982; Springer 2002) – then a different kind of racism was one in which black women were seen as epitomizing an issue such as promiscuity or subjection to strict patriarchal familial codes (Bhavnani 2001). Valerie Amos and Prathiba Parmar (1984) have commented that the 'hysteria' in the Western women's movement surrounding issues like arranged marriages, purdah and female-headed households is 'often beyond the black woman's comprehension'. Similarly, Hazel Carby criticized both the media and feminism for their representation of Asian girls:

> The media's horror stories about Asian girls and arranged marriages bear very little relation to their experiences. The feminist version of this ideology presents Asian women as being in need of liberation, not in terms of their own history and needs, but into the progressive social mores and customs of the Metropolitan West. (Carby 1982: 47)

Additionally, black women pointed out that most white feminists were silent about their own privilege and the history of that privilege – in particular the ways in which white women have benefited from the exploitation of black women, in circumstances that vary from domestic work to sweated labour. The reluctance of white feminists to acknowledge their own privilege meant that racism within and outside the women's movement could not be properly addressed.

These sustained critiques from black feminists had a seismic effect upon feminism. They opened up a focus on differences between women – differences of 'race' and ethnicity, but also differences relating to class, age and disability which had previously been ignored. This involved not simply 'adding in' women of colour but rethinking entire frameworks. Writing about the family Ann Phoenix (1997) pointed out that if feminists simply added black women in while leaving the framework of the argument unchanged this would serve to further pathologize black families, who would be compared to an implicit white norm. If black women's experiences were to be taken seriously the entire theory of the nuclear family would need rethinking.

In relation to representations this meant that processes of classing and racialization had to be examined alongside gender. For some, using a restricted content analytic approach to examine images, it translated merely into disaggregating the category 'women' and producing findings about the shocking invisibility of women of colour on television and in other media. But for most feminist writers concerned with the media it involved thinking about the intertwining of discourses of race, gender, sexuality, class and so on, tracing different patterns of desire, contempt, fear and exoticization. Feminist research on media texts has had to become much more sensitive to a range of discursive constructions in order to avoid complicity with racism as when, for example, earlier writing bought into stereotypes of black masculinity as violent and sexually rapacious (see chapter 4 for a discussion of this in relation to press reporting of rape). It is also beginning to move beyond the notions of 'black' and 'white', to expand the concept of race in ways that break with this civil rights era dualism (Dines and Humez 2003).

A further impact of black feminism has been a new focus on the global within media studies. In a globalizing world there is a sense that the boundaries of the scholarship should not be set by national borders and that attentiveness to difference should include different global locations. Ien Ang (2001) has argued that the majority of Western feminism's most straightforward ideals are totally embedded in beliefs and assumptions that may make no sense to other women, for example, assumptions about individualism. Aihwa Ong (1988) contends that while claiming to be oppositional most feminist scholarship has fallen prey to a colonial, hegemonic view of the world in which women in developing countries are constructed as fixed in sexualities and natural capacities: the figure of the 'Third World woman' described by Chandra Mohanty (1988). The call for a global focus is a call to acknowledge differences, to listen to other voices, and to stay alert to the flows of power and resistance. Above all, the impact of black and Third World feminist criticism has been to stress the intimate interrelationships between gender, 'race', class and other forms of oppression. As the black US writer Patricia Hill Collins (1991) has put it, these are all linked in a matrix of domination in which there are few pure oppressors and few pure victims.

Interest in difference also, but to a lesser extent, led to a concern with media representations of disability (Klobas 1988; Cumberbatch and Negrine 1991; Barnes and British Council of Organizations of Disabled People 1992; Hevey 1992). Likewise, developments in post-structuralist and postmodernist theorizing and shifts in lesbian, gay, bisexual and transgender politics together produced queer theory, which has had a significant effect on media studies of gender and sexuality (see chapter 2 for discussion). Here, however, I want to turn to the growth of interest in men and masculinities.

Masculinities and media studies

Studies of gender and media were transformed throughout the 1990s by the new interest in masculinity, or, better, masculinities. This developed in the West as a direct result of feminism's sustained interrogation and critique of masculinity. Prior to that, male experience had often been treated unproblematically as human experience, and, historically, most of what passes as history, anthropology, sociology, psychology, literature has been by and about men. What made the late twentieth-century interest in masculinity different was that it made men visible as a *gendered* group.

In the past men as men tended only to be studied if they were regarded as a problem – with predictable classed and racialized pictures emerging, and moral panics about young men, working-class men and black men. But today the study of masculinity focuses on all kinds of masculinities in diverse areas of social life – men working in the City of London as well as male prisoners, policemen as well as criminals. Masculinity studies is a growing area and there are studies of masculinities in the workplace, masculinities and health, masculinity and violence, the representation of masculinities in film and media, fatherhood, and masculinities in education – this last has been a particularly important area of research because it offers a chance to see how boys are produced as masculine subjects.

Like women's studies, research on masculinity has been characterized by a diversity of different perspectives: role theory, psychoanalysis, social constructionist approaches, as well as some distinctive and rather celebratory perspectives from the mythopoetic men's movement associated with the writings of Robert Bly (1990), Sam Keen (1991), and to a lesser extent Steve Biddulph (1995). This mythopoetic movement believes that modern Western men are suffering from a deep malaise, some kind of psychological wound, because they have become alienated from their fathers and from 'deep structures' of masculinity, often constructed around male bonding, initiation rites and warriorhood. The 'gurus' seek to inspire in men a desire for a re-masculinization of culture, through attendance at retreats, workshops and camps in the USA. Much of the writing has a neocolonial feel to it, and Bob Connell (2000) offers a vivid critique of these wealthy, privileged white men travelling the world to ransack different cultures for 'resonant male rituals'.

It is fair to say that this approach has little in common with academic men's studies. Most contemporary writing takes a constructionist perspective, is concerned with specific, contextual studies examining masculinities in different sites, and focuses on masculinity as a performance or masquerade rather than an essential identity. It starts from the notion that masculinities need to be understood *relationally*. Masculinity in general derives some of its meaning from being constructed against femininity, heterosexual masculinities are constructed against homosexual ones, and all specific forms of masculinity get their meaning from being defined against others. Thus masculinities are classed, raced and aged, but also coexist and get meaning in a global postcolonial context.

One of the most important notions in masculinity studies is the idea of *hegemonic masculinity*. This notion comes directly from the recognition that there is no single masculinity but rather multiple masculinities. Hegemonic masculinity is intended to capture the sense that different masculinities are not equal – some are more dominant or powerful than others. Hegemonic masculinity may not be the most common form of masculinity – in fact it is most unlikely to be because only a few men can ever achieve it – but it is dominant in the sense of being socially valued and culturally powerful. As Michael Kimmel has argued of the US context, hegemonic masculinity is what sets the standards for men, is what other men are measured against and found wanting. He quotes the sociologist Erving Goffman:

> A young, married, white, urban, Northern heterosexual, Protestant father, of college education, fully employed, of good complexion, weight and height, and a recent record in sports . . . Every American male tends to look out upon the world from this perspective . . . Any male who fails to qualify in any one of these ways is likely to view himself . . . as unworthy, incomplete and inferior. (in Kimmel 2001: 271)

All men, it is argued, benefit from the 'patriarchal dividend' but some men benefit more than others. ➤

Bob Connell, who coined the term, argues that in any given time one type of masculinity is more highly valued than others. The current form, he argues, is that of 'transnational business masculinity'. This is marked by increasing egocentrism, very conditional loyalties (even to the company), a declining sense of responsibility for others, and the idea of the executive in fast capitalism as a person with no permanent commitments, except to making money. Connell claims that transnational business masculinity differs from traditional bourgeois masculinity by its increasingly libertarian sexuality, with a growing tendency to commodified relations with women. Hotels catering for businessmen in most parts of the world now routinely offer pornographic videos and there is a well-developed prostitution industry catering for male international business travellers.

One problem with the notion of hegemonic masculinity is that it implies considerable uniformity and consensus in values about what form of masculinity is culturally valuable and powerful at any one point. Transnational business masculinity may represent a powerful form of masculinity but so too do military masculinities, sporting masculinities and those associated with 'high science', especially biotechnology and genetics. Are things increasingly fragmented? It would seem that even within the context of the school classroom there are many different types of masculinity competing for hegemony – boys who are good at sports have social power, but so do boys who are in bands, who are good-looking, who are successful with girls, etc. – and the category memberships may not overlap.

Perhaps a recognition of hegemony should be coupled with careful study of local specificities. Taking the example of the school again, we can note that precisely the 'cool pose' (Majors and Billson 1992) that gives young African-American boys their cultural power and status in the classroom and the playground may be a source of problems and discrimination to the same men in the labour market or in relation to wider society.

Masculinity studies has had a significant impact in media studies, literally transforming research on women and media into something that is properly about gender and media. Studies of masculinities examine a variety of different media and genres – men's magazines, films, music videos, advertising, etc. (Wernick 1991; Cohan and Hark 1993; Tasker 1993; Mort 1996; Nixon 1996; Edwards 1997; Jackson, Brooks et al. 2001; Beynon 2002; Benwell 2003; Mackinnon 2003). Current research has a number of concerns. First – as with studies of representations of women – there are concerns about the narrow range of representations of masculinity on offer in the media. John Beynon argues: 'A Martian arriving on planet Earth and not knowing what masculinity was would quickly form the opinion that it was a highly damaged and damaging condition with very few, if any, redeeming features' (Beynon 2002: 143). A number of other writers have been concerned about the potentially damaging impacts on young boys of being bombarded by images that range from violent, muscular Rambo-esque heroes to incompetent figures of fun or contempt – with very little in between (e.g. Hill 1997). (The recent trend for 'revenge ads' and for depictions of men as useless, infantile imbeciles is discussed in chapter 3.)

A second focus has been on the dramatic trend towards idealized and eroticized presentations of male bodies that have transformed the visual landscape over the past two decades. Research variously explores the determinants of this shift in visual culture, the extent to which it challenges well-established rules about 'looking', and its implications in terms of men's self-esteem, challenges to heteronormativity, and so on (Chapman and Rutherford 1988; Moore 1988; Simpson 1994; Mort 1996; Edwards 1997; Gill, Henwood and McLean 2005).

Thirdly there is a new interest in the role media play in constructing new forms of masculinity – new man, new lad and metrosexual are some examples (Gill 2003). Producing reflexive knowledge about gender is one of the key roles played by the media in the twenty-first century which displays (in numerous newspaper and magazine articles and discussion shows) a meta-interest in transformations in gender.

Finally, throughout the 1990s and early noughties whenever one heard the word 'masculinity' in the media, one knew that 'crisis' could not be far behind (Beynon 2002). Thus another key interest has been in examining the media's role in pulling together random unconnected facts – such as the decline in the manufacturing industry, the change in the gender composition of middle-class educational success, and the increasing use of Viagra – to construct a palpable sense of masculinity in crisis (Bordo 1999).

Cultural Politics and Activism

Having focused so far on academic literature I want to look now at the relationship between analyses and cultural politics. I have noted already the striking link in the early women's movement between research and activism. Four decades on, gender studies as well as media studies have become academically institutionalized. Has this led to depoliticization? One key concern is with the growing obscurity of the language through which critique is conducted. bell hooks regrets that so much writing is so opaque and abstract: 'It is sadly ironic that the contemporary discourse which talks the most about heterogeneity, the de- centered subject, declaring breakthroughs that allow recognition of Otherness, still directs its critical voice primarily to a specialised audience that shares a common language rooted in the very master narratives it claims to challenge' (hooks 1990: 25). In a similar vein, Alison Light has argued, 'if the day ever comes that any woman feels that she cannot put pen to paper without being conversant with Lacan's Mirror phase . . . then we may as well stop the bus and get off' (1989: 27). I believe that a commitment to clear, inclusive forms of communication is central to any struggle that seeks to change the world.

A second key issue concerns the fear that the growing sophistication of understandings and analyses of the media can make it difficult actually to take a stance. Have we become sophisticated to the point of depoliticization? Another issue relates to the 'knowing', postmodern, ironic moment in which we find ourselves in the West, when, as Katherine Viner (1999) puts it, taking offence, even at something legitimately offensive, has become an anachronism. In the last few years, representational practices which would once have attracted angry responses have passed into the mainstream without even a whimper. Even pornography is now regarded as a cutting-edge, visually exciting genre – the new 'cool' (McRobbie 2004d).

In the 1970s feminist media activism took many different forms: there were calls for positive images, sticker campaigns, demonstrations against offensive media events such as the international Miss World competition; calls for more women working in the media; demands for women-only media spaces; attempts to develop alternative media; billboard 'guerrilla' interventions, and there were repeated attempts to use the existing regulatory bodies to challenge and change representations of women. There was a huge energy and hunger for change and the women involved achieved an enormous amount. Let's look at some of these political strategies in a little more detail.

Early calls for positive images made perfect sense in the context of the late 1960s and early 1970s in which – as Gaye Tuchman (1978)

observed – women were trivialized, condemned and symbolically anni-
hilated in the media. Against this backdrop, a positive image might be
one in which a woman was not shown as unintelligent, narcissistic
and dependent. A call for positive images was also implicitly a call for
greater diversity in media representations of women – a desire to see
older women, disabled women and black women on television screens
and magazine covers.

Beyond this, however, the campaign for positive images ran into
trouble somewhat. It faltered on the very basic problem that it was
impossible to agree on which images were positive – because the meaning of the image does not reside in the image itself but in its interaction or negotiation of the context in which it is produced and
interpreted. It also broke down because it simply sought to replace one
set of partial representations with another set. As Ali Rattansi (1992)
has argued in relation to 'the stifling aesthetic of the positive image'
in anti-racist literature, this opens up critics to charges of propaganda
and also authoritarianism. Presumably, for the many women who buy
magazines like *Cosmopolitan* or *Marie Claire* each month, a picture of a
glamorous young model or actress is an attractive and positive image,
yet more overtly feminist magazines favour images of faces with 'character', wrinkles and no makeup to meet their particular criteria of
positiveness.

What is positive is *contested*. This is seen very clearly in the struggles
of disabled people over their representation. Traditionally this has
relied on strategies that proclaim 'we are just like you' and depict
disabled people in the conventional settings of 'blissful' nuclear families, or even (in one charity advertisement) at their own wedding! More
recently, however, voices from within the disability movement had
expressed their anger at such restrictive heteronormative definitions
and demanded their right to be queer, to be different (Shakespeare and
Corker 2002).

Interestingly the inverse occurred when the drama *Queer as Folk* aired
in Britain in 1999. Its unashamed attempts to 'transgress heteronormative standards of decorum' (Arthurs 2004) and to acknowledge the
range of queer sexual practices through a group of characters who
were not 'bland, saintly, desexualized mainstream figures who might
as well be heterosexual' (Doty and Gove 1997) outraged some lesbians
and gay men, fearful of the impact of this move away from safe positive
images of homosexual desire.

A different form of challenge took the form of sticker campaigns and
guerrilla interventions into advertising. Stickers declaring 'this advert
is sexist' or 'this image degrades women' were applied to advertising
posters in a range of public transport venues. Guerrilla interventions
were somewhat different: they usually took the form of graffitied

additions to large billboards. For example the car advert slogan 'To Volvo a son' had the phrase 'better luck next time' sprayed across it. Another advert which showed a woman draped across a car attracted the addition: 'when I'm not lying on cars I'm a brain surgeon', and a third which showed only a woman's sleek, stockinged legs emerging from a shell was amended to read 'born kicking!' Such campaigns continue to be used by many women's groups across the world. In Croatia, the organization BaBe (Be active, Be emancipated) sees sticker campaigns as part of a long-term strategy to raise awareness of sexism in advertising. However, in many places in the West, advertisers have become so adept at incorporating critiques that many adverts (as we discuss in chapter 3) already contain disavowals of their sexism, or use slogans which ironically repudiate any potential critique. In this context, it is not clear what effect merely pointing to sexism would have. This is further complicated by the profound breakdown of any agreed notion of what constitutes sexism – just as positive images are contested, so too is any notion of what might constitute a sexist representation. It no longer seems as easy as it once did to make a confident pronouncement about the problems with particular representational practices in relation to gender.

The demand for women-only spaces within the media such as women's programmes and women's pages was another strategy used to challenge the representation of women in the media. This strategy attracted considerable debate between feminists concerned about the ghettoization of women's concerns into a small number of bounded spaces, and those who believed that this was an important starting point to get powerful media figures to take women seriously (Coward 1984; Feldman 2000). Although some people argued the point passionately on either side, in the end a sensible both/and politics prevailed, which acknowledged that the campaign for women-only spaces, *and* the campaign for women's interests to be taken seriously right across the output of the media were not mutually exclusive.

Today the debates have lost their relevance as a consequence of other major shifts. Looking at newspaper history over the past decades, it is clear that the desire to attract more women readers became a driving force for change within the industry. Women were used as a wedge to sell more papers and to attract more advertising, and there has been a trend towards the 'magazining' of the press, with greater and greater emphasis placed upon myriad advertising-rich lifestyle sections largely targeted at women. This 'feminization' of the press makes political demands for women's pages problematic. They are also problematic in the current climate because of the re-naturalization of sexual difference – what I call 'Mars 'n' Venus' thinking, which has already gone a long way to presenting a completely segregated 'his and hers' universe in which 'girls' stuff' is lifestyle, home, cooking and leisure, and the 'boys' stuff' is sports, politics and business. At this particular juncture, a call for separate spaces would therefore have none of the political force it once had, but might, instead, be re-articulated to this commercially driven, sexually differentiated view of the world.

The campaign to get more women working in the media, and increasing numbers in senior positions, has been a crucial aspect of feminist cultural politics. Broadly speaking, it has been phenomenally successful in the West – though not without significant costs and exclusions which relate to race, class and children (see chapter 4). Yet, what has become clear is that the relationship between the gender of media producers (whether journalists, editors, script writers or directors) and the nature of gender representations is an extremely complex one. It is mediated by many intervening institutions and practices, meaning that there is no straightforward relationship between more women employed in the media and 'better' images.

Some women have chosen to struggle for change by using the existing regulatory authorities. In the UK, the Advertising Standards Authority (ASA), the body charged with ensuring that adverts are fair, decent and unlikely to cause widespread offence, is one organization to which feminists have addressed thousands of complaints about sexist advertising. Making one's opinion known to bodies like the ASA, and to broadcasters, is extremely important in raising awareness of concerns about sexism – each call to the duty desk at the BBC, for example, is logged, and complaints about programme content are taken very seriously. However, broadcasters and regulators typically use very different criteria to evaluate the appropriateness or otherwise of media content – relating to questions of decency, obscenity and privacy, rather than gender inequality. In most countries the representation of explicit sex is taken much more seriously than sexism (explicit or otherwise). In a fascinating study of ASA adjudications relating to bra advertising, Dee Amy-Chinn (2006) found that the ones the regulator consistently deemed offensive (regardless of the number of complaints received) are the adverts that break with heterosexual sex and the coital imperative (e.g. by implying masturbation, oral sex or women's complete independence from men) whilst adverts which presented women as objects for male consumption received far more positive evaluations from adjudicators.

In her global report, Margaret Gallagher (2001) looked at the challenges faced by women all over the world in using existing frameworks to contest sexism (often being forced to fall back on guidelines about sexual explicitness). Frequently this draws women into alliances with very conservative organizations, with whom they have little in common. Moreover, Gallagher discusses how arguments about freedom of speech are mobilized by media organizations to claim the rights to represent women as they wish. And, of course, the final defence is always 'if you don't like it you can always switch off'. In a time of increasing deregulation this riposte has a new significance as contemporary neoliberal citizens are exhorted to 'self-regulate'. Increasingly it is only concerns about children's well-being that are deemed to require attention, and, even then, the burden for protecting children is fast being shifted away from media organizations and onto parents (Arthurs 2004).

An enormous amount of energy has been put into creating alternative media: community radio and television stations, feminist, lesbian, gay, bisexual and transgender magazines, Internet sites, etc. Globally, women's radio stations have had a significant impact – particularly in regions where there are low levels of literacy. The Internet has reinvigorated DIY media and there are many thousands, if not millions, of alternative websites, e-zines, spaces for weblogs and the other cyber venues (e.g. BBS) that offer radically different content and opinions from traditional media. Young women's Grrrrl zines are particularly vibrant and inspiring examples of this. Alternative media have a major role to play but the problem is the fact that they are only seen/consumed by a small number of (usually self-selecting) people, and also that whilst offering an alternative they leave the mainstream intact and unchanged.

Besides these strategies there are many other innovative ways feminists, queers, anti-racists, disability activists and others have engaged in cultural politics around representations – instigating prizes for more challenging content, developing media activists kits with checklists for broadcasters and journalists, building greater critical media literacy. Overall, each of the strategies we have considered has made a major contribution, and, taken together, they have produced huge (but uneven) transformations. In some countries (e.g. the Netherlands and Canada) it has become routine for major national broadcasters to have gender equality officers. In others there is much further to go. Moreover, today, in the West, a major sticking point concerns not only what form of activism or cultural politics to advocate, but also, more fundamentally, what – if anything – should be the target of critique. It is to this that I turn in the conclusion.

Conclusion: Debates, Dilemmas, Contradictions

The aim of this chapter has been to review some of the main developments in feminist media studies over the last four decades. It has looked at changing analyses of representations, at audiences and at feminist cultural politics in relation to the media. Throughout, the emphasis has been upon pointing to debates and areas of contestation. In this final section I do not want to present a traditional summary of the chapter, but rather to highlight some further dilemmas within feminist media studies.

It seems to me that compared with the certainty and confidence of early critique, today's feminist media scholar is more tentative, less certain. Looking across the field there is no one single type of critical practice but a diversity, with very different perspectives. There is no agreement about how to interpret contemporary media culture and even a single show such as *Ally McBeal* or *Sex and the City* or *Desperate Housewives* can be read in many competing – indeed diametrically opposed – ways (see chapter 7 for discussion). Moreover, there is no consensus about what critical vocabularies feminist media studies should use, with the usefulness of even long-established notions such as 'objectification' being called into question. What value does the term have at a moment when, far from being objectified, many women are being presented as active, desiring sexual subjects?

Feona Attwood (2004) argues that sexual display has developed more positive connotations in a culture in which female celebrities routinely present their bodies as objects of spectacle which indicate success, confidence, assertive female sexuality and power. In this context, figure 1.1, an advert for Opium fragrance, could be read as signifying sexual autonomy and desire rather than passivity and objectification. Attwood comments that model Sophie Dahl's size (a UK size 16 at the time of the campaign and therefore significantly bigger than most other models) also offered opportunities for the image to be read in a positive, empowering way as strong, curvy and sexy: 'Sophie Dahl's body is . . . available for reading as an emblem of liberation, fun, self pleasure and pride, not only within an older libertarian tradition which celebrates porn, but also for a much wider readership for which sexy images have become the currency of the day' (Attwood 2004: 14).

More broadly, the increasing sexualization of media content is subject to intense debate (Arthurs 2004). For some, it represents a liberation from stifling repression, and a democratization of desire that now includes diverse sexualities and sexual practices (McNair 2002). Others point instead to the uneven gender effects of this, to the re-sexualization and the commodification of women's bodies in the wake of feminist critiques that for a decade or more had neutralized at least more overt examples of objectification, and to the exclusions of this practice – only some (young, fit, beautiful) bodies are sexualized (Gill 2003). Some commentators are concerned about the mainstreaming and 'respectabilization' of pornography (e.g. Merskin 2003; McRobbie

Image courtesy of The Advertising Archives

Figure 1.1 Positive female sexual autonomy or sexual objectivization?

2004d), and the growing sense that almost whatever her other achievements (e.g. Booker Prize nominees, serious TV presenters) any woman
with celebrity status will be required to pose topless for one of the
men's magazines (Viner 1999). It used to be the case that women wanting to make a break into 'show business' would occasionally do nude
modelling to boost their career prospects. Today it seems almost a
requirement of the modern female's CV that she has done at least one
cover shoot or centrefold for *Playboy* or *FHM* (*For Him Magazine*).

Is this a sign of the growing maturity of Western societies in relation
to sexuality, or part of a backlash against feminism? How should the
sexualization of women's bodies be understood, and what are we to
make of the increasingly sexualized presentations of men?

Irony, too, has become a key term in the lexicon of media critique,
but one of its most contested. For some, irony offers some space, some
'room to move', 'room to breathe', a space of playfulness and openness
(McRobbie 1999). Discussing the use of irony in 'laddish' men's magazines David Gauntlett (2002) argues that it provides a 'protective layer'
between lifestyle information and readers, to avoid making men feel
patronized or inadequate. He contends that magazines like *FHM*
(which are saturated in ironic discourse) are fully aware that women
are as good as men – perhaps even better – and that '[T]he putdowns of

women . . . are knowingly ridiculous, based on the assumption that it's silly to be sexist (and therefore is funny, in a silly way) and that men are usually just as rubbish as women' (2002: 168).

An entirely different reading of the same magazines is put forward by Nick Stevenson, Peter Jackson and Kate Brooks. For them, in contrast, irony allows someone to express 'an unpalatable truth in a disguised form, while claiming it is not what they actually meant' (Stevenson, Jackson and Brooks 2000). Or, as Imelda Whelehan puts it, it is

> the way in which a sophisticated media machine can anticipate objections to the content and images it uses and place them in ironic quotation marks, often evoking nostalgic settings to forestall criticism or render the critics speechless, since to attack the object on the grounds of offence is already anticipated by a 'knowing' stance on the part of the image maker. (Whelehan 2004)

Not only are these perspectives very different, but they contain critiques of each other: for Gauntlett, some gender and media scholars just 'don't get the joke' and are not sophisticated enough to see through the irony. From Whelehan's perspective, this position is enacting precisely the same move as irony in a media text: it is defending against critique, and it is moving to silence anyone who wishes to criticize it – since they are already positioned in advance as lacking humour and sophistication.

Perhaps more than anything, however, it is the media's relationship to feminism that is most contested. One of the things that makes the media today very different from the television, magazines, radio and press of the 1960s, 1970s and early 1980s is that feminism is now part of the cultural field. That is, feminist discourses are part of the media, rather than simply being outside and independent critical voices. It is a measure of the success of feminism that many ideas that once required active battles are now accepted as uncontroversial – from the right to work after marriage to equal pay for equal work, from reproductive health rights to the notion that rape can happen in relationships. Today, feminist-inspired ideas burst forth from our radios, TV screens and print media (alongside many anti-feminist ideas). Indeed, it is probably fair to say that most feminism in the West now happens in the media, and for the majority of people their experience of feminism is an entirely mediated one.

Returning to the Opium advert discussed above, for example, it is worth noting that almost the whole debate about it took place in the media – the advert and public responses to it (the ASA received a record 900 complaints) were the topic of newspaper articles, TV talk shows, radio phone-ins and so on. Jennifer Wicke (1998) has argued that in the USA a decline in a women's *movement* has been accompanied by a rise in what she calls 'celebrity feminism' with a star system of media-friendly feminists such as Naomi Wolf or Camille Paglia doing the rounds of American network television to discuss feminist issues and promote their latest books.

This shift to feminism becoming part of media discourse itself produces many different interpretations, and debates about incorporation, recuperation and backlash. Have the media been transformed by feminism, become – in significant ways – feminist? Or have they incorporated or recuperated feminist ideas, emptying them of their radical force and selling them back to us as sanitized products or lifestyles to consume? Is this a moment of backlash or retro-sexism? Or are the media now postfeminist? These are amongst the most contested issues in the field of gender and media at the moment, and in many respects the whole of this book is dedicated to exploring the changing, ongoing relationship between feminism and the media. It is the debates, the dilemmas and the contradictions that make this field so difficult and challenging, but also so interesting and exciting.

2

Analysing Gender in Media Texts

Introduction

THE purpose of this chapter is to introduce a number of different approaches that are used for studying gender and the media. Because the book is primarily about representations of gender in media – rather than media production and/or audience readings – the focus here will be on theories/methods that have been used to analyse media texts. I wrote theories/methods, rather than choosing one or other of the words, because most of the approaches discussed here are both methods of analysis and theories of representation – that is, the approaches are built on specific epistemological foundations such as beliefs about the relationship between 'representations' and 'reality', understanding of how meaning works, and so on. This should become clear early in the chapter when you encounter the radically different understandings of meaning espoused by content analysts and semioticians.

The first part of the chapter deals with what might be understood as the 'standard' approaches media studies uses for analysing texts: content analysis, semiotics and ideological critique. Next, however, the chapter focuses on newly emerging perspectives from discourse analysis and discourse theory, including an empirical social scientific tradition and an approach influenced by the French theorist Michel Foucault. Finally, the chapter examines a group of perspectives that, although not yet well represented by specific studies, pose a radical and critical challenge to previous theories of the relationship between meaning and power (that builds on understandings from discourse theory). Specifically, the chapter looks briefly at the extraordinary importance of postmodernism, postcolonial theory and queer theory for contemporary cultural analysis, picking out some of the ways in which they have already impacted upon feminist media studies.

Content Analysis

'Content analysis' is sometimes used as a generic term to refer to a variety of methods used to analyse texts, but it is generally taken to define a specific type of analysis – a quantitative technique which measures certain aspects of a media text. At its most simple it can be used as a way of 'measuring' the relative numbers of males to females who appear on television, in magazines or in the press. It has often been used in feminist research to provide a measure of the kinds of roles which men and women appear in on TV or the kinds of traits they are represented as possessing. Essentially, it involves counting the frequency of particular kinds of portrayals, using a coding framework that has been created and agreed in advance. The raw data it produces comes in the form of frequencies, which can then be translated into percentages, or analysed for significance using a variety of different statistical packages.

Content analysis has been used to examine portrayals across a range of media and genres including adverts, pop videos, news, drama, computer games, etc. But the approach is not limited to looking at how women and men as groups are portrayed. It can also be a means to document a whole variety of patterns in media, such as the relative amounts of airtime given to different political candidates during an election, the number of times female news interviewees are interrupted compared with their male counterparts, the range of ways in which violence against women is understood, or the portrayal of specific groups of women, such as disabled women or aboriginal women.

By far the largest and best-known examples of content analysis being used to analyse gender are the three Global Media Monitoring projects which took place in 1995, 2000 and 2005 as part of the enormous energy generated by the United Nations Fourth World Conference on Women in Beijing. At the regional and international meetings held to plan for the conference there was a sense of urgency about the need to include media issues in the Platform for Action to be adopted – these had been downplayed in the three previous conferences. The degree of importance attributed to media is reflected in the fact that no fewer than seventy-one countries took part in the systematic media monitoring. Margaret Gallagher has written movingly of its import:

> The significance of this project was enormous. The 1995 Global Media Monitoring Project gave women a tool with which to scrutinize their media in a systematic way, and a means of documenting gender bias and exclusion. The project was unprecedented not simply in terms of its geographical scope, but also in its execution. From teachers and researchers, to activists and lobbyists, to journalists and other media

professionals – some with considerable research experience, others with none – groups and individuals from a wide spectrum of backgrounds contributed to the data collection. In some countries disparate groups co-operated for the first time, united by concern about the portrayal of women in their national media. The process of monitoring their news media proved an eye opening, educational experience for many of those involved. For some it created a new awareness of the pervasiveness of gender stereotyping. For others it provided concrete evidence to support long held personal opinions. (Gallagher 2001: 27)

As this demonstrates, research using a content analytic approach has been enormously valuable over the last thirty years in raising the profile of questions about gender representation in the media, and documenting the narrow and restrictive range of stereotypes used to depict women and men. The relatively low costs of conducting this kind of research – essentially available to anyone with access to a tape recorder, video recorder or the price of a sample of daily newspapers – has encouraged groups beyond academia to undertake studies and has empowered many women to become involved in campaigning on issues around media representation. Today increasing numbers of activist groups use some form of quantitative data collection to document critiques and strengthen their overall arguments. The high status accorded to the quantitative data produced by content analysis has made it a persuasive tool for use with broadcasting/media organizations and their regulators. Indeed, this type of research is still the industry's standard way of measuring and assessing gender representations (as well as the representation of ethnic minorities and people with disabilities). It is used by the major broadcasting corporations across the world and it attracts large amounts of funding.

Content analytic research plays an important role in political leverage and in holding media bosses and programme makers accountable with questions such as 'why do women constitute only 30 per cent of people on television when they make up 52 per cent of the population?' Despite this, many of the approach's underlying assumptions have been called into question by critics. First, the idea that the media act or should act like a mirror for society has been roundly challenged by many media scholars as at best naive and at worst extremely damaging for our understanding of media/gender relations (Cowie 1978; Gledhill 1978; Jaddou and Williams 1981; Betterton 1987; Myers 1987). Rather than reflecting reality, such theorists argue, the media are involved in producing or constructing particular versions of reality in order to make them 'real' and persuasive (such perspectives are explored later in this chapter). Secondly, content analysis's conception of meaning is problematic – particularly its focus upon bias and distortion, with the suggestion that sexism resides in single images such as the 'dumb blonde' or the 'unintelligent housewife'. Not only is this challenged for its accuracy of understanding (i.e. it does not capture how sexism works), but it is also deemed to lead to a problematic form of political action focused on excising 'bad' stereotypes, but leaving the rest of media content intact. Thirdly, the approach does not distinguish between levels of meaning, and, in fact, only ever addresses the manifest content of representations, thus ignoring the way that 'woman' can be used to symbolize an enormous variety of different meanings including stability, comfort, conservatism and sexuality. Indeed, research in the content analytic tradition tells us little about the images it examines, except how frequently they occur. Finally, content analysis tends to gloss over the specificities of representations and offers instead a tale of the persistence of certain well-worn stereotypes (Winship 1981). The major problem with this is its failure to pick up on differences and on how things are changing. At its worst, content analysis may be accused of only telling us what we know already.

Semiotics and Structuralism

Semiotics originated in studies of language, but it can be used to analyse everything that can communicate meaning for example gestures and non-verbal communication, sports, architecture, road signs, flags, fashion, myth, music, all kinds of media texts and much more. It is both a theory and a method, and works by unpacking and making explicit meanings that we all – as lay semioticians – create through our engagement with 'texts' of all kinds.

The term semiology was coined by the Swiss linguist Ferdinand de Saussure (1857–1913), whose lectures were published posthumously as *A Course in General Linguistics* (Saussure 1974). The term 'semiotics' was proposed by the American philosopher Charles Peirce (1839–1914), writing at about the same time. Today the two terms are used more or less interchangeably.

Saussure's work posed a radical challenge to linguistic theory. He argued that semiology should become a new science – 'a science of signs'. He proposed that an analytic distinction could be made between two parts of a sign – the signifier and the signified. He used the term *signifier* to refer to the word or speech sound, and *signified* to refer to its mental concept. Thus, for example, the sign 'snow' was made up of the sound produced by the word snow (the signifier), and the concept soft white matter which falls from the sky (the signified). Saussure argued that there is no natural or inevitable relationship between the signifier and the signified – their relationship is purely arbitrary. Any word could have been chosen to name the soft white matter which falls from the sky; indeed, the fact that snow has different signifiers in other languages – 'neige' in French, 'Snee' in German – illustrates this point. It is important to note that the signified is not the 'thing' which is represented, but it is the mental concept of that object. In practice, the signifier and signified are linked; the distinction is an *analytic* one.

The arbitrariness of the sign

Arguing against traditional word-object conceptions of meaning Saussure contended that the meaning of any word comes not from any inherent or natural relationship between the signifier and signified but *from its relationship to other elements within the system*. The signifier snow gets its meaning by being distinguishable from other words which share some of the same features when written or spoken, such as flow and snot and snore, and the signified derives its sense from its distinction from the mental concepts of sleet, rain, hail and ice. We could have called snow 'snew'; this is perfectly easy to pronounce in English and is not used for any other signified, but it sounds like nonsense because of its lack of relationship to other signs. Sense – or meaning – is a product of relationships and differences within the language as a system. As Saussure put it: 'in language there are only differences without positive terms' (Saussure 1974: 120).

The relationship between signifiers and signifieds is, then, an arbitrary one. But Saussure went further than this. He also suggested that signifieds, concepts, are themselves arbitrary. The world could be conceptually partitioned in an infinite number of ways, but each language makes only some differences significant. Saussure called this the *arbitrariness of the sign*. To use a standard example: whilst the Innuit have a variety of different words for different types of snow, in English we have only one term. There are different ways of interpreting this: philosophers and linguists have argued about the extent to which the concepts which a culture marks as detectable in language are determined by the 'world', and to what extent our language constrains which features of the world we can actually 'see'. Some feminist linguists contend that most languages are inherently patriarchal – they divide up the world conceptually in ways that serve male interests and encode male perceptions, making some of women's experiences invisible (Spender 1985). Before the terms 'sexism' and 'sexual harassment' were coined, for example, women had difficulty in talking about important features of their lived experience – what Betty Friedan (1963) called the 'the problem with no name'.

As this indicates, language, like other forms of representation, is a site of struggle. Some new words – like the many arising out of developments in information technology such as snail-mail and mouse potato – pass into the language uncontested, generating little more than a wry smile from the individual who encounters them for the first time, whilst others, such as 'sexual harassment' and 'political correctness' produce enormous passion and controversy precisely because they encode contested meanings. Saussure challenged the idea that language was a process of naming, in which each object-in-the-world has a name corresponding to it. He was not interested in referents and he recognized that, in any case, many words – for example abstractions like 'freedom' or 'democracy' – have no concrete referent. He argued that all signs are *cultural constructs* that take their meaning from learned, social and collective use. The word snow, for example, is now used in Northern communications technology-saturated societies to refer to white specks on a television or computer screen; at other times it has been slang for cocaine, and so on.

Iconic, indexical and symbolic signs

Saussure was concerned primarily with language. Peirce, in contrast, focused his attention on a whole range of different signs, including pictorial ones. He distinguished between three types of signs – the iconic, the indexical and the symbolic. Iconic signs are signs which resemble the object, person or place being represented. The signifier–signified relationship is one of likeness. Painted portraits constitute an obvious example of an iconic sign, as do documentary photographs, since they are designed to look like the thing being represented. The relationship between these signifiers and their signifieds often appears to be a straightforward one – as expressed by the oft-quoted view that 'the camera never lies'. In fact, they are no less mediated and culturally determined than any other signifier–signified relationship. In order to make sense of any drawing or photograph we have to be familiar with a whole series of learned conventions, which, once acquired, are taken for granted – conventions about scale, perspective, lighting, etc. It is extremely difficult to recognize even the most mundane objects when they are photographed in unfamiliar ways – from unusual angles, with unconventional lighting, from very close up, etc.

Indexical signs are signs that rely on some kind of connection between signifier and signified: smoke, for example, is an index of fire, while profuse sweating is an index of a high temperature. Indexical signs are used extensively in all the visual media, and we have become adept at reading them – knowing, for example, that a representation of the White House is not merely a depiction of a particular building but a sign which stands indexically for the President of the USA, or the

US government, or Washington, or even the USA itself (depending on other contextual signifiers). Liesbet Van Zoonen (1994) has argued that women are frequently used as 'signs', with a young, blonde girl dressed in white signifying (within the codes of Anglo-American television) innocence and probity, and dark-haired women signifying danger and sexuality – a set of codes that was used, for example, in *Dynasty*.

For both iconic and indexical signs there is *some* relationship between the signifier and the signified, even if this is determined culturally; that is, these signs, in being 'caused' by their referents, lack the absolute arbitrariness of the signifiers of speech. However, symbolic signs rely entirely on convention: there is no 'natural' relationship between the signifier and the signified. Advertisements rely heavily on symbolic signs, developing brand symbols to 'stand for' the product. Recently multinational companies have become so adept at the use of symbols that even the presence of particular colours in a landscape can symbolize the product – such as the red and white of Coca-Cola, or the purple of Silk Cut. Music too can act as a potent symbol, evoking the signified of a particular product even when it is played in an entirely different context.

Denotation and connotation

Two other concepts which are central to semiotic analysis are denotation and connotation. Denotation refers to the most literal meaning or to the first level of signification of any particular signifier – for example a picture of a rose denotes a particular type of flower. At a second level, however, the rose has many other connotations – it may indicate love or passion, or the British Labour Party, or a particular county in the War of the Roses (Lancashire). The study of connotation or second-level signification was opened up by the French theorist Roland Barthes. Barthes's essays on many different features of French popular culture dissected everything from adverts and travel books to food and wrestling, exploring the process of second-level signification. Connotative readings of signs, Barthes argued, are introduced by an audience or 'reader' who possesses the appropriate cultural codes. This highlights a very important point about semiotics generally – that the process of semiosis is *culture bound*. The sense of any particular signifier is only meaningful within particular cultural or sub-cultural settings.

Barthes's most famous example of second-order signification comes from his essay 'Myth Today', which elaborates his theoretical and methodological system for analysing popular culture. He describes his encounter with a particular edition of the popular magazine *Paris Match*:

> I am at the barber's, and a copy of Paris-Match is offered to me. On the cover, a young Negro in a French uniform is saluting, with his eyes uplifted, probably fixed on a fold of the tricolour. All this is the *meaning* of the picture. But, whether naively or not, I see very well what it signifies to me: that France is a great Empire, that all her sons, without any colour discrimination, faithfully serve under her flag, and that there is no better answer to the detractors of an alleged colonialism than the zeal shown by this Negro in serving his so-called oppressors.
> (Barthes 1973: 116)

The first level of signification produces the most literal meaning: a black man is saluting the French flag. But, as Barthes argues, at a second level the image works to naturalize French imperialism and to present it as positive – so positive indeed that the black man in the photograph feels not like a victim of oppression, but a proud subject of the French Empire.

Barthes is interested in a particular type of second-level signification: myth. For him, myth is 'depoliticized speech'; it is the transformation of history into nature. Barthes's work on myth has particular relevance for feminist analyses particularly in the field of advertising.

Semiotics and advertising

Advertisements work by constructing myths, in such a way as to endow products with meanings which *appear* to be natural and eternal. The task of semiotic analysis is to show how these sign systems work, to decode them. Semiotic analysis, then, is quite different from content analysis in its approach to adverts. While content analysis looks at the frequency of particular images or stereotypes, and compares them with some notion of an undistorted reality, semiotic analysis is concerned with *how* adverts mean. Judith Williamson's (1978) book *Decoding Advertisements* was the landmark publication for semiotic analyses of adverts. She combined insights from psychoanalysis and Althusserian Marxism to produce compelling analyses of more than one hundred advertisements, as well as explicating a groundbreaking theoretical approach. Williamson was concerned with the 'currency' of adverts – the way in which they permit the meaning of one thing to be expressed in terms of another. They provide a structure which enables language of objects to be transformed into a language of feelings or people. 'Thus a diamond comes to "mean" love and endurance for us. Once the connection has been made we begin to translate the other way and in fact to skip translating altogether: taking the sign for what it signifies, the thing for the feeling' (Williamson 1978). As Robert Goldman (1992) argues, when we recognize an advert as an advert, we recognize a context or framework in which meanings are rearranged, so that exchanges of meaning can take place. If we did not recognize the motive of an advert we would frequently be baffled by its juxtapositions: why is that car dancing? How come those people in jeans can run through walls? What is a giant blackcurrant doing in the road?

Advertisements do not work by imposing meanings upon us or by manipulating us in some crude way. They create structures of meaning which sell products not for their use value, their functional value as objects, but in terms of ourselves as social beings. Through advertising, products are given an 'exchange value' – statements about a particular commodity are translated into statements about who we are and who we aspire to become. Ads are commodity signs which attach to products. Through advertising the exchange value of many products is made to far eclipse their use value. For example, the value of a Rolex as a sign of affluence and success is far more significant to what a Rolex is than its utility as a timepiece (Goldman 1992).

One of the principal ways in which advertisements communicate with us, Williamson argued, is through what Althusser (1984) described as *interpellation* or *hailing*. One of Althusser's major contributions to discussions about ideology was his argument that ideology works by 'constituting concrete individuals as subjects' (Althusser 1984). Recognizing ourselves as subjects is an act of ideological recognition, and it operates through interpellation. Using the example of a street scene Althusser argues that when someone turns around in the street in response to the shout 'hey you there!' that person becomes a subject. 'Why? Because he has recognised that the hail was "really" addressed to him, and that it was *really him* who was hailed' (Althusser 1984: 48)

Williamson suggests that Althusser's notion of interpellation captures precisely what happens in advertisements. Adverts address us through the implied phrase: 'Hey you!' and, as we 'recognize' that we are being addressed so, in that instant, we take on the (ideological) subject position being offered to us by the ad. Lawrence Bardin (1977) suggested three different forms that interpellation in adverts can take – the vocative form (direct address), the imperative (which urges the addressee to become what she is addressed as), and a variety of other more subtle forms which permit identification. Janice Winship (1981) argues that one way in which we can analyse advertisements is to ask: 'who does this advert think I am?' In doing so, we can attempt to lay bare the assumptions about age, gender, 'race' and class around which the advert is based. Chinyelu Onwurah (1987) cites the advertising copy: 'Isn't it nice to be brown when everyone else is white' as a particularly graphic demonstration of assumptions about 'race' in glossy women's magazines. Winship (1981) suggests that we use the technique of reversal when analysing to whom an advert is addressed; this can help to make clear the assumptions that are implicit in the ad. As I will argue in the next chapter, however, reversals have, since Winship was writing, themselves become a mainstay of advertising, and do not necessarily have the critical force they once did.

Using semiotics to analyse an advert

The advert in figure 2.1 shows a photographic image of a contemporary living room with two people seated in the foreground. The man, to the left of the picture, is slightly in shadow, leaning forward with a contemplative look on his face and his left hand placed on the woman's thigh. The woman is wearing a short black lace dress which has fallen open to reveal her left thigh, and black patent shoes with high stiletto heels. Her lips and eyes are made up to accentuate them and light falls across her body. Also in the foreground is a stylish glass table on which chrome hi-fi equipment is laid out. Superimposed on

Image courtesy of The Advertising Archives

Figure 2.1   Experience an unbelievable pleasure

the photo, and placed visually between the man's and woman's heads, is the caption: 'Experience an unbelievable pleasure'. Down the right-hand side of the double-page spread a small printed text describes the 'perfect' experience of one-bit audio by Sharp which is 'set to revolutionise the way we listen to music'.

So much for the denotative meanings. It is the connotations of the photograph that offer the richest material for the semiotic analyst. The room with its polished floor, neutral furnishings and Miro-esque modern painting connotes both affluence and taste. This is reinforced by the attire of the man who appears to be at ease in the situation and whose well-cut, sober suit and glasses suggest status and substantial financial means. In contrast, the woman appears less at ease. She is sitting on a hard chair, leaning back with her spine arched and her legs parted. While he stares into the middle distance (or at the hi-fi?) she gazes at him, as if waiting for him to act or move. The man's hand upon her thigh connotes possession of her. Her attire, gaze and position are strongly coded as sexual, and this is underscored by the lighting in the room which suggests that it is late evening or night.

The advertiser has set its readers a puzzle. In order to produce the desired reading we (the readers) have to fill in meanings, perform what Judith Williamson (1978) calls 'advertising work'. The caption cues us to read the photograph as one in which unbelievable pleasure is being experienced or is about to be experienced. The small printed text at the right-hand side of the photo explains the nature of this pleasure: it comes from listening to music on Sharp's unique analogue and digital technology which allows 'every sound made by every instrument' to be perfectly reproduced. However, without reading the small print, the viewer is invited to make a different kind of sense of the unbelievable pleasure on offer. The woman's body – which could be said to *stand for* sex – seems to be being offered to the man in the photo (and viewers of the image) as the source of unbelievable pleasure for him (and them/us).

The puzzle for the viewer, then, is why this man seems so uninterested. He is sitting close and is touching the woman but his hand seems placed almost carelessly on her thigh and he appears to be somewhere else, absorbed in something that does not involve the woman. The printed text offers a possible explanation of this: 'one-bit audio reproduces more than just the music. It actually recreates the performance space itself'. The puzzle is solved – the man has been transported by the music; its pleasure is so intense that he has forgotten the other potential pleasure awaiting him in the form of the woman's body.

For the semiotic analyst interested in gender a number of critical points can be made about this advert. First, there is the use of the woman's body to signify sex. We are invited to read her presence solely in terms of the promise of sexual pleasure. There are no signifiers of any relationship between man and woman and, in the absence of these, her attire and deportment suggest that she may be a 'call girl' or prostitute bought by him for the evening for his gratification. Perhaps the neutrally furnished room is a hotel room. A clear power dynamic is in evidence between them: she half-sits, half-lies, watching and waiting; he is in control.

The advertisement creates a visual economy in which the woman becomes an object on offer for the man (and for viewers). In the 'currency' (to use Williamson's terms) of the advert an equivalence is established between the woman and the hi-fi: both offer the man unbelievable pleasure. This is reinforced by the lighting and *mise-en-scène* of the advert, with light falling on the woman's bare arms and legs and on the front of the chrome hi-fi. If we answer Janice Winship's question; 'who is the advert addressed to?' in this case the answer is clearly *men*. It is the man who is absorbed in the pleasure of listening to Sharp's sound system – *his* is the pleasure we are alerted to. The woman, in contrast, appears not even to be listening – she is impassive, but with all her attention focused on him. (And it is interesting that Sharp must be so certain that its target audience is male that it risks showing a woman so evidently unmoved by the experience of its one-bit audio.) Likewise, the sexual pleasure on offer is pleasure for the man in the photograph and for heterosexual male viewers. There is no suggestion of mutual pleasuring, and, on the contrary, the woman's body is the commodity (like the hi-fi) that promises men unbelievable pleasure.

Overall, then, in order to make appropriate sense of this advert the viewer has to participate in a meanings system which reproduces highly traditional gender power relations. Regardless of gender or sexual orientation the viewer is expected to adopt a masculine spectating position (Mulvey 1975) and to view the woman as an object offering sexual gratification.

Ideological Critique

A third important tradition within media studies is ideological critique or analysis. Good examples of work in this vein include Angela McRobbie's and Janice Winship's (McRobbie 1977, 1978; Winship 1978) studies of girls' and women's magazines, which look at how magazine discourses are constructed around highly restricted ideologies of femininity centring on romance, domesticity and caring. In addition, a much broader range of work within feminist media studies – characterized perhaps as 'thematic analysis' or merely as criticism – can also be understood as ideological analysis. Susan Faludi's (1992) book *Backlash*, for example, is not formally labelled as a piece of ideological analysis, but its concerns with documenting the ways that the media have sought to attack, discredit and marginalize feminism clearly place it within this genre.

Here the term is used inclusively to refer to a large body of work focused on the connection between cultural representations – meanings – and power relations, affirming the importance of images, values and discourses in constructing and reproducing the social order. A useful general critical definition of ideology can be found in John Thompson's work. He uses the term to refer to 'the ways in which meaning is mobilized for the maintenance of relations of domination' (Thompson 1984: 5).

Analysis of the media's ideological role comes out of a long tradition of Marxist scholarship. At the heart of this work is the wish to understand how it is that social relations based on domination, antagonism and injustice come to be seen as natural, inevitable and even desirable by those who benefit least from them. In Marxist terms, then, the question concerns why it is that the working classes acquiesce in a system which gives them such a raw deal: selling their labour and being paid less than the value of what they produce so that the capitalist class may cream off the surplus value as profit to line their own pockets. Attention to this question by Marx and Engels highlighted several important points – which have been the topic of intense discussion and contestation ever since. First, Marx and Engels argued that the people who own and control the material means of production (factories, workshops, etc.) are the same people who also control the production and distribution of ideas in society. This is not just chance, they suggest, but a key way in which the ruling (capitalist) class secured their own power. The quote below from *The German Ideology* is one of the most celebrated summaries of their position:

> The ideas of the ruling class are in every epoch the ruling ideas, i.e. the class which is the ruling *material* force of society is at the same time its ruling *intellectual* force. The class which has the means of material production at its disposal, has control at the same time over the means of mental production, so that thereby, generally speaking, the ideas of those who lack the means of mental production are subject to it . . . In so far, therefore, as they rule as a class and determine the extent and compass of an epoch, it is self-evident that they do this in its whole range, hence among other things rule also as thinkers, as producers of ideas and regulate the production and distribution of the ideas of their age; thus their ideas are the ruling ideas of the epoch. (Marx and Engels 1970: 60–1)

Marx and Engels also argued that people's consciousness (their ideas and beliefs about the world) is determined by their material life: 'it is not the consciousness of men that determines their existence but the social existence that determines the consciousness.' This was the basis of their materialist theory of ideology, which stressed that ideas are not somehow 'free-floating' but are the product of the groups, social locations and conditions which produce them.

Throughout the twentieth century there was intense debate about Marx's theory of ideology, particularly on the issues of determination versus relative autonomy, structure versus culture and the question of false consciousness. Contemporary media studies inherited a tradition of writing informed by the Frankfurt School, the structuralist Marxism of Louis Althusser (whose work has already been briefly discussed), the culturalist perspectives of Richard Hoggart, Raymond Williams and E. P. Thompson, as well as a body of Lacanian psychoanalytic theory (Hall 1980; Bennett, Martin et al. 1981; Hall 1982, 1986). Today's ideological media critique, however, owes its biggest debt to the work of the Italian theorist Antonio Gramsci.

Gramsci

Gramsci's work – or at least a particular reading of it associated with the Centre for Contemporary Cultural Studies at Birmingham University and at the Open University in Britain – allowed a way out of the 'impasse' represented by the previous debates. Gramsci developed four concepts which are at the heart of current research in media studies. First, he elaborated the notion of *hegemony* to refer to ideological and cultural power. It denotes the processes through which a group or party is able to claim social, political and cultural leadership throughout a society or social formation. Hegemony does not mean domination. Rather, Gramsci emphasized the need to win approval or consent. It is an active, ongoing process which is always temporary and contested.

The second key concept is that of *articulation*. Elaborated by Ernesto Laclau and Chantal Mouffe (Laclau 1977; Laclau and Mouffe 1985) from Gramsci's work, the notion of articulation is a way of thinking about the relationship between different elements of the social structure in non-determinist and non-reductionist ways. It allows us to think in non-essentialist terms about the relationship between one's position (in the social structure) and one's beliefs or actions. In relation to gender, for example, it means rejecting the idea of an automatic link between one's gender and one's attitude to feminism. Thus, simplistic assertions about all men as rapists or patriarchs would be rejected, as would similarly crude statements about women's natural affinity for feminism (which cannot explain why large numbers of women do not consider themselves feminist).

A third contribution of Gramsci's ideas is the notion that ideology is best understood as a *discursive phenomenon*, often fought out on the terrain of fragmented and contradictory common sense, rather than being characterized by clashes between fully formed, coherent world-views.

Finally, Gramsci's ideas have made a contribution to understanding how ideology works *by constructing subjects* – by producing new identities for us to occupy. Rather than seeing this (as most psychoanalytically inspired accounts do) as something that happens once and for all in infancy, Gramsci favoured a more dynamic and historical reading which could take account of the ways that our subjectivities can be made and re-made: in short, we change.

As with the other perspectives discussed so far, a brief example should help to illustrate these key themes. Stuart Hall (1988b) has provided one of the best Gramscian analyses in his work on the ideological power of the governments led by Margaret Thatcher in the 1980s in Britain. Hall argued that Thatcherism was best understood in Gramscian terms as a 'hegemonic project'. This is not to say that it achieved hegemony, nor does it mean that Thatcherism was purely a cultural and ideological phenomenon, but it stresses the importance to the Conservative administration of winning people's hearts and minds, not merely changing economic policy.

The Thatcher government's radical right-wing programme constituted a huge shock and change for many people in Britain at the time, used to a more consensus-based form of politics. But Stuart Hall urged people on the Left not to misread Thatcherism as an alien, external force imposed on the 'masses' from the outside, but instead to recognize its popular appeal. As he put it, Thatcherism made itself 'not only one of "them", but, more disconcertingly, a part of "us"' (Hall 1988b: 6). By addressing certain popular discontents and harnessing or articulating them to its own agenda, it was able to win popular support and, more significantly, to redefine the content of common sense.

For Gramsci, common sense is at the heart of ideology (which also has a more theoretical or philosophical domain). When ideologies come into conflict, the struggle is rarely between fully formed coherent world-views, but instead involves contestation over the meaning and ownership of particular notions – like democracy, freedom or the nation. In Britain during the Thatcher years, for example, there was intense ideological struggle over which of the two main parties could claim to be the 'party of the family'. What was contested was the very nature of the family, with the Conservative Party defining it in 'traditional' nuclear terms, and the Labour Party pushing for a broader, more inclusive definition that would include lone parents, stepfamilies and, in some formulations, gay couples with children. The task for the Labour Party was to wrest 'the family' from a traditional chain of connotations, and to build it into discourses favourable to Labour. The key point is that both political parties wanted to claim to have the true interests of the family at heart and wanted to harness this to their political project.

Hall argued that Thatcherism represented a particular articulation of liberal free-market discourses and conservative themes of tradition, family, nation, respectability, patriarchalism and order. He called the resulting mix 'authoritarian populism'. His main interest was in accounting for how it was that Thatcherism took hold of the popular imagination so quickly and so pervasively. It did so, he argues, by articulating popular discontents to its own project; something that was emphasized by the deliberate use of ordinary language – what Brunsdon and Morley (1978) describe (in another context) as 'popular ventriloquism'. Vivid metaphors, analogies and illustrations featuring 'U-turns', 'handbags' and homespun wisdom from the domestic arena helped to sediment Thatcherite ideology in common sense consciousness. A similar process can be seen with President Bush's use of baseball metaphors.

Above all, Hall argued that Thatcherism worked by creating new subject positions and by transforming subjectivities. It deliberately sought to detach people from their existing points of identification and to reposition them in new sets of discourses which hailed them as 'concerned patriot', 'self-reliant taxpayer', 'respectable home owner', and so on. Indeed, in this way, Thatcherism did nothing short of *remaking subjectivities* – as a central part of winning consent or achieving hegemony.

Gramsci's ideas have proved a powerful tool for understanding representations of gender in the media, allowing us to go beyond the study of single images to examine patterns and themes in representations. His work allows us to attend to the dynamic qualities of ideology – its mobility and fluidity; the fragmented nature of subjectivity; and the significance of winning consent for particular identities through struggle. As such, it can help us to understand (for example) the multiple and contradictory ways in which contemporary young men are addressed by the media – as new men, lads, new fathers, metrosexuals, etc. – and to analyse the struggle between these subject positions. In order to do this effectively, though, a more fine-grained approach is often needed, and it is this that we turn to next.

Discourse Analysis

The terms 'discourse' and 'discourse analysis' are as hotly contested as 'ideology' and 'ideological analysis'. Discourse analysis refers to a huge variety of approaches including critical linguistics, social semiotics, ethnomethodology and conversation analysis, speech act theory and a number of post-structuralist approaches to texts and history. In this chapter two broad traditions of discourse analysis will be examined. First, we will focus upon a tradition developed over the last two decades in the social sciences as a way of rigorously analysing a variety of different texts. Next we will look at Foucault's ideas which constitute a different – historical or genealogical – discursive analysis.

Discourse analysis (in the first sense) has been developed in recent years by scholars in sociology and social psychology (Potter 1987; Wetherell 1992; Speer 2005). It is useful to think of it as having four main themes: a concern with discourse itself, a view of language as constructive and constructed, an emphasis upon discourse as a form of action, and a conviction in the rhetorical organization of discourse. First, then, it takes *discourse* itself as its topic. The term discourse is used to refer to all forms of talk and texts, whether it be naturally occurring conversations, interview material, or written or broadcast texts of any kind. Discourse analysts are interested in texts themselves, rather than seeing them as a means of 'getting at' some reality which is deemed to lie behind the discourse – whether social or psychological or material. Instead of seeing discourse as a pathway to some other reality, discourse analysts are interested in the content and organization of texts in their own right.

The second theme of discourse analysis is that *language is constructive*. Potter and Wetherell (Potter 1987) argue that the metaphor of construction highlights three facets of the approach. First, it draws attention to the fact that discourse is built or manufactured out of preexisting linguistic resources. Secondly it illuminates the fact that the assembly of an account involves choice or selection from a number of different possibilities. It is possible to describe even the most simple of phenomena in a multiplicity of different ways. Finally, the notion of construction emphasizes the fact that we deal with the world in terms of constructions, not in a somehow 'direct' or unmediated way; in a very real sense, texts of various kinds construct our world. This basic social constructionist point highlights the connection of discourse analysis to post-structuralist and postmodernist approaches more broadly. It marks a break with traditional realist models of language in which it is taken to be a transparent medium.

The third feature of discourse analysis is its concern with the *action orientation* or function orientation of discourse. That is, discourse analysts see all discourse as social practice. Language, then, is not viewed as a mere epiphenomenon, but as a practice in its own right. People use discourse to do things – to offer blame, to make excuses, to present themselves in a positive light, etc. To highlight this is to underline the fact that discourse does not occur in a social vacuum and it is oriented to specific interpretive contexts.

Finally, discourse analysts treat talk and texts as organized rhetorically (Billig 1987, 1991). Discourse analysts see social life as being characterized by conflicts of various kinds. As such, much discourse is involved in establishing one version of the world in the face of competing versions. This is obvious in some cases – politicians, for example, are clearly attempting to win people around to their view of the world, and advertisers are attempting to sell us products, lifestyles and dreams – but it is also true of other discourse. The emphasis on the rhetorical nature of texts directs our attention to the ways in which *all* discourse is organized to make itself persuasive.

An increasing number of media scholars are adopting discourse analytic approaches (Montgomery 1986; Fairclough 1989; Scannell 1991; Fairclough 1995). In my own research on gender in popular radio I used discourse analysis to examine how broadcasters accounted for the fact that there were so few women working as presenters or DJs (Gill 1993). At the time, fewer than one in ten radio presenters was female. The research was carried out in two independent (i.e. commercial) pop radio stations in England which were typical in this respect: one employed no female presenters and the other had only one, whose show was broadcast in the early hours of the morning – the so-called 'graveyard shift'. Male radio presenters and programme controllers were interviewed and asked a whole range of questions about their role, responsibilities, view of the audience, freedom and autonomy, career progression – as well as a number of questions about the lack of women DJs.

The analysis involved careful reading and rereading of transcripts and attempts to code responses, paying attention to variability and contradiction. Six interpretive repertoires were identified which the broadcasters used to account for the lack of women in presenting roles. These were organized around the following ideas:

- women just do not apply (for the job of presenter);
- the audience prefer male presenters;
- women don't have the right skills for radio presentation;
- women who want to become broadcasters all go into journalism;
- women's voices are wrong;
- daytime radio is 'housewife radio' so it is better to have a male presenter.

The broadcasters all drew on and combined these different repertoires, moving between accounts when it felt right to do so. Thus one moment they might assert that the reason for the lack of women at the station was that no women applied or sent in demo tapes; the next they would regretfully explain that actually the issue was audience objections, or the fact that women's voices did not sound appealing on radio.

One of the things that attention to the fine detail of discourse was able to show was how carefully these accounts were constructed. They were, for example, full of disclaimers about sexism (such as 'I'm not being sexist but . . .'), and other rhetorical devices designed to head off potential criticisms of their own sexual politics or the equal opportunities practices of the radio station. The interviews were also characterized by multiple strategies to make their accounts persuasive – for example, detailed stories or narratives to act as warrants, the use of scientific terms to lend credibility and objectivity, the deployment of 'extreme case formulations' and so on.

The analysis focused attention on the way that the accounts were designed to make the lack of women appear to be natural, self-evident and – regrettably – beyond the control of the radio station. All the accounts constructed the reasons for the lack of female presenters as lying in women themselves or in the preferences of the audience. The role of the radio station was rendered indivisible in these accounts, and discussions of employment practices and institutional sexism were conspicuous by their absence. In this way, broadcasters were able to present themselves as non-sexist, while they simultaneously justified the lack of women at the radio station where they worked.

What the analysis showed, in sum, was the subtlety and the detail of the way that discrimination was practised: at no point did any one of the interviewees say that they did not think women should be employed as radio presenters – on the contrary they were keen to stress their positive attitude to female presenters and to suggest that they were (to quote one) 'looking hard' to appoint women. However, what they produced were accounts which justified the exclusion of women, while simultaneously protecting themselves against potential accusations of sexism. The research concluded that a kind of 'new sexism' was in operation, which shared a number of features with 'new racist' discourse (Barker 1981).

Foucaultian Approaches

Since the late 1980s another type of discourse analysis has had a profound impact on cultural theory: that associated with the French writer Michel Foucault. Foucault was interested in the development of modern power from the sixteenth century onwards, and specifically in understanding the shift from feudal forms of control to a new distinctively modern political rationality. His work has transformed contemporary understandings of power. Rather than seeing power as a top-down phenomenon, a 'thing' that some people wield and others are oppressed by, Foucault conceptualized it using the metaphor of the capillary or grid: it is not uniform or centralized but runs throughout the whole society.

Whilst in the feudal period power was individualized in the person of the king or sovereign who had absolute authority, Foucault argued, in the modern epoch it is dispersed, impersonal and productive rather than simply repressive:

> If power was nothing but repressive, if it never did anything but say no, do you really think that we should manage to obey it? What gives power its hold, what makes it accepted, is quite simply the fact that it does not weigh like a force which says no, but that it runs through, it produces things, it induces pleasure, it forms knowledge, it produces discourse: it must be considered as a productive network which runs through the entire social body much more than as a negative instance whose function is repression. (1980: 119)

Among the most important influences of Foucault's work in cultural and media analysis has been his critique of the notion of ideology, and his analysis of the power–knowledge nexus. Foucault rejected the Marxian emphasis on the distinction between ideology (understood as falsehood) and science or truth. He argued that it was not possible to divide up representations into those that are true and those that are false, and he was more interested in 'truth effects' and how they are linked to power. Moreover, rather than seeing science as 'innocent' and 'truthful' Foucault was concerned with the ways in which the newly emerging human and social sciences were themselves enmeshed in, and central to, power relations. For Foucault, modern power was intimately connected with the production of new knowledges which had a regulatory function – for example through the categorization and measurement of more and more areas of human life and experience, rendering them knowable and manipulable, as well as through the production of new subjects such as the hysteric, the schizophrenic, the homosexual, etc.

Peter Miller and Nikolas Rose (1997) have used this insight about power/knowledge in their analysis of the way that advertising and marketing developed together with the 'psy disciplines'. Following Foucault, they reject the idea that advertising is simply about creating and imposing 'false needs' but instead examine the way in which newly emerging psychological techniques and knowledges were mobilized to chart and anatomize (in minute detail) people's passions, desires and behaviours. Miller and Rose's insightful analysis of the Tavistock Institute of Human Relations in the post-war period in Britain highlights a number of distinct ways of understanding the consumer – psychoanalytically, psychologically and as a 'rational' shopper – which each constructed or configured the consumer in a radically different way. Rather than simply describing what was already there, Miller and Rose argue, these new perspectives and the technologies associated with them quite literally brought them into being:

> This charting does not merely uncover pre-existing desires or anxieties: it forces them into existence by new experimental situations such as the psychodynamically interpreted group discussion, that enable them to be observed, it renders them thinkable by new techniques of calculation, classification and inscription such as 'flavour profiling' and hence makes them amenable to action and instrumentalization in the service of sales of goods. (Miller and Rose 1997: 31)

Other recent work on the 'psy complex' has focused on the rise of popular therapeutic discourse as a form of regulation. Ian Hodges (2001, 2003) in his analysis of radio advice programmes uses a Foucaultian approach to examine how the shows provide an interpellation within which subjects recognize themselves as requiring therapeutic transformation; incite the caller to engage in particular techniques of the self such as monitoring and measuring their own conduct; and provide normative models of conduct such as the well-adjusted individual, the functional family, etc. The growing literature on talk shows affirms this and examines the operation of power in the incitement to 'tell all' or 'confess' on TV (see chapter 5). Rather than conceptualizing talk (e.g. about sexuality) as 'liberation from repression', Foucaultian analyses stress the roles that 'confession and testimony play within the machinery of discipline and power . . . The encouragement to "confess" on TV or anywhere else is a fundamental part of modern systems and regimes that govern sexuality' (Probyn 1997a).

Foucault's work has also made an important contribution to feminist media studies through his notion of *disciplinary power* – in which power is conceptualized as circulating through ever finer channels, invading the body and seeking to regulate every aspect of its functioning. Foucault's work focused upon the operation of discipline in specific institutions like the factory, prison, clinic and military, but a number of feminist writers have developed his ideas to examine forms of discipline that are not tied to single institutions but cut across a variety of social spheres and spaces such as the family, workplace, media, etc. Sandra Lee Bartky has argued that feminine bodily discipline is often institutionally unbounded:

> The woman who checks her makeup half a dozen times a day to see if her foundation has caked or her mascara run, who worries that the

wind or rain may spoil her hairdo, who looks frequently to see if her stockings have bagged at the ankle, or who, feeling fat, monitors everything she eats, has become, just as surely as the inmate of the panopticon, a self policing subject, a self committed to a relentless self surveillance. This self surveillance is a form of obedience to patriarchy. It is also the reflection in woman's consciousness of the fact that she is under surveillance in ways that he is not, that whatever else she may become, she is importantly a body designed to please or to excite. There has been induced in many women, then, in Foucault's words 'a state of conscious and permanent visibility that assures the automatic functioning of power'. (Bartky 1990: 80)

Foucault's analysis of surveillance and self-discipline, building on the idea of 'the panopticon' (a design for a prison in which individuals are isolated but know they can always be seen) has proved a particularly fruitful metaphor for feminist analyses of the operation of femininity as a discipline. Adverts and women's magazines have been identified as key sites of this form of power in a society increasingly oriented towards the visual media. Their representations of normative femininity form part of the 'public habitat of images' that works to discipline and regulate women's relationship to their own bodies. Bartky (1990) suggests that images of normative femininity have replaced the religious tracts of the past and now operate as a form of discipline acting on all classes of women throughout the life cycle. A key challenge has been to understand how this disciplinary power works, how women engage in self surveillance, and to theorize this in ways that do not render women only as passive, docile subjects (Sawicki 1991; Bordo 1999).

Feminine bodily discipline has this dual character: on the one hand, no one is marched off for electrolysis at the end of the rifle, nor can we fail to appreciate the initiative and ingenuity displayed by countless women in an attempt to master the rituals of beauty. Nevertheless, in so far as the disciplinary practices of femininity produces a 'subjected and practised', an inferiorized, body, they must be understood as aspects of a far larger discipline, an inegalitarian system of sexual subordination. This system aims at turning women into the docile and compliant companions of men just as surely as the army aims to turn its raw recruits into soldiers. (Bartky 1990: 75)

Some writers have argued that gender itself is a disciplinary technique: Judith Butler (1990) famously regards it as a 'regulatory fiction', while Teresa de Lauretis (1989) argues that gender is the product of various social technologies including film and media. Both writers have been profoundly influenced by Foucault, both engage with contemporary texts of various kinds, and both pose the question of how to think about gender *beyond the limits of sexual difference.*

Foucault's notion of *normalization* has also been a valuable one in analyses of gender and media. Since the seventeenth century and the birth of statistics (the science of the state), the state has been amassing more and more details about every aspect of populations' lives. The power to regulate through description, measurement, calculation of differences between individuals and the norm has taken over from simple sovereign power. Increasingly, appeal is made to statistical measures and judgements about what is normal rather than absolute notions of right and wrong. These procedures of normalization operate upon every aspect of our intimate lives from the cradle to the grave, rendering into norms our frequency and type of sexual intercourse, the number of times each year we consult a doctor, our consumption of units of alcohol, how often we watch television, our weight and body mass index, etc., etc. Such discourses are central to an increasing number of media products, from magazine quizzes to advice columns and reality TV shows, as we are invited to survey and discipline the self by comparing our own conduct with what is 'normal' (Currie 1999).

Finally, Foucault's *methodology* – in particular his later genealogical approach – has had an important influence on some media analysts. His work refuses mono-causal explanations, single totalizing stories, and he attempts to write 'histories of the present' that disrupt the sense of obviousness about the way things are: 'The genealogist tries to rediscover the multiplicity of factors and processes which constitute an event in order to disrupt the self-evident quality ascribed to events through the employment of historical concepts and the description of anthropological traits' (quoted in McNay 1992). In contemporary media studies this emphasis can be seen in Sean Nixon's (1996) analysis of the development of new sexualized ways of representing the male body in the late 1980s. Drawing on Foucault's approach, his achievement is to show that the emerging representational practices for signifying masculinity had multiple points of origin – in advertising, photography, fashion, retailing, etc; they were not the result of one single change (see also Gill 2003).

Postmodernism, Postcolonialism, and Queer Theory

Foucault explicitly rejected the terms 'post-structuralist' and 'postmodernist' to describe his work. Nevertheless his ideas have been extremely important to and influential within these bodies of work – taken up by feminist postmodernists, postcolonial writers and queer theorists. In this final section of the chapter we look briefly at these traditions and their importance for media studies.

Postmodernism, postcolonial theory and queer theory cannot be described as approaches in the way that content analysis, semiotics and discourse analysis are; they are not methods that can be applied to single texts or straightforwardly deployed to analyse a corpus of representations. Rather they are best thought of as critical orientations to textual analysis, ways of reading critically or against the grain, 'writing back' and making political interventions. In key respects they also challenge the distinction between criticism and cultural production, and postmodern, postcolonial and queer are used as frequently to designate cultural products and their creators as modes of critical inquiry, for example a postmodern building, a queer film, a postcolonial novel.

Postmodernism

Postmodernism has been one of the most debated terms of the last decades. As the cultural theorist Dick Hebdige (1988) has noted, the term is 'overloaded' – bearing the weight of many different meanings. For the purpose of clarity it can be useful to think of postmodernism as having four different types of meaning:

Postmodernism as artistic movement   Probably the most specific way in which postmodernism is used is to refer to an artistic movement in painting, literature, music and architecture. The term was first coined by a group of artists and critics working in New York in the 1960s (including the composer John Cage and critic Susan Sontag). They wanted a term that would distinguish what they were doing from what they saw as 'high modernism' which they believed had become exhausted and rendered safe through its institutionalization in the academy, the gallery system and international art markets. In order for art to play its proper questioning and subversive role, they argued, a new movement was needed that would be as radical as Expressionism or Cubism or Dadaism had been at the beginning of the twentieth century. They called this movement postmodernism (see Foster 1985 for a helpful discussion).

Postmodernism as cultural trend   A second way in which postmodernism is used is to refer to general cultural trends that go beyond art and architecture. The media and popular culture are often described as postmodern and this is a way of suggesting that they are characterized by some of the following features: a mixing of forms from high culture and popular culture and, more significantly, a breakdown of agreement about the criteria for judging cultural worth; pastiche, bricolage, fragmentation and genre mixing; intertextuality; knowingness;

nostalgia; irony; preoccupation with the surface/aesthetic values – looks, fashion, spectacle – rather than depth (see Featherstone 1991 for further elaboration).

Postmodernism as historical epoch   Some people use the term postmodernism to refer not to trends or styles of cultural or artistic movements but to designate a historical shift beyond modernity. The dates for a shift vary according to different theorists, but broadly speaking focus upon the period from the late 1960s onwards. The change is understood as having been driven by a move into a distinct period of (late) capitalism, characterized by changes in the organization of work and production – including a shift from Fordism to post Fordism, increasing globalization of capitalism, and a move to much more flexible forms of production consumption and accumulation (Harvey 1990; Jameson 1984).

Postmodernism as epistemological crisis   The notion of postmodernism is also widely used to signal a crisis in the ability of philosophy to underwrite knowledge production. The crisis – and thus postmodernism – was prompted by a number of factors. First, feminism and movements against racism and colonialism all challenged the claim of philosophy to speak about universal subjects. Together, they highlighted the fact that the supposedly universal knowing subject at the heart of philosophy was in fact historically and socially situated – and was invariably and implicitly a white, First World, male subject. Secondly, the notion of the unified rational subject, built on enlightenment ideas about the autonomy of reason and the equation of mind and consciousness, was called into question by psychoanalysis which stressed the pre-eminent position of the unconscious and of fantasy and desire in understanding human action. Thirdly, post-structuralist ideas, and in particular ideas from discourse theory, challenged the basis of the entire enterprise of philosophy – namely the possibility of representing reality. As we have seen, discursive theories argued that language is not a neutral, transparent medium which can be used to reflect or represent the world, but is active and constructive. Such approaches recast social life as thoroughly textual so that, rather than language merely representing truths about the world, the very idea of truth came to be understood as an effect of discourse. Fourthly, postmodernist theorists problematized the grand narratives or meta-narratives – ideas of History, Reason, Science, Marxism as too 'big', too universalistic and totalizing (Lyotard 1984). Moreover they were constructed from binary oppositions which constituted a central organizing principle of Western philosophy – for example, nature/culture, emotional/rational, female/male. Deconstruction showed how these binaries worked by projecting all the chaos and disorder onto the subordinated of each binary pair – hence feminist oppositional slogans such as 'I won't play nature to your culture' (Weedon 1987). This crisis has had an enormous impact across arts, social sciences and humanities – interrogating the very nature of knowledge production. Two bodies of work which have 'pushed' the crisis are postcolonialism and queer theory.

Postcolonialism

Like postmodernism, the term postcolonialism is used in multiple, overlapping and contradictory ways – for example, we can distinguish historical, literary and psychoanalytic variants and even hybrid postcolonialisms. Early uses of the hyphenated form were used to designate a specific historical moment after colonies secured their independence – a moment of decolonization and the end of direct territorial control. However, the usefulness of such a definition is called into question by ongoing complex forms of intervention and control in the New World (Dis) Order: structural adjustment policies, aid tied to political reform, nation building, the 'liberalization' of the global economy – these could all be read as new forms of colonization (to say nothing of increasingly aggressive Anglo-American foreign policy and the 'War on Terrorism'). As Anne McClintock (1995) has argued, the 'post' in postcolonial may be prematurely celebratory and a variety of neocolonialisms are in play (see also Hall 1996; Spivak 1988). Today, the term is used less to signify the end of colonialism than to locate postcolonial theory in 'the historical fact of European colonialism' and to 'reject the diffusion of the term . . . to refer to any kind of marginality at all' (Ashcroft, Griffiths and Tiffin 1995).

It is important to note that the 'post' in postcolonialism is not necessarily the same as the 'post' in postmodernism – precisely because of the former's location in the brutal material reality of colonialism. Indeed, a potent postcolonial critique of postmodernism is in fact its Eurocentrism – its irrelevance to, or, worse, violence to the vast majority of the world's people whose experiences are not in the least 'postmodern'. Notwithstanding this, there are significant shared themes. Foucault's notion of power/knowledge has been at the heart of postcolonial theorizing. For European imperial powers 'knowing the Other' was central to political and economic control, and was achieved through the development of a colonial sociology concerned with categorizing and differentiating its subjects.

The postmodernist/deconstructive project of exposing the binaries on which Western thought depends is also central – in explicitly political terms – to postcolonial theorizing. Edward Said' s groundbreaking study of Orientalism is perhaps the classic example of this, showing how Orientalism as a discourse depended on a binary relationship with 'the Occident': 'Orientalism is more particularly valuable as a sign of European-Atlantic power over the Orient than it is as a veridic discourse about the Orient (which, in its academic form, it claims to be)' (Said 1985: 6). As Trinh Minh-ha (1991) has argued, the meaning of 'Third World person' (or 'colonized subject' or 'blackness') cannot be specified independently, but comes from its contrast with a silent binary-other. The task of postcolonial writing is not to reverse the binary relationship – colonizer and colonized, centre and periphery – but to displace binary discourses altogether:

> Without a certain work of displacement, again, the margins can easily comfort the centre in its goodwill and liberalism; strategies of reversal thereby meet with their own limits . . . By displacing, it never allows this classifying world to exert its classificatory power without returning it to its own ethnocentric classifications. (Minh-ha 1991: 17)

The job of the postcolonial intellectual is to trouble or upset or interrupt, to analyse and disrupt the representational practices that make such epistemic violence possible. Ien Ang likens him or her to a party pooper:

> The diasporic intellectual acts as a perpetual party pooper here because her impulse is to point to ambiguities, complexities and contradictions, to complicate matters rather than provide merely for solutions, to blur distinctions between coloniser and colonised, dominant and subordinate, oppressor and oppressed. (Ang 2001: 2)

Most postcolonial work, then, is (like most postmodernism) committed to a radical anti-essentialism. Its project is not to reclaim or give voice to the experiences of the oppressed or colonized. Indeed, answering her own question – can the subaltern speak? – Gayatri Spivak (1988) is sceptical of whether it is possible to recover a subaltern voice that is not a kind of essentialist fiction. She argues that postcolonial intellectual work must avoid reproducing it as merely another unproblematic field of knowing (see also Hall 1988a on the problems with the 'essential black subject'). The tactics of postcolonial writing are largely deconstructive rather than making counter-hegemonic claims. They aim to disrupt, to focus on the 'in between', to create 'the third space', to emphasize hybridity (Bhabha 1990, 1994).

Within media studies, the impact of postcolonial theory has been felt in a variety of ways (although there is still some considerable way to go before its transformative potential is met). There has been the emergence of 'new' constituencies, politico-regional articulations such as Chicana/o and Latina/o cultural studies – albeit positioned against 'nativist essentialism' and identity politics (Quinonez and Aldama 2002). Postcolonial theory has also generated renewed attention to the 'politics of location' (Mohanty 1988) in a postmodern world where any overarching sense of who 'we' are has become problematic and contentious. Ethical and political questions about representing Others are on the agenda (though without the impact they should have) and there is a new focus on interrogating whiteness (Carby 1982; Frankenberg 1993; Fine 1996; Gilkes, Kaloski-Naylor et al. 1999; Ware and Back 2002; Fine 2004). 'Globalization' has become a central topic of analysis, with theorizations that attempt to challenge the global/local binary and examine complex flows of power and resistance (Gillespie 1995; Morley and Robins 1995). Interestingly, postcolonial theorizing has also led to a revitalization of 'political economy' approaches which focus not only on the cultural power of multinational corporations but also on their economic power, globalized employment practices, etc.

Queer theory

Since the early 1990s, queer theory has also had a significant impact in media studies, particularly on those traditions of textual analysis with origins in the humanities. Like postcolonialism, its political intent and impact have been to disrupt and destabilize rather than to advance alternative truth claims. There are now 'queer readings' of everything from Shakespeare to Bridget Jones, and 'queer' can be used as a verb – thus public spaces can be 'queered', as can film-making practices, modes of consumption, etc. (Sinfield 1994).

Queer theory emerged as the complex outcome of a number of different factors – the influence of Foucault's ideas, particularly his work on the history of sexuality; the shortcomings of identity-based liberation politics for lesbians and gay men; and the exigencies of activism around the AIDS crisis. 'Queer' is often used as a shorthand to refer to 'lesbians, gay, bisexual, transgender' (LGBT). As Stephen Epstein puts it, the term:

> offers a comprehensive way of characterising all those whose sexuality places them in opposition to the current 'normalising regime'. 'Queer' has become convenient shorthand as various sexual minorities have claimed territory in the space once known simply, if misleadingly, as 'the gay community'. As stated by an editor of the defunct New York City queer magazine Outweek, 'when you're trying to describe the community, and you have to list gays, lesbians, bisexuals, drag queens, transsexuals (post-op and pre) it gets unwieldy. Queer says it all.' (1996: 150)

But 'queer' is much more than this: its import is less in providing an inclusive term to help magazine editors, than in marking a break with previous 'minoritarian' and subcultural models of activism in which lesbians and gay men saw themselves as oppressed minorities with similar claims to minority ethnic groups. It signals a new kind of political engagement framed in terms that are more explicitly confrontational to the heteronormative order. Moreover, it foregrounds the instability in the supposedly stable relationship between sex, gender and sexual desire. Above all, queer theory constitutes an attack on the notion of stable identity as a foundation for theory or political action.

Among the most influential contemporary queer theorists are Judith Butler, Eve Kosofsky Sedgwick, Theresa de Lauretis and David Halperin (De Lauretis 1984, 1989; Butler 1990; Sedgwick 1991; Butler 2004). These scholars have all been profoundly influenced by post-structuralist and postmodernist thinking (as well as – to varying extents – psychoanalysis). They are sceptical of the notion of the unified, coherent and autonomous subject, seeing it as an ideological fiction. Subjectivity is not a pure essence but is constituted in and through discourses and social structures. Lesbian, gay, bisexual and trans subjectivities are no exception – and thus should be regarded as provisional and contingent rather than fixed. From this perspective a position that regarded LGBT as stable identities would always be problematic – no matter how progressive its intent. Not only is it 'wrong' (that is, inaccurate) from any position influenced by postmodern thought, but it is also politically dubious because homosexuality is never an autonomous category but is part of a binary that works to privilege and stabilize heterosexuality.

This reading owes a great deal to Foucault. For him, the category 'homosexual' was a product of both the agents of social control (e.g. psychiatrists and sexologists) who defined it in the late nineteenth century, *and* the people who mobilized around it to attempt to reverse or contest its negative construction. Although this activism challenged the meaning of homosexuality, it also helped to solidify the very idea of a binary. This illustrates the complex nature of power/knowledge and the intimate relationship between power and resistance.

A further way in which the focus on lesbian and gay identities was regarded by queer theorists as problematic was on account of its multiple exclusions. As Robert Corber and Stephen Valocchi (2003) have argued, the field's 'focus' cannot account for practices such as cross-dressing, sadomasochism and transsexualism, not defined by the gender of object choice, and, in this way, lesbian and gay studies does not address the full range of non normative genders and sexualities. Moreover, in practice, the idealized subject at the heart of many lesbian and gay discourses has repeatedly been identified as a white, middle-class, able-bodied, young male.

Like the 'party-pooping' postcolonial intellectual, the queer theorist's/activist's job is to interrupt and disrupt the smooth functioning of the heterosexual/homosexual binary, with the aim of dismantling it. Judith Butler's work has been central to this project and has also secured an ongoing dialogue between feminism and queer theory (Weed and Schor 1997). In her book *Gender Trouble*, Butler reversed the feminist understanding of the relation between sex and gender – a relation in which (biological) sex was understood as providing the foundation for (social/cultural) gender. Butler argued that 'sex itself is a gendered category'. It is not the means of underwriting gender, but one of gender's most powerful effects. Butler's work severed the idea of a necessary connection between sex, gender and sexuality and argued that identities are performatively constituted by the very expressions of gender and sexuality that are thought to be produced by them. Her argument is not a humanist one: what is conceptualized is not role-playing in which a knowing subject 'behind' the performance controls the enactment of gender. More radically, Butler is suggesting that it is the repeated performance that produces gendered subjectivity. Because of this, the knowing performance of drag or camp can be used to disrupt and subvert the process and draw attention to the performance of gender and sexuality.

Queer readings of media texts – like some postcolonial critique – highlight the importance of the heterosexual/homosexual binary to their functioning, and/or show how homosexuality is key but repressed. Another powerful critical tool is the notion of heteronormativity which refers to the ways in which particular structures privilege heterosexuality. It allows for the possibility that there may be modes of organizing sexual relations between straight people that are not heteronormative and, conversely, patterns of organizing gay and lesbian sexual relations that are. A good example of this might be the US sitcom *Will and Grace*, in which the sexual aspects of homosexuality are completely erased and the two protagonists – a straight woman and a gay man – are presented as ABM (all but married). Indeed, it could be argued that most media representations of LGBT persons and lifestyles are deeply heteronormative and represent little challenge to the existing structures of gender and sexuality.

Conclusion

This chapter has covered an extraordinary amount of ground. It has tried to convey the range of different approaches that can be used for studying gender representations, from those, like content analysis, which regard gender as something that can be unproblematically quantified, to those, like discursive, queer and 'post' theories, that regard its construction as inextricably linked to historically produced binaries about race, colonialism and sexuality.

It is hoped that this chapter, like the previous one, offers a useful foundation for the discussions that follow. But a word of caution is needed: it is not always possible to neatly identify the approaches being used in analyses of actual media texts. This is partly because very often analysts do not name or make explicit the approaches they are using or because they are theoretically pluralist and draw on more than one approach. It is also because the impact of each of the approaches has been felt well beyond its specific domain. In particular, discourse theory and postmodern approaches have had reverberations across media studies. Sometimes I have pointed this out, highlighting, for example, the impact of Foucault's ideas on how talk shows or magazines are understood. But word constraints together with an absence of published material have meant that this is not always possible. The challenge for you – the reader – is to use the tools provided here to think through for yourself how the different approaches conceptualize the issues. How might queer theory understand the emergence of 'new lad' imagery? Is postmodernism useful for making sense of contemporary advertising? What might a postcolonial critique of chick lit look like? – and so on. In posing these questions the key point of this chapter should become clear: namely that the different perspectives produce different knowledge about the media. Quite simply, they make the world knowable in different ways.

3

Advertising and Postfeminism

ADVERTISING is inescapable and ubiquitous in Northern/Western societies, and increasingly elsewhere too. It is estimated that the average US citizen sees or hears 3,000 adverts each day (Kilbourne 2000). When you translate that into the notional time spent 'interacting' with adverts, and work it out as a fraction of a lifetime, the results are sobering; Kilbourne puts the figure at approximately three years in the average lifetime of a North American. It is clear that adverts are at the heart of our social existence. Indeed, the magnitude of advertising's influence has been compared to that of education and organized religion (Lazier-Smith 1989). It constitutes a 'vast superstructure' (Williamson 1978) and is, according to Leiss, Kline and Jhally (1986) the most consistent body of material in the mass media.

As well as having a huge influence on audiences/consumers, advertising is also key to media production. It is central to the entire political economy of the media. At the start of the twenty-first century, advertising revenues fund all but a few remaining state-run or community broadcasters, as well as the lion's share of newspaper and magazine publishing, and, increasingly, worldwide web content. Advertising influences – both directly and indirectly – the kinds of programme that are made and not made, and whether a new magazine title will survive in the market. It is often said, for example, that television networks produce few programmes aimed at the elderly since they do not represent a group that can be easily 'sold' to advertisers, whereas young, upwardly mobile people with considerable disposable income are the individuals that most networks attempt to seduce, court and nurture. It may be an obvious point but it is worth making: advertising has a profound impact on the entire shape and content of contemporary media.

Perhaps more than any other type of media content, advertising has been the target of extensive feminist critique and discussion (Van Zoonen 1994). As Sut Jhally (1987) has argued, this is partly because gender ideology is the single biggest resource for advertisers. Since the late 1960s there has been considerable feminist scholarship examining advertising, and it has also been the object of much feminist activism, with campaigns ranging from boycotts of companies using women in demeaning or offensive ways in their advertisements, protests to regulatory bodies against specific advertising campaigns, sticker campaigns highlighting women's anger at the way they are portrayed in adverts, to acts of semiotic 'guerrilla' graffiti – rewriting advertising copy in amusing and subversive ways.

The aim of this chapter is to review some of the early studies on gender and advertising, and also to consider in detail the way that some of these feminist campaigns, and the broader cultural shift created by feminism, have impacted on advertising. Specifically, the chapter is designed to explore the way that advertisers responded to feminist anger at always being addressed in terms of idealized, perfect images of unattainable femininity, and developed new advertising strategies that partly appropriated the cultural power of feminism, while often emptying it of its radical critique. The primary focus of the chapter is on contemporary advertising, and it explores a number of key shifts in regimes of representation away from depictions of women as happy housewives or sex objects, towards what might be understood as *postfeminist* representations in which confident, sexually assertive women dominate, irony is ubiquitous, and men's bodies are presented as erotic spectacles almost as much as women's.

The chapter is divided into three broad sections. In the first, I look at how advertising is changing, and how, in turn, resistance to advertising is changing. The second section focuses on gender in advertisements, and reviews the most important studies of advertising from the 1970s and 1980s, highlighting their key findings. It examines the extent to which these earlier studies have anything to say about contemporary advertising, and explores some of the trends which prompted advertisers to rethink their strategies. The third section is by far the longest of the chapter and looks at ten of the most important themes of postfeminist advertising. These include the shift from sexual objectification to sexual subjectification, the rise of queer chic, and the proliferation of sometimes vicious revenge adverts directed at men. The themes do not exhaust an analysis of contemporary gender in advertisements, and in the conclusion there will be brief discussion of some of the other key shifts.

Advertising in the Mediascape

Advertisers, media companies and other businesses are becoming increasingly entangled and interdependent. We live, as Andrew Wernick (1991) puts it, in a 'promotional culture'. This can be seen clearly at the level of consumption whenever a new film targeted at children is launched, and is accompanied by every kind of product tie-in imaginable, from clothes, toys, school equipment, magazines and furniture, to a myriad of different kinds of food and drink products – Bugs Life potato chips, Toy Story pizza, Harry Potter cakes, and so on. Venturing to almost any local (global) supermarket shows that this phenomenon is not limited to children's products: new *diet* Chardonnay was perfectly timed to coincide with the launch of *Bridget Jones: The Movie*, and a myriad of snack foods are repackaged to coincide with the World Cup or the Olympics. More and more, advertising is becoming part of the production process of everything from cookies to cars to movies. In this way it influences the very look, design, smell, taste, feel and capacities of the product, rather than being a separate add-on function brought in to sell the product after it has been produced and packaged.

Advertising is changing rapidly, with consequences for media content, social relations and global capitalism. Changes include the increasingly blurred differentiation between advertising and other activities – marked by the coining of neologisms. We now have 'retailtainment' and 'advertorials' to cite just two examples of new hybrids which are redefining previously stable categories.

New forms of advertising are emerging too, partly as a result of the growth of the Web. Viral advertising and interactive advertising have both taken off and become mainstream within the last few years. Levi's advertisers studied the ways in which underground party/'rave' promoters drew crowds with flyers, lamp-post stickers, and so on. The agency then set up a viral advertising programme that used these means, and also pirate radio stations, to broadcast 'secret information' on where to find the new line of jeans. The idea behind the campaign was to create a sense of 'sneaking' the Levi's name into the hottest clubs, street scenes and websites (Berger 2001). Interactive advertising, using the extraordinary explosion of mobile and Internet technologies, is also routine – many campaigns now feature telephone numbers or website addresses, before they even mention the product – generating anticipation and interest through tantalizing slogans or arresting images. Interestingly, many of the 'spoof' adverts which anyone with a mobile phone or e-mail account will receive, are today likely to have been produced by the agency itself, in parallel with the actual campaign. Agencies know that they can rely on people to circulate witty, sexual or amusing spoofs amongst their friends via these technologies achieving a saturation rate they could only dream of with their actual advertisement. We live in an era of 360 degree branding, as the advertising agency Ogilvy and Mather put it.

Advertising is increasingly global, and has become one of the most powerful forms of global communication. Many large companies have established global brand images and even own and control the use of the brand colours in the environment (e.g. the red and white that Coca-Cola have branded as their own). Other companies have experimented with 'localizing' their advertising production so that the products may be made to fit more harmoniously into a specific national, cultural, ethnic and religious setting. Either way it is hard to overestimate the significance of the role being played by advertising both economically and culturally in the processes of globalization.

Alongside these other changes resistance to advertising – and to global capitalism – is also changing and taking on some new forms (Klein 1999; Carty 1997). The extract below shows part of the correspondence between the NikeCorp and one individual from Massachusetts who attempted to take up their 'special offer' to 'personalize' his trainers – requesting that the word 'sweatshop' be sewn on under the swoosh. What is striking about this example is the connection that is made between the company's alleged practice of using sweated, child labour and the 'liberatory' feel of its advertising campaigns. The entire correspondence was circulated globally by e-mail in early 2001. As one forwarder wrote: 'this will now go round the world much faster and farther than any of the adverts they paid Michael Jordan, more than the entire wage packet of all their sweatshop workers in the world to do . . . I normally avoid making a plea to pass on these things, but this time I say: just do it':

> From: 'Personalize, NIKE iD'
> To: xxxxxxxxx
> Subject: Your NIKE iD order
>
> Your NIKE ID order was cancelled for one or more of the following reasons:
>
> 1) your personal ID contains another party's trademark or other intellectual property
> 2) your personal ID contains the name of an athlete or team we do not have the legal right to use
> 3) your personal ID was left blank. Did you not want any personalization?
> 4) your personal ID contains profanities or inappropriate slang, and, besides, your mother would slap us.
>
> If you wish to reorder your NIKE ID product with a new personalization please visit us again at www.nike.com
>
> To 'Personalize, Nike iD'
> From: xxxxxxxxx
> Subject: My NIKE iD order
>
> Greetings,
>
> My order was cancelled but my personal NIKE ID does not violate any of the criteria outlined in your message. The personal ID on my custom ZOOM XC USA running shoes was the word 'sweatshop'.

Sweatshop is not
1) another party's trademark
2) the name of an athlete
3) blank, or
4) profanity

I chose the ID because I wanted to remember the toil and labour of the children that made my shoes. Could you please ship them to me immediately.

Thanks and happy new year

From: 'Personalize, NIKE iD'
To: xxxxxxxxx
Subject: Your NIKE iD order

Dear NIKE ID customer

Your NIKE ID order was cancelled because the ID you have chosen contains, as stated in the previous e-mail correspondence, 'inappropriate slang'. If you wish to reorder your NIKE ID product with a new personalization please visit us again at nike.com.

Thank you, NIKE ID

To 'Personalize, Nike iD'
From: xxxxxxxxx
Subject: My NIKE iD order

Dear NIKE ID

Thank you for your quick response to my inquiry about my custom ZOOM XC. USA running shoes. Although I commend you for your prompt customer service, I disagree with the claim that my personal ID was inappropriate slang. After consulting Webster's dictionary, I discovered that 'sweatshop' is in fact part of standard English, and not slang The word means: 'a shop or factory in which workers are employed for long hours at low wages and under unhealthy conditions' and its origin dates from 1892. So my personal ID does meet the criteria detailed in your first e-mail.

Your website advertises that the NIKE ID programme is 'about freedom to choose and freedom to express who you are.' I share NIKE's love of freedom and personal statement. The site also says that 'if you want it done right . . . Build it yourself.' I was thrilled to be able to build my own shoes, and my personal ID was offered as a small token of appreciation for the sweatshop workers poised to help me realize my vision. I hope that you will value my freedom of statement and reconsider your decision to reject my order.

Thank you.

The correspondence continued until Mr xxxxxxxx withdrew his request.

Gender in Advertisements

One of the first major studies of television advertising was conducted by the National Organization of Women, who published the results in the *New York Times Magazine* in 1972 (Hennessee 1972). The study analysed more than 1,200 commercials shown on US television over an eighteen-month period. It found that more than one-third of adverts showed women as domestic agents who were dependent upon men, and nearly half portrayed women as 'household functionaries'. The study also reported many examples of women depicted as 'decorative objects' and portrayed as 'unintelligent', and it highlighted the fact that men occupied almost all the authoritative roles in adverts.

When this study was first published, a number of objections were raised about its professionalism and credibility. In particular, the validity of coding on subjective criteria such as dependence or intelligence was interrogated, as was the reliability of judgements made by large numbers of untrained coders (see Gunter 1995). These are fair questions to raise about the rigour of any study. However, what appears striking in retrospect is how the NOW study prefigured the results of almost two decades of subsequent research. Throughout the 1970s and 1980s, study after study found the same consistent and pronounced pattern of gender stereotyping in adverts in the US, UK and elsewhere: women were predominantly shown in the home, depicted as housewives and mothers; they were frequently shown in dependent or subservient roles; and rarely provided an argument in favour of the advertised products with which they appeared. In contrast, men were portrayed in a range of settings and occupational roles; as independent and autonomous; and were presented as objective and knowledgeable about the products they used. (See Gunter 1994 for summary.)

Clear patterns relating to attractiveness and authority were identified across studies, with women presented as visually attractive and men as authoritative figures. One common way in which this was analysed was by examining the use of voice-overs. Studies consistently showed that male voices were used in between 80 and 90 per cent of voice-overs (e.g. Livingstone and Green 1986; Furnham and Bitar 1993). In fact, research by Lovdal (1989) found that when women's voices are employed in adverts they are most frequently used to address cats, dogs, babies, children and female dieters – rather than the population at large.

When we look not just at the generic group 'women' but at specific groups of women, the picture can seem even more depressing. Older women are conspicuous by their absence in most advertising, and when they are shown they are depicted in a narrow range of (often unflattering) stereotypes such as gossip, interfering mother/mother-in-law. Women outside the heterosexual norm will also not see their lives reflected in advertising. Invisibility is the norm, with this challenged – problematically – by a growing number of representations of highly sexualized 'lipstick lesbians', usually kissing another woman (see discussion in next section).

Black women are frequently portrayed in crude stereotypes, often signalling animalistic sexuality, exotic 'otherness' or 'soul'. Representations of women of African origin frequently play on themes of 'darkness' and sexuality, for example Tia Maria's After Dark adverts, and Options cocoa drinks adverts, in which both the woman and the drink are signified as 'hot chocolate'. When women of Asian origin are shown, sexual submissiveness and sexual services are often indexed – not least in the airline adverts that have been a notorious site of this stereotype. Increasingly, sexist and racist images of women are globalizing. Michelle Lazar (2004) argues that to appeal in different global markets identikit images of pan-Asian femininity are being created, which 'blend between East and West' constructing a 'globalised consumer sisterhood' through purchase of particular products. This marks a new chapter in a long history of advertising's relationship with colonization, in which the rest of the world is offered up in (often sexualized) commodity form (Williamson 1986c).

A landmark study by the sociologist Erving Goffman (1979) provided another way of coding gender differentiation in advertisements, concentrating on the way in which non-verbal signals communicated important differences in male and female power. Examining magazine and billboard advertising, Goffman analysed several key features of the representations of men's and women's bodies in advertisements. He concluded that adverts frequently depict ritualized versions of the parent–child relationship, in which women are largely accorded childlike status. Women were typically shown lower or smaller than men and using gestures which 'ritualized their subordination', for example, lying down, using bashful knee bends, canting postures or deferential smiles. Women were also depicted in 'licensed withdrawal': slightly distanced from a scene, gazing into the distance, not quite there. The predilection of advertisers for showing women looking into mirrors, with only the reflection captured, is another way of achieving this, which additionally conveys the message that women are narcissistic.

Goffman also identified clear differences in the kinds of touch that women and men in adverts employ. While men's touch was functional and instrumental – reaching out and grabbing that shaving foam or hair gel – women's was light and caressing and often seemed to have no purpose at all. In fact, even when the product seemed to require some action from the person using it, as in the case of shower gel, men would be shown lathering up busily, while women were routinely depicted making only a small circular movement on one shoulder. Women were shown touching themselves constantly, especially on the face, and were also depicted running their fingers gently along a range of products. In a recent advert, a young woman is even shown gently caressing a sanitary pad, a look of far-away wonderment on her face – presumably marvelling at the ingenuity of its 'wings'!

Goffman's work has been developed by many other writers to examine the body's presentation in advertising. Perhaps the major insight of subsequent feminist work has been the analysis of how 'cropping' is used in adverts. Many studies have highlighted the way in which women's bodies are fragmented in adverts, visually dissected so that the viewer sees only the lips, or the eyes, or the breasts, or whatever (G. Dyer 1982; Coward 1984). This frequently mirrors the text in which women's bodies are presented simply as a composite of problems, each requiring a product-solution. The effect is to deny women's humanity, to present them not as whole people but as fetishized, dismembered 'bits'. Interestingly, as I discuss later, this is one area where advertising imagery is changing: while cropping used to be the sole province of women's bodies, it is now, increasingly, used to depict men's torsos too – headless and legless 'six-packs' taking their place next to women's dismembered bodies.

A number of studies have discussed cropping in terms of violence. Jean Kilbourne argues:

> Adverts don't directly cause violence . . . But the violent images contribute to the state of terror . . . Turning a human being into a thing, an object, is almost always the first step towards justifying violence against that person . . . This step is already taken with women. The violence, the abuse, is partly the chilling but logical result of the objectification. (Kilbourne 1999: 278)

Many adverts use images of violence or the suggestion of violence to create a frisson of risk and danger. As Grainger and Jackson have argued: 'In a world inundated with media messages . . . Advertisers have been forced to invent new strategies in order to identify their products and arrest your attention. Arguably, one such strategy has been the appropriation and exploitation of violence' (1999: 515, quoted in Carter and Weaver 2003).

Anthony Cortese (1999) has collected together several examples of what he calls 'mock assault' in adverts, including an ad for Karl Lagerfeld perfume in which a frightened-looking, sexualized woman is portrayed backed against a wall, while a powerful muscular man (seen only from behind) bears down on her. The notion that this is pleasurable seduction is disavowed by the woman's posture and facial expression and the scene is instead reminiscent of shots from film and television of violent sexual attacks on women. Often a male body does not need to be in the frame for violence against women to be implied – shadows routinely create similar sinister and threatening effects. This can also, of course, be achieved with words. In 2003 the car maker Audi used the slogan 'He has the money, he has the car and he'll have the woman' in its marketing campaign in France, while Suchard promoted its chocolates with a nude model and the words 'You say no, but we hear yes' (Henley 2003). There appears to have been a striking increase in violent imagery in adverts in recent years, and Judith Williamson (2003) has argued that the portrayal of male–female relations in adverts increasingly draws on troubling sadomasochistic imagery. 'Porno chic' (McNair 2002) has become a mainstay of advertising, constructed around the figure of the provocative child-woman, who is usually extraordinarily thin, vulnerable looking and portrayed in a highly sexualized manner.

Several scholars have argued that advertising representations of gender changed significantly in other apparently more positive ways in the 1990s (e.g. Goldman 1992; Macdonald 1995). A study by Furnham and Skae (1997) in the UK found that women were more likely to be portrayed in the workplace, to be accorded status as authorities and to be represented as independent individuals than they were in previous decades – although most other features of their presentation remain as before. European research suggests that sexism is mutating from its older more obvious forms to become more subtle and masked (Kivikuru 1997; Hrzenjak et al. 2002). In Central Europe, the transformations towards a market economy after the collapse of the Berlin Wall in 1989 have resulted in a new stereotype of women as sexual objects (Marinescu 1995; Roventa-Frumusani 1995).

More generally, the traditional image of 'wife-mother-housewife' is now being replaced by images of sexually assertive, confident and ambitious women who express their 'freedom' through consumption (Kivikuru 1997; Macdonald 1995). Rather than the 'sex object' being one image of womanhood among several available options (well, OK, two or three available options), increasingly *all* representations of women in adverts are being refracted through sexually objectifying imagery: in the boardroom and in the bedroom, in the kitchen and in the car, wife and mother or executive or pre-teenager, women are being presented as alluring sexual beings. The 'splitting' of yesteryear, in which women were divided into safe, reassuring, motherly figures located in the home, and young, free, sexy symbols in the workplace has given way to a style of representation in which every woman must embody all those qualities. This is the new superwoman: intelligent, accomplished, effortlessly beautiful, a wonderful hostess and perfect mother who also holds down a demanding professional position. As Jean Kilbourne (1995) notes, women are now expected to meet standards of physical perfection that only a mannequin could achieve.

Perhaps this explains why one of the most consistently popular images of womanhood among heterosexual boys and young men is Lara Croft, a computer-generated simulation with legs like skyscrapers and a 34DD bra fitting. Lara proved so appealing to the men and boys who were the predominant buyers of the Tomb Raider computer games that Smith-Kline-Beecham purchased the rights to use her image in their commercials for Lucozade. When asked to play Lara in the film of Tomb Raider, the actress Angelina Jolie spoke of the incredible range of technological and cosmetic techniques that were required to reconstruct her likeness.

Unlike real models, 'cyber babes' like Lara Croft have no physical imperfections, do not have 'bad hair days' and make absolutely no demands. A competition for cybermodels called 'Miss Digital World' was reported as just as sexy as the real thing 'but without the catfights and backstabbing' (*Metro*, 23 November 2004). The first true virtual supermodel, Webbie Tookay (2K, intended to signal the year 2000), created in 1999 by designer Stephen Stahlberg for the Elite agency, is described as having myriad advantages over real supermodels: 'she will never age, gain weight, develop cellulite or throw a tantrum.' The designer continued: 'Like most men, I wanted a woman who would be physical perfection without the mental and verbal grief . . . I must confess I tweaked the result to shave the chin or make the bosoms a tad larger. And she never talks back!' (Stephen Stahlberg, quoted in the *Guardian*, 27 July 1999). The misogyny of this account is chilling – perhaps all the more so because of its humorous, laddish tone. It represents an example of the way that contemporary sexism is changing to take on knowing and ironic forms – forms in which the hatred of women can easily be disavowed (if challenged), and the finger pointed accusingly at the 'uptight', or 'humourless' feminist challenger.

Advertising and Postfeminism

Advertising has changed constantly throughout its history, in response to changes in the economy, technology, fashion and social relations. But the shifts that it has undergone since the late 1980s have been particularly significant, as developments in information and communication technologies, the emergence of a new generation raised on computer games and MTV, and the growing confidence of increasingly 'media-savvy' consumers forced a radical rethink of previous advertising strategies. In his excellent analysis of advertising, Robert Goldman (1992) argues that advertisers needed to respond to three problems. First, there was the problem of 'sign saturation' – the fact that in affluent societies people were continually bombarded by images, signs and brand names to such an extent that many individuals began to suffer 'sign fatigue' – like its millennial sibling 'compassion fatigue', it shows itself in exhaustion and indifference. The sheer number of competing signs had engendered a kind of weary cynicism among consumers to which advertisers responded by attempting to produce ever more shocking or arresting images.

The second related problem was viewer scepticism – consumers' increasing resistance to being told what to buy or what to think, and their growing sense of themselves as sophisticated decoders of advertising's messages, able to 'see through' its manipulations (regardless of whether or not this was the case). Taking on board consumers' alienation, advertisers began to produce adverts which incorporated critiques of the entire enterprise of advertising. 'Don't believe the hype' advertising explicitly attacks the codes and claims of advertisements, mocking everything from the employment of focus groups, to the use of athlete endorsements, and the suggestion that buying the product will make one more attractive. A clear example can be found in the Sprite adverts of the late 1990s which assert 'image is nothing; thirst is everything' and tell people that if they want a badge of identity they should become a security guard. Similarly adverts for Amstel beer exhorted consumers *not* to buy the product.

Other responses included: adverts which passed themselves off as art works; the growth of 'oddvertising' (Berger 2001) using surreal and irrational images and narratives; the inclusion of the iconography of political dissent; the development of reflexive adverts which mocked the rules and codes of advertising; and a move towards what I would call 'reality advertising' (which preceded the rise of reality TV by several years), featuring grainy home video footage (or, in fact, expensive film footage designed to look like home video), 'street' scenes designed to connote authenticity, and the use of 'imperfect' models to capture an accessible level of cool and 'kick-off' against the 'artifice' of other adverts.

All of these changes deserve more attention than they have received to date (but see Berger 2001). But here I must focus on the impact of the third cause of the shift identified by Goldman: advertisers' need to respond to increasingly vocal feminist critiques. As we have seen, from the beginning of the second wave, feminists had identified advertising as one of the key sites for the production of sexist imagery. Throughout the subsequent decades women voiced their anger about being treated like objects to be visually consumed. By the end of the 1980s, advertisers were beginning to recognize the significance of women's hostility to being objectified and fed with unattainable, idealized images of femininity, and they started to rethink their advertising strategies. This was also prompted by women's increasing financial independence – which meant that advertisers needed to address them in new ways: it is no good showing women lying on or draped over a car, for example, if you want to sell that car *to women*.

Goldman (1992) argues that advertisers' response was to develop 'commodity feminism' – a bid to incorporate the cultural power and energy of feminism while simultaneously 'domesticating' its critique of advertising and the media. Inspired by this analysis, what follows attempts to unravel some of the elements of the shift, examining ten key features of representations of gender in contemporary advertise-ments. These are (1) the appeasement of women's anger; (2) the use of more edgy and authentic-looking models; (3) the shift from sex objects to desiring sexual subjects; (4) the focus on being and pleasing ourselves; (5) the articulation of feminism and femininity in adverts; (6) the eroticization of male bodies; (7) the development of queer chic; (8) the use of gender reversals in adverts; (9) revenge themes; and (10) attempts to re-eroticize gender difference.

Addressing and incorporating feminist anger

One response by advertisers to feminist critiques of unrealistic and idealized images has been to address the criticisms directly in adverts. An advert for a Pantene (L'Oréal) hair product, for example, headlined with the slogan 'Don't hate me because I am beautiful', tackling head-on women's anger about constantly being addressed by unattainable images of female beauty. Other leading cosmetics houses followed suit using copy that downplayed the importance of beauty – such as Elizabeth Arden's 'my best feature is my big, beautiful, sexy brain'. Such strategies have the advantage of facilitating the continued portrayal of flawless fashion models alongside written copy which seems to suggest that their beauty is beside the point. Even the Storm modelling agency promoted itself in this way, producing an image of a beautiful woman defaced in ink with a moustache, beard and black-ened teeth, and the headline 'models so beautiful, you'll hate them for it'. The mock graffiti simultaneously conveyed the idea that the agency did not take itself too seriously, as well as suggesting that Storm models were so attractive that even this could not hide their beauty. The only other copy in the advert was a telephone number for bookings.

A particularly interesting and influential example of this theme is to be found in a series of Nike adverts run in 1993 and placed in women's magazines in the UK. One showed a cute pink and white toddler with the caption asking: 'when was the last time you felt really comfortable with your body?' The implication being, of course, that it was some-time before your second birthday! This advert explicitly addresses women's insecurity about living up to idealized images of women's bodies, and the text suggests that buying Nike goods will contribute to women feeling good about themselves. I want to discuss another in the series of adverts in a bit more detail (see figure 3.1 overleaf). This featured a photograph of six women (one of whom is holding a baby), all naked except for a white muslin loincloth. The caption reads: 'it's not the shape you are, it's the shape you're in that matters', implicitly reassuring women about being judged yet again by their appearance, something that is reinforced by the text:

> Where is it written that unless you have a body like a beauty queen you're not
>   perfect?
> You're beautiful just the way you are.
> Sure, improve yourself.
> But not in the pursuit of an impossible goal.
> A synthetic illusion painted by the retoucher's brush.
> Get real.
> Make your body the best it can be for one person.
> Yourself.
> Just do it.

This text, then, incorporates a critique of advertising images even as it itself advertises Nike goods. By kicking off (to use Judith Williamson's 1978 phrase) against adverts that suggest that 'unless you have a body like a beauty queen you're not perfect' and by drawing attention to the artifice and trickery of those adverts (which achieve their illusion via the retoucher's brush) it claims the status of authenticity. It employs an assertive and upbeat feminist tone, which is explicitly addressed to challenging the tyranny over women's appearance, and suggests that women should not be judged by their looks or their 'shape'. Moreover, it offers an apparent endorsement of feminist critiques of unrealistic media images ('the pursuit of an impossible goal'), its very slogan implying that Nike shares women's anger: 'Get real'. However, the linguistic text is undercut by the photographic text. The advertiser's preferred reading of this is that it shows a diversity of differently shaped women. In fact, all the women are very slim (differing slightly in height, but little else), all are white, young, apparently able-bodied, and conventionally attractive. They look exactly like the images which the text claims to reject, and they are photographed using precisely the soft focus and lighting techniques criticized in the text as 'synthetic'.

One of the ways in which this advert appears to be different from the generation of adverts it succeeds is in the tone it adopts. Whilst most adverts work by highlighting some way in which we could improve

Image courtesy of The Advertising Archives

Figure 3.1   Is it the shape you are or the shape you are in that matters?

ourselves (have glossier hair, more kissable lips, etc.) this advert *seems* to be telling women that they are fine: 'you're beautiful just the way you are.' But as semioticians have made clear, the meaning does not reside in the text, but in the interaction between the text and the reader. We have to fill in, to do 'advertising work' to make this advert meaningful, and as we do so we may construct the desired meaning: that we will feel this good about our body only if we buy Nike products. The positive tone which feminism used to address women is, then, taken up and offered back to us on condition that we buy the commodity being sold.

In this advertisement the critique of tyrannical media images is fore-grounded to such an extent that it may be possible to miss the fact that Nike are not promising women freedom from being judged; on the contrary, they are merely shifting the criteria by which women will be assessed. It will no longer be 'the shape you are', but now 'the shape you're in'. A new form of tyranny is on offer, and if you want to compete you had better buy Nike sportswear. The fetishization of fitness is arguably more pernicious than that of appearance because we are interpellated as morally responsible for how well we do. If we don't have the looks of a fashion model we may be less socially valued but it's not entirely our fault. But if we don't 'keep in shape' we are culpable: we let ourselves go – the most dreaded sin of contemporary affluent societies. The advert urges us to reject external templates of beauty, whilst simultaneously enrolling women in a regime of disciplinary power in which they become morally responsible for disciplining their own bodies, and where beauty work is redefined in terms of health and pleasure (see Coward 1984; Bordo 1993).

Edginess and authenticity

If one response to feminist critiques has been to confront women's anger directly, another has been to move away from the perfect beauty of models, to use more ordinary-looking people, or, alternatively, individuals with unusual or striking looks. The shift towards 'edginess' can be seen in various parts of popular culture including fashion, music and film, and reflects a disenchantment with the bland, packaged, squeaky-clean nature of popular entertainment. It is also evidence of the increasing speed with which 'alternative' looks, values and lifestyles are commodified in late capitalist society.

The films of the Spanish director Pedro Almodovar are one locus of the interest in 'edgy'-looking people. Almodovar's female characters are notable for their striking and asymmetrical appearances, a world away from the (predominantly) blonde, bland perfection of Hollywood. Similarly, in high fashion, edginess has become the defining feature of many collections, particularly in the wake of Alexander McQueen's 1999 show in which disabled models featured exclusively. His venture – captured in a special issue of the style magazine *Dazed and Confused*, edited by McQueen – generated considerable controversy, with some seeing it as a final recognition of difference, giving visibility to people who are routinely rendered invisible in the media, and others problematizing the way in which disabled people were made visible as exploitative, fetishistic and dehumanizing.

Undeniably, McQueen has had a profound effect on the fashion industry as a whole and there are modelling agencies purely devoted to handling 'edgy' models, for example the Ugly agency in London, as well as sections of magazines routinely dedicated to clothes being modelled by ordinary readers.

What is perhaps surprising is how *little* edginess in popular culture has impacted on advertising, or, to put it another way, how minutely female models must differ from the norm of 'perfection' in order to earn the tag 'edgy'. Berger (2001) cites examples of advertising agencies pointing out that their model has freckles as 'evidence' of their move away from tyrannical images of female beauty! Similarly, every time a cosmetics company chooses a woman over forty to be the 'face' of their products, for example Madonna, Isabella Rossellini or Andie McDowell (hardly 'ordinary' women) it makes the national and international news. It is clear that most women are quite simply too 'edgy' ever to appear in advertisements. Women of colour remain largely invisible, their presence organized semiotically to convey a highly restricted range of meanings, such as 'soul' and authenticity, or sexual availability and promise. Older women are, if anything, seen even more rarely in mainstream media advertising – outside of daytime television commercials for mobility aids or specially targeted financial products. When they do appear they are often targets of critique or derision, as in a series of adverts for BT Openworld which ran in the British 'quality' press in 2003, which showed a middle-aged woman apparently leaning over a garden fence, with the headline 'is gossip keeping you from your customers?' The text explains that 'chatterers' are clogging up Internet traffic and may be preventing 'you' from going online for important business uses. One thing is clear, the 'you' being addressed is not a woman over forty.

One brand which did notably break the mould is Dove. In 2004 it launched a series of global campaigns centred on the theme that 'beauty comes in many shapes and sizes and ages', and showing 'ordinary' women. In one advert in the UK a group of women dressed only in identical white knickers and bras were shown smiling under the headline 'firming the thighs of a size 8 model wouldn't be much of a challenge'. In another series of adverts pictures of pleasant-looking and attractive women (but not models) were shown with two tick boxes giving options for viewers to respond, for example, 'fit' or 'fat', 'wrinkled' or 'wonderful'.

Like the Nike campaign discussed in the previous section the adverts highlighted women's distress at being offered only 'narrow stifling stereotypes' and suggested that Dove's claims about the product (various kinds of firming cream, lotion or gel) were more genuine than those of their competitors – through such slogans as 'our latest Dove firming results (and we haven't cheated the figures)'. Accompanying all aspects of the campaign was a web address which invited women to sign up to the Campaign for Real Beauty which featured photographs celebrating the diversity of women's beauty, a report on young women and body image, plus discussion amongst ordinary women about idealized images. The adverts were notable for generating debate and extensive media coverage about their departure from the use of very thin models, though many commentators also noted the relative slimness of the women used and their uniformly attractive appearance. The Dove advertising was also notable for pioneering the use of a 'campaign' to sell its product. But the irony of selling creams to slim and firm the body on the back of a campaign for real beauty was not missed by everyone.

Image courtesy of Ogilvy & Mather, Chicago

Figure 3.2   Attacking the beauty myth . . . to sell beauty products

From sex object to (desiring) sexual subject

One of the major shifts in advertising over the last decade or so has been the shift from the portrayal of women as *sex objects* to the portrayal of women as *active and desiring sexual subjects*. Nowhere has this been more clear than in the billboard advertisements for bras which seem increasingly to dominate the urban landscape. In 1994 Eva Herzigova's advert for Playtex Wonderbra hailed us with a quotation from Mae West: 'Or are you just pleased to see me'. The first part of the quotation – the implication that the male viewer had an erection – was left out, for us to fill in. This was no passive, objectified sex object, but a woman who was knowingly playing with her sexual power. Similarly, the confident, assertive tone of a Triumph advert is quite different from earlier representations: 'New hair, new look, new bra. And if he doesn't like it, new boyfriend.'

This advert, like others in the series, including one which claims Triumph is 'The bra for the women's movement', has a feminist veneer, a cool and assertive tone. This woman knows what she wants, and she is going to get it: her boyfriend should feel lucky to have her (in a bra like this), and if he does not appreciate her (it), he will be replaced.

What this represents is the idea that women can gain control through the commodification of their appearance – that by acquiring a particular 'look' (by buying the right bras, makeup and accessories) they can obtain power (Goldman 1992). As one bra advert put it very clearly, 'I pull the strings'. On one hand it constitutes a recognition that gender power relations *are* partially lived out at the level of appearances; more disturbingly, though, it represents a shift from an external judging male gaze to a self-policing narcissistic gaze. It is a move to a new 'higher' form of exploitation: the objectifying male gaze is internalized to form a new disciplinary regime: 'The spectator-buyer is meant to envy herself as she will become if she buys the product. She is meant to imagine herself transformed by the product into an object of envy for others, an envy which will then justify her loving herself' (Berger 1972).

As Robert Goldman argues, adverts like these offer women the promise of power by becoming objects of desire. They endow women with the status of active subjecthood so that they can then *choose* to become sex objects because this suits their 'liberated' interests. In this way, sexual objectification can be presented not as something done to women by some men, but as the freely chosen wish of active (confident, assertive) female subjects. As I will argue later, one of the most disturbing aspects of this profound shift is that it makes critique much more difficult – precisely because the objectification is no longer seen as imposed from outside, but rather is self-chosen.

This dialectic of envy, desire and power is significant for what it conceals – namely the 'diverse forms of terror experienced by women who objectify themselves':

> There is the mundane psychic terror associated with not receiving 'looks' of admiration – i.e. of not having others validate one's appearance. A similar sense of terror involves the fear of 'losing one's looks' – the quite reasonable fear that ageing will deplete one's value and social power. A related source of anxiety involves fears about 'losing control' over body weight and appearance . . . And there is the very real physical terror which may accompany presentation of self as an object of desire – the fear of rape and violence by misogynous males. (Goldman 1992: 123)

This argument fits well with Naomi Wolf's study of the divisiveness of 'beauty oppression' – a secret 'underlife', a 'vein of self-hatred, physical obsessions, terror of ageing, and dread of lost control' which is poisoning and undermining women (Wolf 1990). The beauty myth attacks women physically and psychologically and leads them to willingly submit to regimes of torture (e.g. dieting and cosmetic surgery) which, she argues, make practices like foot-binding seem innocuous by comparison.

Advertisers have fetishized and commodified female sexuality, associating it with beautiful, young bodies who want to have lots of (heterosexual) sex. Contemporary femininity is constructed as a *bodily characteristic*. No longer associated with psychological characteristics and behaviours like demureness or passivity, or with homemaking and mothering skills, it is now defined in advertising and elsewhere in the media as the possession of a young, able-bodied, heterosexual, 'sexy' body. This is a profound shift and is captured in yet another bra advert in which displayed across a prominent cleavage are the words 'I can't cook. Who cares?' The voluptuous breasts here, then, are much more important than 'traditional' feminine skills. Is this progress? we might want to ask. Myra Macdonald (1995) notes that foreplay is in danger of being removed from the bedroom to the shopping mall. But it is important to note that only *some* women (beautiful, slim, young) are attributed sexual subjecthood: 'By attending to media representations, we might easily forget that fat, ugly, disabled or wrinkled women have sexual desires, too, and that stretch marks are not incompatible with sexual pleasure' (Macdonald 1995: 190).

Being ourselves, pleasing ourselves

Intimately connected to the depiction of (some) women as active, desiring sexual subjects is the idea that when women construct themselves as sexual objects they are simply 'pleasing themselves'. The bra adverts discussed above are emblematic of a shift in advertising generally: women are presented not as seeking men's approval, but as pleasing themselves and, in doing so, they *just happen* to win men's admiration. Another good example is found in a South African advert for She-bear lingerie which featured an attractive young white woman wearing only her lingerie and a nun's habit and rosary. The slogan, 'wear it for yourself' ties the brand identity to women who dress for themselves rather than for men – even if they are not nuns!

There is a kind of auto-eroticism at large, which has accompanied the shift to internal regulation/discipline, in which women appear to celebrate their own fetishization. Indeed women in adverts are so hyper-sexualized and narcissistic that they are presented as irresistible, even to themselves. 'If he's late, you can always start without him' declares one advert in which the *mise-en-scène* constructs a picture of seduction, complete with carelessly abandoned lacy underwear, but in which a sexual partner is absent. This is not genuinely celebrating the pleasures of masturbation for women but is designed to show how sexy the product is, and how aroused it will make you feel.

In an advert for a Gossard bra a young woman is depicted lying dreamily in some straw or grass, wearing only a black translucent bra and pants. The text reads: 'who said you can't get pleasure from something soft'. This cues us to read the photograph as one in which she is 'getting (sexual) pleasure', as well as jokily implying that men may not be necessary: she gets her pleasure from her underwear. Here is an example of an advert which emphasizes women's pleasure, and directs us to the redundancy of men in achieving it, but which uses a form of representation which is familiar from pornography: the woman is pictured from above, almost naked and pleasuring herself (or at least being pleasured by her underwear). In 'pleasing herself' she is also (just by chance?) pleasing the many heterosexual men who may have consumed very similar images in porn.

This is captured brilliantly in Jacky Fleming's (1996) satirical cartoon about the advert. In the first frame a heterosexual couple is shown standing in front of two large images of young attractive women in their underwear. The woman says: 'I don't know why you're staring like that, Adrian, these adverts aren't FOR men. They are meant to be for WOMEN and they make us feel cheekily confident about being sexy in a raunchy but fun loving postfeminist sort of way . . . And there's a lot of humour involved too.' In the second frame, the same man is shown again in front of the posters but this time with a male friend. (We assume) he has just reported his partner's explanation. 'Tell you what mate,' says his friend, 'if this is feminism we've been backing the wrong horse!'

This trend goes wider than advertising alone – it is at the heart of many postfeminist discourses. Kate Taylor, a sex columnist for the men's press, argues that young women already see themselves as equal to men: 'they can work, they can vote, they can bonk on the first date . . . if a thong makes you feel fabulous, wear it. For one thing, men in the office waste whole afternoons staring at your bottom, placing bets on whether you're wearing underwear. Let them. Use that time to take over the company. But even if you wear lingerie for you, for no other reason than it makes you feel good, that is reason enough to keep it on' (the *Guardian*, 23 March 2006). Here, then, two understandings of dressing in a particular way are offered: you might be doing it to make yourself feel good, or you might be doing it so as to distract (implicitly shallow/weak) men who will waste so much time thinking about your underwear that they won't notice that you have overtaken them in the career stakes, and, indeed, maybe even taken over the whole business. This is 'power femininity' in which self-objectification is not an indicator of the power of cultural expectations about how women should look, but in fact a strategy of 'empowerment' (Lazar 2006).

Fay Weldon has also attacked feminism for making women feel guilty about wanting to look attractive. In direct opposition to Naomi Wolf, she asserts that young women today have been freed of the tyranny of beauty, and that beauty, far from being a source of oppression, is a means through which women can feel more confident. This may be a seductive argument – especially for women who have little other power – but there are major problems with it, not least its individualism, the setting up of competition between women, and the caricature of feminism (as emanating from a 'feminist headquarters' somewhere in North America). However, it is a good example of the postfeminist trend to present women as entirely autonomous agents, no longer constrained by any inequalities or tyrannies, who can some-how freely choose to 'use beauty' to make themselves feel good. Fay Weldon puts it succinctly: 'Young girls seem to be getting prettier all the time. There is a return to femininity, but it seems to me that most girls don't give two hoots about men. It is about being fit and healthy for *themselves* not for men' (quoted in *The Observer*, 25 August 1996; emphasis in original).

Of course the idea that in the past women dressed in a particular way purely to please men is ridiculous: it suggests a view of power as something both overbearing and obvious which acted upon docile subjects. But this pendulum shift to the notion that women just 'please themselves' will not do as a substitute – it presents women as completely free agents, and cannot account for why, if we are just pleasing ourselves, the resulting valued 'look' is so similar – hairless body, slim waist, firm thighs, etc. Moreover it simply avoids all the interesting and difficult questions about how socially constructed ideals of beauty are internalized and made our own.

The disingenuousness of the claim that women are in any simple sense 'pleasing themselves' in making lingerie purchases is interest-ingly highlighted in another advert for Nancy Ganz bodyslimmers. Showing a slim and curvaceous woman's body from the neck down clad in a black basque and stockings, the advert's text (in white over the image) reads: 'while you don't necessarily dress for men, it doesn't hurt, on occasion, to see one drool like the pathetic dog he is.' Here, then, the advertisers dared to make explicit what is left implicit in most adverts – namely that by purchasing this sign of independence and autonomy, women would also (fortuitously) bring 'men' to their knees. Another lingerie advert which drew attention to the traffic-stopping/accident-inducing effects of such eroticized representations of women was on display on a large billboard in Hong Kong whilst I was there in 2004. Showing a woman in red underwear on all fours in a standard porn-shot, the slogan made no reference whatsoever to the product, but simply advised 'Coco says please drive carefully'. Moreover, returning to the 'thong' example, it is worth noting that when the fashion for G-strings was replaced in late 2005/early 2006 by the rise of 'boy shorts', beauty writers across the magazine industry heaved a collective sigh of relief. Their jubilation at not having to wear or promote uncomfortable 'wedgie-inducing' underwear any more retrospectively gave the lie to earlier claims that it was all about women pleasing themselves.

Research by Shuna White and Margaret Wetherell (1987) on discourses of body shape found that young women tended to present *themselves* as immune from influence of cultural constructions of femininity, but presented *others* as being affected by them. In a society which prizes individualism (and flatters people that they can 'see through' adverts) it is not surprising that the women they interviewed felt extremely uncomfortable with the idea that they might be influenced by adverts or other media images of feminine desirability. Advertisers have taken this on board. They now suggest to women that by buying a particular product they will not be buying into a conventional, socially sanctioned type of femininity but will be purchasing a sign of their own individuality, and pleasing themselves – no one else.

More broadly it is part of the shift, discussed by Warren Berger (2001), towards a new style of advertising whose injunctions are to be yourself, to reinvent yourself, to follow your heart, to be proud, to be an individual, to live to the full, and so on. Berger (2001) argues, following Geoff Weiss, that the major brands have become our new philosophers, in a time in which selling is packaged in 'new commandments' about how to live our lives, such as 'Long Live Dreams', 'Think Different', 'Experiment', etc.

Articulating feminism and femininity

Clearly, many of the profound shifts we have seen in adverts in recent years are a direct consequence of feminism. The focus on individual rights, the emphasis on personal empowerment, the upbeat, assertive tone, and the quasi-therapeutic injunctions to be yourself and please yourself, are all responses to the extraordinary cultural power of feminism. How, then, should we make sense of this? Does the active, confident and individualist tone represent some kind of progress over earlier depictions of women as passive objects? Has feminism reached a rapprochement with advertising? Could it even be said that advertising has become feminist?

I think such a conclusion would be premature. Advertising simultaneously uses, incorporates, revises, attacks and depoliticizes feminist themes and ideas. The concept of articulation (introduced in chapter 2) is useful for understanding this process and showing how adverts bring together elements from different discourses (including feminism) and connect or yoke them ideologically.

There are many different ways in which the cultural power of feminism is appropriated in adverts (some of which we have examined already). One way is to render feminism as a visual style or look. Goldman (1992) argues that just as traditional femininity is portrayed through a narrow range of signifiers, so now is feminism conjured up through an increasingly predictable lexicon – shoulder pads, brief-case, location in a professional environment, etc. Advertisers assemble signs which connote independence, freedom and bodily autonomy, and link them to purchase of commodities. In this way, feminist goals like independence and control over one's own body are emptied of their political significance and sold back to us as choices about what to consume. Thus, far from being straightforwardly 'positive' images, the newer representations are implicated in 'commodity feminism' (Goldman 1992): we are invited to become liberated and to take control of our own lives by acts of individual consumption – rather than collective struggle for social and political change. Feminism, signified in this manner, becomes just another style decision.

Another way in which advertisers directly draw on feminist ideas is through the use of feminist (sounding) discourse in their adverts. As long ago as 1986, for example, Club 18–30 took the pro-choice abortion campaigners' slogan 'A woman's right to choose' to market their holi-days. Since then the 'recuperation' of such discourse within advertis-ing has become commonplace, with 'feminism' – or rather a feminist gloss, emptied of its political implications – being used to sell every-thing from sanitary towels to cars.

Feminism, then, is being used to sell products in precisely the way that women's bodies have long been used – as advertisers try (when it suits their interests) to recuperate feminism and articulate it to the product they are aiming to sell. The notion of recuperation is a slightly problematic one because it implies a finality to the process of the reworking of meanings (Macdonald 1995). However, it is a useful correc-tive to the view which sees advertising as 'becoming feminist' or simply 'reflecting' feminist ideas. Advertising is involved in what Jameson (1984; in another context) described as the 'cannibalization' of ideas: it may wear a feminist mask today if that will help it to sell, but it may well wear a different mask tomorrow. Less than ten years after employ-ing 'A woman's right to choose' as their slogan, Club 18–30 had aban-doned their feminist pretensions and were advertising their major destination as 'Beaver Espana' and reminding us that 'it's not all sex, sex, sex, sex, sex, sex, sex (etc.) there's a bit of sun and sea as well'.

Robert Goldman (1992) points to three additional ways in which advertisers have sought to articulate feminism and femininity, and to construct a detente between them. In the first and most obvious way, visual signifiers of female success such as briefcase, business suit, car, own home, etc. are connected to signifiers of traditional femininity such as long hair, makeup, conventional attractiveness, so as to imply that there is no tension between being a successful and powerful woman who is taken seriously, and being sexually attractive to men. The subject of some feminist perspectives, then, who is juggling competing demands on her and is striving to be taken seriously as a woman, is recast in some advertisements as a kind of superwoman – powerful, respected, successful as well as effortlessly beautiful and desirable (and in some cases also a perfect mother).

Adverts now frequently portray women and men in positions of formal parity – particularly in office environments. However, as Goldman (1992) points out, advertisers are increasingly recognizing a need to dispel the anxieties which this produces in some men (and women). In a further inflection of the articulation of feminism and femininity, he argues, many adverts explicitly reassure consumers about the nature of this 'new woman'.

> Everyday you win. More independence. More success.
> But you still cry at sad movies.
> You still believe in the power of love at first sight.
> And you think fragrance should be all flowers and feelings.
> Because being a woman – is everything.
>   (Advert for *Pique*, quoted in   Goldman 1992: 108)

This advert for fragrance is a good example. Goals coded as feminist – success, winning and independence – are here purposefully reconciled with feminine codes of romance. It is not so very different from the 1970s bra ad slogan 'Underneath they are all lovable', reassuring viewers that inside every power-dressing feminist is a soft-hearted, incurable romantic.

A third way in which femininity and feminism are articulated is slightly more complex: it suggests that feminism can be an asset in pursuing the goals of femininity. Magazine adverts aimed at women frequently use this discourse. Goldman (1992) quotes an advert for *Cosmopolitan* in the *New York Times*:

> Three dates in I got the non-commitment speech. 'You're wonderful but I'm not ready for a relationship.' Fine, I said, and we kept dating. One night I had to cancel because of a heavy meeting next day. He was astonished. Two weeks later I went on a business trip to France. He was in shock. Two months later – right this minute – he's the most attentive man I've ever known. I didn't plan to be hard to get . . . I really *have* been *busy*. My favorite magazine says don't play games . . . just play your career for all it's worth and a lot of other things will fall into place. I love that magazine. I guess you could say I'm That Cosmopolitan Girl.

In this example, the young woman's pursuit of her own career makes her less accessible, which serves in turn to heighten her boyfriend's desire for her, and thus gives her greater control in their relationship. 'That Cosmopolitan Girl' is not being manipulative by *playing* hard to get, she is serious about her career. In this way, her pursuit of feminist goals (or, at least, goals encoded as signifiers of feminism within the discourse of advertising) makes her more, rather than less, attractive to men in a way that harks back to notions that women should ration their presence and not be too 'available to men'. In a new twist to this articulation of feminism and femininity some adverts now suggest that not only is there no conflict but that traditional feminine skills are precisely what women need in order to achieve career success and financial independence. A print advert for a major high street bank in the UK, for example, shows an attractive woman in her thirties laughing and playing with her two young children. The copy reads: 'I manage a family, I'm sure I can run a business'. This is interesting in appearing to value traditional women's work (caring for children) and suggesting that this work and running a business are similar – indeed, that business management is 'child's play' compared with running a family. What it renders invisible, of course, is that the woman pictured will probably end up running a business *and* managing a family – carrying out a 'double day' that is rendered invisible by superwoman imagery.

Eroticizing men's bodies

It is not just the representation of women in advertising that has undergone important shifts in recent years; the portrayal of men has changed too. In fact, one of the most highly visible changes in advertising in the last decade or so has been its use of a growing number of images of the male body. Where once women's bodies dominated advertising landscapes now men's are taking their place alongside women's on billboards, cinema screens and magazines. However, it is not simply that there are more images of men circulating, but that a specific kind of representational practice has emerged for depicting the male body; namely an idealized and eroticized aesthetic showing a toned, young body. What is new about this type of representation is that it codes men's bodies in ways that give permission for them to be looked at and desired. To use a phrase from film studies, men's bodies are now coded in many adverts (and in other sites) as 'to be looked at', to be the object of women's and other men's gazes (Cohan and Hark 1993; Jeffords 1994; Mulvey 1975).

The *locus classicus* of this kind of representation in mainstream media was 'Launderette', an advert for Levi's 501s which first aired in the UK in 1985. The advert featured Nick Kamen undressing down to his boxer shorts in a late-1950s launderette, against the soulful soundtrack of Marvin Gaye's 'I heard it through the grapevine'. What was so striking about this advert when it was first produced was that it represented Nick Kamen's body in an explicitly sexual and highly eroticized way. The camera followed his 'striptease' – intercutting it with looks from the people in the launderette – and lingered on his smooth muscular torso in a way that had previously been reserved for women's bodies. The advert provoked a huge amount of discussion among the advertising industry, journalists and academic commentators, and arguably launched a mode of eroticized representation of the male body that has subsequently become routine and taken for granted. (Sales of Levi's jeans reportedly increased by 700 per cent after the advert was shown, and the company could not produce them fast enough to meet demand.)

The catalysts for this decisive shift in visual culture were many and varied (see also chapter 6). On one hand, a variety of popular movements from feminism to popular psychology to environmentalism were pressing the case for a reinvention of masculinity along more gentle, emotional and communicative lines, and there was a growing appetite for a 'new man'. Additionally, the gay liberation movements in Western countries were gaining confidence. The economic significance of the 'pink economy' was helping to produce an increasing range of representations of the male body in gay magazines and popular culture – and part of the shift can be understood in terms of these 'going mainstream' (Moore 1988). Moreover, the shift had significant economic determinants. Retailers, marketers and magazine publishers were keen to open up new markets and had affluent men in their sights as the biggest untapped source of high-spending consumers (Edwards 1997). Style magazines like *The Face* helped this enterprise by producing a new visual vocabulary for the representation of men's bodies, and this too opened up space for eroticized practices of representation (Mort 1996; Nixon 1996).

The eroticized or fetishized representation of male bodies – or parts of bodies – in adverts is now completely normalized and no longer prompts questions or discussion within or outside advertising (except for regular expressions of concern about the effects of such images on men's body-image and self-esteem). What, then, are the characteristics of this representational practice? Rather than a diversity of different representations of the male body, most adverts belong to a specific generic type. The models are generally white, they are young, they are muscular and slim, they are usually clean-shaven (with perhaps the exception of a little designer stubble), and they have particular facial features which connote a combination of softness and strength – strong jaw, large lips and eyes, and soft-looking, clear skin (Edwards 1997). This combination of muscularity/hardness and softness in the particular 'look' of the models allows them to manage contradictory expectations of men and masculinity as strong and powerful but also gentle and tender – they embody, in a sense, a cultural contradiction about what a man is 'meant to be'.

Clearly, then, advertising offers very specific representations of male bodies. Older bodies are strikingly absent. There are strong and persistent patterns of racialization to be found in the corpus of eroticized images. White bodies are over-represented, but they are frequently not Anglo-American or Northern European bodies, but bodies that are coded as 'Latin', with dark hair and olive skin, referencing long histories of sexual Othering and exoticism. Black, African-American and African-Caribbean bodies are also regularly represented in the highly eroticized manner, but these bodies are usually reserved for products associated with sport, drawing on and reproducing cultural myths about black male sexuality and physical prowess. In turn, the bodies of Asian men are rarely represented in this way, again drawing on racialized myths about sexuality – in this case the supposedly asexual nature of the Asian male. In a study of adverts in *Men's Health* magazine in Finland and the USA, Hakkala (2001) found the men shown were muscular with 'rectangular' faces. They were invariably shown alone and were symbolic of independent, hegemonic masculinity.

It is worth noting that when men of African origin are represented in an eroticized manner in advertising they are much more likely than their white counterparts to be well-known sportsmen or celebrities rather than anonymous models. Peter Jackson (1994) has argued that the British campaigns for Lucozade (the glucose drink) in the early 1990s which featured two black sportsmen (John Barnes and Daley Thompson) were successful because they relied on viewers' assumed knowledge of the particular personalities of the men, rather than simply plugging into (potentially threatening) racial myths. England soccer player John Barnes and Olympic athlete Daley Thompson represented the 'acceptable' face of black masculinity, constructed from viewers' shared appreciation of the dignity, sportsmanship and good humour of these men. Their inclusion did nothing to challenge the underlying racial logic of representation, but constituted them as separate and particular. 'The judicious choice of Barnes and Thompson establishes a range of "positive" associations between masculinity, athleticism and style, shorn of the more threatening associations of a stereotypically anonymous and rapacious black masculinity' (Jackson 1994: 57). The same can be said of the more recent use of black celebrities and sportsmen, such as Thierry Henri.

As the eroticized presentation of the male body has become mainstream, there has been an increase in the range/type of masculinities presented. The hairless, muscular models described above still predominate, but alternative, more obviously homocrotic, images can also be found, as well as representations of thinner, more vulnerable-looking male 'waifs'. Dior broke taboos in 2003 in using a naked man in its adverts in some European countries. Almost as significant as the showing of his penis was the presence of abundant facial and body hair on this model – marking a departure from earlier representations of the male body.

Queer chic

Another important change in advertising in the last decade or so has been the growing prevalence of representations of lesbians and gay men (and, to a much lesser extent, bisexuals and transgendered persons). In June 2004 Commercial Closet, a Web-based organization that monitors gay-themed adverts, had no fewer than 1,700 adverts from thirty-three countries in its database. This proliferation is partly the result of flourishing LGBT creativity in the wake of HIV and AIDS, the growing confidence of queer media, and the recognition by companies of the significance of the 'pink economy'.

However, before welcoming unequivocally this shift in visibility, it is worth examining it in a little more detail. What is striking is the way in which queerness is aestheticized and fetishized in advertising, rather than being treated as merely a different sexual identity. In fact, it is extremely rare for lesbians or gay men to be presented without comment in a situation where advertisers would usually use an opposite-sex couple; there are very few adverts in which queerness is simply normalized or mainstreamed. Instead, it is increasingly signified through a *hyper-sexualized chic*.

A significant part of the increase in representations of homosexuality is accounted for by adverts with a 'lipstick lesbian' theme in which two extraordinarily attractive, conventionally feminine, young women are shown kissing or touching or in a mutual embrace. Recent examples include Sisley fashion in Britain, and Lucky Strike cigarettes in Spain. It is worth thinking about this not only as pushing at the boundaries of acceptability of lesbianism in the media, but also as a response to feminism. One way of reading the proliferation of this kind of eroticized imagery is as a sexualized display designed primarily for heterosexual men, frequently drawing on well-established codes from pornography. It might also be interpreted as a means for companies to continue to objectify and sexualize women's bodies but to evade charges of sexism – for how can it be sexist, they might argue, if it's about women's mutual desire.

In this way, the sexualized depictions of lesbian women are often linked to the 'pleasing ourselves' discourse discussed earlier. In one cinema advert for lingerie, designed by Saatchi & Saatchi, a gorgeous, naked woman steps into her bedroom, and slowly puts on her sexy black underwear. Later, dressed in a black suit, she enters a restaurant, shots of her earlier dressing routine intercut with appreciative looks from men in the restaurant. She then joins her short-haired companion, of whom we see only a back shot, and they exchange a passionate kiss. Only then is it revealed that the woman's companion is another woman. The question 'Do men deserve this?' is then flashed up on the screen, followed by the answer: 'No'. The advert is, according to its creative director, aimed at women who 'please themselves and who do not necessarily want to please men' (quoted in Lee 1996). However, whilst its explicit message is that Boisvert lingerie is too good for men (they don't deserve it), it is scarcely credible that the advertiser's only target audience is affluent lesbian women. Instead, like many of the bra adverts discussed earlier, it is drawing on one of the oldest heterosexual male fantasies in the book – that of watching women engage in intimate sexual conduct – whilst implying that the purchase of this underwear is actually all about women pleasing themselves and each other. As Veronica Lee (1996) has noted: 'Far from men receiving the message: "we don't need you boys", they might clearly get the message "Another woman just panting for it".'

It is sobering to note that lesbian women rarely appear in mainstream adverts *except* in this highly sexualized manner. In contrast, gay men are rarely portrayed kissing or even touching. There are some notable exceptions (e.g. various campaigns for Smints and Calvin Klein's Guitar Kiss in which the men embrace – albeit rather chastely), but for the most part gay men are signified primarily through stylish and attractive appearance and patterns of looking. Indeed, it often seems as if gay masculinity is primarily a style identity, not a sexual one, signified by attractive bodies and faces and beautiful clothes. This is not to deny the pleasures offered to gay male audiences, nor to downplay the transgressive significance of presenting male bodies as objects of desire, as passive, and sometimes even vulnerable (R. Dyer 1982; Simpson 1994; Edwards 1997; Buchbinder 1998). But advertising's preoccupation parallels the long-standing criticism of representations of gay men on television as asexual – that is, only allowed to exist on network TV on condition that they never actually engage in the practices that define their sexual identity. *Will & Grace* is perhaps the most obvious example of this, with the two main protagonists depicted using tropes normally reserved for old, bickering heterosexual couples. Will and Grace are ABM (all but married) – the more so in later series as the storyline about the baby is developed.

Interestingly, gay men in adverts often appear as objects of straight women's desire (rather than other gay men's desire). A frequent theme (see next section) is female sexual disappointment at discovering that the attractive man she has been eyeing up is gay. This was used in a famous 1997 advert for Lynx deodorant in Britain that attracted huge publicity and a cult following. More recently, the theme has developed into what Commercial Closet call 'queer world' advertising. A good example is 'Astrology', an advert for a Siemens mobile phone. The scenario is as follows:

> A young woman arrives alone to a packed dance club. As she enters the dancefloor, a scantily dressed woman longingly looks at her, and a moment later a muscular guy grabs her and begins dancing close.
>
> They dance erotically, and she grabs her breasts as they look deep into each other's eyes. She notices a necklace he is wearing that appears to be the astrological symbol of Gemini, the twins, and pulls out her mobile phone. While still sexily dancing with him, she smoothly goes to an astrology website to test her compatibility with the guy and it says they're a 'perfect match'. She also notices the first woman smiling from over his shoulder.
>
> A narrator says, 'you know there's a sexy way to connect to the Web. But whatever you do with the new Siemens C35, be inspired.'
>
> At that moment, another more boyish guy, who is apparently with the first one, shows up and it becomes clear that the necklace implied he was gay instead of a Gemini.
>
> But no matter, because she turns her head and there is the woman whom she keeps catching eyes with. The last shot is of a sly smile on her face as she looks to the woman and nods her head. The tagline: 'Be inspired'. (quoted on www.commercialcloset.org)

Discussing this advert, Commercial Closet call it 'one of the most gay positive commercials from Europe . . . Amazingly, as a lipstick lesbian and a gay man both play straight for a moment, it turns out that everyone is gay. No one is left unhappy at the end as both have partners.' Undoubtedly this 'queering' of what appeared to be a straight space was experienced as enormously pleasurable and transgressive for many lesbian and gay viewers. Nevertheless, the casual switching between sexual orientations could also be viewed as trivializing sexual identities (unless the advert is read as one in which the man and woman are both bisexual – which really *would* mark a real departure!). Other commentators on the Commercial Closet site read the advert as one in which the women were not lesbian at all, but 'competitive friends', chasing a guy who turned out to be gay – the common narrative discussed already.

It is fair to say that many adverts that feature gay themes continue to do so in a very homophobic way. One example is 'Meet the Parents', an advert for Dockers jeans that intertextually references the film of the same name. In this advert, a young man arrives at the extravagant home of his wealthy girlfriend, walking arm in arm with her. After greeting him, her mother walks behind the man and slyly checks out his behind. As they are sitting at the enormous dinner table, the young man suddenly gets a playful foot between his legs. His girlfriend nearby smirks, but then he looks at the mother who is also smiling coyly – the young man himself is wearing a reserved smile. Still uncertain whose foot it is, he then turns to the father, who has a stoic look on his face except that he raises his eyebrows. The music soundtrack dramatically turns to a discordant horror sound. The younger man has lost his smile and raises his eyebrows as well. In the end, it is not made clear whose foot it is. What is clear, however, is that homosexuality is here signalled (albeit humourously) as the focus of fear and repulsion. This is still the case in many adverts, in which 'we' as viewers are hailed through a discourse that both assumes and perpetuates homophobia. The representation of transgender people and bisexuals is, in many ways, even worse, with the former frequently portrayed as predators, Queens, paedophiles or pornographers, and the latter often depicted as duplicitous cheaters.

Overall, then, while homosexuality is much more visible in advertising than it was ten years ago, it is signified through highly specific, highly sexualized codes. Queer chic can seem to add 'edge', risk and sexiness to products that are often associated with straight men and traditional sexism. It is for this reason that adverts for beer, alongside more predictable products like fashion and fragrance, have increasingly deployed this style.

Gender reversals

The shifts discussed so far provoke an important question: are we witnessing a reversal in patterns of gender representation in which women are shown as confident, empowered individuals and men as sexual objects coded for visual consumption? The idea of gender reversals is something that advertising has been preoccupied with in recent years, and not just in terms of sexual objectification. Adverts for a variety of products have shown us women wielding power in senior management positions, and men struggling to clean the bath or to cook dinner. However, what is interesting about most of the adverts of the last decade has been their attempts to reassure viewers that – despite appearances – traditional gender relations remain unchanged (an argument not dissimilar from some feminist claims!) When 'new man' is shown cooking, for example, in partnerships with a woman coded as equal, the emphasis is usually on selling a product that will allow him to 'cheat' – to appear to have produced an elaborate and delicious meal from scratch, but in fact to have merely heated something pre-prepared (having spent the rest of the time indulging in some appropriately male pursuit such as watching the football). In this (all too familiar) type of advertisement, the woman always 'finds him out', but gives an indulgent shrug to show that she doesn't mind and loves him anyway – and gender power relations are restored to the status quo. Such adverts may be perceived as offensive to men, with their implication that it is beyond the wit of the average male to cook a meal or to clean the kitchen floor. However, often they are equally insulting to women who are set up as 'nags' or as needlessly demanding.

Perhaps the strongest case for gender reversals can be made in relation to adverts which use sexualized imagery. At one level, the mere fact that men's bodies are now routinely shown in a sexually objectified manner constitutes a kind of reversal in gender relations. But the objectification of male bodies has not led to a decrease in the objectification of women's. Feminist anger about being objectified in advertisements has not brought about an end to this practice, but merely its extension to men – we are all objectified now.

Despite advertisers' interest in playing with the idea of gender reversals, it is hard to think of examples of adverts in which the potentially subversive implications of this are followed through without some attempt either to reinstate the social order or to punish those who transgress it. A common device for defusing the threat to normative heterosexual gender relations is humour. An old advert for 'Options' hot chocolate drinks illustrates this. It shows an alluring, long-legged black woman apparently trying to make up her mind which of a number of flavours of hot chocolate she will have. A sachet of each different flavour (e.g. chocolate orange, chocolate mint) is held by each of a number of barely clothed men, posed as if on the catwalk, and the woman is depicted making a difficult (but nevertheless arousing) decision between each man-drink – a soundtrack is playing 'decisions, decisions'. She finally decides, takes a sachet and the men walk off screen (as though models on the runway). The 'punchline' of the adverts occurs in the following frame when each of the men reappears modelling an identical kettle, and the woman wonders 'now who shall I get to pour it?' The 'joke' that concludes the advert serves to defuse the potential challenge/anxiety presented by having men portrayed as mute sexual objects in a mode borrowed from the beauty pageant or catwalk. Any erotic charge is undercut by laughter in a way which does not have parallels in the reverse situation.

A similar process can be seen in a recent and long-running advert for Diet Coke on British television (and elsewhere). In this advert a number of attractive women (in their mid-thirties) turn up in an unspecified office environment claiming to be there for their '11 o'clock appointment'. The camera cuts between their arrival in reception and their seat in the waiting room in which each of them is depicted in a state of obvious sexual anticipation (licking lips, breathing heavily, rearranging hair, etc.). Only then does the camera reveal the cause of their arousal – an attractive labourer, *sans* T-shirt, pausing to drink his Diet Coke on a scaffold outside the window. The choice of labourer is an interesting one since men in the building trade have become iconic signifiers of a particular kind of 'in your face' sexism. Where once building workers ogled women, the advert playfully suggests, now women ogle them! However, as in the Options example, the camp and exaggerated desire of the women and the comic nature of the 11 o'clock appointment serve to place the advert in humorous, ironic quotation marks. The exchange of looks between the females and the male are not equivalent, and are not straightforward reversals of patterns of power involved in men's looks at women. This is partly because each individual gaze operates in the context of our collective knowledge about the politics of looking – captured in John Berger's famous phrase 'men look at women and women watch themselves being looked at' (Berger 1972). It is also weighted by a long cultural history of the beauty myth in which women are subject to constant scrutiny and assessment of their appearance. No single instance of women looking at men could reverse that, nor – without this history – does it have the authentic, referential quality of examples of men looking at women.

David Buchbinder (1998) discusses three adverts aired on Australian television that explore this terrain of the gaze and power. The commercials are for Underdaks, a brand of men's underpants. The adverts all have the same narrative: they are set in an airport, at the scanning device through which all passengers must pass. The scanner is supervised by a woman security officer and the scene opens with a handsome, muscular young man walking through the scanner and setting off the buzzer. The officer asks him to remove his shirt, which he does, but the buzzer sounds again as he walks through the scanner. This time the officer asks him to remove his trousers: 'He looks at her in exasperated disbelief but complies, striding through the gateway, this time without further incident. As he passes by the officer, he looks down at her with an expression combining smug triumph and challenging insolence' (Buchbinder 1998: 15). The whole episode has been watched by another female security officer who comes over as the man saunters off, and reaches into the pocket of the first officer. Pulling out an electronic device (that sets of the scanner's buzzer) she says to her colleague 'one day you're gonna get caught!' Next, the camera shows the man, still dressed only in his underpants, striding away and turning to look back at the two women, again an expression of triumph and challenge in his gaze. As we watch him disappear from sight we hear the final line of the commercial, spoken by the first officer, and it is this that differs in each version of the advert. In one version, the officer says (suggestively) 'nice . . . luggage'. In another she says (forlornly) 'he's probably gay', and in the third she comments 'one day I'm going to get lucky' (Buchbinder 1998: 16).

The advert is notable in representing the male as 'docile to female command, and as available to the female gaze' (Buchbinder 1998). In doing so it also facilitates an active homosexual gaze. The advert might be said to combine the representation of the eroticized male body and the depiction of women as active desiring sexual subjects (discussed earlier), particularly in the line 'one day I'm gonna get lucky', which suggests a libidinous female sexuality unconstrained by notions of traditional femininity. However, as Buchbinder notes, 'the very articulation of female desire in this case also marks that desire as frustrated' since she has clearly not 'got lucky' yet, despite routinely playing this trick. This signals an imbalance in the power of men and women which is also evident in the complex exchange of glances. While as an airport *officer*, the woman has the power to undress the beautiful male stranger, her power as a *woman* is not sufficient to subordinate him – he is exasperated, but looks *down* on the woman (Goffman's point about relative size again), and his looks are insolent and triumphant. He maintains an active subjecthood, depicted in his posture and defiance, and is not, finally, rendered an object.

It is interesting that precisely the questions of power and mutual looking explored in film theory are the subject of adverts like this. Janice Winship (2000) argues that adverts which endow women with power offer a different scopic regime than earlier adverts, and frequently take as their topic the politics of looking that have been problematized by feminism.

Revenge adverts: the battle of the sexes

In the period of turbulent gender relations that has characterized the last decade, another emergent theme in advertising has been the notion of gender war and revenge. Rather than playfully reversing gender roles, revenge adverts put the supposed love–hate relationship between men and women – 'battle of the sexes' – centre stage. At the innocuous end of the continuum, adverts for Volkswagen lamented, 'if only everything in life was as reliable as Volkswagen', and compared men unfavourably with cars, while Renault adverts cheekily – and repeatedly – suggested that 'size matters'. A humorous tone was also found in Fiat Punto's 2001 television campaign. It showed a young, good-looking, heterosexual couple driving through a European city. The woman (who is driving) glances at her boyfriend every so often and notices that he is staring out of the window at every attractive woman he sees in the street. Getting evidently ever more irritated by this, she finally stops the car, winds down the window, and proceeds to passionately kiss a handsome male passer-by. This, the advert tells us, is the 'spirita di Punto', a spirit that is perhaps a hybrid of feminism, revenge fantasy and sheer *joie de vivre*, but which nevertheless suggests that simply turning the tables is the only solution.

Other adverts, however, are considerably more threatening and even vicious. In one example, high heels are used as a symbol of women's power and sexual dominance, with the effect of threatening a man. The advert – for Lee jeans – showed a naked man lying prone, his head just outside the shot, and a woman's boot pressed on his buttocks, its stiletto heel hovering menacingly close to the man's anus and testicles. The violence of the imagery is reinforced by slogan: 'put the boot in', designed, the creators of the adverts said, to draw attention to the fact that the jeans are 'bootcut'. The advert created a storm of controversy in Britain where it was seen by millions on prime billboard sites. Newspaper columnists demanded to know whether any company would dream of representing a woman in such a way, and, if not, why it was acceptable for a man. Some even suggested that the pendulum of gender power had swung so far the other way that men now required a dedicated governmental minister to protect their interests.

A number of other adverts have contributed to the perception by some men that they are being unfairly attacked. In Britain, Budweiser's low-calorie beer was advertised in posters in which attractive young women mocked the target audience's beer bellies – for example, 'I don't chase men who can't run away'. Male commentators argued that the adverts 'reduced' men to their appearance and implied that being overweight meant that they are not worthy sexual partners – something, of course, implied about women for decades, but somehow overlooked by the commentators until it happened to men! In Japan, a public-service campaign to promote men's role in the family showed well-known and highly respected Japanese men engaged in various fathering activities, with the bold headline: 'you can't call a man who doesn't care for his child a man' – generating considerable anger among some men (Berger 2001).

Earlier in this chapter, I discussed the widespread prevalence of (threatened or implied) violence against women in adverts. Increasingly, men seem to be the target of violence as well – frequently perpetrated by women. As Myra Macdonald (1995) has argued, it seems as if the fantasies on offer to women today are those of taking revenge against men and getting away with it. This is a perversion of real feminist aims, which, in none of their myriad formulations, have been about simply turning the tables on men and engaging in tit-for-tat aggression.

Janice Winship (2000) discusses two campaigns which feature violence against men – Nissan's 'Ask before you borrow it' and Wallis's 'Dress to Kill' campaign. In the Nissan campaign men are shown as subject to violence against their genital regions, for having used their partner's car without first asking permission. In one advert a man is holding his hands to his groin as if to protect his genitals from being kicked. In another, a newspaper clipping featuring the real-life

'Bobbitt' case (in which a woman cut off her unfaithful partner's penis) is presented. Nissan's advertising agency defended the adverts, saying that they were not about violence towards men, but about women 'feeling much stronger than ever before' and being free to react towards men however they want (quoted in BBC 2003). Similarly the Lee jeans advert was championed as emblematic of 'the prevailing Girl Power mood in Britain' (quoted in BBC 2003).

Winship (2000) argues that the 'Dress to Kill' campaign for Wallis was rather different in that it foregrounded questions of the male gaze, as discussed in the previous section. In these adverts looking at women is shown as having fatal consequences for the man himself or for another man. In 'Crash', for example, a male driver staring at a woman in the street crashes his expensive sports car. In another Wallis ad, the unsuspecting client is about to have his throat slit by a barber distracted by a woman outside the window. In all the adverts men look at women at their own or another male's perilous expense, but the woman herself is oblivious. Winship contends that the adverts are 'evidence of shifting and contested relations between men and women' and are precursors to a possible feminine identity constructed less around desire/desirability than around autonomy/dependency (Winship 2000). But she also notes that the adverts are ambiguous, for, despite foregrounding the dangers of looking, offering a symbolic revenge to women who have felt constantly surveyed and objectified by men, they nevertheless also rely upon a sexualized stereotypical representation that is designed precisely for the male gaze that is ostensibly challenged.

Mars and Venus: making patriarchy pleasurable

In some way the flip side of the notion of the battle of the sexes and in some senses its extension is the idea, popularized throughout the nineties and early noughties, that men and women are separate but complementary species. According to the title of John Gray's (1992) book, which captured the zeitgeist, 'men are from Mars and women are from Venus' and any tension or conflicts between us should be understood by reference to the fact that we are metaphorically creatures from different planets. Men and women are fundamentally different, Gray argues, and the key to happiness and success is to recognize this, rather than fighting it.

> Martians value power, competency, efficiency and achievement. [Meanwhile, over on Venus] they value love, communication, beauty and relationships . . . Instead of being goal-oriented women are relationship oriented; they are more concerned with expressing their goodness, love and caring. (Gray 1992: 22)

Given the staggering popularity of Gray's books, the huge number of copycat manuals, and resonances with other key theories of innate gender differences, such as evolutionary psychology, it is not surprising that this notion has taken hold in advertising in recent years.

The most straightforward iterations of this idea are in adverts for gender-typed products which construct all-male or all-female environments. Berger (2001) describes such adverts as being themed according to group pride: beer commercials, for example, may show a world of male camaraderie organized around complicity in getting women 'off men's backs' for an afternoon so they can watch the football and have a few beers with their mates. The recent, award-winning adverts for Budweiser, Berger suggests, build pleasure and pride around African-American speech patterns – the lilting question 'Whaassup?' – and construct a community of men via the telephone: 'having a Bud, watching the game', is the reply.

This may be understood as the commodification of an 'alternative', marginalized speech pattern, which was previously ethnically bounded, but is now regarded as the epitome of urban cool. It is also partly a recognition of the extent to which black male identities are increasingly perceived by young people as more 'cool' than any others (Majors and Billson 1992; Connell 2000; Frosh, Phoenix and Pattman 2002).

One of the features of the Mars/Venus discourse that particularly interests me is its attempt to re-eroticize sexual difference. It not only asserts that there are natural psychological sex differences (a highly contested claim in itself, refuted by considerable research evidence), but also that these alleged differences are profoundly pleasurable, if only we could recognize their existence instead of resisting. In this twin argument, then, Mars/Venus thinking not only reifies psychological sexual difference but also freezes in place unequal power relations. Advertising which draws on this effectively works by making patriarchy pleasurable. Like the Mars/Venus industry as a whole, adverts in this vein must be understood as a response to feminism. Such commercials have attempted to take feminist criticisms of unequal gender relations and repackage them in such a way as to make them a source of pleasure. A good example of this is to be found in a series of adverts for the 'lad mag' *FHM* magazine (see chapter 6), targeted at 18- to 34-year-old men which I first saw in the London Underground in the mid-1990s.

In one, five or six spectacularly beautiful and scantily clad women are depicted on a (*Friends*-style) sofa under the banner headline 'He took me to heaven and back'. Underneath the photo of the women is some text which appears to be a transcript of what they are saying to each other. The impression given is that we are privy to a private and intimate conversation between women – the subject of which is men. The 'conversation' ranges over a variety of 'male failings' – the way they don't put the lavatory seat down after going to the bathroom, for example, or the way they stare at 'girly' calendars. But the tone of criticism is humorous and affectionate and presents men as mildly irritating but lovable. In this way feminist arguments about male behaviour and privilege are apparently acknowledged, but are trivialized and re-presented as merely endearing quirks or eccentricities on men's part. The adverts trade on the idea that men and women will never really understand each other – summed up in the slogan for the magazine: 'it's a guy thing'. But whilst a feminist might note the same observable phenomenon and ask why society is organized in this way, these adverts suggest that it is a natural and inevitable rather than a social phenomenon.

This advert and the others like it are extremely interesting because they do seem to acknowledge common female complaints or concerns about male behaviour. They resonate with many women's experiences. They are also appealing to women because they assure them of their superiority (e.g. their maturity relative to 'childish' men) and are organized around displaying women's triumph. In the advert about the 'girly calendar', for example, the woman got her own back (as she saw it) by using 'his' porn calendar to line the cat's litter tray! However, the adverts also serve to reassure men on a number of levels – not least the anxieties that men have about women's get-togethers being forums for character assassination or sexual undermining of men. In representing a world of women to men, the adverts confirm that yes, indeed, this type of conversation does take place, but that your girlfriend or wife will come home afterwards and still love you. It constructs a homo-social world of female bonding that is no threat to men, but is compliant to patriarchal norms of gender and heterosexuality (Storr 2003). At a more general level, of course, the adverts also suggests that the *FHM* reader will 'get a girl' like one of these.

Conclusion: A Final Word from our Sponsors

Irony means never having to say you are sorry

No discussion of contemporary advertising would be complete without mentioning irony – that catch-all device that allows advertisers to have their cake and eat it: to present titillating and sexist images of women while suggesting that it was all a deliberate and knowing postmodern joke. 'That is not an objectified image of a half-naked woman; it is an ironic comment on 1970s advertising, or, more specifically a hilarious send-up of the dumb blonde stereotype!'

Irony is everywhere in postmodern consumer culture, and advertising is no exception. It allows adverts to defend against critique by self-consciously drawing attention to their ironic status. Frequently, today, irony is wedded to nostalgia and to retro-sexism (Whelehan 2000; Williamson 2003). The use of a 'period style', usually 1950s, 1960s or 1970s, allows sexism to operate freely under the cover of a nostalgic preoccupation with the past. Williamson argues: 'Retro-sexism is sexism with an alibi: it appears at once past and present, "innocent" and knowing, a conscious reference to another era, rather than an unconsciously driven part of our own' (Williamson 2003). Besides locking a vocabulary of critique of sexism into the past, Williamson argues, it allows troubling sexually objectifying images to be seen as cutting-edge and radical, rather than exploitative.

This is where irony links to another of the underlying trends in advertising (and across contemporary popular culture or generally): the expansion of the 'pornosphere' (McNair 2002). 'Porno chic' or the 'pornographication of the mainstream' (McNair 2002) is transforming representations of women. From time to time examples of this cause public outrage – most famously in the case of the advert for Opium perfume which depicted a prone Sophie Dahl, cupping her breast and arching her back, apparently in the throes of orgasmic ecstasy (see figure 1.1). But much more significant than any individual example is the ongoing and routinized borrowing from porn idioms, poses, *mise-en-scène* and vocabularies which can be seen across advertising. The fact that the models speak a language of empowerment in no way detracts from the impact of this shift – indeed it serves merely to defend against critique. Subjectification, it might be argued, is just how we 'do' objectification today. But women are still located in their bodies, indeed *as* bodies, albeit voraciously heterosexually desiring ones, as in conventional pornography.

This returns us to the question of how much has changed. I hope that this chapter has shown that there have been profoundly import-ant shifts in advertising in recent years: many adverts today construct gender entirely differently from their counterparts in the 1970s and 1980s. Feminism has clearly had a major impact on advertising, as has the gay movement, though, in both cases, this has not resulted in many adverts which could be characterized as straightforwardly femi-nist or as challenging homophobia.

But in the focus on what is new, on the novel constructions of gender and sexuality to be found in adverts, it is important not to lose sight of the fact that many things have also stayed the same. New stereotypes have not necessarily displaced older ones but may coexist alongside these, or perhaps merely influence their style. Thus in figure 3.3, an advert for a 2004 motor show, the women are not smiling, prone and submissive as they would have been twenty years ago, but instead

Image courtesy of Haymarket Exhibitions Ltd and Emap Automotive

Figure 3.3   Advert for a 2004 motor show

present an image of femininity that is a hybrid of soft porn and action-adventure computer games. But in the shift from passive to active, from smile to pout, from submissive to empowered, the link between cars and sexy women is not severed but merely given a gloss for the twenty-first century. Sexy 'babes' are still selling cars.

4

News, Gender and Journalism

THE critical examination of news has been a central concern of media studies for decades, but it is only relatively recently that this interest has involved a sustained focus upon gender. Earlier analyses focused on what made news, the criteria for newsworthiness, why some events are headlined and others are ignored entirely, and how, given all the things that are happening in the world at any one time, a few are selected to become news stories. Research on 'news values' pointed to the powerful 'event orientation' of news (meaning that *processes* were often ignored); its focus upon social, political and cultural elites, and also upon elite nations (captured in the cynical newsroom observation that one death at home is equal to 100 elsewhere in the West, and 10,000 in the rest of the world); the 'personalizing' tendencies of news; and the overwhelming importance of a small number of official sources for news – from whose perspective news stories are usually told (e.g. defence departments or military briefers during war, government or police departments in relation to protests, etc.) (Cohen and Young 1973; Galtung and Ruge 1973; Whitaker 1981; Curran and Seaton 1981).

Many matters of undoubted global significance never make the news. Each year in the last decade approximately 40 million people in the developing world have died from entirely preventable causes – mainly from starvation, lack of clean water or readily curable infectious diseases. As protesters from Afghanistan to the Gaza Strip have observed in their chants: 'here it is September 11th every day'. Yet this information about people's lives rarely made it to the world's newspapers or television screens, because it did not fit with current news values, or with the time/event/visual requirements of contemporary news. By contrast, countless apparently inconsequential happenings were given vast amounts of coverage – the dresses worn by female Hollywood stars, footballers' affairs, or the sexual proclivities of television presenters. Studies of news have revealed its highly constructed nature, and showed that it is no more a simple reflection of reality than a soap opera or a women's magazine. Rather, news is a cultural product that reflects the dominant cultural assumptions about who and what is important, determined by 'race', gender, class, wealth, power and nationality, and about what social relations and arrangements are deemed normal, natural and inevitable. It is not surprising, then, that most news is designed for, about and by men.

What makes something newsworthy? How are women represented in the news? Do female journalists tell different stories from their male colleagues? Is television news being 'dumbed down'? Are we witnessing the 'feminization of journalism'? These are just some of the questions considered by this chapter, which aims to address journalism as a profession, the representation of women and gender issues in the media, and the recent and ongoing transformation of news from public service to market-led, consumer product. Additionally, it examines in detail news reporting of one issue: sexual violence against women.

The chapter is divided into four substantive sections. The first considers the representation of women in news, highlighting their relative invisibility in news stories, and the sexualizing and trivializing ways in which they are portrayed. Particular attention is given to the coverage of female politicians. Next, the chapter turns to the profession of journalism, noting the increasing numbers of women in its ranks, but also the emergence of new patterns of discrimination alongside persistent 'old-style' sexism. Examining the claim that news is being 'feminized', the chapter looks sceptically at the notion that female journalists produce 'different news' than their male colleagues. The third section of the chapter explores some of the ways journalism is changing, and looks at the rise of 'infotainment' or 'newszak', discussing its origins and its impacts on the nature of news. Finally the chapter turns to an analysis of the reporting of sexual violence against women, showing the misleading and distorted picture of the nature and incidence of rape found in news presentations.

Here is the News . . . about Men

In 1995 the first extensive cross-national study of women's portrayal in the media – covering newspapers, radio and television in seventy-one countries – found that only 17% of the world's news subjects (i.e. newsmakers or interviewees) were women (Media Watch 1995). The proportion of females was lowest in Asia (14%) and highest in North America (27%). Women were least likely to appear in news stories about politics, government, business or the economy, and most likely to feature in discussions in the more traditionally feminine domains of health and social issues, as well as arts. This Global Media Monitoring Project gave the first truly international picture of women's under-representation in news. A follow-up study in 2000 found that the percentage of female news actors had only increased by 1% to 18%. And in 2005 the figure was still only 21%. Even in those countries doing 'best', women only represented just over a quarter of news actors, and across many aspects of political and economic life women were quite literally invisible. Men constituted 86% of spokespeople and 83% of experts, while women were more than twice as likely as men to be portrayed as victims (Global Media Monitoring Project 2006).

One response to this finding might be to suggest that it simply reflected reality – a reality in which women are still absent from positions of power and responsibility in many domains. However, this argument does not stand up to scrutiny: even in Scandinavian countries where women's participation in decision-making and public life is high (for example, in Sweden women constitute 43% of the national Parliament) they were still dramatically under-represented in news media (Eie 1998). Eie's study found that there was not a single category of television programming in which women outnumbered men, but that they were most likely to be found in children's programmes.

Another riposte to the 'reflecting reality' argument comes from research in Cambodia, discussed by Margaret Gallagher (2001). Gallagher notes that the long-term effect of the Cambodian war has meant that women represent 64% of the adult population, 55% of the labour force (the highest female participation in the world) and that one-third of all households are female-headed. Despite this, only 6% of news items were about women. Moreover, some 22% of items in the press about women were categorized as 'obscene' by the International Federation of Journalists and the Women's Media Centre of Cambodia. A clear finding of research in this field, then, is that news does not reflect reality, but presents a consistently more male-dominated view of society than exists in actuality.

However, it is not just small numbers of women in news that is cause for concern, but also the ways in which women are portrayed when they do become 'newsworthy'. One consistent finding is that most news about women focuses on their physical appearance – indeed many newspaper editors seem incapable of printing a story featuring a woman without some evaluation of her attractiveness, or at least a description of her age and hair colour. Gaye Tuchman's description of one of the unwritten laws of media reporting seems as depressingly true today as it was in 1975 when she wrote it: almost whoever she is the media will represent a woman in one of two ways – in terms of her domestic role or her sexual attractiveness. This goes for female politicians and 'ordinary women' as much as for the entertainment celebrities who increasingly fill our daily papers.

In Britain the tabloid newspapers routinely feature many photographs of young, attractive women in each edition, scantily clad, and frequently photographed in colour (while news about men usually has black and white images, except – increasingly – in sports pages). The quality broadsheets are quickly learning to follow this trend, using large photographs of young women (often on the front or back page) with often an extremely tenuous connection to the news story being reported. A survey by Women in Journalism in 1999 found that of all the photographs judged 'not relevant' to a story – that is, just put in to give the piece a 'lift' – 80 per cent feature young women. Research elsewhere produced similar findings. A study in China pointed to the fact that women's *images* were much more likely to appear than their actions or opinions: 'while men are speakers to the readers, women tend to be gazed at by readers' (Yuan 1999: 4).

The flip side of this is that women who for whatever reason do not conform to the media's requirement that they be 'eye candy' are subjected to regular vilification. The viciousness with which women are attacked if they do not meet the normative modes of attractiveness demanded by the press is chilling. When the story of President Clinton's relationship with Monica Lewinsky broke in the UK it was greeted with a chorus of 'ugh – how could he', rather than any political or ethical debate about the behaviour of an incumbent president. Sarah Ferguson, former wife of Britain's Prince Andrew, has also been the target of a barrage of press hostility about her appearance; notoriously *The Sun* newspaper set up a telephone poll inviting male readers to vote for 'who you would rather date . . . Fergie or a goat' (quoted in Franklin 1997: 4). Even the Hollywood actress Kate Winslet found herself subject to attack by the popular press: after starring alongside Leonardo di Caprio in the film *Titanic*, she was dubbed 'Titanic Kate' and some newspapers printed diet plans for her to follow. It is hard to avoid the conclusion that for much of the press a woman's worth is based entirely upon her sexual attractiveness.

One simple strategy that can help to understand what is going on in news reporting of women is to compare it with how men are portrayed. Unlike women, men are very rarely described in terms of their physical attractiveness. Indeed, when men's appearance does become a topic deemed newsworthy it is much more likely to be reported at a meta-level or at one remove – thus the phenomenon of David Beckham's sex symbol status will be discussed, not his body itself, or his body will only be described as part of a wider story about how young boys are emulating his style. Compare this to the reporting of the equally famous Kylie, whose bottom has been declared by the press 'an area of outstanding natural beauty' and who regularly has column upon column devoted to lascivious descriptions of her body. (And the same can be said about most other female pop-stars and Hollywood actresses.)

It is interesting to note that when men *are* subjected to evaluative descriptions of their appearance the purpose seems frequently to disparage them or trivialize their point of view. Anti-war activists protesting against an attack on Iraq were frequently given this treatment in early 2003, even by columnists in the liberal 'quality' papers. Writing in the *Guardian* in January of that year David Aaronovitch described a prominent campaigner as 'a lovely looking lad' and went on to describe his (blonde) hairstyle, before attacking the naivety of his position.

Examining such examples of the ways in which comments about men's appearance are deployed helps to show that there is nothing innocent about sexualized representations of women; they are part of the operation of power which trivializes women's perspectives and keeps them 'in their place'.

Gender, politics and news

A key focus of research in recent years has been the way in which those women who have made it into senior positions of high public office are treated by the media, compared with their male counterparts. It is fair to say that the results of this research are not encouraging. Female politicians receive significantly less coverage than their male colleagues, even when their relatively small numbers are taken into account. Moreover the ways in which they are depicted fits the patterns associated with the portrayal of women generally, in stark contrast to the representation of male parliamentarians. Women's age and marital status are routinely commented upon in news reports, women are frequently referred to only by their first name, photographed in domestic rather than parliamentary settings and have their physical appearance obsessively picked apart by journalists (Ross 2002). Walkosz and Kenski (1995: 10) were forced to conclude that in the USA the very first female member of Congress Jeanette Rankin provided the blueprint for coverage which continues today whereby 'the press focused on what she looks like and wore, not what she stood for or accomplished'.

In a comparative study of female parliamentarians in Britain, South Africa and Australia, Karen Ross offers countless examples of the media's obsession with what women look like, and many angry reflections on it by female politicians: 'Women are never the right age.

We are too young, we're too old. We are too thin, we're too fat. We wear too much makeup, we don't wear enough. We are too flashy in our dress, we don't take enough care. There isn't a thing we can do that is right' (Dawn Primarolo MP, quoted in Ross 2002: 90).

Perhaps even more shocking is the fact that almost identical judgements were made by male politicians, and women in all three countries reported repeated comments on their age, appearance and (lack of) credibility from colleagues, for example 'she is looking even blonder today', 'your skirt is too short', and 'isn't this past your bedtime' (all quoted in Ross 2002). In November 2005 the would-be leader of the British Conservative party, David Davies, outraged a senior female interviewer by discoursing on the topic of whether blondes or brunettes were more fun, but his subsequent contrition (such as it was) focused mainly on the fact that his wife had brown hair, when he had gone on record as saying he preferred blondes! This supports Ross's argument about the way in which the institutions of Parliament and the media work together to demean and humiliate women and to undermine their power and credibility.

Besides appearance, another key theme of the reporting of women in Parliament was the repeated focus on their gender roles, domestic and childcare responsibilities. Female politicians reported routinely being asked: 'who is looking after your children?' And even when questions appeared sympathetic, framed in terms of how they managed to 'juggle' home and work, the subtext was 'almost always condemnatory' (Ross 2002). As the British Labour MP Glenda Jackson put it: 'If a woman goes out at six o'clock in the morning to clean offices to keep her family together, to raise her children, she will be presented as a heroine. If she wants to run that office she will be presented as an unnatural woman and even worse, as an unnatural mother' (quoted in Ross 2002: 87). It is interesting to note that even the topic of sexism in politics could itself be used as the way of not taking female politicians seriously. As one commented, 'I am ready to throttle the next journalist who asks me about toilets and creches in the House of Commons' (quoted in Ross 2002: 156). She felt this way because the barrage of questions about her lifestyle and work environment left no time for any discussion of policy initiatives – the reason she became a politician in the first place!

One of the things this highlights is the flexibility of the sexism deployed against women, in which different stereotypes could be invoked and mobilized for different purposes, and even apparently supportive questions or comments could be used to undermine women. Another example of the flexible practice of stereotyping can be seen in the reporting of the first female Mayor of Mumbai, India.

The Media Advocacy Group found reporting of her appointment filled with layer upon layer of contradictory stereotypes. Thus a commentary would note with relief that she 'doesn't fit the stereotype of someone in a position of power', but go on to say that 'she behaves like a typical housewife, rather than an aggressive hungry go-getter' and 'unlike rabid feminists she is not anti-men'. Discussing this coverage, Margaret Gallagher (2001) notes that so much time was spent establishing her as a happy housewife that viewers never got to hear about her plans or goals in her new position.

A further important finding of much research into the portrayal of powerful women explores how they are subject to pervasive double standards and also frequently trapped in a double bind situation. An example of the reporting of the large number of women who entered the British Parliament in the late 1990s should help to illustrate both issues. When, in 1997, 120 women won parliamentary seats and New Labour swept to power under Tony Blair, a now infamous photograph pictured the new Prime Minister surrounded by a sea of women, with the headline 'Blair's babes'. Many inside Parliament now argue that this photo opportunity was ill judged, managing to both infantilize and sexualize female politicians at the same time. It set the tone for the reporting of women in the aftermath of the election. However, quite quickly 'Blair's babes' gave way to another style of reporting that was even more critical of female Labour MPs. 'Babes' became 'clones' or 'Stepford wives' as journalists increasingly sought to argue that they were simply 'yes-women', without independent political convictions or minds of their own, who would always, unthinkingly, support the government.

The issue came to a head when large numbers of female MPs voted with the government to support cuts in welfare benefits to single parents, provoking enormous disappointment and cries of 'betrayal' from people who expected their female Labour MPs to take a more feminist position. At this moment a press not hitherto noted for its feminist credentials launched into an attack on those MPs, characterizing them as weak, unprincipled 'yes-women'. But the many hostile columns targeted at female MPs at the time had little to do with feminists' genuine disappointment about the outcome of the vote, and everything to do with calling into question women's entitlement to serve as elected representatives. In this way, an issue of significant interest to feminists was seized upon opportunistically by sections of the media to serve as a vehicle for vitriolic sexism.

Newly elected female MPs found themselves in a double bind: they were attacked as 'Blair's puppets' or 'Stepford wives' if they showed loyalty to the government, but faced even greater hostility if they did not. Given the criticism that met women who voted with the government on benefit cuts (and many other issues), one might have expected the media to champion or celebrate those women who did not and remained true to their conscience. But far from it: the media reserved its greatest ire for those women who would rather resign over a point of principle than 'unthinkingly' support the government. In sum, women found themselves 'damned' whichever stance they took.

In Britain, one of the female MPs most frequently attacked by the press is Clare Short, who formerly led an (unsuccessful) attempt to have pictures of topless models removed from daily newspapers. This was greeted with extraordinary hostility by sections of the press who used her allegedly unattractive appearance to cast doubt on her credibility to speak on the issue, and suggested that she was motivated by a combination of envy (of attractive 'page three' models), prudishness, and a desire to spoil people's fun. When, in 2003, she lost her Cabinet position after criticizing Prime Minister Tony Blair's decision to attack Iraq, *The Sun* ran a (political) obituary to her which featured a photograph in which her head was grafted onto the body of a much younger topless model. The double-page spread headlined 'SHE LEFT SPITEFULLY, ALL CREDIBILITY GONE', included vilification for her 'treachery' and 'backstabbing', for giving up a child for adoption early in her life, and for being 'frumpy' and a 'killjoy' (13 May 2003). Compare this to the reporting of Robin Cook MP's resignation on the same issue, which earned him plaudits about his integrity and statesmanship.

War reporting is another area replete with sexism that often operates through sexualization. During the US bombardment of Afghanistan in late 2001, *The Sun* headlined with 'KICK ASS', alongside a photograph of a young model displaying her 'ass' (Branston 2002). Similarly, newspapers often sponsor models' visits to entertain and boost the morale of troops overseas.

A number of interesting studies have explored gender issues in the coverage of Hillary Rodham Clinton. Brown and Gardetto (2000) argue that as First Lady she was constructed as a kind of 'gender outlaw' because she stepped outside the conventional image of wife and citizen (notwithstanding early attempts to address such expectations by sharing cookie recipes!). When she sought political office in New York, coverage shifted to depict her as over-ambitious and power hungry. It was only when she attained the status of 'wronged wife' in the aftermath of her husband's relationship with Monica Lewinsky that she received consistently sympathetic media reporting. As Parry-Giles (2000: 221) points out, this leads to a troubling conclusion: 'we are to fear women with power, yet admire women with the status of victim.'

The Gendered Cultures of Journalism

Having examined some common patterns in the representation of women in news, it is now time to turn to the production of news and to the culture of journalism. Historically, journalism, like other media professions, has been very male dominated, and, although this is now changing, there is still persistent evidence of both horizontal and vertical segregation. *Horizontal segregation* refers to the way that media industries and different roles within them are segmented along gender lines, with women concentrated in low-status parts of the industry (e.g. local papers and women's magazines), and in particular types of role (e.g. administration and support). *Vertical segregation* is a way of capturing the fact that even when in the same general field (e.g. television production) they tend to be concentrated at lower points in the hierarchy, while men dominate senior management. Marked pay differentials still exist between women and men for the same work. It is well known that even the most highly paid Hollywood actresses, like Julia Roberts or Catherine Zeta Jones, earn significantly less than their male counterparts and this is reflected throughout the industry with 'scandals' hitting the headlines with monotonous regularity.

Since the late 1980s some research has indicated that gender segregation may be changing (Creedon 1993; Van Zoonen 1998; Sreberny-Mohammadi and Van Zoonen 2000). Creedon pointed out some years ago that women constitute more than half of journalism students in the US, and argued that some fields – like advertising and public relations – were becoming 'pink-collar' ghettoes, dominated by white women (see also Beasley 1992; Sebba 1994). However, this in itself is not necessarily cause for celebration. Lafky (1989) argues that we are witnessing 'occupational resegregation': women are moving into previously male-dominated fields only to discover that their growing presence has led to decreased status and erosion of pay. Moreover, newer, more complex patterns of discrimination are emerging. Beasley (1992) found that women journalists were less likely to be married or in long-term partnerships than their male colleagues, suggesting that part of the price such women pay for their career success is its impact on long-term relationships. Women were also significantly less likely to have children: a fact noted by all the research which has looked at this question (e.g. Lafky 1991; Seighart and Henry 1998). A simple numerical increase in the numbers of women producers or directors or journalists, then, cannot be taken as straightforward evidence of greater equality, since for women, but not men, achieving this seems to involve major sacrifices in other parts of their lives. While men can and do expect to 'have it all' – career, partner, children – most women in senior media positions still face a stark choice.

One reason for this is to be found in the culture of media work, especially news journalism. Part of journalists' professional ideology requires them to be available twenty-four hours a day and to be able to travel anywhere at a moment's notice – not something easily reconciled with family responsibilities for men or women. Many news organizations offer little or no parental leave, and make clear their hostility to women who take time off to have children. Anecdotes about women who were sacked while on maternity leave (technically illegal, but nevertheless not uncommon) abound within the industry, as do reports of editors' decisions that young women are a 'bad risk', take lots of leave and then don't come back. As Piers Morgan, then editor of the *Daily Mirror*, put it, only half joking, at a meeting organized by Women in Journalism:

> We just sack them. I think we all play by the book and there are set ways of doing this. There is no question if one of your top people falls pregnant, it's a pain in the arse, of course it is, you don't want to lose them for six months. It's even more irritating if they bang out five, one after the other, and you don't see them for four years, of course it is, and I'm afraid for 20 who get pregnant, come back and behave impeccably in that respect there will always be one who doesn't. (Women in Journalism debate, October 1998, transcript of proceedings)

The attitudes of decision-makers within the industry constitute a significant barrier for women seeking to gain entry or hold down a position. Liesbet Van Zoonen (1994) documents many international examples, including one blatant case of the 'casting couch' syndrome: 'And then the vice president came over and stood so close to me that his nose was nearly touching mine, and said: "we don't have anything right now, but we could probably arrange something. Do you fuck?" ' (quoted in Van Zoonen 1994: 52).

Sexism does not always take such obvious forms, but there are countless examples of men appointing 'in their own image' (e.g. the 'favourite son'), reporting feeling 'less comfortable' with female colleagues, and using 'old boys' networks' as a means of recruiting staff. Paternalistic attitudes are also still rife in the newsroom, and many editors find the idea of sending a woman to cover a war or conflict unpalatable. Many others, however (particularly in television), invert the older paternalistic forms of sexism and now deliberately recruit women to posts of foreign and war correspondent, believing that a woman's presence in a conflict zone will add to the frisson and drama of war reports. An article in *The Times* noted: 'the world's war zones are chock-a-block with would-be Kate Adies risking their lives for minor stations in the hope of landing the big story because they know what the major networks want is a front-line account from a (preferably pretty) woman in a flak jacket' (quoted in Van Zoonen 1998: 44).

Interestingly, veteran war reporter Kate Adie herself recently criticized this trend, arguing that television is trivializing news by hiring female reporters with 'cute faces and cute bottoms, and nothing else in between' (quoted in the *Guardian*, 30 January 2003). Moreover, it takes very little for a woman to be discredited as a war correspondent. When the *Express* journalist Yvonne Ridley was captured by the Taliban in October 2001 it provoked a chorus of misogynist comments from journalists on other papers, concerning both her ability and – even more worryingly – her entitlement *as a mother* to be doing a job that placed her at risk: 'Is her copy so marvellous that she thought it worth making her daughter an orphan? . . . This may be a strange war, but it is a proper war, not a gender war. We want information, not pictures of blondes in khaki' (*The Scotsman*, 10 October 2001, quoted in Magor 2002). Research has yet to document any cases in which a man's role as a father challenges his rights to work as a journalist.

The laddish atmosphere of newsrooms also constitutes an important barrier to women entering the profession. A masculine culture of hard drinking, lewd jokes, and pornography consumption alienates and antagonizes many female recruits. The *Guardian*'s political reporter Joanna Coles (1997) has argued that the behaviour of her male colleagues covering the general election in Britain was worthy of a dispatch in its own right. She likened the journeys on the campaign bus (on which journalists hitched a free ride) to a 'minor stag party' with male journalists and camera crews leering at pornographic material previously downloaded from the Internet, sharing cans of lager and sniggering whenever a woman happened to wander down the aisle of the bus towards them.

Liesbet Van Zoonen (1998) has also documented some of the initiation rites that new females in the newsroom have to undergo, involving porn, suggestive comments and sexist jokes, during which the woman in question has to prove that she can take it and be 'one of the lads'. This is not just something junior women are subjected to either. In January 2003 it was announced that Rebekah Wade was to take over as the first female editor of *The Sun* newspaper. The next day the topless page three model was described as 'Rebekah from Wapping' (Wapping being the part of London where most national newspapers including *The Sun* are produced). Coincidence? It seems unlikely. Rather the male staff of *The Sun* seemed to be sending a jokey yet hostile message to their new female boss: you may be the editor of a national newspaper but you're still just a pair of tits to us.

In the USA, a marketing campaign for CNN anchor Paula Zahn was similarly problematic. It showed her profile and lips with a voice saying 'where can you find a morning news anchor who is provocative, supersmart, oh yeah, and just a little bit sexy'. The words PROVOCATIVE and SEXY flashed on the screen, and the sound of a zipper being unzipped was heard when the music finished (Chambers, Steiner and Fleming 2004).

Women face pervasive double standards: they are expected to be able to do the job as well as a man, and to be 'one of the lads', but they are also required to deploy 'feminine wiles' to get the stories that men cannot. Female journalists are often referred to dismissively as 'honey pots': sent on assignments involving a 'sting' in which they are instructed to use their femininity to elicit some information which could not be obtained in the usual way. Perversely, some editors are able to present this double standard as an 'advantage' for women!

Because of the obstacles they face, women have had to be creative to enter media professions and often have entirely different career trajectories than their male colleagues. For example, women are much more likely than men to use a secretarial route as a way of gaining access to work in television production, performing menial tasks and giving 110 per cent in order to get noticed and be given an opportunity to participate in production (see Baehr 1996). A major study of women in the cultural industries in Australia (Swanson and Wise 1998) found that women were also significantly more likely than men to be self-employed and freelance. Women in the media are increasingly constructing flexible careers, developing their own occupational portfolios in order to compete in a sector in which men still dominate the senior positions.

Do women produce different news from men?

Increased employment of women within senior and creative media positions is an important goal in its own right. But from the point of view of portrayals of gender, a key question is what difference – if any – women in the industry make to the kinds of representations that we see, hear and read every day. Does employing more women lead to 'better' representations of women, as many people implicitly assume? Do women produce news that is feminist – or even just feminine?

Many journalists and commentators argue that they do. It is often asserted that women tell stories that would otherwise be ignored, that they have different ethical values from men that are evident in their reporting, and that they are particularly concerned to look at the human effects of the stories they are covering (e.g. crime or unemployment). In a report for Women in Journalism that investigated this issue Linda Christmas concluded that both *what* women journalists regard as newsworthy and *how* they report it differs from men. She argued that the large-scale entry of women into journalism is changing the nature of news to focus on human-interest stories, health, education and family matters, as well as fuelling an increase in confessional journalism, and the blurring of a distinction between news and features:

> Even when women select the same news content as men they write it in a different manner. Women want news that is 'relevant', news you can 'identify with', news that is explained in terms of their lives. Issues therefore are 'personalised', or 'humanised' in order that the reader understands the relevance. This move recognises:
>
> - that women prefer to communicate with the reader; they put readers' needs above those of policy makers and other providers of news;
> - that women tend to be more 'people' oriented rather than issue oriented;
> - that women place greater importance on seeing news 'in context' rather than in isolation; and
> - that women like to explain the consequences of events' (Christmas 1997)

Claims like these are often underpinned by an unexamined essentialism (i.e. the view that men and women are entirely different) or – in a more politicized variant of the argument – by a feminist standpoint position (Harding 1993). From this perspective, it is argued that by dint of their subordinate status women have gained a kind of 'double vision' which allows them to see the view from above *and* from below and thus to produce fuller, fairer and more accurate representations. Some variants of this argument do not go so far as to assert that women have an epistemological privilege (i.e. an ability to produce *better* knowledge), but simply stress the fact that women have *different* perspectives because of their different lives. According to this view, they observe things which men literally could not see, and therefore can create characters and storylines and news reports that women find far more convincing and subtle than those constructed by men.

Persuasive though this argument may be, it should be treated with scepticism. For one thing, it relies on the assumption that women constitute a homogeneous group, and that the key division in society is between men and women. In fact, women are not just different from men but are also different from each other, and there is no reason to suppose that the influx of white, middle-class, heterosexual women into journalism, scriptwriting or broadcast production will produce any improvement at all in the representations of black, working-class or lesbian women. Certainly, I have not noticed a decline in stereotyping of single 'welfare mothers' or black working-class women as the British press has taken on more and more female columnists. On the contrary, the liberal 'quality' papers offer a cloyingly white, middle-class view of the world in which the role of female writers' seems to be primarily to produce an endless cycle of hand-wringing articles about the trials of the school run, whether or not to have little Oliver immunized or buy him brand name trainers, and whether you can still call yourself a feminist if you buy sexy lingerie/shave your legs/wear makeup, etc. If the structural position of cultural workers is deemed to make a difference to the kinds of representation produced, then the key will be diversity in terms of social class, 'race' and ethnicity (among other things) as well as gender.

However, even this may not necessarily translate into 'better' representations because this argument about difference ignores the significance of both ideology and the market. Those people who succeed in media organizations tend to be those who take on the professional values and ideologies of those organizations: they are professionally socialized in a variety of formal and informal ways to think, write, produce or direct in a particular manner, which invariably reflects the interests of the dominant culture. Our very notions of what constitutes news, for example, or what makes good television are shot through with assumptions about gender, 'race', class, geography and so on. To this extent an individual's social location or origin may not be as significant a determinant of how a media product turns out as one might expect. Add to this the conservatism of the market for cultural products, manifest in the desire for sequels in film or for copycat sitcoms in television or intermedia agenda setting (the way that different media look to the others for guidance about whether something is newsworthy) in news, and you have a recipe for 'more of the same', almost regardless of who is producing it.

Van Zoonen (1998) argues that what research on women and news values reveals is the force and pervasiveness of widely shared stereotypes about women. She notes that men share the view of female journalists as interested in different news, and reporting it differently. But when research looks at the practice of journalism, rather than perceptions of interests, only two small differences emerge: female journalists are more interested and oriented to audience needs than male journalists and they tend to look more for female spokespersons. All the other putative differences disappear. Apart from being wrong, Van Zoonen suggests, arguments about gender differences in news values end up producing a situation in which women get given stereotypical or traditionally feminine, low-status assignments, thus helping to create and perpetuate the very myth being explored. Many female journalists are actively struggling to avoid this kind of pigeon-holing, to be allowed to write about politics or economic policy, rather than being ghettoized in the advertising-rich lifestyle sections of newspapers and television broadcasts.

Looked at from this perspective it is possible to make a case that is diametrically opposed to Christmas's argument: that is, rather than the entry of women leading to the feminization of journalism, it is the transformation of journalism that is leading to greater numbers of women entering the profession. The growing presence of women in journalism, then, may be the outcome not the cause of changes that are transforming the news industry as a whole. Below, I examine some of these transformations.

The Changing Profession: Casualization, Media Management and the Rise of the Columnist

One of the most dramatic shifts in journalism over the last two decades has been the casualization of the profession. A large proportion of the content of newspapers is now produced by freelancers working from home. This is vastly cheaper for employers who have no office or equipment costs and bear none of the real costs of employing someone – national insurance, health and maternity benefits, pensions, etc. According to Franklin (1997), financial restructuring within the industry is responsible for this shift, and in the UK three-quarters of freelancers previously held staff journalist posts from which they were made redundant. Such individuals went from well-paid salaried positions to freelance status in which they are 'piece workers', paid by the word, and are remunerated only for those pieces that are used. It hardly needs stating that such insecure employment is not likely to foster probing or critical analyses – let alone large-scale investigative reports, which involve significant investments of time and resources. It has become a truism to note that had Bernstein and Woodward been working as journalists today, we would probably never have known about the Watergate scandal.

Another aspect of the restructuring of journalism has been the dramatic growth of PR and media relations firms and their impact on news content. Recent studies have revealed that such sources exercise a huge influence in structuring the range and profile of editorial content (Franklin 1997). PR has expanded while traditional journalism has been shrinking, with the result that press officers have considerable power to set news agendas. We are living in the age of spin. The editor of *PR Week* has argued that 50 per cent of broadsheet papers' news is sourced by press officers, and that the figure for tabloids and local papers is considerably higher (quoted in Franklin 1997). Many journalists who entered the profession with a view of it as a scrutineer of authority, a powerful fourth estate, find that the reality of their work today is more humdrum and often involves little more than rewriting press releases. As Franklin notes, media editors in press and broadcasting increasingly acknowledge the operation of a two-tier system in which 'top-quality reporters engaged on complex and important news gatherings' represent an elite, alongside a mass 'lower tier of editorial assistants who can deal with rewrites, obituaries, wedding reports, etc.' (Franklin 1997: 51).

The third major change in journalism over the last decade has been the rise of the columnist. Views, it is sometimes said, have replaced news. Columnists are not experts or specialists in a particular area of journalism, but generalists, adept at expressing their opinion on an endless range of topics, able to 'sound off' about anything and everything on a weekly or even a daily basis. Some newspapers hire 'serious' columnists to write reflective pieces about world affairs, but the vast majority of columnists work by the fixing on one feature of one news report and building an edifice of claims and counterclaims around it. The nature of such writing is that in order to be persuasive and saleable it must claim to identify or examine a general phenomenon, but this is usually built from only two or three examples: a columnist might note that Kate Winslet and Catherine Zeta Jones have both had babies recently, and ask 'so are we witnessing a Hollywood baby-boom?' There are thousands of examples of this style of column in newspapers every day: men are the 'new women' because they have to take care of their appearance now; spot the new trend for 'toy boys' as older women date younger men; why a gay man makes the best friend a heterosexual woman can have; etc., etc.

What is important about these stories is that they illustrate a shift in the nature of journalism – a shift from reporting to interpreting. Many journalists have become cultural intermediaries (Featherstone 1991) devoting time not to meticulous reporting of newsworthy events, but to describing and exploring shifts in tastes, values, feelings, beliefs, aspirations, mores and behaviours. Such writers regard their role as being to pick over and analyse every aspect of human behaviour from the bedroom to the street, to find or create a pattern in what they see, and to narrate the story of who we are back to us in compelling – and preferably new – terms. In this hyper-reflexive moment a single event may be random, but two instances of it are highly suggestive and three constitute a major trend – whether that trend relates to male 'bad lad' pop-stars getting married, celebrity women in their forties having babies, or a 'middle youth' magazines closing down.

In addition to 'trend stories', two other types of column are worthy of note. First the confessional sub-genre constructed around a first-person account of some harrowing experience (fighting cancer or HIV, being in prison, having an abortion etc., etc.). Secondly the 'provocative' column/rant designed to make readers angry or to court controversy. Mayes (2000) has argued that 'therapy news' is in ascendancy, and feelings are increasingly prioritized above careful reporting of facts. After the 7 July 2005 bombings in London, for example, a huge amount of media coverage focused on foregrounding the emotions of people involved, whether victims or emergency service workers, in a way that was quite different from the reporting of tragedies or disasters one or two decades earlier. This is connected to the rise of therapy/confessional culture more generally (see chapter 5).

Trend stories and the backlash

From a gender perspective, it is striking to note that many of the new columnists are female. Zoe Heller argues that there are three types of 'new girl writing': first, the amusing 'home front' column in which women cheerfully write about lazy husbands and accident-prone children ('mum, Johnny has a marble up his nose!'); second the 'stern comment' piece, taking a feminist-ish perspective on public affairs ('when was the last time the Foreign Secretary changed a nappy?'); and third the 'daffy girl' piece in which a young-ish single female confides the vagaries of her personal life ('never try shaving your legs in a moving taxi'). What is perhaps significant overall, however, is the preponderance of stories *about gender*, which seek to document and make sense of changing relations between men and women.

Today's newspaper columns bear a powerful resemblance to the 'trend stories' that Susan Faludi argued were part of a far-reaching backlash against feminism. Faludi set out to explore a paradox in popular culture. She noted that on one hand women were constantly being told that they 'have it all' and 'all the battles have been won', but on the other an equally powerful message was being sent to women which said 'you may be free and equal now, but you have never been more miserable'. Faludi (1992) observed a 'bulletin of despair' posted everywhere from newspapers to films to doctors' offices. Its message was (superficially) different every day, but the underlying theme was that feminism is bad for your health, your relationships, and your psychological well-being.

> Professional women are suffering 'burn-out' and succumbing to an 'infertility epidemic'. Single women are grieving from a 'man shortage'. The New York Times reports: childless women are 'depressed and confused' and their ranks are swelling. Newsweek says: unwed women are 'hysterical' and crumbling under a 'profound crisis of confidence'. The health advice manuals inform: high powered career women are stricken with unprecedented outbreaks of 'stress induced disorders', hair loss, bad nerves, alcoholism, and even heart attacks. The psychology books advise: independent women's loneliness represents 'a major mental health problem today'. (Faludi 1992: 2)

Fifteen years on from Faludi's research, the press is still full of trend stories, warning career women of the risks of 'superwoman burn-out' and of the dangers awaiting their children in the guise of irresponsible nannies or abusive childminders, fragile emotional lives, and poorer SATs results. To avoid this women are invited to join the 'new housewives' who had well-paid jobs, but 'gave it all up to push a pram to the shops. Why? Because it's fun' (the *Guardian*, 12 December 2002).

As Faludi documented, the trend stories come in pairs – one to flee and one to join – and columns are built around stark contrasts with clear take-home messages. On one side of the balance sheet is exhaustion, 'a diet of Marks and Spencer ready meals', 'fleeting telephone exchanges with her husband', 'no sex', 'salary spent on the nanny, cleaner and dry-cleaning bills' and the 'terrible knowledge' that her son's first word was 'taxi' (to take a typical example from the *Guardian*, 12 December 2002). On the other is relaxation, pleasure, freedom, the satisfaction of knowing her child is being brought up by 'the person who loves him most', along with – presumably – a rich partner (though this prerequisite is rarely mentioned). A double-page feature in *The Observer* (Sunday, 4 July 1999) starts with a warning that working mothers will 'weep' when they hear about the lives of the 'new housewives', and constructs a story of neighbourliness, community harmony and domestic bliss. Each perfect day of fun, play and mutual emotional nourishment Naomi spends with her child is capped off by 'an adult supper and a bottle of wine' when Naomi's husband gets home at 9 p.m. 'This', the journalist tells us, 'they linger over, while exchanging notes about their respective days.' It is a major accomplishment of the columnist (Maureen Freely) that staying at home to care for young children and having dinner ready for a husband who gets back from work at 9 in the evening can be made to seem both pleasurable and new. But today's columns are all about reporting (or is it constructing?) new trends.

Another current – and long-running – favourite is the 'men are in crisis' trend in which feminists appear again in the role of evil-doers, responsible for everything from male underachievement in schools, to unemployment, health problems, high rates of male suicide, and that catch-all 'emasculation'.

It is not that I would argue that many men are not facing difficulties, or that the life of the stay at home mum (with rich partner) is without its attractions. On the contrary, there are clearly grains of truth in both these accounts and they speak to real and deeply felt longings and experiences for some women. But what is at issue is both the way the stories are told – the lack of real evidence, the manifold exclusions of different women's experiences, the transformation of one or two personal anecdotes into a 'trend', the ethnocentricism and stubborn inattention to changing economic necessities, and so on – and the political effects of these columns day in, day out. In the shift from reportage to interpretation gender relations have become perhaps the prime topic of 'news'.

The New Journalism

These changes have contributed to what has become known as the 'new journalism'. Every generation seems to have its 'new journalism', often celebrated as a riposte to previous or existing journalistic styles and regarded by its champions as more in touch, authentic and immediate – for example, 'gonzo'. However, the 'new journalism' of the late 1990s and early twenty-first century is more often lamented than celebrated (Langer 1997). It is regarded as the product of ever more competitive media environments, the triumph of market reforms over public service, changes in the regulation of media (deregulation or regulation with a 'lighter touch') and rapid technological change.

Kevin Glynn (2000) argues that the origins of today's journalistic style can be traced back to the USA in the 1950s. In the wake of the quiz show scandals, television networks tried to improve their tarnished reputations by expanding news and current affairs programming in an attempt to garner prestige and respectability. However, the dramatic expansion of this type of programming meant that producers had to develop new ways to increase television journalism's appeal. The political and social conflicts of the 1960s (the civil rights movement, protests against the Vietnam war, etc.) offered the perfect opportunity for developing new styles that generated broad appeal through emotionally intense narratives 'that emphasized high impact images at the expense of official commentary' (Glynn 2000: 21). New grammars of photography as well as an emphasis on immediacy and being part of, rather than detached from, the action, were central to this style.

The rise of local news was also key to the transformation. The local television 'news family', built around an attractive mixed-sex couple had a profound effect upon national and international news programming, and has become colloquially known as 'Ken and Barbie news'. The phatic communication practised by this style of news was at least as significant as the information conveyed; local news programmes signalled the beginning of the flirtatious banter between presenters dubbed 'happy talk'. News broadcasts became informal and intimate – part of the shift to what Norman Fairclough (1995) calls 'synthetic personalization' across a range of different social domains.

Technological changes in the form of lightweight, easy-to-operate cameras and sound equipment, and portable satellites, also had their impact upon emerging styles of news reporting. But far more important was the role played by the growth of satellite and cable television – both in its impact upon competition between networks, and its shift towards news values rooted in entertainment rather than public service. After CNN was launched in 1980, the three major network broadcasters in the USA lost 10 per cent of their audience for news, and responded by attempting to further popularize their programmes through news stories deemed relevant and engaging to people's everyday lives, rather than through abstract notions about what the public 'should know'. Television news became part of the ratings war, and had to win audiences, attract advertisers and make a profit as much as any other type of programming.

The news that resulted from these changes has become known as 'newszak', 'bonk journalism', 'infotainment', or simply 'tabloid news' – the idea being that nearly all sections of the press, radio and television have become tabloidized. What, then, are the characteristics of this news? Bob Franklin argues:

> Journalism's editorial priorities have changed. Entertainment has superseded the provision of information; human interest has supplanted the public interest; measured judgment has succumbed to sensationalism; the trivial has triumphed over the weighty; the intimate relationships of celebrities from soap operas, the world of sport or the Royal family are judged more 'newsworthy' than the reporting of significant issues and events of international consequence. Traditional news values have been undermined by new values; 'infotainment' is rampant. (Franklin 1997: 4)

For Franklin, the emergence of 'newszak' represents the beginning of the end for foreign reporting, investigative journalism and serious parliamentary reports. More fundamentally, it erodes a number of the key tenets of journalism – the commitment to rational, objective reporting, to informing the public about matters of importance, and to furnishing information necessary for citizens in a democracy. In place of this public sphere model of journalism, Franklin argues, a market-led model has come to prominence. This prioritizes entertainment over information, and will always favour dramatic visual images of action (preferably involving car chases or helicopters) over serious in-depth reporting. It regards its audiences as consumers not citizens, and it sees itself as answerable to commercial imperatives not public service ones. In the USA, news bulletins are now organized according to the results of 'market testing' about what viewers want, rather than any other notion of what constitutes news. In the UK, the head of programming at the Carlton television network is reported as saying that he would cut *World in Action* (one of the few remaining documentary series) if it got low viewing figures, even if its programme makers had uncovered serious miscarriages of justice (Franklin 1997).

Meanwhile, his colleague in charge of news at Channel 5 argued that his mission was to prevent news from being 'painful', by offering less politics and more consumer, sports and entertainment news to viewers.

News broadcasts are becoming increasingly preoccupied with style and presentation, and with the possibilities afforded by new technologies – flashy virtual studios, impressive graphics, and live two-ways by satellite link-up. Often the performance of immediacy and liveness seems to take precedence over any actual information conveyed (much of the time simply repeating what has been said in the studio link). A 'responsive' interactive quality is also becoming central to many news broadcasts, which invite e-mails, text messages and phone calls during the 'show' on a variety of questions posed by the news reader/host – for example, 'should George Bush attack Iraq, even without another UN resolution?' – a selection of which are read out later.

Kevin Glynn (2000) argues that tabloidization is intimately connected to postmodernism, with its prioritization of images over the real, scepticism about key modern categories (for example, distinctions between public and private, reality and representation), fragmentation and eclecticism, and the growth of incredulity towards grand narratives. Of the trend towards tabloid news, he contends:

> It prefers heightened emotionality and often emphasizes the melodramatic. It sometimes makes heavy use of campy irony, parody and broad humour. It relies on an often volatile mix of realistic and anti realist representational conventions. It resists 'objectivity', detachment, and critical distance. It is highly multi discursive. It incorporates voices frequently excluded from 'serious' news and often centres on those that are typically marginalized in mainstream media discourse. The 'bizarre' and the 'deviant' are central to its image repertoire. . . . It frequently violates dominant institutional standards and procedures for the production and validation of 'truth'. It thrives on the grotesque, the scandalous and the 'abnormal' . . . Tabloid media simultaneously de-familiarize the ordinary and banalize the exotic. (Glynn 2000: 7)

One of the postmodern features that can be seen very clearly in contemporary television news broadcasts is the blurring of fact and fiction, and, more specifically, the use of generic conventions from different kinds of entertainment product in news – such as cliffhangers, action sequences, detective stories, etc. Recently, this pattern of generic borrowing has been intensified by the trend to use music behind some reports. The idea seems to be to get us to feel rather than think. As a Dutch executive producer puts it: 'A news bulletin without tears is not a really good one' (quoted in Van Zoonen 1998: 43).

Table 4.1 Traditional and contemporary news presentation

Old style news	Newszak
serious	trivial
rational	emotional
information	entertainment
abstract	personal
literary	visual
modern	postmodern
public interest	human interest
factual	blurring fact and fiction
investigative	infotainment
measured judgement	sensationalism

Table 4.1 captures in outline some of the contrasts between older-style journalistic values and the values of contemporary newszak. Obviously, it is important to remember that these are ideal types, general tendencies, rather than fixed properties to be found in any single news broadcast or newspaper. As Simon Jenkins has observed, 'there is always a golden age of journalism and it was always when the person discussing the subject came into newspapers!' (quoted in Franklin 1997: 6). This acerbic comment alerts us to the need to beware of nostalgia – particularly nostalgia for a mythical journalism that never existed – a point also made forcefully by John Langer (1997) who criticizes the common 'lament' about news, and argues that 'the other news' (about fires, accidents, beauty contests, celebrities, peculiar occupations and hobbies, lost children, romantic adventure and changes of fortune) has long been a feature of news.

From Langer's perspective, it is important to subject this type of news to ideological analysis (just as much as news about political conflict, industrial disputes and racism) rather than simply to bemoan the passing of a bygone era.

One of the sets of questions that urgently requires addressing is the relationship of discourses of gender, 'race' and class to the new journalism. On the one hand, its preoccupation with surface, beauty, sex, and celebrity hardly seems to offer hope for those interested in progressive social change. But on the other, it marks a break with an 'old style' of news that was often patronizing, imperialist, deferential to politicians and royalty, and deeply implicated in the maintenance of the status quo. It is important not to idealize the older tradition of journalism, and to look at both the opportunities and the challenges represented by new journalistic styles. This means that studies of news and gender should examine not only those obviously weighty and serious issues such as the representation of female politicians or the reporting of violence against women, but should also look at the 'trivial' pieces that increasingly dominate newspapers. How do lifestyle articles on dieting or bullying construct gender? In what ways might reporting of celebrities like David and Victoria Beckham reinforce or challenge conventional gender scripts? What spaces – if any – do new journalistic styles leave for new and different voices or perspectives to be heard? How is the decline in deference to authority connected to gender? On this last point, for example, it might be noted that while respect for politicians and public servants may be decreasing, scientists 'discovering' or explaining natural gender differences are often treated with a respect that borders on reverence (particularly with the recent explosion of media interest in evolutionary psychology). This illustrates above all the need for careful and specific research that can explore the complex ways in which gender and new journalism interact.

News Reporting of Sexual Violence

The sexual objectification of women's bodies has been a major topic of research across a range of media (see chapter 3 on advertising). But it represents a particularly grave concern in relation to news reporting of sexual violence against women. Studies from across the globe have highlighted the ways in which news reports of rape and sexual assault sensationalize sexual violence, give a distorted view of its incidence and nature (for example focusing disproportionately on attacks by strangers, on unusual or bizarre assaults, and on those perpetrated against young women), trivialize women's experience of the attack, and report rapes in a manner that is designed to be titillating or arousing. Female victims are frequently described in highly sexualized terms – 'sexy 21-year-old', 'blonde beauty', 'blue-eyed schoolgirls', etc., with descriptions that bear little relationship to the woman's experience of the attack – such as 'fondled her breasts'. Moreover the photographs used to illustrate reports of rape are often deliberately provocative. An example from South Africa illustrates this well. In reports about a woman who was bringing rape charges against four men, newspapers ran stories which headlined 'Girl a "willing partner"' and 'Sex party' which told the story of the attack entirely from the perspective of the four accused men. Reporting focused on the ordeal that *they* had been through since the allegations, without consideration of the woman's experience. The men were photographed fully clothed, while the woman was presented naked – in a video-still taken on the night of the alleged rapes (Gallagher 2001).

This is shocking but it is far from uncommon. In Britain, *The Sun* is one of a number of popular papers that features a daily 'pin up' – a photograph of a young, topless woman – on page three. In her study of 840 press reports of sexual violence over a three-month period, Cynthia Carter (1998) found that several articles about rape were placed directly beside this photograph (in contravention of an agreed code of practice), and that nearly half were in the pages either side of the photographs, indicating a clear strategy to use reports of rape as part of a sexualized 'news' package. My own less extensive analysis of random samples of British tabloid newspapers reveals that even when rape stories are not juxtaposed with the page three model they are frequently placed on the same page as other 'sexy' representations of women, as in an example from *The Mirror* (15 January 2003), in which an article that reports on the discovery in a drain of clothes and a mobile phone belonging to a 21-year-old woman widely believed to have been raped and murdered is placed next to a story about the growing popularity of a chain of sex shops – illustrated by a photograph of a woman in one of its lines of black lacy underwear.

In the remainder of this chapter I want to look in detail at how the press report sex crimes, and how media reporting both feeds into and feeds upon the criminal justice system. The point is to illustrate how the media and the police, courts, and so on, work together to construct particular, problematic understandings of sexual attacks, their victims and perpetrators.

Rape in the criminal justice system and the media

Rape is a crime of violence designed to humiliate, debase, overwhelm and control a woman. It involves invasion of parts of a woman's body normally reserved for pleasure, intimacy and, for some women, for childbearing. Many women regard rape as a form of torture. Ironically, this is sometimes accepted in times of war, when rape may be regarded as a crime against humanity, but not when individual women are subject to the same experience in peacetime. Rape is regarded by the vast majority of women as extremely traumatic, and can leave long-term psychological as well as physical scars.

Over the last three decades the women's movement has generated increased awareness about sexual attacks against women, and rape is now appreciated as being a major crime. The rape reform movement has been successful on many fronts in bringing drastic changes in law, courtroom procedure, evidence gathering, crisis counselling and victim care. More generally, it has proposed a model for understanding rape that directly and purposely opposed traditional conceptions of victims, attackers and the nature and meaning of the crime, rejecting the view that rapists are motivated by lust, that female victims contribute to their attack, and that rapists are best understood as lone, deranged psychopaths, in favour of an understanding that situates sexual attacks in the context of a male-dominated society.

Today, elements of both types of conception of rape are widespread, and public understanding of sexual attacks is replete with contradictions. On the one hand, crimes of sexual violence evoke widespread horror and disgust, yet, on the other hand, there is still a pervasive belief in the idea that women are in some way guilty or responsible if they are raped – they were dressed provocatively, they were out alone at night, they 'led the man on', etc.

Together, the media and the criminal justice system have played a powerful role in sustaining this view of women. For some judges it would seem that only if you are the ideal victim – who, it would appear (contradictorily), is white, middle-class, married, a virgin, and a housewife with children – do you escape denigration. This view is reinforced by media reporting of rapes which shows clear evidence of a 'hierarchy' of crime news: 'Women who . . . are battered, raped or even murdered appear to be journalistically unimportant unless they are white and middle-class, or if they can serve as a warning to other women' (Meyers 1997: 98). In the UK, stories highlighting individual judges' sexism hit the news-stands every few months. In 1990 Judge Cassell was forced to take early retirement after his comments and sentencing in the case of a man who had raped his twelve-year-old stepdaughter. Cassell said that it was understandable for a man with a healthy sexual appetite to be driven to such behaviour, as his wife was pregnant and had lost interest in sex. He sentenced the man to probation.

Closer scrutineers of judicial behaviour might observe that the most unusual feature of Judge Cassell's case was his enforced retirement. Action is rarely taken against individuals in a profession in which one prevailing view seems to be that 'no' does not always mean 'no'. As Judge Wild put it in his direction to the jury: 'Women saying no do not always mean no. It is not just a question of how she says it, how she shows that makes it clear. If she doesn't want it she only has to keep her legs shut and she wouldn't get it without force and then there would be marks of force being used' (quoted in Kennedy 1992: 111). It is worth noting that evidence of force *is not* always sufficient to convince courts that a woman has been raped, since bruises can be presented by the defence as having resulted from 'vigorous sex play'. Indeed, Helena Kennedy QC (1992) has documented cases where even *gang rape* is passed off as the woman having 'liked it rough'. The British judiciary hit an all-time low in 1992 when one of its senior judges described a ten-year-old girl who had been sexually assaulted as 'no angel', with the implication that she was partly culpable. Jane Ussher (1997) has documented many similar examples in which girls as young as five and seven are castigated: 'I am satisfied we have here an unusually sexually promiscuous young lady. And he [the defendant] did not know enough to refuse. No way do I believe [the defendant] initiated sexual contact.' In this case the judge was sentencing a man for sexually assaulting a five-year-old girl (quoted in Ussher 1997: 390).

Reliable figures about how many women have been raped are extremely difficult to find and interpret. Sandra Walklate (2001) points out that two different measures are often confused: *incident rates* – which refer to the number of incidents occurring during a specified time period – and *prevalence rates* which refer to the number of incidents occurring over a lifetime. Studies of the prevalence of rape suggest that between one in six and one in four women will experience rape during the course of their lifetime, and one in three will experience sexual assault in the UK. In the USA a large survey in 1990 found 13 per cent of women claiming that they had been raped – and of these only a quarter had reported it (quoted in Ussher 1997). This mirrors findings of the British Crime Survey (quoted in Walklate 2001) which noted that only 13,000 sexual offences against women were reported to the police, out of an estimated 60,000 in one year.

The number of rapes being reported to the police has increased dramatically over the last three decades. Indeed, since 1985 reports of rape increased by 400 per cent in Britain. However, this increase has to be treated with caution. It may not necessarily mean that more women are being raped, but may be a consequence of higher reporting rates due to increased awareness, and more supportive treatment by the police (for example the introduction of 'rape suites', guarantees that female officers will be assigned to female rape victims, etc.). What is very clear, however, is that, despite increasing reporting of rape to the police, convictions for rape are not increasing. Rape has the lowest conviction rate of any serious crime, with fewer than 6 per cent of cases brought to court resulting in a conviction. Given that only a fraction of incidents of rape are reported to the police, and that only a fraction of these get to court, the finding that so few rape cases end in a conviction is very worrying. It represents a tiny proportion of sexual attacks against women. A report published by the police and Crown Prosecution Service Independent Inspectorates in April 2002 found that the system failed rape victims at all stages, and noted that women who had been raped were more likely than any other crime victims to have lost confidence entirely in the criminal justice process. The report concluded that more sensitive treatment of victims was crucial to securing a conviction. It recommended introducing specialist prosecutors for rape cases, better training for police and prosecutors, and instructions to prosecuting counsel to challenge offensive cross-examination by defence counsel.

The report did not deal with media coverage of rapes, but it is clear that news reporting is also a key part of the jigsaw, for it is here that public understanding of sexual violence is at least partly constructed. Research on media reporting of sexual attacks highlights a very small number of discourses or myths which are drawn on repeatedly in coverage (Benedict 1992; Cuklanz 1996; Moorti 2002). Taken together, these systematically misunderstand rape, provide justifications for male behaviour and work to blame the victims. It is to these structuring myths that we turn next.

Rape myths in news reporting

Discrediting the witness/victim: women's reputation   One of the most pervasive and established beliefs about rape is that victims in some way provoke it – by their dress or conduct. So entrenched is this myth that even some rape victims accept it, along with many lawyers, journalists and police. The myth works to circumscribe the range of women's behaviour that is deemed acceptable – such that dressing up for a party, walking somewhere alone, or being friendly to a man can all be constructed as blameworthy.

Another important aspect of this myth is that women can be depicted as having 'deserved it' if they did not protect themselves against 'normal' (i.e. uncontrollable) male lust. Women's behaviour is pathologized, while the view of men as 'testosterone timebombs' just waiting to explode is treated as unproblematic. In court, women's sexual history can be discussed, and even their underwear exhibited in order to discredit them or to show that – because she was wearing a lacy bra or a string – a woman was actively interested in pursuing sex and therefore consented. In much press reporting the defence's argument is unproblematically reported, and comments made about the victim are unquestioningly reproduced – as when it was revealed that the alleged victim of a campus rape had been known as 'slut of the year'. All subsequent reporting in the tabloid press used this epithet and even the scare quotes around it scarcely detract from the main message that the woman was 'easy' or 'loose' and therefore must have consented.

The use of sexualized language to describe female victims is well documented (Sootnill and Walby 1991). Benedict (1992) has noted the key role which language like this plays in press reporting:

> Men are never described as hysterical, bubbly, pretty, pert, prudish, vivacious, or flirtatious, yet these are all words used to describe the female victims of cases I have examined . . . Male crime victims are rarely described in terms of their sexual attractiveness, while female crime victims almost always are . . . [E]ven policewomen and female detectives were described as 'attractive' or 'pretty'. (Benedict 1992: 20–1)

She asks us to imagine press reports saying 'Vivacious John Harris was attacked in his home yesterday' or 'Handsome, blond detective Paul Robinson took the witness stand today'. Of course, we cannot.

It is instructive to compare the reporting of sexual attacks on women and girls with those on men and boys. In these cases, instead of the *victims'* behaviour or dress being commented upon, *the occupation or position of authority* held by the *attacker* is made salient – for example 'Kinky copper' or 'Vicar's night of shame' or 'Headmaster in boys sex romp'. There is never any consideration that the behaviour of the boys or men who are victims might have contributed to the assault on them, and no suggestion, for example, that it might be understandable that a teacher, faced with a gym full of boys in shorts, might be unable to contain his feelings of lust. In short, male victims of sexual attack are depicted as blameless, and the rape, in these cases, is treated as being a crime related to power rather than desire. It is worth noting also that when rapes of boys or men are reported in the media neither the victims nor the crimes are so graphically described (Caputi 1987).

Rape is sex: the triviality of unwanted sex   The idea that rape is 'just' sex lies at the root of most other popular discourses about rape. It ignores the fact that rape is a physical attack, and encourages the belief that it should not be taken seriously as a crime. Helen Benedict (1992) cites many instances of this myth in the public domain, including this comment by Texas Republican candidate Clayton Williams while running for Governor in 1990: 'if it's inevitable, just relax and enjoy it.' This ignores the fact that rape is a forced attack, during which time the victim is assaulted, threatened and often in fear of mutilation or murder. 'Rape is to sex like a punch in the mouth is to a kiss', said a teenage victim of rape quoted by Benedict (1992: 14). A particularly pernicious aspect of this myth is the suggestion that the woman *enjoyed* being raped, something that defence lawyers almost routinely suggest in court. A new and sinister development – especially in the context of growing numbers of reports of date rape – is the use of feminist-sounding discourse by defence counsel in the courtroom to suggest that the pressures on women's sexual reputation mean that they 'have to' say no, when, in fact, they wanted to have sex with the accused; from this perspective the apparent refusal was simply an attempt by a woman to maintain an untarnished sexual reputation (and not to get labelled a slut) rather than an unequivocal statement.

Rapists are usually black and/or lower-class   Racist myths about black male sexuality have a long history – dating back at least to the era of slavery. Between 1880 and 1940 one of the most common 'justifications' given by white mobs for the lynching of black men was that they had raped or 'despoiled' a white woman: 'white women were the forbidden fruit, the untouchable property, the ultimate symbol of white male power' (Dowd Hall 1983). White women were depicted as pure and innocent, whilst black men endured a mythology which still persists about their sexual appetites, their lack of self-control, and their desire to punish white men by raping 'their' women. In fact, most rapes occur between members of the same ethnic group – with the notable exception of rapes during wartime.

Black women who have been raped suffer disproportionately as a result of this mythology. They face: 'both the rape myths that confront all women, and stereotypes of black women as more likely to have consented to sex, more sexually experienced and less likely to be psychologically damaged' (Kennedy 1992).

In very extensive analysis of the reporting of sexual violence over four decades, Soothill and Walby (1991) found many examples of racism. They noted that news photographs of alleged rapists were much more likely to be used when the defendant was black, contributing to the steady drip, drip, drip of racist assumptions about sexual violence. Discussing the way in which reports of rape are sometimes articulated to other political agendas, they examined coverage of what became known as the Brixton gang rape in which themes about gang rape, 'light' sentencing and 'race' were systematically yoked together to produce an image of 'rampaging black youths threatening white girls and being treated too leniently by the courts' (Soothill and Walby 1991).

As bell hooks (1982) and Patricia Hill Collins (1991) have pointed out, anti-racist struggles have also privileged black men's experiences at the expense of black women's, such that the lynching of black men is regarded as iconic of racism, while the rape of black women by white men receives attention as a sexist practice but not also (as it should) as a racist one.

The attacker is motivated by lust   A further myth about rape is that it is perpetrated by men who become overwhelmed by their feelings of sexual desire. The male attacker is assumed to be full of pent-up sexual feelings, and is driven beyond normal self-control by the lust engendered by a particular woman. This myth has been challenged repeatedly by the rape reform movement, but still has a hold in public consciousness and is often implicit – if not explicit – in press reporting. In fact, rapists are not motivated by desire but by anger or by the need to humiliate and dominate women. Rape is about power, not sexual gratification. This can be seen from rapes of men which are carried out overwhelmingly by heterosexual men, not as an expression of frustrated desire but as a means to degrade or punish their victim (Lees 1996).

The flip side of this fundamental misunderstanding about the nature and causes of rape is that women are blamed for their 'attractiveness'. Indeed, as we have already seen, even children can be presented as 'seductive'. A frequent theme of legal defences (particularly in sexual murder cases) is provocation – which can include anything from teasing the defendant, to refusal to have sex with him. In one example cited by Soothill and Walby (1991) the press reported that a twelve-year-old girl who had been stabbed to death by a seventeen-year-old youth had 'provoked' her death by failing to reveal her age prior to sex play. Frequently reports made the assumption that women should be willing to provide sex for interested men. For example, *The Sun* headlined with 'Landlord's death lust for girl', in which the strapline was 'Lodger shunned sex'. By using the word 'shunned', *The Sun* gave the impression that the normal occurrence would be for a woman to have sex with her landlord. Similarly, in a case where a man killed a female hitchhiker, *The Sun* headlined with 'Hitchgirl spurned sex', again suggesting that normally such a situation would produce willing partners.

In this myth, then, women (even little girls) are all-powerful and men are vulnerable. As one judge put it, 'we are all liable to fall, gentlemen; we must be lenient'. He made this comment while sentencing a man for sexual assault of a seven-year-old girl (quoted in Ussher 1997).

Jane Ussher notes there is an irony that women are positioned as inviting or even asking for rape if they follow the traditional feminine masquerade – makeup, high heels, etc. As she points out, there is an interesting 'reversal of the more ubiquitous notion that femininity is "natural"; here it is implicitly positioned as something about which women have a choice' (Ussher 1997: 391).

Women cry rape for revenge   Another idea that is central to both the criminal justice process and to news reporting of rape is the idea that many women simply 'make up' accusations of rape – perhaps to get attention or as a way of disavowing a sexual encounter that they regret and for which they do not wish to take responsibility. It is hard to overestimate the importance of this idea in relation to rape; it would not be an exaggeration to say that all rape claims are viewed through this sceptical lens – which constitutes a major barrier to women reporting sexual attacks, since many fear, quite rationally, that they will not be believed. Moreover, procedures have been established across a whole range of institutional settings to deal with men's fear of false accusation of rape. Chaperoning systems in hospitals, for example, are not designed to protect female patients from being raped, but male doctors from false accusation of rape.

Underlying this fear is the spurious belief that false accusations are easy to make and hard to rebut. In fact, the opposite is the case: rape has the highest standards of evidence of any crime, and juries are frequently warned about the dangers of relying on the victim's testimony alone, and advised not to convict on the basis of uncorroborated evidence. Given that this is often all there is in rape cases, it is small wonder that conviction rates are so low.

Undoubtedly a tiny minority of women do make false accusations of rape, but there is no reason to suspect that false allegations about sexual attack are any more common than those for any other crimes, and many reasons to expect them to be far less common. As many feminists have asked, why would any woman submit herself to intrusive examinations, hostile public scrutiny of her sexual relationships and moral behaviour, and stigmatization, only to watch the alleged rapist go free in 94 cases out of 100?

Rapists are deranged strangers   The final myth that structures media reporting of rapes is the idea that 'real rape' means stranger rape. Talking here about fictional depictions of rape, Lisa Cuklanz (2000) identifies the 'basic formula' which is also implicit in most news reporting:

> The victim is attacked by an unseen rapist who clamps a hand over her mouth, grabs her forcefully or throws her to the ground, and speaks lines filled with threats, sexist stereotypes, and outmoded ideas about women and sexuality. Brutal violence is often suggested by the use of weapons, through the post rape appearance of the victim, or through the inclusion of an unusual modus operandi that involves restraints, weapons or strange marks on the victim's body. The beginning of the attack often emphasises the rapist's intense depravity . . . The rapists are depicted as identifiably outside the mainstream through their language, clothing, habits or attitudes. (Cuklanz 2000: 6)

From her extensive analysis of rape representations in the media Cuklanz (1996; 2000) concludes that fictional representations of rape have done consistently better than news media in portraying victims sympathetically and offering an understanding of feminist ideas about sexual violence. A similar evaluation is offered by Sujata Moorti (2002), who compares news reports of rape unfavourably with TV talk-show treatments.

The news media's portrayal of rapists as identifiably sick and depraved strangers offers a very misleading picture of rape. In fact the vast majority of rapes are committed by friends, relatives, neighbours or someone else known to the victim. Over a twenty-year period the numbers of attacks which fit the basic 'stranger danger' plot identified by Cuklanz have stayed stable, while acquaintance rape has increased dramatically (CPS study, 2003). Yet while the numbers of rapes carried out by someone known to the victim have soared, the news media have persisted in reporting only the small minority of crimes that fit the classic rape formula. The available evidence shows that most rapes are not reported as news at all; only the most atypical cases, often with bizarre or horrific violence, received prominent coverage, and gruesome sexual murders are disproportionately over-reported compared with their actual incidence (Carter 1998). Ordinary rapes, it seems, are simply not deemed newsworthy.

From their analysis of over 3,000 reports about sexual violence, Soothill and Walby (1991) found that coverage was organized around three distinct moments – the hunt or search for the attacker (in those minority of cases where police established that a crime had been committed); the courtroom; and, for a few infamous cases, the post-conviction. In reporting of sexual attacks by strangers the construction of a beast was central to the story. The sex beast would be constructed through links with other crimes – perhaps of a similar nature, or in the same area, or involving the same sort of victim. These links are often made in the press *before* they are made by the police (if at all) – so they tend to be written in the passive form, for example 'Fears are growing that the rapist could be the same as the man in the M42 rape' or 'Speculation is growing that there may be links with the unsolved murder of two children in the area twelve years ago.' Sometimes links will be correct – at other times they will not. But the point is that construction of links with other crimes is crucial to a 'good' sex beast story.

The second stage involves providing a label for the man, such as 'beast', 'fiend', or 'monster'. Sometimes the man will be named after some distinctive feature of the crime – for example, M42 rapist, or the balaclava rapist.

The third stage in the construction of a sex beast story is the making of symbolic links with previous fiends – such as the Yorkshire Ripper, Dracula, Hannibal Lecter, etc. – whether they are factual or fictional is largely insignificant. The important point is that the story begins to trade on the horror of these other cases. After that, *any* future incidents are described in terms of previous ones, for example 'Ripper-style', 'Fox-like'. Soothill and Walby note that in the same year as the notorious rapist Malcolm Fairley ('The Fox') was convicted hardly a rape was reported which was *not* treated as if it was some kind of copy-cat offence – that is, *all* reporting about rape was refracted through the lens of this one particular case.

Contrasting sharply with this focus on the depraved stranger as the major source of danger to women has been a highly selective reporting of so-called 'date rapes'. By focusing on a small number of notorious cases (such as the William Kennedy Smith trial in the USA and the trial of Austin Donellan in the UK) news media have repeatedly suggested that most accusations of date rape are without foundation. Katie Roiphe's book *The Morning After* (Roiphe 1993), which attacked 'victim feminism' and argued that many accusations of rape were simply the product of consensual sex regretted afterwards, received acres of favourable coverage.

Taken together, the media's discrediting of date rape and the focus on sick strangers have produced a completely distorted view of the nature and incidence of rape.

Sex Crime News in the Twenty-First Century

These myths about rape have been distilled from the findings of research on the reporting of sexual violence (e.g. Soothill and Walby 1991; Benedict 1992; Meyers 1997; Ussher 1997; Carter 1998; Kitzinger 1998). Not all of them will appear in every report of sexual violence, and there is considerable variability between different papers and the style of coverage of different crimes. Nevertheless, it is fair to say that these notions continue to structure a good deal of the reporting of rape and other sexual crimes, even in the twenty-first century. An example will help to show how these myths are deployed in actual reports.

In February/March 2004 the press in Britain was dominated by the reporting of two sexual violence stories. One concerned the trial of Antoni Imiela, dubbed by the press 'the M25 rapist' because of the proximity of his attacks to this major motorway. Imiela was convicted of the rapes of at least eight women, and sentenced to seven terms of life imprisonment in March 2004. As the Imiela trial was going on, another sexual violence story hit the news-stands: this was the claim by three women that they had been sexually assaulted by six premiership footballers (from Leicester City club) in a room in a Spanish hotel.

On 5 March 2004 the London newspaper *Metro* juxtaposed both stories in a double-page spread on pages 4 and 5 (see Box 4.1 with the Imiela story). Looked at together they contain all the myths we have discussed. The main headline about the Imiela trial reads INSECURE CHILD WHO BECAME MONSTER. In this article Imiela is constructed as a sex beast or monster, whose 'twisted urges' and 'pathological hatred' stemmed from feelings of insecurity and from his experience of being bullied at school. A 'criminal psychology expert' is quoted as saying that 'rapists can be driven by feelings of inadequacy. They rape to feel in control.' And a psychological discourse is also used to describe his 'deluded mind' and 'desire to humiliate'. The article seems designed to show that Imiela is abnormal. The impression of someone made

Box 4.1 Sex beast imagery is still selling papers

INSECURE CHILD WHO BECAME A MONSTER
Serial rapist Antoni Imiela believed his victims deserved to be attacked, it was revealed yesterday.

Psychiatrists suggested his twisted urges stemmed from a troubled background and feelings of inadequacy.

Imiela, who is 5 foot 6 inches, may have harboured childhood feelings of hatred for his own body which fuelled his desire to humiliate vulnerable victims.

In his deluded mind he blotted out the reality of what he did by convincing himself they were as guilty as he was.

His first attack on a ten-year-old girl in Ashford, Kent, shocked the town – and sparked an argument between Imiela and workmate Darren Arnold.

Mr Arnold said that, after reading an article about the rape in a cafe, he commented that he would kill the rapist if his child had been the victim.

He stormed out after Imiela calmly said: 'Maybe she deserved it.'

The judge ruled the evidence too prejudicial to put before the jury. . . .

Three victims noticed that Imiela had a small penis and Dr Anthony Beech, a criminal psychology expert at Birmingham University, said it may have helped turn him into a serial rapist. He added: 'Rapists can be driven by inadequacies. They rape to feel in control.'

Those who knew Imiela spoke of his 'pathological' hatred of authority. The nature of his job on the railways – working long hours and travelling – allowed him to visit prostitutes.

One colleague recalled how he boasted about a vice girl who 'was 18 but looked younger'.

Imiela was born in Lübeck, western Germany, in 1954 and spent part of his early childhood in a refugee camp.

The family moved to Britain in 1961 and settled in Newton Aycliffe, County Durham. He was bullied at school over his German origins and beaten by his father. He was sent to borstal at 15 for robbery and in 1988 he was jailed for 14 years for armed robberies.

Source: Metro, 5 March 2004.

monstrous by his father's brutality and by his traumatic childhood is reinforced by the juxtaposition of the photographs – one showing Imiela as a pleasant-looking young boy; the other the 'monster' he became. The other articles on the page report on interviews with his family, his victims, and the police. To complete the focus on sexual violence, a separate article at the bottom of the page reports on the failings of the police in the handling of the case of Ian Huntley, jailed for the sexually motivated murders in 2002 of two eleven-year-old girls, Holly Wells and Jessica Chapman – a case that provoked national grief and revulsion.

Meanwhile on the opposite page an entirely different story about alleged rape is told. Here there is no 'sex beast' discourse at all, but rather one in which the women making the claims are treated with suspicion (which, unusually, turned out to be justified in this case). Although not allowed to print their names, the paper describes the women who made the rape allegations as 'African-born' – thus indexing the racist myths discussed earlier – and 'thought to live in Germany' – also significant in the context of old antagonisms, frequently and deliberately reworked in relation to football. Much of the tabloid coverage of this incident was strikingly xenophobic, casting the rape claims as an attack on the British nation. Reporting of the three women speculated that they were prostitutes and that they consented to sexual relations. In contrast, the footballers were frequently characterized as innocents, who had been falsely accused and were, as *Metro* put it, 'devastated'.

Here, then, we can see how the myth about women 'crying rape' is mobilized, as is the notion that the alleged attack was in fact consensual sex. Furthermore, racist and nationalistic themes are significant in the reporting. Bearing in mind Soothill and Walby's (1991) observation about the preponderance of photographs of black defendants in the press, the pictures here are also significant. Whilst the article is working hard to present the footballers (unlike Imiela) as 'normal guys' who are 'shocked' at how they have been 'wronged', it nevertheless uses an image of Sinclair (the one black player amongst them) that might challenge this interpretation. More than twice the size of the other photos this (out of context) photograph indexes a long iconography of racism, showing Sinclair in a manner that looks aggressive and animalistic. In this way, perhaps unwittingly, the photograph promotes a different understanding of the rape allegation than that which is explicitly constructed in the written text.

The case against Imiela resulted in his conviction and imprisonment, while the charges against the footballers were dropped, after it was decided that there was no case to answer. In reports of both cases, though, long-established and well-worn notions about the nature of men, women and rape were deployed which resonated with the myths uncovered by previous research. Despite important recent improvements in the criminal justice system's responses to sexual violence, media reporting of rape remains powerfully framed by some outdated and pernicious discourses that are at best unhelpful and at worst dangerous.

Conclusion

This chapter has looked at how news is changing in the early twenty-first century, driven by market pressures to become a consumer-friendly entertainment product. This marks an important shift away from earlier notions of news as a public service designed to educate and inform citizens to enable them to take part in democratic life. Gender has been intimately tied up in this transformation in a number of different and contradictory ways. On the one hand, the desire of newspapers, and radio and television companies to reach bigger markets and to attract advertisers has – alongside political pressures – helped to open up journalism to greater numbers of women, and women now constitute the majority of people seeking to work as journalists. At the same time, however, the large-scale entry of women into journalism has coincided with the radical overhaul of the profession, declines in pay and status, and increasing casualization. Most female journalists today work as casuals or freelancers, paid by the word, and with few rights or benefits.

The shift from a public service to a consumer-led model of news has also been built on the increasing sexualization of news. After a period of ten or fifteen years in the wake of second-wave feminism in which the gratuitous use of women's bodies was held in check, there has recently been a dramatic re-sexualization of news. The popular papers such as *The Sun* or the *Daily Star* in Britain or *Bild* in Germany feature in every edition many pictures of naked or scantily clad young women provocatively posed. Even more widespread across press and television is the tendency to evaluate all women in terms of their physical attractiveness, whether they are pop-stars or politicians.

Discussion of gender issues has itself become a central part of the shift in news, and features about the entrenched difficulties between men and women, 'new' problems faced by either sex, or 'scientific' discoveries about gender are a mainstay of all news media. In the shift in their role from reporters to interpreters contemporary journalists document (or construct) 'trend stories' about gender with tedious regularity. While superficially interesting and engaging these are invariably light on evidence and seem often to operate as part of a backlash, for example seizing upon stories of one or two high-profile women who gave up work when they had children, to announce the arrival of 'the new housewives'. The media hunger for simple tales of gender from evolutionary psychology, together with the epidemic of news features bemoaning the crisis of masculinity, also show how a kind of 'sociology-lite' is transforming news into a key site of discourses about gender.

Alongside this talk of change, however, there is much that remains the same. This chapter has highlighted the pernicious myths that continue to structure much news reporting of sexual violence against women. It has shown how news reports systematically misunderstand and distort the facts about the nature and incidence of rape, and contribute to a climate in which most rapists get away with their crime.

The key for studying gender and news is to examine both the continuities and the changes, and, above all, to remain alert to the ways that assumptions about gender and assumptions about news are intimately intertwined.

5

Talk Shows: Feminism on TV?

In the best-selling 'chick lit' novel *Game Over* (Parks 2001), the post-feminist protagonist, Jocasta, works for a cable television network that has fallen on hard times. Faced with an ultimatum from her boss that she must devise a ratings-winning show or face the consequences, Jocasta is plunged into despair. She tries anxiously to think of something that hasn't been done before or of an old formula that can be given a new twist. Alas, she is unable to come up with a single original idea and looks set to lose her job, until Josh, her best friend, comes to the rescue. Chatting casually about how common it seems to be for people who are about to be married to 'hook up' again with an ex-partner, he inadvertently hands Jocasta her million dollar idea. *Sex with an Ex* is born.

Sex with an Ex is a hybrid of many genres including game shows, reality TV and the confessional talk show. The show works by 'testing' about-to-be-married couples by staging meetings between one partner and his or her ex, and pushing to see if he or she can be 'tempted'. Invariably they are, and the show consists of playing the tape of the 'temptation' and 'fall' to the three protagonists – in front of a studio audience – and filming the inevitable tears, accusations and rage when the betrayal becomes clear.

Sex with an Ex is a fictional television programme (at least for now – till a producer with a glint in the eye reads the novel, or Parks options the TV rights). But it might as well be real. It contains all the ingredients of any number of contemporary talk shows and reality TV – a focus on ordinary people, the privileging of personal experience, the display of raw emotion, the audience as both participants and spectacle, and an emphasis on confrontation. All this is orchestrated by a host seeking to arouse the guests and audience to anger, grief, jealousy, joy or any other display of heightened emotion. As Laura Grindstaff (2002) puts it, the primary aim of such shows' producers is to get 'the money shot' – the moment when the guest breaks down in tears, shouts out in anger, or has to be restrained from hitting another guest.

'Cold open – no music, no applause!' the director shouted. 'Three! Two! One! *Roll tape!*' The camera was tight on the first guest, Karen, a victim of childhood molestation, who spoke of the abuse that she suffered as a child every holiday when her uncle came to visit. Her voice was high and clear, with a faint southern accent. Diana, the show's host, prodded her for more details, and Karen obliged, tears welling up in her big brown eyes. I could feel the tension rise in the control booth; we were simultaneously horrified by her suffering, incredulous that she would discuss it on national television, and elated that she was doing so with such visible emotion – especially with the November ratings sweeps just around the corner. When the woman broke into sobs describing the time her uncle 'shared' her with a friend, the look of triumph on the producer's face told me that this show was indeed a 'sweeper'. (Grindstaff 2002: 19–20)

It is no surprise that a fictional heroine of the noughties should choose to produce a reality/talk show, for these are ubiquitous, a mainstay of TV schedules. Cheap to produce, they are hugely popular, enormously influential and highly controversial. It used to be the case that if you wanted to disparage a cultural product you likened it to a soap opera; today the dismissive analogy is with talk shows – both genres, it should be noted, are associated with high numbers of female participants and viewers, and this is no coincidence. Indeed, many of the terms used to condemn talk shows – cheap, easy, sleazy – are also words laden with negative associations for female sexuality.

But for those interested in gender the reasons for studying talk shows go far beyond this. For talk shows are at the centre of a range of key contemporary debates: about empowerment, democracy, sexual and racial diversity, shifts in media discourse and the transformation of the public–private divide. How should the shift from expert discourse to personal testimony be understood? Do talk shows represent the confessional for our time? Have they come to constitute a new feminized public sphere? What kinds of gendered, 'racialized' and classed identities do talk shows make available to audiences and participants? Are they redefining the very nature of the political? These are just some of the questions that have animated contemporary debates about talk shows and which this chapter sets out to address. The chapter is divided into six parts. Initially, it will present a brief history of talk shows, tracing their origins in a number of different forms and genres and locating them in the political-economic context of US and UK broadcasting. Next the chapter will discuss a range of different talk shows and present a typology for distinguishing between the very different – and increasingly differentiated – televisual products. The next two sections examine the dominant theoretical tools applied to talk shows – Habermas's notion of the public sphere, and Foucault's ideas about confession, discipline and normalization – paying particular attention to gender and sexuality. Finally a number of key feminist debates will be explored concerning empowerment, the ideological position of talk shows, the representation of 'raced' and classed identities in talk shows, and the personalization of the political.

First, however, it is worth considering some of the public debates about talk shows – debates that have raged outside the academy – in newspapers, on television, in political forums, charitable and religious organizations, support groups for talk-show participants and even in the US government. These arguments, this talk about talk shows, is important in its own right. It not only helps to illuminate how talk shows are understood, but is itself increasingly reflexively involved in talk-show production, for example when talk-show hosts decide to showcase their guest counselling services in response to public criticisms that individuals are exploited by talk shows and offer little or no psychological support. Moreover, public discourse about talk shows points to the wide range of potential ways of watching these programmes, including camp and ironic appropriations of their much-censured 'trashiness'.

Talk-Show Controversies

It is difficult to think of a genre that has aroused more controversy than talk shows. Reality TV is, increasingly perhaps, a strong equal contender. A common criticism (of both genres) is that they manipulate and exploit their guests, using – and often ambushing – them for dramatic effect and then simply dumping them without any concern for their well-being. As one commentator put it, 'Asking a producer to describe manipulation is like asking a fish to describe an aquarium' (quoted in Grindstaff 2002). The notorious murder of Scott Amedure in 1995 following an appearance on the *Jenny Jones* show gave chilling substance to such criticisms. Amedure's killer, Jonathan Schmitz, was told that he had a secret admirer and was invited to an episode of the show about secret crushes. Schmitz, who is heterosexual, was apparently devastated to find that his admirer was a gay man, and felt that he had been publicly humiliated. Three days after the episode was taped he shot and killed Amedure.

Schmitz was convicted of second-degree murder, but a subsequent civil trial found Warner Brothers – which owns the *Jenny Jones* show – guilty of negligence and fined them 25 million dollars. Part of the case against the company rested on the inadequacy of their psychological profiling which had failed to pick up on Schmitz's unstable and volatile character or his homophobia. Whilst an extreme example, the case also pointed up the need for post-show support for talk-show participants, and the American Psychological Association has suggested a code of conduct to define what constitutes informed consent for participation and to urge long-term post-appearance counselling.

Another set of criticisms of talk shows have centred on their status as 'reality'. In 1999 the BBC show *Vanessa* was axed, after it was revealed that some guests on the show were fakes who had been deliberately recruited from entertainment agencies and then coached to appear as feuding sisters, victims of abuse or any other category of guest. There have been similar scandals in the USA, and here the concern raised is about exploitation of the *audience*; the betrayal of their right to trust the authenticity of programmes that claim to deal in 'reality'.

Alongside specific concerns about the veracity of programmes or the treatment of guests, however, a number of much broader accusations have been made about talk shows' effects on contemporary culture. One perspective has it that talk shows are leading to the debasement and degradation of American culture (and presumably the cultures of other countries where they are shown). They are denounced as crude, tasteless and pornographic, as freak shows and purveyors of perversion, and have inspired endless comparisons to garbage cans, toilets and brothels (Grindstaff 2002). According to Vicki Abt, talking about your problems on daytime television is like 'defecating in public' (quoted in Grindstaff 2002: 23). In the USA, one company invited people to send in their household rubbish with the promise that it would be forwarded direct to Jerry Springer, the talk-show host who was also awarded the 'silver sewer' medal for 'cultural pollution' (Stenner and Lunt 2005).

Senator Joseph Lieberman and William Bennett in the USA joined forces in the mid-1990s to use the neo-conservative think tank Empower America to campaign against the new generation of talk shows. Lieberman argued that they were 'pushing the envelope of civility and morality in a way that drags the rest of the culture down' (quoted in Shattuc 1997: 142). The conservative position vacillates between two – in my view, somewhat contradictory – poles. In the first, talk shows are blamed for 'defining deviancy down' and effectively normalizing acts of deviancy or perversion that would previously have been regarded as abhorrent or outside the bounds of normal behaviour. In the second, however, talk shows are charged with voyeuristically presenting people as freaks – presumably of interest because of how far they depart from the norm. Either way, the charge of moral corruption is laid at the door of talk shows.

One of the most telling and frequently repeated statistics about talk shows is that more people in the USA watch them than vote in national elections. As we will discuss later, this has led to debate about whether talk shows constitute a new public sphere. But it has also produced an array of concerns about the potential threat to democracy posed by the talk show. Neil Postman (1986) has argued that we are in danger of 'amusing ourselves to death', and that talk shows represent a diversion from the real and important matters that the public should be addressing. A slightly different point is made by Jill Nelson. She accuses talk shows of a lack of social consciousness and of threatening collective understanding of contemporary issues by focusing entirely on their individual manifestations without any sense of their social and political context. In this respect, she argues, talk shows are 'the stormtroopers of the Right' (quoted in Shattuc 1997: 224).

Closely linked to this criticism is a view which understands talk shows in terms of class exploitation – the exploitation of those most vulnerable in society, who are rendered into a spectacle for the better-off. Barbara Ehrenreich points out that you will not find investment bankers bickering on *Ricki Lake*, nor will you see Montel Williams recommending therapy to sobbing professors: '[Guests] are so needy – of social support, of education, of material resources and self-esteem – that they mistake being the centre of attention for being actually loved and respected' (1995: 92).

Whilst there is something patronizing in Ehrenreich's suggestion that guests are unable to distinguish real love and respect from the glitz of a talk-show appearance, the spectre conjured of a society voyeuristically consuming its most disadvantaged members is a powerful one. This position stands out from most of the other critiques in making class salient. In contrast, many other stances appear to speak from an implicit position of class superiority, or, to put it in terms that borrow from Judith Butler and Pierre Bourdieu, to use talk about talk shows to *perform their middle-classness*. As Kevin Glynn (2000) observes, the almost homogeneous hostility of white middle-class commentators towards talk shows should make one rather suspicious: is it, in fact, thinly disguised class antagonism? The use of the term 'poor white trash' to refer to talk-show guests and audiences would uphold such an interpretation, as well as reinforcing racial hierarchies by suggesting that colour, poverty and degenerate lifestyles go together so naturally that when white people behave in this way 'their whiteness needs to be named' (Grindstaff 2002: 263). These issues will be returned to later in the chapter.

The final widespread public criticism of the talk-show phenomenon is the set of views that argues that as well as *dumbing down* talk shows are *numbing us down*. John Dovey (2000) points to the paradox that as both our thinking about the self and our experience of selfhood become ever more subtle and complex, television seems to offer us ever more tabloid or cartoon versions of the self, constructed around simple polarized images. Other commentators argue that talk shows portray people 'talking at each other, not to each other, interrupting each other constantly, and rarely listening at length to what others have to say' (Coombes, quoted in Glynn 2000: 199). Moreover, our constant bombardment by the commodified anger and pain of talk-show guests is said to desensitize us to real suffering and ultimately to blunt our affective responses into numbness. Taken together, these criticisms charge talk shows with having deleterious effects upon communication, of caricaturing the self, and of harming us emotionally by reducing our capacity for empathy.

The Roots of TV Talk Shows

Some of these criticisms will be familiar to readers as part of more generalized moral panics about television (and indeed every new medium). But many of them pertain to a phenomenon that is quite novel: ordinary people talking about private and emotional matters in front of audiences of many millions. Before the 1980s there were very few 'ordinary people' on television. There were experts, celebrities, politicians and actors, but being on TV usually required some authority or special claim to appear. As Elayne Rapping puts it, from the 1950s onwards television gave us 'white middle-class men . . . assuring us that they knew best' (Rapping 1995: 378).

Over the past two decades, television's output has been transformed by a combination of political, economic, regulatory and technological shifts. The development of cable and satellite networks; deregulation, privatization and increasing international competition; and the manufacture of relatively cheap and lightweight cameras and recording equipment all contributed to the rise of 'first-person media' (Dovey 2000). Writing about the Italian situation, Rita Crisci (1997) has carefully charted the impact of the war between private networks (mainly Finnivest Mediaset) and public (RAI) channels on television's *palinsesti* (schedules), documenting how competition produced a profound shift towards melodramatization, and increasing reliance upon romance, confession and emotional realism in public as well as private networks (see also Barile and Rao 1992; Petley and Romano 1993).

As Crisci shows for Italy and Glynn (2000) and Dovey (2000) have argued for the USA and the UK respectively, the development of daytime talk shows was a central part of this shift. However, the genre did not arrive from nowhere, and had a number of precursors or influences. Chief amongst these was the radio talk show, which dated back to the 1930s and typically featured a combination of host, experts and 'ordinary citizens' in conversation. Wayne Munson

(1993) documents a shift in the 1970s from political/public-issue shows with predominantly male participants to a new kind of phone-in talk show with a younger and more female audience and a focus upon interpersonal relationships. In the USA, such shows attracted a lot of critical comment and became known informally as 'topless radio'. However, long before that there were radio advice shows on every aspect of home management, food preparation and childrearing, uniformly targeted at a female audience listening in the home (see Mitchell 2001 and Barnard 1989 for discussions of 'housewife radio', and Moores 1988 for a discussion of the feminization and domestication of radio).

These radio genres were themselves descended from the press, and bore close similarities to advice columns targeted at women. Jane Shattuc (1997) has traced the impact of the tabloid press on contemporary television talk shows as far back as the seventeenth century, though her particular focus is on the socially conscious 'yellow journalism' of the nineteenth century which combined vivid and colourful prose with a populist emphasis on the injustices done to the 'average' American. Comparing Pulitzer headlines in 1884 with daytime TV's talk-show titles 110 years later, she finds an astonishingly similar tone and a parallel interest in crime and deviance.

A third distinct precursor to today's talk shows are the true confession magazines that were first launched in the early twentieth century and continue to the present. As Laura Grindstaff (2002) points out, these have been overlooked in most genealogies despite their striking similarities with talk shows. The emphasis is upon first-person accounts of misfortune and suffering and their headlines sound remarkably like topics on daytime shows: 'My Doctor Made Me his Sex Slave', 'Raped by the Boy Next Door', 'I Sent my own Father to Prison' and 'My Little Girl's 3 Words: He Hurts me' (quoted in Grindstaff 2002: 54).

The two or other notable antecedents of television talk shows are carnival freak shows and nineteenth-century theatre, vaudeville and early cabaret. The similarities relate both to the construction of the entertainment and to the forms of spectatorship implied or invited. Gamson (1998) notes that key elements of the freak show are quite deliberately recreated in contemporary talk shows, for example the sensational promotional strategies and the counterpointing of the experts and 'freaks', etc. (see also Bogdan 1988). Moreover, both the carnival freak show and the theatre in the early nineteenth century were places of refuge 'where the normative restrictions of the society were relaxed' and people were allowed to 'act out themselves with much less inner and outer restraint than prevailed in society' (Levine 1988: 68).

In addition to these specific 'ancestors' of today's talk show, a broader – but ultimately more important – influence came from the rise of new social movements in 1970s and 1980s, and in particular the feminist movement. It was feminism that brought onto the agenda almost all the issues that are the everyday topics of talk shows – childhood abuse, violent partners, destructive relationships, low self-esteem, restrictive norms for female appearance and behaviour, eating disorders . . . the list could go on. As Elayne Rapping (1996) has argued, this litany of problems had existed for a long time; what feminism supplied was a sense of the 'not rightness' of these things, which turned them from 'facts of life' into political problems. Feminism was also involved – at a still broader level – in the postmodernization of Western societies, helping throw into crisis all the old certainties, tradition, and meta-narratives, to produce a situation in which everything is 'up for grabs'.

Classifying Talk Shows

The variety of talk shows available on daytime television is as diverse as the forms that prefigured them. It makes little sense today to speak of 'the talk show' as if it represented a self-evident single genre; as talk shows have developed, so the differences between them have proliferated. In this section I will present a rough typology to help differentiate between talk shows.

There are many different ways of categorizing talk shows – some typologies are chronological, others are thematic, some work only for one national context, others aim to be more encompassing. Whatever their rationale, categorizations are never innocent or merely descriptive, but, as we saw in chapter 2, are always involved in ordering, excluding and making one version of the world persuasive; they are, in short, inevitably involved in the power/knowledge nexus. But that doesn't mean that they aren't helpful!

Here I am going to present a three-way classification of talk shows that differentiates between the audience discussion programme, usually organized around debates about public and political issues; issue-oriented shows of the therapeutic genre which focus on personal problems and dilemmas; and confrontational talk shows – often dismissed as 'trash TV' – where the emphasis is less upon problem solving than on the spectacle of emotional conflict. These shows differ not only in their substantive focus, but also in the geography and design of their sets, the nature of the host's authority, the kinds of interaction they invite or permit, and the age, class, ethnic and gender composition of their audience.

The audience discussion show

This type of show usually consists of a single host who orchestrates discussion with an invited studio audience made up of 'ordinary people' with direct experience of the topic being considered, and a number of 'experts' (e.g. psychologists, doctors or lawyers). In such shows the host generally introduces the topic or question and then – quite literally – runs through the audience with a microphone, soliciting the views of experts and the personal testimonies of others. At the beginning of the show it is clear that participants have been 'primed' to speak – the host addresses them by name and solicits their contributions directly. However, after the first few turns, there is considerably more spontaneity, signalled by frequent interruptions and requests to speak. The task of the host is skilfully to keep control of the talk, while weaving a complex story from the diverse audience contributions.

As Livingstone and Lunt note, this type of programme often moves between different modes of discourse – variously assuming the discursive patterns of the debate, the therapy session or the romantic narrative:

> In the audience discussion programme, as in the romance, we start with a social problem which directly affects the studio audience, who represent the inhabitants of the 'kingdom' . . . The host plays a central role as the hero who undertakes to solve the problem affecting the kingdom (the public) and restore social order (through advice, understanding or validation of experiences). Consequently, he or she strides through the mythical kingdom (studio), setting out on a journey of discovery, brandishing his or her sword (microphone). On the way, the hero encounters those who can offer information and advice, and those who hinder by posing problems and undermining information . . . Having attained the goal – an understanding, a decision, a body of evidence – the hero returns triumphant to the community in need, for whom social order is restored and celebrated. (Livingstone and Lunt 1994: 59–60)

Compared with the two other types of talk show to be examined, audience discussion shows have received relatively little attention. Most writing has been concerned with what is understood as the erosion of the authority of the experts in such shows, and there is considerable speculation about the long-term effects on the culture of privileging experience as the primary source of knowledge. Closely linked to this are the debates about talk shows as the new (electronic) public sphere which will be discussed in the next section. There is relatively little feminist literature on audience discussion shows.

The therapeutic genre

The therapeutic genre is best exemplified by *Oprah*, which is made in the USA and shown in sixty countries. The show's format is consistent: 'Winfrey introduces each episode by reading an outline of the day's topic to camera, talks to guests, solicits a few questions from the audience, brings in some expert opinions, and then alternates guests', experts' and audience members' comments while she roams around the audience with a microphone' (Squire 1997: 100). The studio audience for *Oprah* is predominantly female, as are the experts who appear on the show, 80 per cent of whom are women (Shattuc 1997). Episodes are split between those focusing explicitly on psychological issues such as obsessions, addictions or destructive relationships, those which focus on broader social issues such as unemployment or the rise of girl gangs, and a miscellaneous category including celebrity interviews and makeover shows.

Whatever the focus of the show, however, *Oprah's* discourse is primarily psychological. Every topic – from unemployment to the experience of celebrity – is framed in psychological terms, usually highlighting individuals' feelings. *Oprah* – as well as *Sally Jesse Raphael*, *Geraldo* and other 'therapeutic' shows – is suffused with psychoanalytic language: repression, desire and denial are workaday concepts for such shows, which draw eclectically from Freud, American ego psychology, rational emotive therapy and cognitive behavioural approaches. These are mixed together with a smattering of American 12-step programmes (e.g. for recovering from alcoholism) and a large pinch of faith in the healing power of talk. The narrative of each show works towards psychological closure – feeling better because of having expressed oneself, brought an issue to public attention, or unpacked a difficult issue to come to a better understanding of what one really wants.

Those concerned about the widespread use of psychological techniques outside the therapy room (by people without training) point to the dangers of the shows' use of role-play and therapeutic techniques in forums where guests are under intense pressure to perform in front of audiences that (in *Oprah's* case) often number 20 million. More generally, there are concerns about the superficiality of talk-show interventions and the focus on behavioural change at the expense of deeper psychological understanding – for example, 'compulsive shoppers' on *Oprah* are offered a range of behavioural incentives and penalties for saving money but without any consideration of what might have caused their unrestrained buying in the first place (Shattuc 1997). The shows require that individuals have an active and conscious cognizance of their 'problems' before coming on the show – they must already self-identify as (for example) 'Women who Love Too Much' or 'People who are Obsessive Fault Finders', and the idea that these are fixed attributes is reinforced by the constant use of captions which telescope an individual's character or problem in one easy-to-understand phrase. Moreover the entertainment functions of the show mean that points that are easily generalizable take precedence over any deeper understanding of an individual's particular dilemmas – shows move quickly from an individual case to broader advice such as 'tips for raising self-esteem' or 'ways to help your child avoid bullying'. Often experts will have their own stock-in-trade set of therapeutic tips, lifted from their most recent book – for example, an attorney of family law, featured on *Sally Jesse Raphael*, repeated the mantra 'negotiate, communicate, compromise' as the basis for all problem-solving (10 December 2002). (All transmission dates are for broadcasts in the UK.)

The therapeutic genre of talk shows has been a particular focus of feminist interest. Some commentators have seen in such shows elements of a potentially feminist televisual experience – a preponderance of female hosts, guests and experts, a focus on topics of particular concern to women, a space for women to talk about their own experiences, an atmosphere of affirmation and affiliated listening. Others, by contrast, have written about the overwhelming normativity of the shows, their relentless psychologism, and the way in which talk shows evacuate any of the political aims of feminism in exchange for a totalizing focus upon disease and therapy models. All these issues will be explored later in the chapter.

Confrontation talk: 'trash TV'

Jane Shattuc (1997) argues that the talk shows that were born in the 1990s should be understood as reactions to the previous generation of talk shows. They pushed at the boundaries and implicit taboos of establishment shows like *Oprah* and *Sally Jesse Raphael*, and sought to engage a different audience – younger, more economically disadvantaged, and more likely to be from a minority ethnic group. Shows like *Ricki Lake*, *Jenny Jones* and *Jerry Springer* took established talk-show topics like infidelity or abuse and 'recycled' them, pushing them to extremes. If, on *Oprah*, you were invited to discuss men's extramarital affairs, then on *Jerry Springer* these would feature a lesbian grandmother, a pregnant mother-in-law, or a transsexual brother.

The difference in the form of address is apparent immediately: a shift from concerned-sounding titles expressed in the third person to exclamations in the first and second person – '*I* married a gay man', '*You* slept with your husband's brother', 'Surprise: I'm dating your mom!' – expressed in colloquial, urgent and often aggressive terms.

This is redolent of the language of 'confrontalk' shows more generally. These have largely dispensed with the experts who lent the other types of show legitimacy and institutional credibility, and guests and studio audience speak in non-standard forms borrowing heavily (in the USA) from African-American and Hispanic speech patterns. Participants constantly interrupt each other, speech is excited and at high volume, and the amount of swearing means that audiences at home often hear almost constant bleeping as expletives are 'disguised' – which makes for an extremely fragmented viewing experience.

The body language of guests and audience is also strikingly different from other talk shows:

> The physicality of the guests erupts on-screen: they strut and saunter in, they shake their fists, they stand off, nose to nose. They try to hit one another and are pulled apart by the host and security guards, or they play the victim who has suffered at the hands of lovers or family members or been abused by life in general. They shout and weep, they curse and insult and offend each other, and they tell stories of betrayal, sexual promiscuity and abuse, abandoned children, drunkenness, drugs, and every other kind and combination of deviancy that can be imagined. (Haarman 2001: 60)

Another key difference between these talk shows and the audience discussion or therapeutic genres is the position accorded to the audience. As Louann Haarman notes, whereas in the other talk shows the audience in the studio in some sense stands for the audience at home – it forms, in Peck's (1995) terms, an 'identificatory bridge' – in the newer, more confrontational type of talk shows audience members in the studio are positioned on different footings from viewers at home. Their loud chanting, placard waving in support of one guest or another, and angry interventions are constructed as part of the spectacle, as much as the stories of the guests. In an episode of *Jenny Jones* about people who are ashamed of their sibling's appearance ('Sister, Kick that Tired Gear' – 29 November 2002), for example, the studio audience was asked to vote on each 'frump' by holding up a placard in response to the chant 'is she tight or ain't she right?', as well as shouting out their appreciation or hostility. The camera spent almost as much time dwelling on the audience's reaction to each woman, as it did on the protagonists in the confrontation (usually two sisters).

The shift from audience as participants to audience as spectacle is a significant one, particularly in the light of the demographic makeup of studio audiences for shows like *Ricki Lake* and *Jerry Springer* – who are predominantly young, working-class, and female, with a preponderance of African-American audience members. It could be argued that they are being made into a spectacle to be consumed by white, middle-class America. As some commentators have pointed out, in racially and class-segregated societies like the USA watching *Ricki Lake* may be 'middle America's' only exposure to a culture from which it has been economically and geographically separated: 'the spectacle of so many unfamiliar gestures, hairstyles, fashions, and bits of jargon may shock politicians whose previous contact with people like these has come from statistical samples and made for TV movies' (Stephen Schiff, quoted in Shattuc 1997: 140). Yet perhaps this 'shock' is valuable, and such shows construct and celebrate an 'uncomfortable' nation. 'They do reveal Americans who act outside conservative polite behaviour: uneducated poor people, ghetto blacks who refuse the King's English, gays who resist being family men, lesbians who flaunt their desire, and seemingly nice middle-class whites who are not what they appear to be' (Shattuc 1997: 145). We will return to this debate later in the chapter: it hinges upon an analysis of what kind of visibility marginalized and disadvantaged groups are allowed to have, and the extent to which they are objectified or commodified, or allowed to control their own representation.

'Race' is central to the production of the talk shows that came to prominence in the 1990s. Although the production staff on such shows are, like those in the rest of television, predominantly white, well-educated and middle-class, the product being aimed for is one that is 'black' – where black signifies 'street' and street equals 'hip'. 'Black' terms, slang, body language and so on are routinely appropriated by white guests and hosts – Ricki Lake, in particular, affects a discourse in which she is always 'hanging' with her 'home girls', her 'sisters' or 'girlfriend' and routinely borrows from the black hip-hop lexicon.

The question here, of course, is what it means when black forms of speech and cultural practices are performed by powerful white individuals who want to appropriate the 'coolness' of doing/being 'black' but can do so free from any of the negative consequences that affect young African Americans (cf. Majors and Billson 1992 on the 'cool pose'; Frosh, Phoenix and Pattman 2002 and 2000).

Perhaps the biggest difference between this type of talk show and the other two genres is that they have largely – though not entirely – abandoned any pretensions to therapeutic content and any attempt to deal with social issues connected to injustice. As Shattuc (1997) has argued, these shows are gutted entirely of political content, and the emphasis instead is on youthful and in-your-face rule-breaking. There is little pretence at objectivity and the shows clearly side with one person against another: 'You ruined our marriage' or 'I'm going to keep my baby'. The 'morality' on such shows is heavily controlled and highly orchestrated – from the 'warm up' act onwards. Ian Hutchby (2001) shows that there are a variety of characteristic structures of talk in the show that deliberately facilitate confrontation – for example, the way that participants are introduced (as complainants), the host's deliberate emphasis on acts as particularly complainable, and the manner in which respondents or antagonists are introduced. In *Ricki Lake*, this is almost always done through a rhetorical question to the audience. We will have heard all about guests X's wrongdoings, and then Ricki will turn to the audience and ask 'do you want to meet X? Shall we bring him/her out?' The audience roars its assent.

Analysing the *Jerry Springer* show, Greg Myers (2001) outlines the four stages of conflict building and resolution within the show. These involve defining and representing stances; making the stances controversial; making the controversy dramatic – a story with a build-up of tension and a climax; and, finally, making the controversy meaningful at a broader level, by generalizing from the particulars of the story. The third stage – in which the controversy is made more dramatic – often involves an ambush in which a guest is brought into an unexpected confrontation. Frequently, guests are invited to appear on a show, but are misled about its topic, and then find themselves ambushed by a former lover, friend or spouse. The *Jenny Jones* show in which Jonathan Schmitz was introduced to Scott Amedure is one example of this. In another notorious example a woman was invited to appear on the *Jerry Springer* show having been told that the show was about marital reconciliations, and that her husband wanted to get back together with her. In fact, the woman was brought on – to screams of abuse from a 'primed' audience – to be told by her ex-husband and his new partner to 'get out of their life'. According to Stenner and Lunt (2005) you can now see an average of sixteen ambushes per hour on American television.

Ambushes represent one way of making conflict dramatic. Other theatrical devices employed on the shows include dramatic forms of revenge, retaliation, punishment and discipline. Guests are often 'given a taste of their own medicine', put in the stocks, or sent to terrifyingly real 'boot camps'. The theatricality of interpersonal conflict has spawned countless comparisons to wrestling matches. Grindstaff (2002) argues that whereas shows like *Oprah* were built upon the 'feminine money shot' – the pornographic fetishization of empathy and tears – the newer, more tabloid and theatrical shows, developed a masculine version based on anger and aggression. In a notorious incident on the *Geraldo Rivera* show in 1988 about 'teen hate mongers' a chair was thrown and a fight erupted centred on a group of white supremacist youths. In the ensuing brawl (quickly broken up by security guards) Geraldo's nose was broken. However, rather than halting the taping, Rivera immediately taped two more shows, the fresh blood on his face and shirt a dramatic testimony of his commitment to 'real' controversy and conflict. In short, as Acland (1995) observes, the fight and its visible aftermath fitted perfectly with the demands of the newly emerging genre.

Clearly, there are profound differences between the three types of talk show discussed here. But these differences change over time. In the mid-1990s, in response to the new wave of conflict-based talk shows, *Oprah* and *Geraldo* moved to differentiate their product, by taking the moral high ground. Oprah dropped conflict-based topics entirely and focused on 'moral and spiritual uplift' while Geraldo Rivera created a 'bill of rights and responsibilities' to help encourage more ethical production practices (Grindstaff 2002). However *Sally Jesse Raphael* took quite another route, instead closing the distance between her own – originally therapeutic-style – show and the new kids on the block. Her show aired its first ambush (about cheating husbands) in 1990 and the first 'family feud' soon after that. The two key points to note here are both the dynamism and change among talk shows, and their influence upon each other. Although this tripartite typology is useful, then, it is also worth remembering that all the shows draw on a wide repertoire of different discursive styles and borrow extensively from each other and from other media products.

Talk Shows as the New Public Sphere

One of the most passionate debates about talk shows concerns their status as the new public sphere. As James Curran has argued: 'television has eclipsed Parliament as the central forum of national debate. It is now the principal channel of communication in the public space between the state and the home, the main means by which citizens engage in a collective conversation that influences public opinion and the direction of society' (Curran 1997: 193). The question is to what extent television is fulfilling the functions allotted to it. Does it form a collective community of citizens or does it, as some have suggested, simply 'gross out and titillate' (screen analyst, quoted in Dovey 2000: 17).

On one side of the debate are those who argue that talk shows are the contemporary equivalent of salons and coffee houses, forums in which free and open debate takes place, and where people gather to discourse on matters of importance. Paddy Scannell (1989, 1991) argues that radio and television have profoundly re-socialized people's lives, both through the construction of national public time and by bringing into the public domain private experiences and pleasures. Forums like talk shows have contributed to the extension of public life by opening speech from a narrow and restricted class to a more relaxed, sociable and widely representative mode. Speech on talk shows is informal and spontaneous, and anyone – regardless of their qualifications – can join in. This represents a democratizing move in which even the traditional boundaries between host and audience are being broken down (Carpignano, Anderson et al. 1990). As Steve Clark puts it, 'the world in broadcasting appears as ordinary, mundane, accessible, knowable, familiar, recognisable, intelligible, shareable and communicable for whole populations. It is talkable about by everyone' (quoted in Dovey 2000: 158).

In some variants of this upbeat argument the public sphere represented by talk shows is seen as a 'counter' public sphere or an oppositional or feminine public sphere – where voices not heard in traditional political forums speak out, and where forms of knowledge not valued in mainstream political culture (e.g. experiences or emotional knowing) are confirmed. Jane Shattuc summarizes this point:

> The shows not only promote conversation and debate but do away with the distance between audience and stage. They do not depend on the power of expertise or bourgeois education. They elicit common sense and everyday experience as a mark of truth. They confound the distinction between public and private. The shows are about average women as citizens talking about and debating issues and experience. (Shattuc 1997: 93)

Against this is a body of critique which rejects the notion that talk shows constitute a new public sphere, feminized or otherwise. From this perspective, the apparent openness and democracy of the talk shows is fake. Critics point to the careful screening of talk-show guests and the way in which potential participants are rejected because they are too old (for the advertisers' demographic) or 'not emotional enough' (Boggs and Dirmann 1999). The talk is highly controlled and confrontation is orchestrated by talk-show staffers selecting people on opposing sides in any debate so as to make dramatic television.

Boggs and Dirmann point out that even in audience discussion-style shows only a very narrow range of topics is discussed and that many issues – such as poverty or the environment – are regarded as too dull and/or complicated. In this way, 'highly charged issues of minor social importance take precedence over crucial global and domestic problems' (Boggs and Dirmann 1999: 75). The structure of talk shows favours superficial banter and quick responses rather than a balanced exchange of views or a more critical reflection on issues. One of the consequences of this, they argue, is that radical ideas – particularly those on the left of the political spectrum – which are unfamiliar and require explanation are automatically ruled out of bounds.

This critical position owes much to Jürgen Habermas, whose book *The Structural Transformation of the Public Sphere* (1992) is central to these debates. Habermas documents the rise of the public sphere in Europe in the seventeenth and eighteenth centuries where it existed in the independent space of civil society that lay between and outside of the state and capital. The defining feature of the public sphere for Habermas was its independence from any sectional interests. The discourse in it was based upon rational critical discussion, closely related to the free press and a precursor of the new forms of democratic political organization that emerged at the end of the eighteenth century. Habermas charts the decline of the bourgeois public sphere as it was colonized by commercial and bureaucratic forces in the eighteenth and nineteenth centuries with the advance of monopoly capitalism. A key target of his contemporary critique (along with other Frankfurt School theorists) is the media which serve as a 'tranquilizing substitute for action' for the 'uncritical masses' (1992: 164). According to Habermas, the divisions between capital, the state and the public sphere have disappeared and the mass media increasingly substitute for independent public thought, *producing* public opinion while claiming merely to represent it. Critical public debate has been replaced by public relations, with the media-managed spectacle of domination masquerading as democracy, and consumerism substituting for citizenship.

Habermas's ideas have received considerable discussion. Feminist criticisms have centred on his definition of the public sphere and its implicit contrast with private spaces, which are less valued. Nancy Fraser (1989) has argued that the *gender subtext* of his work is negative towards women – it places high importance on the masculine public spaces of rational debate and little or no importance on the private (and traditionally feminine) space of the home (see also Johnson and Lloyd 2004). Habermas has also been criticized for his deeply bourgeois notion of the public sphere, in which the mode of speech required is that of the upper classes, and the procedures and models for consensus are explicitly bourgeois (Glynn 2000). This notion not only denigrates working-class public spaces and popular culture within Western democracies, but it is also based upon a far from innocent claim about the irrationality of many cultural practices outside the modern West.

Habermas – like other Frankfurt School theorists – is also often accused of 'nostalgia', and of writing a 'lament' for a golden age in the past (which may not even have existed). Yet those who make this criticism are usually not without similar psychological and political investments themselves. Indeed, just as the Habermas-influenced criticisms of talk shows can be read as a political lament about their failure to constitute a *proper* public sphere, so the arguments which *champion* talk shows are often utopian expressions of hopefulness about the possibility of 'resistance' (be it feminist, working-class, queer or whatever) in popular culture. Writing at the height of the Thatcher era in Britain (and the Reagan–Bush era in the USA) Judith Williamson (1986b) suggested that social theorists of the Left were so disappointed by 'the people's failure' to challenge the New Right in the ballot box, on the streets or in trade union struggles, that they sought instead to find resistance in popular culture. They looked for (and found) 'strands of subversion' in everything from fashion to soap opera, argues Williamson. There is a parallel here with contemporary writing about talk shows. As late capitalism has produced Western populaces alienated and turned off by traditional politics, some commentators look hopefully to forums outside the traditional political arena for evidence of revitalized public discussion and critique.

Livingstone and Lunt (1994) argue that the media in general and talk shows in particular are taking on new roles: they are acting as spokespersons for the people to talk back to the government and elites; they are offering forums in which politicians can be held directly accountable to the public (for example, when they appear on audience discussion programmes and are questioned about what they are going to do about any particular issue); and they represent a social space for communication among the public itself. Talk shows are part of a broader shift from an authoritarian model of discourse to a more populist and democratic style (Scannell 1991; Fairclough 1995). Perhaps more significant than whether or not they could be said to constitute a new public sphere is the way in which talk shows are redefining the nature of public space and re-drawing the boundaries between private and public. Compared with twenty years ago, television now deals with matters that would previously have been entirely outside its purview: sexual dysfunction, child abuse, domestic violence, and so on. As Jon Dovey (2000) comments, when the scandal of President Clinton's relationship with Monica Lewinsky hit the newsstands he heard more detailed discussions of the Presidential member than he could ever have imagined – a topic that would previously have been deemed taboo and unfit for public consumption was suddenly all over television and a matter for everyday conversation. There is a key sense in which what was once private has become public, and talk shows have played an important role in this – though it is found across the media (as we saw in chapter 4), such that personal vicissitudes like illness, bereavement, divorce, giving birth, etc. have become standard journalistic fare and have spawned an entire new genre of autobiographical/confessional literature.

What has changed, then, is not simply the topics that can be discussed in the media but the way in which they are discussed. The new dominant mode is one in which subjective experience and emotional expression become the guarantors of truth and authenticity. After witnessing the outpouring of emotion that followed the death of Princess Diana, Nicci Gerard argued in *The Observer* that the 1990s gave birth to 'a revolution of sentiment; a revolution for the therapy age where subjectivity is our only certainty and sorrow our greatest claim to heroism' (see also Mayes 2000).

This claim is certainly supported by most of the research on talk shows which examines the different ways in which expert knowledge and ordinary people's discourse are positioned. This body of scholarship points to the privileging of subjective experience, and the difficulty for experts to establish their credibility. Livingstone and Lunt summarize the issues:

> Experts speak for others while the audience speaks for themselves. [I]t is difficult for experts to construct an authentic and credible persona on the screen, and yet authenticity and credibility, rather than, say, intellectual argument or verified experience, are, simultaneously, being constructed as the rules of the discourse. As experts are trained to develop arguments carefully, at length, citing supporting evidence, rebutting refutations and noting qualifications, they are doomed to failure in discussion programmes. They appear fragmented rather than whole, cold rather than warm, and alienated rather than authentic. (Livingstone and Lunt 1994: 129–30)

Haarman (2001) notes that unreserved aggression towards experts is such a recurrent feature of the audience discussion show that it might be considered a generic trait. It is reflected most obviously in the radically different uses of language. In the face of a compelling and emotionally articulated personal story, the abstract, technical, generalizing discourse of experts does not stand a chance. Wayne Munson (1995) argues that this is because the expert knowledge of doctors, psychologists or family law attorneys really is inadequate next to the complex experiences and emotions presented by guests. However, discourse analytic research suggests that the privileging of personal experience is itself a complex interactional achievement, and is not something that is self-evident:

> The key point is that the 'triumph of common sense' is not simply because experiential narrative *necessarily* affords some romantic claim to authenticity . . . Personal experience is, after all, as discursive a construction as any other. Rather interactional conflict in talk shows is highly structured around televisual requirements and for the most part these are pursued by the host as the agent of the broadcast network. (Wood 2001: 87)

The persuasiveness of 'personal experience', then, is not simply a matter of giving participants a voice, but involves the complex transformation of that experience into a public performance, co-produced and dramatized by the host (Thornborrow 2001).

The position of experts in the therapeutic genre of talk shows is somewhat more ambivalent than on audience discussion shows. On *Oprah* four out of five experts are female, and Winfrey also attempts to promote black 'organic intellectual' expertise on the show – clearly as a deliberate, affirmative strategy. Nevertheless there are many moments in the shows when experts' comments are treated with scepticism by the host and when Winfrey deliberately identifies herself with the audience's perceived position by saying, for example, 'we find that hard to believe, don't we, audience?', a tone of incredulity in her voice.

Experts are by no means always discredited on such shows, but they occupy a fragile position. They must offer insights about individuals' experiences and must also make points that illustrate the general (usually psychological) underlying issues at stake. But in doing so they must be careful not to make their language too abstract or to move too far from the concrete – often painful – emotional stories produced by guests. As most experts are by definition middle-class professionals, they must also manage delicate issues of class difference and distance from the audience. Above all, they are located in a forum in which a new 'regime of truth' that foregrounds individual subjective experience is evolving. It is to this Foucaultian argument that we turn next.

Talk Shows as the 'New Confessional'

Foucault's ideas have been widely taken up as a way of understanding contemporary talk shows. In particular, many commentators have made an analogy between Foucault's discussion of the confessional and the therapeutic genre of talk show in which individuals tell their personal stories, speak out about private lives and 'confess' on TV about their destructive relationships, childhood abuse, or secret bingeing. The key question at the heart of these discussions is the extent to which talk-show confessions are implicated in the practice of power.

As we saw in chapter 2, Foucault argued that the confession is foundational for the Western sense of self. 'The obligation to confess is so deeply ingrained in us that we no longer perceive it as the effect of power constraints upon us; on the contrary, it seems to us that truth, lodged in our most secret nature, "demands" only to surface' (Foucault 1978: 60). We are encouraged to 'speak out' – 'it will make you feel better'; confession is regarded as cathartic, purifying and empowering. However, Foucault argues that the assumption that liberation results from talk, that confessions are the opposite of repression, and that 'truth' eradicates power is fundamentally wrong. Instead – most notably in *The History of Sexuality* – he shows how power operates through the production of knowledges and that the confession is 'at the heart of the procedures of individualization of power':

> The confession became one of the West's most highly valued techniques for producing truth. We have since become a singularly confessing society. The confession has spread its effects far and wide. It plays a part in justice, medicine, education, family relationships, and love relations, in the most ordinary affairs of everyday life, and in the most solemn rites; one confesses one's crimes, one's sins, one's thoughts and desires, one's illness and troubles; one goes about telling, with the greatest precision, whatever it is most difficult to tell. One confesses in public and private . . . Western man has become a confessing animal. (Foucault 1978: 59)

From a Foucaultian perspective, then, talk shows might be seen as a practice of power – people are urged to tell all to liberate themselves, but in the process become bound ever more tightly into a web of power, in which individuals increasingly police and discipline themselves.

However, recent writing has begun to question the usefulness of reading talk shows through Foucault's analysis of the confessional. Dovey argues that – while valuable – Foucault's account is 'too neat, too totalising and too closed a model' (2000: 106). In contrast to the centralized process of Catholic confession, he argues, television offers many different modalities of speaking of the self, not all of which are confessional. Indeed, many of the ways in which guests on talk shows speak are *anything but* guilty confessions, but are proud and assertive declamations. A further difference between the confession and the talk show is in the top–down therapeutic logic of the therapist/interlocutor and patient/confessor. As Jane Shattuc argues, the power relations in contemporary talk shows are 'far more complex and vertiginous than Foucault's':

> Who is the therapist? The expert? The host? The studio audience? Who are the patients? Those on stage with the reductive name tags such as 'female gang member', 'incest survivor', and 'husband locked her to bed'? Or 'we' the viewers? Or Oprah, who routinely confesses her abusive childhood and displeasure with her body? And to what degree are the confessions, emotions and interactions understood as 'truth'? (Shattuc 1997: 113)

The confession is an enclosed, private process, secret and therefore immune from the democratizing possibilities of open speech in the public sphere. Talk shows represent confession as an open discourse in which intimate speaking is 'validated as part of the quest for psychic health, as part of our right to selfhood' (Dovey 2000: 107). Does this increase or decrease the operation of power within it? Glynn (2000) takes the latter position, arguing that in talk shows there is no authority who requires the confession, 'prescribes and appreciates it, and intervenes in order to judge, punish, forgive, console and reconcile'. Moreover, such authority – according to Glynn – would rarely go unchallenged in talk shows:

> Whereas the Foucaultian confessional is a site for the affirmation and enforcement of dominating truths and normalizing judgments, talk shows characteristically engender a mutability of truth and identities, a multiplicity of voices, the transgression of norms, and the spontaneous eruption of forces that emanate from society's excluded formations. (Glynn 2000: 218)

Where one stands in the debate depends to some extent on whether talk shows are perceived as imposing normative judgements or not. For some, talk shows are a space where 'freaks talk back' (Gamson 1998) while for others they enact 'a drama of social inclusion', bringing back errant individuals into the fold (Acland 1995) and working to recuperate them to a particular model of moral and psychological health (Dovey 2000).

This is an important debate and we will return to it to focus explicitly on gender, 'race' and sexuality in the final section of this chapter. But a crucial point to note first is that no *particular* normative judgement needs to be made in order for talk shows to be implicated in power relations. That is, far more significant than any single, particular position normalized by the talk show is the totalizing normativity of psychotherapeutic discourse. So dominant is this that it could be said to be the major truth/power effect of television talk shows. What we are seeing in talk shows is nothing less than the remaking of common sense in psychological terms. To this extent, whether or not a show comes out in favour of gays' right to marry or women's rights to segregated HIV services is of less significance than the fact that we are encouraged to think about such issues *only* in psychological terms.

This represents a new 'regime of truth'; the rise of what Nikolas Rose (1989) calls 'the therapeutic culture of the self'. Talk shows sustain and help to bring into being a new concept of the self as an inner state which needs to be monitored, supervised and taken care of through psychological techniques that allow the person to purge, relax, stay calm and reach a state of (individual psychological) well-being. This notion of the individual is perfectly suited to neoliberal democracies where discourses of structural inequality or power difference are fast disappearing and individuals are exhorted to live their lives through notions of autonomy, self-reinvention and limitless choice (Walkerdine, Lucey et al. 2001). As Nikolas Rose puts it, contemporary neoliberal subjects 'bear the serious burdens of liberty'; however implacable the constraints upon them may be, it is their responsibility to render their lives meaningful as if each life trajectory were 'the outcome of individual choices made in the furtherance of a biographical project of self-real-ization' (Rose 1996; Walkerdine, Lucey and Melody 2001).

Talk Shows and Women: Televisual Feminism?

In this final section I want to return to some of the feminist debates about talk shows. As we have seen already, feminist writers have been central to the debates about talk shows as the new public sphere or the new confessional, but there are also a number of other issues of key importance to debates in feminism. My aim here is to examine three questions that have provoked most debate:

1 Are talk shows empowering for women (and other marginalized groups)?
2 Where are they situated ideologically or normatively?
3 What have talk shows done with the notion that 'the personal is political'?

Empowering women?

Elayne Rapping argues that 'there is something exhilarating about watching people who are usually invisible – because of class, race, gender, status – having their say and, often, being wholly disrespectful to their "betters"' (Rapping 1995: 38). This happens all time on talk shows when women, people from minority ethnic groups, and those at the bottom of the socio-economic heap tell their stories and challenge or defy experts in front of audiences of millions. A key question that has emerged, therefore, is the extent to which talk shows could be said to be empowering for traditionally marginalized groups.

On the 'pro' side of the debate are those who argue that a central part of empowering people involves giving voice to those not usually heard within the mainstream and allowing them to speak in their own words. Talk shows do this, it is argued, and enable sex workers, victims of child abuse or people who practise domination and submission in their sexual relationships to tell their own stories to the viewing public. As well as giving voice, they also make visible bodies which defy normative standards of femininity, reject discipline and transgress boundaries (Glynn 2000). More than this, the mere fact that talk-show hosts, experts, guests and studio audiences are predominantly female itself represents a challenge, and talk shows break up the almost homogeneous white middle-classness of most other television.

Corinne Squire (1997) argues that talk shows' claim to be empower-ing rests not simply upon the fact that they give voice to or make visible people outside the mainstream, but also because they are largely constructed from women's perspective. Shows like *Oprah* and *Sally Jessie Raphael* address topics concerned with women's experience of living in an unequal society in almost every episode. Shows focus on issues like domestic violence, eating disorders, sexual abuse, fathers who won't support children, discrimination against fat people, and the oppressiveness of dominant images of the female body. The shows present (liberal) feminist arguments about problems in relationships and the difficulty of combining work and childcare. Notwithstanding this, writing about *Oprah*, Squire cautions against a too easy celebration:

> Might women's disempowerment, against which the show defines itself, nevertheless be its most powerful message? A narrative of empowerment structures each episode, but the shows' repeated accounts of victimisation often seem to overwhelm them. After the daily success story of women getting their lives in order, you know that tomorrow you will start off once more with the harrowing experiences of women whose lives have been taken from them by abuse, illness or poverty. (Squire 1997: 102)

Perhaps *Oprah* is more successful in relation to 'race'? Most talk shows avoid discussions of 'race' and racism and deploy a systematic 'colour blindness' (Frankenberg 1993; Williams 1997). By failing to challenge racial stereotypes the shows often simply reinforce an implicit racism, as when Geraldo did a programme on gang members and almost all the guests were black or Hispanic – but the topic of race was absent. Against this background Oprah Winfrey's show is very different. Presented by an African-American woman who is one of the richest women in the world and who owns the production company which makes the show, it promotes black experts, black success stories and has a number of episodes devoted to discussion of topics of particular interest to black audiences (from intra-community discrimination to black hair and skincare issues). Winfrey's book club is also known for promoting new works by black women authors.

As Squire notes, Winfrey mostly avoids any overt discussion of racial politics, but she does use her authority as host to cast doubt on problematic claims or to 'ironize' particular kinds of talk. In a show on dating, for example, she treated with scepticism a white man's talk about why he only dates black women: 'it's that melanin that got you' (quoted in Squire 1997: 104).

Winfrey's position as a black woman in the white-dominated world of talk shows (and television in general) means that she is subject to considerable pressure to 'represent black people', an impossible task and an unfair 'burden of representation' (Mercer 1994). She has been subject to criticism for presenting a face that is too acceptable and unthreatening to powerful white interests, and also for colluding with the white racist imaginary's view of African-American men. Clearly she is located in an impossible position in relation to this last criticism, since if she chose to do a show on 'fathers who walk away from their kids' and did not include any African-American guests she would be accused of excluding them, yet by including them she falls prey to the accusation that she is reinforcing white prejudice against 'irresponsible black fathers'.

It is perhaps when 'race' is *not* explicitly mentioned that *Oprah* may be most empowering to black viewers – when, quite simply, the show inverts the 'white as norm' standards of mainstream US culture and uses a black family to represent 'the family', a black adopter to highlight adoption issues, or a black attorney as a representative of lawyers. This serves to mainstream black people's perspectives rather than to treat them as particular or sectional interests. It flows from what might be understood as *Oprah*'s humanist anti-racism, which tends to focus on what 'we' all share by dint of being human, rather than the differences between 'us'.

A third argument in favour of the talk shows-as-empowerment thesis is that guests and participants manage to interrogate socially authoritative knowledges and to bring challenging issues onto the public agenda. Gloria Jean Mascarriotte argues that the fact that there is so much condemnation of talk shows suggests there must be something a bit subversive going on: 'the critical comments are usually off-the-cuff condemnatory remarks aimed at the sight of women talking, women taking pleasure in talking, even when it is about painful subjects' (Mascariotte 1991: 82). Kate Bornstein, a lesbian transsexual and a frequent talk-show guest, sees her appearances as part of a battle to establish how her cultural identity is represented. Although she compares the shows to nineteenth-century freak shows, she argues: 'what's different now is that we, as freaks, are doing the speaking' (quoted in Shattuc 1997: 93).

Talk shows and normativity

What matters as much as whether the 'freaks are doing the speaking' is the way they are allowed to talk and how they are positioned within the discourses of the show. When I think about this issue I am reminded of an old 'Lefty' postcard. It showed a TV discussion programme where the host was announcing: 'and now, to ensure a politically balanced discussion, let me introduce a wild-eyed Trot from the lunatic fringe.' The 'joke' in this cartoon lies in the terms of the introduction which promises balance but aims to ensure that anything the socialist says will be heard as wild-eyed lunacy. Does something like this happen in talk shows? How are the agendas managed? Do anti-normative messages get created and heard?

Like Bornstein, Kevin Glynn (2000) argues that talk shows are forums where people constructed as 'deviant' can talk back and control their representation. In a detailed analysis of a *Donahue* show about people in sexual relationships that involved domination and submission, he documents the ways in which guests were able to use their public platform to resist and refute normalizing labels. Numerous audience members and telephone callers to the show complained about the 'sickness' and 'abnormality' of the guests. But the guests were quick to produce alternative accounts of their sexual identities, redefining labels like 'dysfunctional'. For example, the dominatrix Miss Jacqueline admonished the audience: 'could we *not* use the word "beat-up", because we, we prefer . . . saying "spanked" or "whipped" or "tied up". We're not beating anybody up' (quoted in Glynn 2000). She continues, asserting that the S/M scene is

> about mutual consensuality. All of us up here on stage are into the scene in a very, very responsible way. We talk about things up front . . . We don't coerce anybody. It's all about mutual enjoyment. It's about having fun. And it's really a very intimate relationship, because you are expressing to people your innermost selves . . . It's not about pain, it's about pleasure/pain. It's about expressing little things about yourself. A lot of the people that I see like to cross-dress, for instance. (quoted in Glynn 2000: 194)

By producing a resistant, counter discourse in dialogue with a normalizing one, Glynn argues that talk-show guests often educate others to better understand and respect their differences (and according to Patricia Priest (1995) this is one of the most important reasons participants give for appearing on a talk show). Glynn believes that talk shows are best understood not as 'spaces where already fixed identities come into collision, but as sites were different actors negotiate the articulation of their own identity formations' (Glynn 2000: 195).

He cites another example of this happening in a *Ricki Lake* show about gays. He reads the 'banter' between the self-styled queens on stage and the straight men in the audience as 'playfulness' that undercuts heterosexual fear and loathing of gay and lesbian sexualities. But he treats the talk show as a decontextualized world and does not consider anything that happens outside of it. Even if the straight audience did behave playfully (and I am sceptical that this is the only reading) there is no reason to believe that this attitude will endure after the 'performance' is over.

In his excitement about the possibility of resistance offered by talk shows, Glynn (2000) neglects to differentiate between different types of show. However, it is clear that his ideas about the negotiation of identity surely cannot apply to the confrontational genre: in these shows it is exactly the point that people are brought into conflict from fixed and reductive identity positions. There are also sobering ripostes to this optimistic position in analyses of audience discussion and therapeutic genre shows. An analysis by Deborah Lupton (1994) of another *Donahue* show offers a more pessimistic reading. Lupton examined a show that featured opposite-sex couples in which one partner was identified as bisexual. She argues that the programme operated with a double standard whereby guests were invited to 'confess' to their bisexuality (as a positive and empowering form of self-expression) only for this to be framed subsequently by Donahue within a discourse of moral indignation. According to Lupton, Donahue constantly reinforced the position of his audience as 'normal', while highlighting the abnormality and Otherness of bisexual guests. She concludes: 'such shows can be regarded as the modern equivalent of the stocks as well as the secularised version of the confessional, in which offenders are held up to public ridicule and chastised for their sins, accepting their punishment in return for experiencing a cathartic release of guilt' (Lupton 1994: 61–2).

This reading is supported by Squire's analysis of *Oprah* which highlights the thoroughgoing heterosexism of the show and suggests that bisexuality is presented as a 'special kind of problem' – 'a con' (Squire 1997; see also Hemmings 2002). More generally, Dovey (2000) argues that the normative conservatism of such shows is particularly active around sexuality (see also Mclaughin 1993 on talk-show discourses about prostitution; Rapping 1995 on eating disorders, and Blum-Kulka 2001 on the depoliticizing effect of the Israeli talk show *With Meni*).

Elspeth Probyn (1993) has introduced a political economy note into the debate by highlighting the position of most talk shows in daytime schedules aimed at housewives. The intersection of talk-show topics with the promotion of domestic consumer goods, she argues, creates an effect that simultaneously disrupts and reinforces 'normal domesticity'. In the UK, where US talk shows like *Jenny Jones* and *Sally Jesse Raphael* are shown back-to-back on Sky 1 (the cable and satellite network) the adverts are disproportionately skewed to the poorest socio-economic groups, with an extraordinary preponderance of commercials for loan companies who offer to clear debts for those with a bad credit history or even a county court judgment against them. As Janice Peck (1995) points out, the need to be perceived as 'advertiser-friendly' exerts a powerful influence on what can and cannot be said on talk shows. But since most talk shows practise 'self-censorship' and are constructed around normative social values for other reasons as well, it is impossible to separate out advertisers' effects on the final product.

The personal as political

Finally I want to turn to the question of how talk shows are positioned in relation to the feminist principle that the personal is political. In one sense the debt of talk shows to feminism is clear: they have appropriated wholesale the methods of the consciousness-raising group. But in consciousness-raising groups part of the purpose of talking about the private, the intimate and the everyday was to break women's isolation by showing that they were not alone (or 'going mad') in feeling a particular way; to explore the patterned nature of women's experience; and to locate this politically so that problems such as feeling like a prisoner in the home or not enjoying sex with one's husband were regarded not simply as personal but also as political; and to do all this in a safe context of negotiated confidentiality.

I want to argue that talk shows have entirely sold out this principle, and instead have turned it on its head. Rather than politicizing the personal, today's talk shows personalize the political, reframing every issue in individualistic terms and erasing any sense of the social or political.

Janice Peck (1995) analysed a thirteen-part series on anti-racism on *Oprah* and argues that the interplay between discourses of liberalism, therapeutic psychologism and Protestantism worked to reproduce racist assumptions under the cover of anti-racist intentions. Above all, she argues that these three discursive resources inherently favoured individualistic understandings of racism and made it very difficult for participants who wanted to formulate the causes and consequences of racism in social or political terms. Peck sees this as part of a wider problem of 'containment through personalization' in which experiences are often understood as producing 'toxic shame' which needs to be overcome through confession rather than set in a social context. In the world of talk shows, she argues, all problems seem to be amenable to therapeutic intervention.

> Therapeutic discourse translates the political into the psychological – problems are personal (or familial) and have no origin or target outside one's own psychic processes. Compare this to the language of politics: there is a difference between saying 'I'm ill, I've been abused, I need recovery' and saying 'I'm angry, I'm oppressed, my exploitation is based on structural inequalities in our society, I share this experience with others with whom I must work for social change.' (Peck 1995: 75–6)

The point here is not in any sense to disparage therapeutic interventions (they are important), but rather to point to the way in which pseudo-therapy is replacing any sense of politics or any understanding of the broader contexts in which experiences take place. As Epstein and Steinberg (1996) argue, the daily fodder for many talk shows is the variety of ways in which heterosexual relationships can go wrong, yet these issues are mostly discussed without any reference to gender inequalities, and tend to be refracted instead through references to family dysfunction or unresolved issues from childhood. What we are seeing, Lois McNay argues, is the 're-privatization' of issues raised by feminists, queers and others:

> These discourses of 're-privatization' operate by absorbing elements of oppositional discourses and thereby depoliticizing them. Thus, discourses of re-privatization seek to contain issues that have only recently become an issue of public debate, such as gay and lesbian rights or wife battering, by returning them to the private realm and hence depoliticizing them. (McNay 1992: 87)

By relentlessly individualizing and psychologizing their topics, and by wilfully avoiding/refusing the horrific yet banal patterns of abuse, victimization and suffering that they daily parade before viewers, 'the shows are a dead end and they are meant to be. They lead nowhere but to the drugstore for more Excedrin. They work to co-opt and contain real political change' (Rapping 1995: 382).

Conclusion

Talk shows are just one example of a wider move to reality-based programming and first-person media that includes docu-soaps, emergency service TV, and reality shows like *Big Brother*, *Survivor* and *Temptation Island*. With the increasingly blurred distinction between fact and fiction, the exponential growth in the numbers of shows featuring ordinary people performing themselves, and the relentless personalization and sexualization of every topic, television in the new millennium could be said to be reinventing itself. Talk shows have played a key role in this.

This chapter has shown that most feminist writing is equivocal about talk shows – and it is easy to see why. They appear to 'give voice to normally voiceless women: working-class women, housewives, lesbians, sexually active older women among others' and 'they articulate the frustrations of women's subordination in a "man's world"' (Shattuc 1997: 136). But the 'empowerment' and 'visibility' they offer are problematic. Writing about how talk shows deal with lesbian, gay and transgender sexualities, Joshua Gamson (1998) notes the emphasis on tolerance/hostility, so that queer identities are accepted, but only if you 'keep it to yourself', 'don't flaunt it', etc. – in other words, do precisely what queer activism set out to challenge. He comments:

> All told, talk shows make 'good publicity' and 'positive images' and 'affirmation' hard concepts to hold. They offer a visibility that

> diversifies even as it amplifies internal class conflicts, that empowers even as it makes public alliances between various subpopulations more difficult, that carves out important new public spaces even as it plays up an association between public queerness and the decay of public decorum. Talk shows suggest that visibility cannot be strategized as either positive or negative, but must be seen as a series of political negotiations. (Gamson 1998: 113)

Talk shows offer opportunities for 'resistant' discourses to enter mainstream popular culture, and particularly for people constructed as 'deviant' to offer their own accounts of their identities and practices. However, this comes at the cost of having to endure repeated verbal abuse ('you are sick/abnormal/disgusting/should be ashamed of yourself', etc.) and, moreover, 'freaks' are often recuperated to a normative notion of health and morality within the shows. Even in their most progressive moments, talk shows rarely go beyond a general 'live and let live' philosophy in which 'tolerance' is the greatest virtue and politics is erased.

Perhaps the most significant impact of talk shows is the part they have played in the redefinition of the public/private divide. Like feminism itself, talk shows have helped to make public issues that were once silenced and taboo, and have rendered them 'talkable about by everyone', as Dovey (2000) puts it. But, as we have seen, the shift from repression to confession is by no means an innocent one, but involves new forms of discipline and regulation. Above all, it has involved the blanket production of an individualistic, therapeutic model of the self – a self that must be monitored, advised, disciplined and and brought 'into recovery'. As Elayne Rapping notes, the apparently apolitical nature of this discourse represents perhaps its most powerful political force:

> Do you hate your body or your husband, and yet can't seem to stop eating or putting up with him? Well, never mind the causes of these feelings, or whether they are justified or not; 'here is a set of rules for managing them,' said the experts of recovery. 'Keep your mind on these rules every day for the rest of your life and don't let anyone or anything distract you from them, because they are all that matters and they are the key to your very survival.' And it is this message which makes the movement not apolitical as it seems, but highly political, in a most reactionary and repressive way. (Rapping 1996: 7)

6

Gender in Magazines: From *Cosmopolitan* to *Loaded*

MAGAZINES are a major part of the media landscape. They accompany us from (just out of) the cradle all the way to the grave, and it is striking that even those aimed at two- and three-year-old children offer remarkably polarized gender scripts: action, transport, adventure for boys; beauty, kindness and princesses for girls. Magazines represent an enduringly popular medium, whose appeal has not been diminished by all the technologies, from radio and film to television and the Internet, that have superseded them. There can be few people who do not read a magazine on a fairly regular basis, whether it is one devoted to a hobby or interest, a stage of life, or a gender-based identification. Indeed, both the 'magazining' of newspapers and the increasing tendency of businesses of all kinds – from supermarkets to mortgage lenders – to produce their own magazines is testimony to the popularity of the form.

This chapter is concerned with gender in magazines. It takes as its focus three broad categories of magazines – teen magazines such as *Jackie*, *J17*, *Bliss* and *Sugar*, and the newer 'baby sister/daughter' spin-offs from *Cosmopolitan* and *Elle*; magazines aimed at adult heterosexual women; and the rapidly expanding men's magazine market. The chapter is divided into four parts. In the first I discuss the notion of ideology as it has been used to study magazine discourses, and emphasize the importance of a political economy perspective in understanding contemporary magazines. Next the chapter looks in detail at teenage magazines charting the ambiguous shift away from ideologies of romance to newer codes based on consumption, beauty and celebrity boy-watching. The proliferation of different types of problem pages is also discussed. The third section turns to women's magazines, but rather than looking at one or two in detail it examines a number of key debates concerned with contradiction and coherence, pleasure versus oppression, text versus audience, and the relation between women's magazines and feminist discourses. Finally, the chapter presents a brief history of the 'new wave' of men's lifestyle magazines, and an account of the construction of new forms of 'laddish' masculinity. The chapter asks how the grow-ing popularity of lad mags should be understood – for example as a backlash against feminism, a reaction against the figure of the 'new man', and a particular classed and racialized articulation of masculinity.

Ideologies of Femininity

The Marxist notion of ideology (discussed in chapter 2) has been used very fruitfully in analyses of women's magazines. The notion directs us to look not only at magazines' content, but at the powerful commer-cial organizations behind their production. It highlights the import-ance of political economy in making sense of magazine texts. Magazines are simultaneously cultural texts, parts of increasingly concentrated media empires (with most of the market dominated by only a handful of companies), and a means of selling highly specific blocks of consumers to advertisers.

It is difficult to exaggerate the importance of advertising to maga-zines. For one thing, their content is dominated by advertisements, with on average 50 per cent of women's glossies dedicated to adver-tising spreads. The September 2003 issue of *Glamour* (UK edn), for example, has 160 full pages of adverts – and that does not include sponsored competitions or special promotions which account for a further 20 pages. Magazines' profits come from the sale of advertis-ing space, with only a small proportion generated by the cover price. This means that magazine publishers have to attract as many adver-tisers as possible, and they do this by creating content that attracts the 'right kind' of readers who can then be offered to advertisers to entice them to spend their money there, rather than in another part of the media landscape. In some cases the desirable readership represents a specific niche (e.g. people who are passionate about photography or canal boating), but generally the most sought-after readership is young, aspirational or upwardly mobile, and with lots of disposable income. In a brochure produced for advertisers, the publishing director of the UK's best-selling women's glossy, *Glamour*, reports that it has attracted more than half a million readers like this: 'The readership is of the highest quality – with an average age of 27, these readers are upmarket, high spending and aspirational – all the attributes that advertisers are looking for' (Simon Kippin, *Glamour*, The Philosophy and Profile). *Glamour* women, he continues, have an average household income of £45,000 per year, they buy a fashion item every eight days and a beauty product every nine days. They take holidays twice a year and they need a glamorous car to project their personality and get them around their busy lives. In short:

> *Glamour* is
> For successful, independent, modern women who know how to have fun, how to dress and how to spend
> They do: shopping, friends, bars, travel
> They don't: window shop, stay at home, have a problem spending
> They buy: clothes, shoes, makeup and jewellery. Their vices? A new handbag every month for each new issue of Glamour
> They are: ABC1C2 women aged 18–34.
>
> (*Glamour*, The Philosophy and Profile)

As well as delivering this desirable demographic to advertisers, magazine publishers sell the friendly and intimate relationship they have established with their readers. Thus *Glamour's* publishers, Condé Nast, are able to report that the magazine's readers trust *Glamour* and turn to it for advice on what hair and beauty and fashion products to buy. Above all, magazines offer an environment that is conducive and sympathetic to the adverts they run.

This can mean many different things. There are a few well-documented examples of publishers making promises to powerful advertisers that their competitors' products will not appear, or, even more problematically, that editorial material will deliberately enhance claims made in adverts. Janice Winship (1987) reports on one example from *Woman* magazine in 1956 in which the manufacturers of nylons (tights/pantyhose) placed an expensive double-page spread on the explicit understanding that there would be no mention of natural fibres elsewhere in the magazine!

Though such agreements undoubtedly continue to be made, today such outcomes are much more likely to be the result of 'normal', 'informal' and 'networked' practices than to be formally imposed. This is because the worlds of magazine and fashion and beauty companies are thoroughly intertwined. Beauty editors routinely receive huge boxes of free gifts from the cosmetics companies eager for their new product to get a write-up; fashion editors 'borrow' clothes from designers, fashion houses and clothes stores to photograph or describe; travel companies pay for fashion shoots on the understanding that the airline, hotel or company get a credit, and so on. In an era of 360 degree branding (see chapter 3), and the triumph of Public Relations (see chapter 5), direct imposition is no longer necessary; through routine practices it is understood that if L'Oréal's agency has spent £50,000 on an advert for a new mascara, the product will almost certainly be mentioned in the beauty editor's advice on 'how to make your eyes look bigger'.

More broadly, the magazines' 'sympathetic' environment means that adverts will not be experienced as interruptions, breaking the flow, but as part of the flow. As Ellen McCracken (1993) has argued, increasingly there is a blurring between adverts and editorial content. This is facilitated by advert placement – emphasizing formal and thematic links, for example by haircare adverts next to articles on haircare, etc.; editorial tie-ins – McCracken (1993) notes that even horoscopes can be used in this way, quoting a special feature on Caribbean holidays in which almost every star sign was told to look forward to opportunities to travel(!); brand reciprocity and the quoting of adverts (e.g. using photographs from adverts but without the caption, or importing copy from an advert as if it were unproblematically factual; shared language, tone, colour, and style; and advertorials, advertising promotions and special tie-ins. Indeed, McCracken (1993) argues that women's magazines as a whole can be regarded as covert adverts. Part of their aim is to win consent for particular constructions of femininity.

Women's magazines share a number of important features: they tend to address readers as equals and friends and to adopt an intimate tone; they are organized around the shared pleasures and labours of femininity; they are invariably constructed in opposition to masculinity (focused on what women share by dint of being women) and are also structured by implicit exclusions relating to age, 'race', sexuality and class; and they adopt a language of individualism, with an emphasis on personal solutions at the expense of collective social or political struggle.

Notwithstanding the similarities, the notion of ideologies of femininity also draws attention to the different versions of femininity on offer in different magazines. There is an immense difference in the femininity constructed in *Woman* magazine and that constructed in *Cosmo*, for example, with one organized around nation and tradition, the pleasures and difficulties of home, and success as a wife and mother, and the other focused on sexual relationships, beauty and career success.

The same magazine can also change significantly over time. As Janice Winship (1987) has argued, women's magazines offer survival skills to cope with the dilemmas of femininity at particular moments in time. Thus, *Woman* adopted a feminist tone in the 1940s during wartime, emphasizing independence and work outside the home. But in the 1950s it celebrated the return to family life and the virtue of the housewife, encouraging women to make their homes even cleaner and more inviting through the purchase of the new consumer goods and domestic appliances (Johnson and Lloyd 2004).

Although the basic ingredients of the woman's magazine as we know it today were already established by the early part of the twentieth century (Ballaster, Beetham et al. 1991), social, political and economic transformations, including the rise of feminism, the advent of the birth control pill and the entry of large numbers of women into the labour market, have wrought major changes. Since the early 1990s there have been a number of discernible shifts in the content of women's magazines. These include:

1 An increasing focus upon *celebrity* – seen in both the launch of new magazines and the transformation of existing magazines to reflect/contribute to a culture ever more fascinated and preoccupied with the lifestyles, diets, body care regimes, marriages and sex lives of Hollywood stars.
2 The dramatic *sexualization of the body*, underwritten by the beauty industry, with the emphasis upon the look (and feel) of the female body as the key site of femininity (Bartky 1990; Wolf 1990).
3 The increasing *adoption of feminist* registers or discourses across magazines, with a stress upon being in control and pleasing yourself.
4 A focus on *work* outside as well as inside the home, with attention placed upon activity, juggling and organization. Winship (1991) notes the rise of a 'new traditionalism' alongside a tone of 'brisk efficiency', offering a fantasy of being able to work, bring up children, produce spectacular dinner parties, and also fit in regular 'home projects' such as creating a garden pond or a mosaic.
5 An increasing emphasis on *heterosexual sex*, with sexuality presented as a key focus of attention in order to please men and to fulfil oneself.

These changes can be seen very clearly in magazines aimed at teenage girls, and it is to these that we turn next.

Teen Mags

In her groundbreaking analysis of *Jackie* magazine in the 1970s, Angela McRobbie (1977, 1978) identified romance as the dominant theme, pervading everything. An iconography of 'great moments' of romance was found in all the stories, with images of 'the proposal', the 'engagement ring' and the 'wedding day' particularly favoured. Romance eclipsed sex (which was often portrayed as dirty or sordid) and instead was presented in terms of its social effects – for example the status of being part of a couple, paired with a handsome boyfriend, or able to flash one's engagement ring. McRobbie argued that the messages conveyed were relatively stable across issues – namely, a girl has to fight to get and keep a man; she can never really trust another female unless she is old and hideous; and yet, despite this, romance and being a girl are fun (see also McRobbie 1991).

Today that version of femininity would be hard to find in magazines aimed at teenage girls. The code of romance has given way to a focus on pop, fashion, beauty and (celebrity) boy-watching.

One of the most significant changes (discussed briefly in chapter 3) is the increasing space devoted to pictures of boys and young men, almost always pop or soap stars. The cover of *J17* announces: 'The biggest celeb boys issue ever' and promises 'Busted: As you've never seen them before' and 'Soap studs: the boys from the box reveal their hidden talents' (September 2003). The suggestion of sexual revelation seems to open up an opportunity for active heterosexual desire, and, as McRobbie has argued, the magazines 'offer one of the few cultural spaces in which girls can stare unhindered and unembarrassed at pictures of boys' (McRobbie 1991: 171). However, despite the magazine's claims to show us things we've never seen before, the boys and men appear fully clothed and striking dominant poses. There is no equivalent to the sexual objectification of women in men's magazines. Instead, the commodity on offer is *knowledge about boys* – their likes, dislikes and embarrassing moments. In each feature, girls are invited to imagine themselves as the star's girlfriend, and it appears that, for all the knowing 'let's-see-what's-in-his-boxers' talk, romance is still the key agenda.

The apparent focus on looking at boys and on active sexual subjecthood is undercut by the emphasis on reading boys, and getting to know what they want. *Bliss* promises readers: 'Know boys inside out: Real lads tell us everything', while *J17* has a regular section called boyology which, just as it sounds, is devoted to the study of boys' obsessions, desires and behaviours. Indeed it could be argued that the magazine as a whole is organized around interpreting boys to girls, furnishing girls with information about how they should look and behave to get and keep a boyfriend. The following represents a small selection of the questions that celebrity boys were asked in just one issue of the magazine:

What kind of girls do you go for?
What should a girl wear on a first date?
What turns you off a girl?
Tell us how your perfect girl would dress?
Do boys really love a bad girl?

Sometimes the answer to these questions are framed explicitly as guidance to girls, for example 'my advice is to keep it natural and stay girlie', says D-Side's Ryan in *J17* (September 2003). But mostly the responses are presented as personal, idiosyncratic preferences, even when they conform to the most predictable and stereotypical heterosexual masculine desires, such as large breasts, high heels, etc. The revelations from the boy band Busted, for example, included things like 'I love the whole revealing your body thing. I like a girl in an open low-cut top' and 'I've always liked a girl in a pair of really low combats and a vested top – a bit rock chickish.' Whether framed as advice or merely personal preference, taken together, the responses constitute – quite literally – a manual for the production of desirable femininity. In the contemporary era of fractured hegemonies, there is no single template of femininity on offer, and, indeed, boys are actively encouraged to argue about the merits of 'quiet girlie girls' versus 'bad girls' and a whole host of similar distinctions. The presence of alternative femininities and contradictory injunctions helps to mask the ideological nature of the texts (it is as if they are saying, 'see, we are not promoting just one way of being a girl') and to obscure the fact that underlying all the versions of femininity is the understanding that girls should be evaluated on the basis of their appearance, together with the requirement that they should be thin, beautiful, curvy, with perfect skin and lustrous hair, yet simultaneously not concerned about their appearance and, above all, 'natural'! Moreover, they take for granted the idea that boys and men are holders of social capital, and naturalize girls' anxious solicitation of male opinion and approval – something that sits uneasily with the 'feisty' and positive assertions of 'girl power' elsewhere in the magazines (Tincknell et al. 2003).

In her insightful analysis of four Canadian teen magazines and their readers (*Teen*, *17*, *Young and Modern*, and *Sassy*), Dawn Currie (1999) found that three themes dominated the advice given to girls. Girls were exhorted to be attractive/create a beautiful personal identity; to be knowledgeable about boys; and to do what is right for them – repeatedly expressed as the requirement to 'just be yourself', 'please yourself' and 'do what you want' (cf. chapter 3).

Currie discusses how she was initially heartened by the feminist tone of some of the advice, with its emphasis upon 'doing what is right for you'. However, closer analysis revealed that the incorporation of feminist messages and slogans did not result in alternative meanings about being a woman. This was because the injunction to 'be yourself' and 'express your own desires' was so closely tied to the two other themes. Currie comments: 'Messages which encourage the reader to "accept herself" for what she is, while giving overall emphasis to "getting a boyfriend", can construct a reading context that makes it difficult for readers to accept themselves if they, in fact, do not have a boyfriend' (Currie 1999: 182). Currie also discusses the deeper, more pernicious, logic of control that has accompanied the shift to a focus on 'being yourself'. Her analysis of problem pages shows that agony aunts frequently admonish girls to just be themselves, setting this up (probably unwittingly and with good intentions) as a new tyranny. The result is that failure at personal genuineness becomes a novel problem for girls: I haven't got a boyfriend because I'm useless at just being myself.

The messages about being yourself, being beautiful and being knowledgeable about boys are inextricably linked in teen magazines in a way that is both profound and taken for granted. It operates, Currie (1999) argues, in the form of an assumption rather than assertion in the texts. Thus in the issue of *Bliss* that proclaims 'Know boys inside out', the next cover headline promises '295 style tricks to be a babe'. The link does not need to be made explicit.

Surveying the content of teen magazines over a forty-year period, Currie (1999) noted a dramatic increase in concern with beautification in recent years. There was a twofold increase in adverts for makeup and a threefold increase in adverts for hair products. This fits with Naomi Wolf's (1990) argument that while advertisers in the past capitalized on women's guilt over hidden household dirt they now focus on the never-ending pursuit of beauty. Increasingly, femininity is presented as a bodily characteristic, requiring constant work – and, crucially, constant expenditure on beauty products. As McRobbie puts it, 'the self which is to be improved now requires even more cosmetics and other products to achieve this end' (McRobbie 1991: 144).

What is significant, then, is the extent to which the emergent discourse of feistiness, independence and girl power is tied to consumption – and, specifically, consumption of beauty products. Unlike the girls in *Jackie*, readers of *J17*, *Bliss*, *Sugar*, and *Teen* are not addressed as people preoccupied with the desire to get an engagement ring; rather their 'feminist' independence is constructed around the idea that they are 'born to shop'. Girls' agency is primarily presented in terms of buying things. This has resonances with the figure of the autonomous, active, desiring female subject discussed in chapter 3, whose sexual confidence is constructed in the service of selling push-up bras and coffee.

Perhaps not surprisingly the discourses of teen magazines make implicit and explicit links between buying things and independence, social power and success with boys. However, the other discourse they use is that of fun. As in adult magazines, femininity is presented as requiring constant attention, vigilance and renewal: girls are advised to change the way they look, the way they laugh, or even the way they send text messages, in order to be more appealing to boys. Moreover they are told to update their clothes, change their hairstyles, and never forget to check on the state of their makeup several times each day, applying extra coats of lipstick when necessary. Yet, in a supreme ideological sleight of hand, the work of producing a suitable feminine appearance is primarily presented through a discourse of fun: 'us girls can't live without mascara. But try swapping boring black for one of these bright blue numbers', 'can't decide which polish to wear? Wear 'em all! Choose five shades and paint a toe on each foot a different colour'. The adverts use the same discourse: 'Sun-In – Fun In' says an advert for hair lightener, 'You can have even more fun with new improved Sun-In' (quoted in Tincknell et al. 2003).

My point is not that experimenting with fashion, makeup and hair colour are not fun activities. Of course they can be enormously enjoyable. But what this emphasis on playfulness and fun displaces is the extent to which feminine appearances are normatively expected of girls and women, rather than simply being pleasurable hobbies. Opting out of femininity as a teenager is extremely difficult for girls and entails very significant costs. This can be glimpsed elsewhere in the magazines, for example in the vox pop interviews with readers about fashions in which even teenagers apparently believe that regular pedicures are essential. The emphasis on fun (like the tendency in adult women's magazines to present feminine body care regimes as indulgence or 'pampering') can produce some almost schizophrenic splits in which girls have no language to talk about their own experiences. Currie (1999) reports an interview with Laura, who, as a consequence of worries about her appearance, started wearing anti-ageing creams when she was eleven years old. By the age of seventeen she would not go out of the house without makeup on, yet asked about this by Currie she was only able to respond that wearing makeup is 'fun'.

There is nothing particularly unusual about Laura, and, indeed, when asked about what things make them feel good, girls mentioned how they look more than anything else. Their feelings about themselves and their self-esteem were directly related to their perceptions of how they looked:

> If my hair is working, and my makeup is working, and there's not too many blemishes on my face and I don't feel fat and I don't think I look fat in what I'm wearing, and everything is – not necessarily comfortable – comfortable isn't even an option, really – and I like what I'm wearing and everything is not binding, or I don't feel like I can't do anything in it, like if everything is okay, I will feel great, yeah definitely [great]. I won't go somewhere if I don't feel good about what I'm wearing. (Alison, quoted in Currie 1999: 231)

Against this backdrop of a powerful beauty mandate for girls and women, 'fun' does not seem to capture even remotely the complexity of women's relationship to their own bodies. Rather, the discourse is part of the shift from objectification to subjectification (discussed in chapter 3) in which more and more of the normative requirements of femininity must be presented as freely chosen and pleasurable, and internally motivated rather than imposed or influenced by wider culture.

The sexual content of magazines represents another area where today's teen magazines differ from those of previous generations. Compared with *Jackie* magazine, in which stories ended in a kiss or a marriage proposal (or in anxiety about whether the boy will continue to love you or will find someone else) contemporary magazines feature much more discussion about sex. This has created alarm among some sections of the population, and in Britain in the late 1990s one Conservative MP attempted to introduce legislation that would require a warning to be printed on the front of girls' magazines concerning their sexual explicitness. Interestingly, as Tincknell et al. (2003) point out, there have been no comparable panics about the proliferation of sex in magazines read by young men and boys. Moreover, it is disappointing that the concerns expressed about sexual content always relate to the explicitness of visual or textual material, without any discussion of the context or the nature of the messages conveyed. In the moral panics that occur with monotonous regularity no distinctions are made between material that is violent, coercive, objectifying or consensual, and instead a blanket concern is expressed about the availability of 'too much' sexual knowledge to girls. In this sense, girls' magazines have fallen prey to a similar problem to that which affects health education and safe-sex campaigns in which information about how to put a condom on an erect penis may sometimes be banned on the grounds that it is 'pornographic'.

One of the most striking features of the magazines is a fervent and unquestioned embrace of heterosexuality. The assumption of heterosexual desire is so pervasive and taken for granted that even when girls speak out about their desire for other women this is invariably recuperated to the heteronormativity. A letter headed 'I fancy my friend' which told of two girls' mutual desire, and their wish to repeat their experience of 'getting off with each other' is answered as follows:

> It's common for girls to experiment sexually with each other, but I have to wonder where doing so again will lead. What happens if one of you finds a boyfriend? What if one of you decides it's not really for her? And what if it destroys your friendship (a definite possibility)? Then what? From the sound of it, neither one of you has given the aftermath of such intimacy much, if any, thought. Have an open and honest chat about the situation, and really listen to each other. If my hunch is correct, you'll both agree that your make-out session was fun while it lasted, but the cost of going for the gusto again is way too high. (Melissa Roske, *J17*, September 2003)

It is hard to imagine a less supportive response – and this written by a ChildLine counsellor in an issue with a special report on tackling bullying! Not only does the agony aunt not even question the (hetero) sexual orientation of the girls, but she trivializes their experience and consigns their feelings to 'experimentation' – the other stock response being 'it's just a phase'. The girls are criticized for not having been 'open' or 'honest enough' to have seen the error of their ways and not to have given enough ('if any') thought to the aftermath of their intimacy. Finally the counsellor raises the frightening spectre that it might 'destroy your friendship' and she concludes that it may have been fun, but the costs are 'way too high'. Chief among the causes of these costs, it should be noted, is precisely the homophobia of magazines like this.

In terms of the heterosexual orientation that dominates the magazines, two main discourses for talking about sex predominate. Tincknell et al. (2003) identify these as, on one hand, a coy, knowing and ironic form of discourse, characterized by humour and innuendo and expressed in a 'teen demotic' with neologism and pop ventriloquism. And, on the other, a discourse that draws on sex education frameworks with warnings, prohibitions, injunctions to stay safe and to remember it is 'your body, your heart and your life'. Tincknell et al. (2003) argue that while there is a rhetorical assertion of sexual confidence in the form of frank (or innuendo-laden) references to male bodies and the desirability of pop-stars, there is also a recognition that such knowledge is not *really* owned by readers, through the presence of articles whose primary purpose is to convey basic information. The disjuncture between the sexually assertive and knowing tone in parts of the magazine and the sex education discourse elsewhere can be seen clearly – and poignantly – in the problem pages which have proliferated in recent years. Teen magazines now feature several pages of problems – themed according to love life, body, boy worries, friends and family concerns, and so on. Indeed, McRobbie (1991) has argued that discussion of problems has become one of the main organizing features of contemporary girls' magazines.

In the example in Box 6.1 the letter writer is distressed both at having witnessed something she did not understand (masturbation) and at subsequently being ignored by her boyfriend. Here the agony aunt is called on to supply basic information about what the boy was doing and reassurance about its normality – yet a few pages earlier the boys in the Blazing boy band were being asked about 'the size of their bits' and boasting about how well endowed they are.

A notable aspect of the problem pages is how they continue to position women as responsible for monitoring and sustaining relations with boys, for protecting themselves against problematic (but normal) male behaviour and for defending their bodies and virtue.

Box 6.1 Touchy boyfriend

I'm very worried about my boyfriend. I went around to his house after school one day as a surprise, and ran upstairs to his room. I was outside the door when I heard him groaning. Thinking he had hurt himself I ran in to see if he was all right. To my horror, he was handling his you-know-what and moving it about. When I asked him what he was doing he told me it was nothing and to go home, and since then he won't talk to me. Please help me. I don't want to lose him as a friend.

Answer: It's likely that what he was doing is called masturbation. That's when people – both girls and boys – touch their genitals for pleasure, which often results in an orgasm. Masturbation is very normal: it's one of the best ways to explore your body and find out what you like, and it's perfectly healthy . . . but usually very private. That, I imagine, is why your boyfriend is not talking to you. He's probably horribly embarrassed, not only to have been caught, but by the thought of having to explain himself to you. I think your best course of action is to be extra-friendly and totally normal to this lad. Hopefully he'll relax, and act normal back. If he doesn't, ask him nicely if you can have a quiet word sometime, then draw him aside and say something like: 'sorry I barged in on you the other day. I'm cool, if you are.'

Source: J17, September 2003.

While (as we discuss later) men's magazines facilitate a discourse of hedonistic sexual pleasure seeking, this discourse is not available to women, who are addressed as subjects who must be both physically and morally responsible. In teen magazines, girls are called on to monitor whether they are ready or not for sex, to consider whether the boy is worth it or not, to think about and plan for contraception and protection against sexually transmitted infections, to take steps to protect their sexual reputation, and to behave responsibly towards friends and other women. A little of the emotional labour involved in this constant monitoring and mediating can be seen in the problem in Box 6.1 in which responsibility is placed upon the girl to first understand and then mend the relationship with her boyfriend (even though he is the one who started ignoring her), to be 'extra-friendly' (yet also somehow 'totally normal'), and, if this doesn't work, to seek him out privately specifically to reassure him.

Women's Magazines: Debates and Dilemmas

In this section we will examine some of the key debates about women's magazines.

Contradiction versus coherence

One of the central debates about women's magazines has been the extent to which they are contradictory texts. The notion of contradiction has become a key way of understanding the fragmented nature of ideologies and the (sometimes glaring) inconsistencies between different discourses in magazines. We have already seen in relation to teen magazines the way that a discourse of knowing sexual assertiveness conflicts with a much less confident presentation of girls' sexuality, and also how an emphasis on fun and playfulness in relation to the body in the fashion pages is entirely at odds with many of the anxious or depressed reflections on appearance in the problem pages.

Similar inconsistencies are also found in magazines for adult women. Fashion and beauty advice is often frankly contradictory. One article may suggest that 'good skin' is the result of a complicated regime that involves cleansing, exfoliating, toning, moisturizing, followed by the application of a myriad of products with all the right concealing, sun protection and light-diffusing properties that the modern woman needs – while another, just pages later, will 'reveal' that drinking lots of water, staying out of the sun and getting plenty of sleep is 'the only beauty treatment you need'. Similarly, fashion pages may advise on staying abreast of all the latest trends and updating your wardrobe to include new skirt lengths, new cuts for trousers, the new season's colours and designs, yet they also warn against becoming a 'fashion slave' and suggest that buying a few key classic pieces is the best strategy which will see you through every season.

Perhaps these inconsistencies are not very important when they concern only skincare or clothes. But in relation to discussion of sex, emotional advice and career guidance they take on a greater significance. Sex is one topic on which contradictory advice abounds. There are at least three structuring discourses to be found in magazines like *Cosmopolitan*, *Marie Claire* or *Glamour*. First there is an emphasis on pleasing your man. This is sometimes allied to a second discourse, a kind of sexual frontierism in which the worst thing that can happen to you sexually seems to be 'getting stuck in a rut', and you are exhorted to 'get out of your comfort zone' to try the new and the taboo – whether it is watching porn together, buying sex toys or trying anal sex. Third there is the feminist (or postfeminist?) discourse about sex: 'take charge sexually'; 'quit faking it and tell him what you like' and 'only do things you feel comfortable with'.

These three discourses frequently come into collision. Myra Macdonald (1995) discusses an article in *19* which advises on how to give a perfect blow job. The article notes that many women do not enjoy performing oral sex, but nevertheless encourages women to give it a try because men enjoy it so much. Then, having detailed some 'tricks' that will really turn him on, the magazine adds: 'sexual acts should be mutually enjoyable, not endurance tests or acrobatic feats, so never feel under pressure to do anything you don't want to' (quoted in Macdonald 1995). A decade later such an article would seem old-fashioned – at least in magazines aimed at adult women. In the last few years anal sex seems to have replaced oral sex as the favourite heterosexual taboo for women's magazines. While researching this book I came across many articles about it, attempting simultaneously to create a frisson of risk and danger and to encourage women to 'break the last remaining taboo' whilst also including an obligatory 'feminist health warning' that you should never do anything you don't feel comfortable with.

Janice Winship (1987) argues that women's magazines perform 'ideological juggling acts'. Writing about the weekly magazine *Woman's Own*, she argues that its discussions of marriage are riven with contradictions. On the one hand it addresses its readership as married women, but on the other recognizes that most are not married. It idealizes marriage and does not acknowledge or reflect the fact that one in three such relationships ends in divorce. It eschews discussion of ordinary people's relationship problems, and instead displaces consideration of marital difficulties onto the lives of the rich and famous. Celebrities' marital failures can be blamed on their exceptional lifestyles – the fact that they are not like us. Winship (1987) contends that the contradictions in the magazine's approach to marriage are able to coexist through their distinct spatial location in different parts of the magazine. Marriage may be a topic for humour in the letters page, for sentimental idealization in the real-life 'triumph over tragedy' stories, for distress and desperation in the problem pages, and so on. As long as they are kept distinct, the inconsistencies do not threaten the overall flow of the magazine.

Ballaster, Beetham et al. (1991) suggest an alternative reason why the contradictions are not necessarily regarded as problematic by magazines' readers. They argue that women's lives in patriarchal societies *are contradictory* and that magazines recognize and reflect this. Indeed, they suggest that part of the success of women's magazines lies in their ability to encompass and hold different – and inconsistent – ideas about women's lives.

However, recent research has thrown into question the usefulness of the notion of contradiction for analysing the content of women's magazines. David Machin and Joanna Thornborrow explore the similarities and differences between the forty-four local versions of *Cosmopolitan* that are produced globally. They argue that not only is there a very coherent discourse or ideology within editions produced for each national context, but that the brand as a whole 'constitutes a set of values that works worldwide in spite of local variations' (Machin and Thornborrow 2003: 454). Machin and Thornborrow suggest that as a global brand *Cosmopolitan* is constructed around the idea of the 'fun fearless female' in which agency is linked to sexuality and the body, and problems are easily solved with the help of *Cosmo's* hot tips. The brand is made coherent across contexts as diverse as the USA, Greece and India by depicting women in abstract empty settings (e.g. 'the office' is signified by just a briefcase and a phone) and using low-modality images and text that travel easily. For example, in relation to work an active but naive reader is addressed – someone who needs advice about how to behave in relation to colleagues, how to impress her boss or whether to date a workmate, but whose job itself and necessary work skills are never mentioned.

The *Cosmo* brand is quite coherent, Machin and Thornborrow (2003) argue. It is built from themes about independence and taking control, transgression ('naughtiness') in relation to sex, and pleasing men. Women are presented as fundamentally alone in relation to both sex and work and must hold their own by using the power their bodies and sexuality afford them.

From this perspective women's magazines are much more coherent than they might appear. The contradictions they contain are part of the brand, and they are not simply collisions between conflicting discourses but part of a motivated whole. Machin and Thornborrow argue that despite *Cosmopolitan's* emphasis on taking control 'the main goal of sex for the fun, fearless female remains pleasing men' (Machin and Thornborrow 2003) – and confidence itself may be part of the 'technology of sexiness' (Radner 1999) that the magazine promotes, since 'the thing that men find sexiest is a woman who knows what she wants and isn't afraid to show it' (Machin and Thornborrow 2003). Underneath the contradictions, then, is a coherent ideological position.

This understanding can help to make a different kind of sense of the following extract from *Glamour*, in which Dan Anderson offers 'his advice for mind, body and emotions':

> There are a few tips you can try that will earn you a coveted spot in any guy's Top 5 list. As one male said, 'ball sucking and nipple sucking go down well, and half of hetero men would love a little anal play'. Start out slowly until you're more comfortable. Testicles are very sensitive so handle them gently. With nipples, start with a light nibble then see if he likes it a bit harder. If something doesn't appeal, skip it. Your willingness to try new things lets your partner know you care and will encourage him to try new tricks on you. (*Glamour*, June 2003: 70)

One way of reading this is as contradictory – it draws on all three discourses identified above – pleasing your man, sexual frontierism, and taking control. Yet rather than simply coexisting it could be argued that the discourses work together purposively to privilege men's sexual pleasure. There is an acknowledgement that ball sucking and anal play may not appeal to you, so you may have to start slowly 'until you are more comfortable' (the implication is that you should *get* comfortable). This is followed by advice on the techniques you should employ. If you really are averse to one of these activities then 'skip it', but remember that doing this is an indicator of how much you care for your partner – with the implication that if you love him, you should do it, no matter how you feel about it.

Is this is an example of contradictory injunctions running alongside each other, or is the emphasis on feeling comfortable and only doing what you want just feminist window dressing for a message that prioritizes pleasing men sexually? Contradiction or coherence – the debates continue.

Pleasure versus oppression and text versus audience

Another key debate has concerned the conflict between two ways of analysing magazines – as vehicles for pleasure or as purveyors of oppressive ideology. On one side of the debate are the arguments that point to the pleasures offered by women's magazines as feminine texts that present a distinct and seductive address to women. On the other is the evidence of magazines' deeply problematic representations of sexuality, race and class, and their espousal of oppressive gender ideologies. In these debates one of the problems is that pleasure and ideology are treated as entirely unconnected and separate. This leads to what we might call the 'Guilty Prefaces Phenomenon' in which feminist writers can (and do) express the pleasure and enjoyment they derive from women's magazines, but this is entirely split off from their analysis of those same magazines as bearers of pernicious ideologies. Janice Winship (1987), for example, prefaces her ideological critique of women's magazines with a confession of her secret enjoyment: she is a 'closet reader', and not just for research. Although Winship does return thoughtfully to this point at the end of her book, it exemplifies a trend (particularly in research of the 1970s and 1980s) to keep discussion of pleasure firmly bracketed off from the 'real' analysis. I am reminded of Jill Tweedie's (1984) fictional character 'the fainthearted feminist' who had a similar guilty secret about her consumption of glossy magazines, and always made sure that her copy of *Cosmopolitan* was hidden inside a 'right on' publication like *Spare Rib*. She would retreat to the toilets to read it so that her family did not find her out – truly, then, a closet reader!

A more productive way of thinking about this relationship is to see pleasure and ideology as intimately related. As Ballaster and colleagues put it:

> The construction and maintenance of any social order entails the construction and maintenance of certain pleasures that secure consent and participation in that order. That any cultural form is pleasurable and ideological is, then, neither surprising nor worrying – what else could pleasure be? And how else could ideology work? (Ballaster, Beetham et al. 1991: 162)

The challenge, therefore, is to integrate an analysis of the pleasurable and the ideological nature of magazines. This means rejecting both the Guilty Prefaces Phenomenon and the pendulum-swing tendency, discussed in chapter 1, to map pleasure onto resistance or to see it as inherently transgressive in its own right. It requires attention to the complexity of subjectivities, in which deeply sedimented desires, patterns and fantasies are not simply erased by becoming more critical of the status quo. Jean Grimshaw puts this clearly: 'It is perfectly possible to agree in one's head that certain images of women might be reactionary or damaging or oppressive, while remaining committed to them in emotion and desire' (Grimshaw 1999: 99).

Winship has been critical of feminists' failure to take on board this point and of the punitive suggestion that long-cherished pleasures and 'unsound' desires should simply be banished or repressed. Returning to her guilty preface, she argues:

> Unfortunately, ideologies cannot be changed only by the assertion that they should be. Feminists we may be, but as individuals our emotional responses and our sense of ourselves have been learned within other codes of femininity. In spite of 'knowing better' we also find ourselves behaving and feeling according to other ideological patterns. And it is important that we recognise that contradiction not as a sign of weakness, to be pushed behind our public feminist veneer, but exactly that which feminism has to deal with. (Winship 1987: 140)

The pleasure versus oppression debate relates to a broader issue – namely the tendency to search for one stable, single meaning in texts. Yvonne Tasker (1991) has argued that despite the increasing theoretical sophistication of media studies and the recognition that texts are polysemic, the search for fixed meanings has not disappeared. Critics hunger for 'the' ideological messages or 'the' radical meanings in texts, and look longingly for texts that can be characterized as unambiguously progressive or regressive. This search for certainty leaves no room for ambivalence or for audience creativity. It makes no distinction between the kind of reading that is akin to 'browsing' and that characterized by complete commitment (Moore 1988). Indeed, the audience is neglected altogether by this focus. As Ballaster, Beetham et al. (1991) argue, the lens is on the implied reader of a text rather than actual readers – who bring very different understandings and motivations to their consumption of magazines.

Since women's magazines first became a topic of scholarship there have been a number of attempts to remedy the exclusive focus on textual analysis. McRobbie's (1977, 1978) early research was very important in showing how magazines were used as part of girls' culture, and, in particular, how an emphasis on femininity could be used by teenage girls to challenge the class-based and oppressive features of their experience at school. *Jackie* readers rejected the official ideology for girls (diligence, weakness, quietness and passivity) and substituted a more feminine and sexual code which operated as a form of resistance in the school's context (although it might be understood in terms of complicity in the wider ideological context).

Another important study of magazine-reading is that by Joke Hermes (1995) in the Netherlands. Hermes takes a postmodern approach. She points out that we all enjoy texts in some contexts which we are critical of in others, and calls for greater 'respect' in academic research on genres like magazines. In her interviews with thirty women and fifteen men she found rather different patterns of use and engagement with women's magazines. For women the fact that magazines were 'easy to put down' was central to the pleasures they offered and their 'fit' with everyday life. Hermes identified two main repertoires that organized women's responses. First there was the practical knowledge repertoire in which women stressed the magazine's role as a 'professional journal' for the home, featuring recipes, patterns, tips, etc. as well as film and book reviews and features on new beauty products. Secondly there was the repertoire for emotional learning and connected knowing, through which women stressed what the magazine-reading offered in terms of learning about other people's emotions and problems and about their own feelings, anxieties and wishes. The magazine helped women to construct a fantasy self who would be ready and prepared to help out a family member or friend in the event of illness, divorce or other kinds of crisis. In fact, Hermes argues fantasy is key to understanding the pleasures of magazine-reading for women, as it is situated at a relatively far remove from daily life – and even the practical tips are rarely used. Men, by contrast, read in an 'apologetic' manner, in which their consumption is continually ironized and any pleasures are put in metaphorical inverted commas saying 'I am a reader of a rather dreadful genre and I cannot be identified with it' (Hermes 1995: 60).

Hermes argues that a theory of everyday media use should have two main tenets: 'first, that content is less important than whether or not a genre is accommodating, whether or not it can be fitted into every-day obligations; secondly, content has, in some sense, to be relevant to the fantasies, anxieties and preoccupations of readers (or viewers)' (Hermes 1995: 64).

Dawn Currie's (1999) study of forty-eight Canadian thirteen-to-seventeen-year-olds represents another important piece of work that moves beyond the text of (in this case teenage) magazines. Unlike McRobbie, Currie found little evidence that girls used magazines to combat school ideologies or employed dress as a form of resistance to authority. She found instead that appearance was used as a vehicle for creativity and self-expression, as an indication of group membership, and as a sign of social status. Magazines played a crucial role in furnishing information about 'what is hot' and about the significance of very small details of appearance (which could be used to mark inclusion/exclusion/social status).

Overall, Currie identified three broad reading positions among her sample: those who read with the grain of dominant meanings (the vast majority); sceptical readers who questioned specific aspects of the magazine (e.g. the realism of the adverts, or the use of just one type of model) but who did not reject the overall ideology of femininity produced by magazines; and, finally, the critical readers who believed that adolescent magazines do not unequivocally serve women's inter-ests, refused magazines' judgements of feminine acceptability, and chose role models by criteria not based on values promoted by maga-zine discourse (i.e. good looks and acceptance by men) (Currie 1999).

These audience studies (and others: see Frazer 1987; Ballaster, Beetham et al. 1991) offer ways out of the pleasure versus ideology impasse. They show the importance of looking at both simultaneously and also of moving beyond textual analysis to explore how media texts such as magazines are read and enjoyed in everyday life.

Women's magazines and feminism

The final set of debates concerns the relationship of women's maga-zines to feminism. Here the focus of discussion has been on magazines launched after the rise of the second-wave Women's Liberation Movement, and targeted at women in their 20s and 30s. *Cosmopolitan* remains the iconic example of this type of magazine and the topic of most analysis, but other magazines in a British context include *Marie Claire*, *Glamour*, and *New Woman*. Debates have focused on whether such magazines may be considered to be feminist or whether they have appropriated feminist discourses merely to empty them of their radi-cal force and to recuperate feminism to consumerist or conservative political ends.

Contemporary women's magazines are certainly informed by feminist ideas. They take for granted women's right to work on equal terms and for equal pay to men, to combine career and motherhood, to have access to reliable, safe contraception, to be able to walk the streets safely, and a myriad of other second-wave goals. These ideas – once so contested – have become part of the common sense of magazines aimed at young women. The topics covered by magazines are also similar to those engaged by feminist writers and activists – how to find ways of getting a balance between work and other aspects of life, how to forge successful relationships with partners, ways to experience a satisfying sex life, etc. Moreover, magazines often celebrate women's achievements in work, sport, triumphing over difficulty, contributing to charity, journalism, defeating attackers and so on.

But the look and feel of women's glossy magazines is still quite different from most avowedly feminist texts. Compared with (other?) feminist writing the tone is positive and celebratory. In place of critique there is *joie de vivre* and an optimistic emphasis on women's success. Magazines like *Cosmopolitan* promote a 'can-do' philosophy in which women are represented as able to achieve anything if they work hard enough (and follow the advice, 'cheats' and helpful hints the magazines offer). The work ethic is central – whether it is applied to dieting, haircare, career or sex life (in the generation of magazines launched by *Cosmo* sex has become a new kind of work and a key source of identity). As Judith Williamson has remarked:

> Whatever the drive is that keeps thousands of women – including myself – buying magazines like *Cosmopolitan* every month, it has more to do with improvement than entertainment. Why else should one curl up after a hard day at work with a publication which tells you to 'Shape up for summer – now', 'Tune into that top job', 'Work off that extra weight' and 'Don't daydream, dare to succeed'? ... Whatever the content, the mode of address is the same: check this, aim for that, start this, stop that – the omnipresent imperative ... Fulfilment, for modern woman, seems to be fixed just around the corner, always an article away, on the other side of some giant 'should'. (Williamson 1986a: 55–6)

In an incisive (and hilarious) critique of the discipline of femininity in women's magazines, Williamson counterposes them against Miss Piggy's Guide to Life, which uses precisely the same format of rules, lists and tasks to subvert the emphasis on hard work, investment and deferred gratification. Miss Piggy's guide to dieting, for example, is based on the idea of 'nipping hunger in the bud whenever it appears' (to stave off future overeating) and a typical afternoon's entry is as follows:

3:34   two cookies
4:14   one more cookie

4:51	small handful of peanuts
5:17	slightly larger handful of peanuts
5:44	the rest of the peanuts
6:11	crackers with cheese dip
6:32	breadstick with cheese dip

(And so on)

What Miss Piggy so brilliantly satirizes with her guide to body care, financial management and travelling is the emphasis on individual self-discipline as the key to success and the solution to all women's problems. It is the individualism of women's magazines that many of their critics argue locate them differently to feminism. In *Cosmo*-world there is no account of power or of structural inequalities and no challenge to men. What is promised is individual transformation (being thinner, prettier, sexier, or higher up the career ladder), rather than social transformation. For some feminists this marks a rupture because not all the problems women face can be solved individually. Winship expresses this succinctly, opining that magazines have appropriated 'the cultural space feminism opened up, minus most of the politics' (Winship 1987: 150).

Feminist writers have also pointed to the profoundly heterosexist and racist nature of women's magazines, as another riposte to claims that they are feminist. Forms of sexuality outside the heterosexual norm either do not figure at all, or are presented as social issues rather than forms of sexual desire. The use of eroticized 'lesbian chic' or 'porno chic' imagery in adverts and visuals does not spill over into the written text and seems designed for auto-eroticism/narcissistic consumption, or for the pleasure of the many heterosexual men who magazine publishers know read women's magazines. Interestingly, gay men have been 'rehabilitated' in recent years in magazines and other media. But this has come at a cost of 'de-gaying' and de-sexualization, and, indeed, the 'meaning' of being homosexual has been reduced to being stylish and a gossip. As we've discussed elsewhere in this book, a gay male friend has become a kind of mandatory style accessory for young women, based on the crudest form of stereotyping. Thus the cover of *Marie Claire* (UK edition, October 2003) asks, 'WOULD YOU SWAP YOUR BLOKE FOR A GAY MAN? THINK STYLE AND GOSSIP BUT NO SEX'.

A similar pattern of exclusion and distortion characterizes white mainstream magazines' representations of 'race'. For the most part magazines like *Cosmo* construct an entirely white world – perhaps punctuated by the occasional image of Naomi Campbell or Sonja Wanda. When non-white groups are addressed, blackness is treated as an aesthetic category, rather than a social or political one, with the result that no differences of experience are acknowledged save for those relating to hair and skincare. There is never discussion of racism and no suggestion that readers may be positioned differently in relation to following the magazines' tips for success at work.

Marie Claire is an exception to this pattern. Whilst most of the content is similar to that of the other magazines, *Marie Claire* also features an award-winning 'reportage' section which regularly focuses on women of colour in different parts of the world. Over the years it has reported on a variety of different women, for example, 'The village of 5,000 Virgins (in South Africa); India's female tycoons; 'The secret world of female drugs barons'; 'India's sadhu nuns' ('Seeking salvation through suffering'); and 'The lost world of Shebai in southern China' ('where women sing to get a husband').

These features generate many appreciative comments from readers who like to be informed about women's lives elsewhere in the world and are pleased to be addressed as intelligent and curious rather than obsessed only with beauty. However, the writing, photography and *mise-en-scène* of the reportage pieces constitute, in my view, what we might call a *National Geographic*-style racism – in which the women under discussion are treated as exotic, uncomplicated, close to nature, inherently pure and moral, and so on. 'Cultures' are treated as hermetically sealed (and indeed 'lost' and 'undiscovered' tribes or groups are a speciality) and there is no consideration of the broader processes of global capitalism that might help to make sense of the women's lives. The 100th birthday issue of *Marie Claire* featured 100 images of women from around the world. The five-line commentary noted: 'From Luisa Bisitan who works on a farm in the Philippines, to Joan Collins in her Chelsea Mansion, the women were chosen to sum up the diversity of women's lives across the globe. This special reportage embodies the essence of *Marie Claire* – that all women are individual and equal'.

Fine sentiments indeed, but the endorsement of equality, individuality and diversity is meaningless in the context of a collection of photographs that juxtapose white Western celebrities with 'Julia Esquivel' who ekes out an existence in Guatemala by scouring rubbish dumps. Where is the equality in that? This is diversity postmodern-style (and post-Benetton style) in which any powerful image can be juxtaposed with any other powerful image without any attempt to make sense of it or understand the processes that produced these different lives. It is the 'rich tapestry' school of diversity in which there is the privileged West and then the Rest with their brightly coloured clothes, simple lives and quaint customs (and of course their beautiful, eminently photographable faces – whether etched in lines through hard work and poverty, or young and fresh-faced emblems of innocence).

But even the representations of white, heterosexual women are anti-thetical to feminism, many critics argue. Myra Macdonald (1995) argues that the feminism of magazines like *Cosmopolitan* and *Glamour* is 'skin deep' – a veneer that hides a real agenda based on pleasing men on their own terms. Tincknell et al. (2003) make a similar argument: they point out that alongside the emergence of assertiveness and feistiness as key modes for representing women's subjectivity there has been a parallel re-inscription of women's bodies as sexually available to men.

The ideological configuration of women's magazines is ultimately determined by commercial interests. For some this represents the 'bottom line' and requires that all magazine representations should be understood in the light of 'brute' economic considerations. From this perspective, the representation of the independent woman or the heterosexual desiring female are astute marketing strategies, rather than reflections of a publishing industry becoming feminist. Ellen McCracken (1993) argues that any potential for feminism is always 'undercut' by consumerism – as when black nationalist themes in the US magazine *Essence* are undermined by page after page of adverts for products promoting white ideals of beauty (skin lighteners, hair straighteners, etc.).

Against this negative assessment of glossy feminism, however, we need to counterpose the positive pleasurable address of women's magazines. The emphasis on women's strength, talents, ability to succeed is not 'nothing', and the fact that it is articulated to individual ends does not necessarily render it completely worthless. The problem pages are a case in point. Most problems are experienced as personal (whether it is a partner's infidelity or a bullying boss) and they require solutions in the here and now. Magazines can offer useful and empowering advice to deal with immediate and painful difficulties. Indeed, what would feminism offer in place of this, McRobbie asks:

> Problems may be socially produced but this does not mean we experience them as such. Nor does it mean we do not look around for some kind of relief or resolution. It is unlikely that an advice column which continually pointed to the social origins of feminine discontent would attract enough letters each week to keep going. (McRobbie 1991: 163)

Winship contends that magazines offer a kind of pragmatic feminism. It is not going to produce a women's revolution, but it can perhaps furnish women with 'streetwise' ways to help them negotiate the problems and dilemmas of everyday life:

> Even if a 'street-wise' consciousness is unlikely to change any further into a more overtly feminist politics in these magazines, we feminists

would do well, I think, to read and take heed of what they are offering. We shouldn't just contemplate the many and inevitable ways they are not feminist, but also consider what they might say to feminism. What can we learn from these magazines to enrich a feminist politics? (Winship 1987: 139)

Where one stands on the issue of women's glossies' relation to feminism finally rests on one's understanding of feminism. Why should the texts of second-wave feminism be seen as the purest or even the sole repository of 'true' feminism, Joanne Hollows (2000a) asks pertinently: why is this body of texts, largely written by white, middle-class, First World academic women, the 'canon' against which popular texts are compared and found wanting? Has not this 'canon' itself been repeatedly shown to be based on exclusions of class, 'race' and disability/able-bodied mess? And is it not the product of a distinct historical moment, rather than a timeless philosophy? Angela McRobbie (1999) cautions against holding onto an idea of one fixed, authentic form of feminism – showing how this inevitably leads to anger and disappointment that the daughters of second-wave feminists are not like 'us' (them), as well as a failure to recognize new forms of feminism. Writing about the phenomenon of the ladettes – groups of women who out-lad the guys and subject them to cruel evaluations such as 'look at the state of that arse, two out of ten', McRobbie argues:

> This kind of reverse sexism can also be seen as a riposte to an older generation of feminists whom the younger women now see as weary, white and middle-class, academic and professional, and certainly not spunky, vulgar or aggressive. Coming across as loutish and laddish is a provocation to a generation of feminists now established as figures of authority . . . To these young women official feminism is something that belongs to their mothers' generation. They have to develop their own language for dealing with sexual inequality; and if they do this through a raunchy language of 'shagging, snogging and having a good time,' then perhaps the role this plays is not unlike the sexually explicit manifestos found in the early writing of figures like Germaine Greer and Sheila Rowbotham. The key difference is that this language is now found in the mainstream of commercial culture – not out there in the margins of the political underground. (McRobbie 1999: 122)

Such arguments make the case for treating 'popular feminism' like that of magazines on its own terms, rather than comparing it with a reified notion of a true feminism (against which it is always deemed a failure). Hollows (2000a) suggests that second-wave feminists have promoted the idea that feminism and femininity are incompatible, even oppositional. This underpins much feminist critique, which she sees as moralistic, and based on the desire to privilege the 'feminist expert'. Instead of seeing 'true' feminism as co-opted or recuperated or neutered in some way by its entry into the popular domain, Hollows suggests that it is more useful to regard feminism and femininity as being brought into new articulations – the political outcome of which cannot be specified in advance. This is essentially a Gramscian perspective which regards popular culture as a site of struggle, from which new meanings are created (see chapter 2). One of the implications of this is that, although the economic 'last instance' exerts a determining effect, this is not the end of the story; the fact that magazines are commercial ventures does not mean that they may not also be spaces for progressive ideas or cultural contestation.

Men's Lifestyle Magazines

In recent years there has been a growing interest in magazines aimed at men, particularly in the UK. This is partly attributable to the more general focus upon masculinities across the arts, humanities and social sciences, and partly the result of the sudden proliferation of lifestyle titles targeted at men in the 1980s and 1990s, for example *Arena, GQ, Loaded, FHM, Maxim*, and *Men's Health*.

For many years people working in the fashion, magazine, advertising and retailing industries had fantasized about the creation of a magazine that could be targeted at affluent male consumers, but it was seen as an impossible dream (notwithstanding the success of older titles like *Esquire* in the USA). In 1986 an article in *Campaign* (the British advertising industry's journal) noted: 'Men don't define themselves as men in what they read [but] as people who are into cars, who play golf, or fish . . . Successfully launching a general interest men's magazine would be like finding the Holy Grail' (*Campaign*, 29 August 1986). Men, it was argued, lack self-consciousness about their sex (the 'male as norm' phenomenon identified by feminists) and whilst they bought magazines about photography or outdoor pursuits there was scepticism about whether they would buy a title organized around being a man, rather than a specific hobby. A second problem concerned the tone such a magazine should employ. Women's magazines, as we have already noted, had long adopted the formula of treating their readers as friends, with a familiar, intimate tone, but this was seen by people within the industry as potentially threatening to heterosexual men because of its homosexual undertones.

A number of factors helped to produce space for the new generation of men's lifestyle magazines in the 1980s. On the one hand they were influenced by the 'gender quake' produced by feminism and other social movements (including gay liberation). Feminists had articulated a desire for a new kind of masculinity based less on the old-style patriarchal model and more upon egalitarianism, communication and nurturance. Men were changing, and heterosexual partnerships were, for the younger generation at least, being forged along different lines: fewer couples married and more women worked outside the home. The old 'breadwinner'/'homemaker' ethic was giving way to something more egalitarian in ethos (although this was very uneven in terms of its effects upon practices).

In the mid-1980s the National Magazine Company, aware that its market leader *Cosmopolitan* was read by a large male audience (primarily the partners of its female readers), launched *Cosmo Man* to try to reach this market directly and to deliver them to advertisers queuing up to sell them cars, hi-fis, designer clothes, sportswear, financial services, fragrances and the new category of 'male grooming products'. In the event, however, *Cosmo Man* failed catastrophically. In part this may have been due to the failure of the producers to understand men's particular reading practices – specifically, the ironic distancing discussed by Hermes (1995; see last section). But Sean Nixon (1996) argues that it was also attributable to the 'identity crisis' at the heart of *Cosmo Man*'s understanding of their implied reader: the new man. The magazine was not clear whether it was addressing the caring, sensitive 'new man' who was the *Cosmo* woman's 'ideal' partner or whether it was targeting the 'commercial' figure of 'new man': affluent, narcissistic and preoccupied with fashion and consumption. The tension between these competing versions of the new man addressed by magazines can be seen right across contemporary discussions of masculinity and partly sowed the seeds for his subsequent cultural displacement by more 'laddish' forms of masculinity (Beynon 2002).

Alongside the impact of progressive social movements on the emergence of men's lifestyle magazines were a number of other factors. These included economic changes, notably the restructuring of the economy away from traditionally male occupations in manufacturing and towards service sector jobs; the rapid growth in retailing, in which men were targeted as the 'new' market; and shifts in political ideology, represented by the rightwards turn in North America and European democracies, exemplified by the election victories of Ronald Reagan, George Bush Senior and Margaret Thatcher (Edwards 1997).

More broadly the success of the magazines can be understood as the outcome of the trend towards consumer society, combined with the gradual transformation of the relationship between masculinity and consumption. Despite the long-established association between masculinity and production, and femininity and consumption, Tom Pendergast (2000) argues that as early as the launch of *Vanity Fair* in the USA in 1892 and *New Success* in 1918 there were powerful versions of masculinity organized around consumption, as men were invited to see themselves as 'malleable potentialities, capable of achieving multiple expressions through the goods they purchased and the way they presented themselves' (Pendergast 2000). Bill Osgerby suggests that the early twentieth-century commodity culture was an uncertain field for (heterosexual) masculine identity and required considerable efforts to ward off its 'lavender whiff' (suspicions of homosexuality and effeminacy). But it was nevertheless quite possible for men to 'step into the world of consumerism and narcissistic style' (Osgerby 2003: 72). Discussing the launch of *Esquire* magazine in the USA in 1933, he notes its editor's reassurance that the content and presentation would allow the magazine 'to take on an easy natural masculine character – to endow it, as it were, with a baritone voice' (*Esquire* editor, quoted in (Osgerby 2003: 69).

In the UK, the first attempt to launch a men's lifestyle magazine was *Men Only* in 1935. It combined articles about heroic masculinity with style features and pictures of female nudes. In this way consumption for men was promoted in an atmosphere not threatened by suspicions of homosexuality. Barbara Ehrenreich makes a similar point about the launch of *Playboy* in 1953. She argues that 'the breasts and bottoms were necessary not just to sell the magazine, but also to protect it' (Ehrenreich 1983: 51).

The 1950s is regarded as a key decade for understanding the dramatic intensification of the relationship between masculinity and consumption (Ehrenreich 1983; Segal 1990; Mort 1996; Osgerby 2001). The post-war consumer boom created a rapid expansion in the advertising industry, media and new service sector and saw the emergence of new class fractions who distinguished themselves from more traditional established class groupings partly by means of their consumer choices. In France, Pierre Bourdieu (1984) argued that a class of 'new cultural intermediaries' broke away from the puritanical morality of duty associated with the 'old' middle class and elaborated in its place a set of values organized around consumption, pleasure and fun. For Ehrenreich (1983) *Playboy* magazine became the 'bible' for the men who dominated this class fraction; its individualistic, hedonistic, consumption-oriented ethic of personal gratification represented a rebellion against the 'old' figure of male as breadwinner and family provider and opened up a space of libidinous fun and lascivious consumption, albeit premised on troublingly sexualized and objectified representations of women.

What this brief review should indicate is both the way that the relation between masculinity and consumption progressively deepened over the twentieth century, and also the increasing proliferation and fragmentation of representations of masculinity. Whilst there was never one single 'hegemonic masculinity' (Connell 1987, 2000), by the 1980s the templates of masculinity on offer were increasingly diverse, influenced by the factors discussed above as well as by different musical movements, changing fashions, and accelerating globalization. As John Beynon notes of the present moment: 'Perhaps what we are currently witnessing at the start of the 21st century is nothing less than the emergence of a more fluid, bricolage masculinity, the result of "channel hopping" across versions of "the masculine" ' (Beynon 2002: 6).

One important precursor of and influence upon the 'new wave' of men's magazines launched in the 1980s (e.g. *GQ* and *Arena*) was *The Face* magazine, created by Nick Logan in 1982. It promoted itself as a style magazine rather than men's magazine, although the vast majority of its readers were male, and was organized around fashion, music and any kind of social commentary deemed to be chic enough to fit in its pages. Nixon (1996) argues that *The Face* developed a new aesthetic: it was not just *about* style, but it was emblematic of stylishness itself, creating a new vocabulary for fashion photography – a vocabulary, significantly, that extended the notion of style to include fashion spreads of menswear and advertising for body products targeted at men as well as women.

The style press exercised two key kinds of influence, then – first in opening up space for fashion/lifestyle magazines aimed at men, and secondly in pioneering radically new ways of representing masculinity. Arguably, however, the two 'problems' that industry people had identified did not disappear. The residues were clearly visible in men's magazines in the 1980s, and are still visible today. Anxieties about how to address heterosexual men were resolved in two ways: first through the adoption of a 'laddish' tone which enabled male editors and journalists to address readers as 'mates', and secondly through an almost hysterical emphasis on women's bodies and heterosexual sex, juxtaposed alongside avowedly homoerotic photographs. As Tim Edwards (1997) has argued, this allowed magazines to appeal directly to a gay audience, while still defensively asserting the heterosexuality of their text.

By the early 1990s, however, this project was becoming increasingly strained, in part because of the growing confidence of the gay movement and the increasing number of magazines targeted at gay men (Edwards 2003). The association of *GQ*, *Arena* and *Esquire* with the figure of the new man was giving way to a more 'assertive articulation of the post-permissive masculine heterosexual scripts' (Nixon 1996, 2001). The pages of the magazines were marked by an increase in sexualized imagery and sexual scrutiny of women, and a significant change of editorial tone. This was clearly visible on the covers of the magazines, which moved away from featuring well-known male actors, musicians, etc. to a focus on scantily clad female models or celebrities. In a widely reported press release, Condé Nast, the magazine's owners, announced: 'GQ is proud to announce that the New Man has officially been laid to rest (if indeed he ever drew breath). The Nineties man knows who he is, what he wants and where he is going, and he's not afraid to say so. And yes, he still wants to get laid' (January 1991).

In a characteristically reflexive move, one of the first attempts to make sense of how masculinity was changing was itself published in *Arena* magazine (O'Hagan 1991). Part sociological analysis, part 'ladifesto', this article sought to expose the 'myth' of the sensitive, caring and non-sexist new man, and celebrate the arrival of his hedonistic, libidinous, postfeminist alter ego. O'Hagan argued that new lads were new men who can't quite shake off their laddishness. Quite different from their 'boorish/tribal/drunken' 'prehistoric predecessors', new lads were intelligent enough to 'tell you how misogynist the new David Lynch film is' but might do so primarily as a seduction strategy. Smart and knowing, the new lad 'aspires to new man status when he is out with women, but reverts to old lad type when he's out with the boys. Clever, eh?'

Aspects of this new masculine script, particularly the unashamed sexual objectification of women, increasingly dominated the men's lifestyle magazines in the late 1980s and early 1990s. But it was with the launch of *Loaded* and the relaunch of *FHM* in 1994 that 'laddism' found its most distinctive voice.

Loaded

The story of the founding of *Loaded* magazine has taken on the status of myth. The apocryphal tale has it that James Brown and Tim Southwell came up with the concept at a football match. They sought to create a magazine that would reproduce the feelings of euphoria and male camaraderie that were familiar from the terraces and from after-match drinking sessions. Bored and irritated by the existing men's lifestyle magazines, they took inspiration for their tone – and some of their content – from the British tabloid newspaper *The Sun* and from the music press. Theirs was a young, loud, hedonistic celebration of masculinity. They spoke to men in their own language, and they addressed men in terms of their assumed interests in beer, football, women and 'shagging'. James Brown argued that *Loaded* expressed what would have come out 'if you'd picked me up and shaken everything out of my head' (Crewe 2003: 100). The first editor's letter set out the magazine's concerns:

> *Loaded* is a new magazine dedicated to life and liberty and the pursuit of sex, drink, football and less serious matters. *Loaded* is music, film,

relationships, humour, travel, sport, hard news and popular culture. *Loaded* is clubbing, drinking, eating, playing and living. *Loaded* is for the man who believes he can do anything, if only he wasn't hungover. (*Loaded*, April 1994: 3)

As Ben Crewe (2003) has argued, the sexual politics of the magazine were in place from the first issue, which featured photographs of Liz Hurley, a homage to hotel sex, porn channels, etc., a 'travel' feature recounting cheap cocaine and cheap women, and the Miss Guyana bikini contest. The attitude towards women was enthusiastically predatory, unabashed by 'new mannish' concerns. The lads addressed were cheerfully unreconstructed; they were familiar with the terms of feminist critique but unapologetic about their consumption of soft porn and their desire to 'shag' women. This was eloquently captured by the strapline of the magazine: 'for men who should know better'.

There is no doubt that *Loaded* had a profound effect on the magazine industry. A month after its launch, EMAP began a revamp of *FHM* that was indebted to the *Loaded* formula. *FHM* became the market leader; its sales peaking in 1998 at 775,000 – far outselling even the most popular women's glossies. *Loaded* also influenced the dramatic expansion of men's magazines and their diversification into gadget magazines (e.g. *Stuff, T3*), health and fitness titles (*XL, GQ Active, FHM Bionic*) and magazines for older and less laddish male consumers (*Later*).

Its impact was also felt in the growing 'ladification' of existing titles, exemplified vividly by James Brown's move in 1997 to take over editorship of *GQ* magazine. Even the editor of the previously rather staid *Esquire* defended his magazine's growing reliance on a diet of 'babes' in states of undress: 'Any good magazine must offer a balance of content, and part of that balance, if it is to reflect the interests of men, will inevitably be articles on beautiful women' (Peter Howarth, the *Guardian*, 25 November 1996).

The lad mag concept was also successfully exported from the UK during the 1990s, partly on the back of the 'Cool Britannia' phenomenon. In his lively account of the decade Robb (1999) argues that it was the moment when Britain learned to party, and the lad mags spoke the language of street, the pubs and clubs. In 1999 *FHM* was launched in the USA. This is how it was recorded in an article in the *Sunday Times*:

> The troops are being assembled, the invasion plans are well advanced and the general is in place . . . to launch if not a full-frontal assault at least a semi-naked one, to liberate the sensibilities of the all-American male . . . For Uncle Sam, the countdown to the acceptable face of party-time has begun . . . A guy is a guy, wherever he lives . . . A testosterone-charged British sperm is swimming across the Atlantic . . . If the American 'new man' was ever house-trained by feminism to be consid-

erate, sensitive and interested in women's minds rather than their bodies, he is about to be led wildly astray. (*Sunday Times*, quoted in Beynon 2002: 114)

A year later, the American version of *Maxim* broke the 2 million circulation level, making it the most successful ever magazine launched in the USA (Beynon 2002). Elsewhere the lad mags were making similar inroads, and in Germany *Playboy* was relaunched at a new publishing house after witnessing the meteoric success of *FHM* and *Maxim*. *Playboy* was quickly established as Germany's best-selling men's magazine (Werkmeister 2003).

It is difficult to exaggerate the significance of the lad mags. Their influence was felt right across the media – in the confident laddism of radio DJs and the growth of new genres of television, lad shows such as *They Think It's All Over, The Frank Skinner Show* and *Men Behaving Badly*. More broadly, the figure of the new lad became embedded in advertising and popular culture – his multiple articulations in different spaces generating a sense of his solidity and 'realness', making him instantly recognizable as an embodiment of a type of masculinity.

Understanding the lad mags

In the last decade there have been many attempts to understand the impact of the lad mags and to make sense of the apparently novel form of masculinity they constructed. One way of thinking about the figure of the new lad is to see him as a reaction against 'new man'. Ben Crewe argues that the new man with his 'hesitant and questioning stands on sexual relations' was marked out as the antithesis of *Loaded* man (Crewe 2003: 100). New man was derided for his 'miserable liberal guilt' about sexual affairs and presented as insipid and unappealing. By contrast, new lad was presented as refreshingly uncomplicated in his unreserved appreciation of women's bodies and heterosexual sex.

New man was also attacked for his narcissism: 'grooming is for horses', opined James Brown in an early editorial (*Loaded*, July 1995). Interestingly, almost as common are attacks on new man's lack of concern for his appearance – again underlining his 'asexual' nature. Jo Ann Goodwin, writing in the *Guardian*, looked forward to a more red-blooded form of masculinity and argued that new man represented 'the toxic waste of feminism':

> The worst of it is that these men are so unappealing, so unaesthetic, so unsexy. Once you see through the dubious charm of someone 'who really understands women' what you're left with is a man whose clothes are appalling, and who is so busy trying to be supportive he has probably forgotten what an erection is for. (*Guardian*, 13 February 1993)

Above all, new man was condemned as inauthentic. He was presented alternately as a media fabrication or marketing strategy, or a calculating pose by ordinary men to get women to sleep with them. Against this apparent duplicity and hypocrisy, new lad was depicted as honest, open and authentic. In analyses of interviews with readers, Nick Stevenson, Peter Jackson and Kate Brooks (2003) found that the apparent 'honesty' of the lad mags was regarded as their most appealing quality. Male readers said they gave them permission to 'be the man you want to be', without fear of slipping up or making some mistake. The masculinity they constructed was regarded as true to men's real selves, in contrast to the contrived image of the new man.

The cultural ascendance of the new lad has also been understood as a reaction against feminism. From this perspective, the figure of the new lad, constructed around knowingly misogynist and predatory attitudes to women, represents a refusal to acknowledge the changes in gender relations produced by feminism, and an attack upon it. Imelda Whelehan argues that the new lad is 'a nostalgic revival of old patriarchy; a direct challenge to feminism's call for social transformation, by reaffirming – albeit ironically – the unchanging nature of gender relations and sexual roles' (2000: 5). He represents, then, a defensive assertion of masculinity, male power and men's rights against feminist challenges.

In a similar vein, Suzanne Franks (1999) has argued that, as women's roles and identities have changed and expanded into domains previously thought of as male, 'new lad' represents a response which moves men further into the heartlands of masculinity – rather than blurring gender identities. In this sense, the new lad seems clearly to be part of the backlash against feminism across multiple sites and domains (Faludi 1992). It is certainly the case that feminists are vilified within the lad mags As Whelehan put it, 'feminism is emptied of any significance beyond being associated with a bunch of dour, ageing women who only want to spoil men's fun' (Whelehan 2000). 'Feminist' becomes a pejorative word to label, dismiss and silence any women who object to the lad mags' ideology. For example, a letter to *FHM* from a woman called Barbara who wished to object to the magazine's portrayal of women as 'weak, frail, obedient, submissive and sexually available' is dismissed as a 'blundering rant' from 'Butch Babs' (*FHM*, May 2000: 24). Frequently, the magazines dismiss and silence criticism before it is even voiced. For example, in an article concerned with the question of 'how to get your girlfriend to let you come in her face' (*FHM*, April 2000: 89) any possible critical feedback is forestalled with the comment 'now before I get any angry letters from feminists . . . I have asked women and they agree it can be an incredibly rewarding experience'. Another article on getting your girlfriend to have sex when she doesn't want to is also prefaced with the acknowledgement that 'I can imagine what letters I'll get from the Council for Women or other busybodies' (*FHM*, July 2000, quoted in Pring-Ellis 2001).

Jackson, Stevenson and Brooks (2001), however, suggest that the new lad may be a more ambiguous figure than straightforward backlash accounts suggest. Perhaps a useful analogy may be made with the rise of 'muscular heroes' in action cinema during the late 1980s and early 1990s (e.g. Arnold Schwarzenegger, Sylvester Stallone and Bruce Willis). One reading of the state of action movies at this time was that they were classic 'backlash texts', which were concerned with bolstering hegemonic masculinity in the service of right-wing US foreign policy under Reagan and Bush. Moreover, they seemed to threaten to erase women from acting roles in films altogether. However, an alternative reading put forward by Yvonne Tasker (1993) is that the films should be understood in terms of the difficulty of maintaining masculine physicality in the microchip era. Thus the muscular masculinities on offer simultaneously reassert, mourn and hysterically state male power, whilst also parodying it.

In their more upbeat account of the popularity of lad mags, Stevenson, Jackson and Brooks suggest that they are 'caught between' 'an attempt to construct masculinity as a form of fundamentalist certitude, while simultaneously responding to a world where gender relations are rapidly changing . . . an awareness that oldstyle patriarchal relations are crumbling and a desire to reinscribe power relations between the different genders and sexualities' (2003: 122).

Much of this ambivalence is handled through the abundant use of irony in the magazines. Where new lad differs from older-established misogynist scripts is precisely in the knowingness of his sexism. As Bethan Benwell has argued, the 'one great trump card' played by the new lad magazines 'anxious to proclaim the power of masculinity but simultaneously to preserve an intelligent post-feminist political identity' was the use of ironic distancing (Benwell 2003). While irony in relation to the new man was designed to provide a safe distance between the reader and less traditional sexual scripts, with laddism irony functions primarily as a means of subverting potential critique. Irony allows you to express an unpalatable truth in a disguised form, while claiming it is not what you actually meant (Stevenson, Jackson and Brooks 2000).

Irony, it seems, means never having to say you're sorry. Much of the time, as Benwell (2003) notes, the irony is not something 'directly recoverable' from the text at all. It operates at a more global level, indexing the knowledge that the sexism in new lad culture is ironically, nostalgically and perhaps even harmlessly meant.

Jackson, Stevenson and Brooks (2001) point out that irony also offers an *internal* defence against ambivalent feelings. They discuss the variety of distancing strategies male readers of the lad mags deployed in accounts of their magazine consumption, with the emphasis upon rebutting the potential charge that they take themselves or the magazines too seriously. My own research with Karen Henwood and Carl McLean, in which we interviewed 140 men between fifteen and thirty-five, found similar disavowals, such as claims that the magazines are only ever purchased for a train journey, or flicked through in a dentist's waiting room, or just bought 'for a laugh' (Gill, Henwood and McLean 2000).

Benwell (2003) argues that the 'ambivalent masculinity' constructed in magazines such as *Loaded* and *FHM* can also be seen in the perpetual oscillation between a discourse of traditional heroic masculinity and a discourse of the fallible, self-deprecating, anti-heroic masculinity. Whilst the sporting stars, male celebrities and interviewees involved in dangerous activities such as war photography are treated to unequivocal admiration for their bravery and heroism, columnists deploy a contrasting anti-heroic, self-deprecating tone for themselves. Thus, for example, an article in *Loaded* about an Outward Bound course starts with: 'seven brave men were set to battle the elements. But they couldn't make it so we sent this lot.' It goes on to detail in humorous terms the fear, clumsiness and abject failure of the writer to complete the course. Similarly, an article in *FHM* about auditioning to be a porn star presents the writer distinctly short of phallic omnipotence. He attempts James Bond suaveness ('raises an appreciative eyebrow' at his sexy co-stars) but 'can think of precisely nothing to say'. Unable to get an erection he is humiliated by being called 'Drooperdick' instead of 'Super Dick' (quoted in Benwell 2003). Such articles seem to suggest that the power and privilege associated with traditional masculinity is unreachable, or at least a struggle to attain. It mocks the phallic masculinity of porn magazines and draws attention to masculinity as an ongoing masquerade, always liable to failure or exposure.

The question is, as Benwell observes, whether the ambiguity reflects 'an unwitting schizophrenia' or whether it has a more deliberate and strategic function. Does the anti-heroic unmasking of masculinity work to threaten male power or to repudiate it and therefore reinforce it? What exactly are the effects of the relations between different discourses of masculinity? This returns us to the question asked earlier in the chapter about women's magazines: contradiction versus coherence? Do the lad mags merely present a collage of different representations of masculinity or do they constitute motivated wholes? What role is irony playing?

Let us address these questions through an analysis of one article in *FHM*. The article is entitled 'Help! My woman is broken! Her sexual malfunctions and how to fix them'. This type of article is the closest the lad mags come to offering an advice column and it is done in humorous terms. Anything else, as Stevenson, Jackson and Brooks (2003) have argued, would seem 'too preachy' for their audience. The article is characterized by a tone of detachment and refuses an emotional register. This is facilitated by the structuring analogy between women and cars: 'Like the secondhand banger in your drive-way, a few years down the road and the missus may begin to rust. *FHM* suggests some fine tuning.' Women here are presented as a series of compartmentalized problems: 'she won't give head', 'she won't play with herself for you', 'porn is taboo', and so on.

The matter-of-fact and humorous way in which these problems and their solutions are presented gives them a strong rhetorical force. The implication is that all women are like this and that all male readers will recognize these problems. The article assumes a commonality of values between the reader and text and in doing so implicates readers in a common ideology of sexism. Women are not once referred to as women throughout the article and instead they are called 'missus', 'little lady', 'po-faced prude', and, most frequently, just 'her' or 'she'. The use of pronouns is significant in inviting generalized identification and underlining the common sense of viewing women in this way. The other terms are characterized by a slightly nostalgic quality, reminiscent of 'naughty' seaside postcards.

A number of problematic ideas about gender relations pervade the article (besides the overall notion that women 'go wrong' and may need to be traded in for racier models). First, there is the assumption of natural gender difference: 'For the fairer sex masturbation is different'; 'sexually explicit films aren't interesting for women . . . the ladies are thought to like artistically pleasing scenes'. These sorts of comments play on the idea, popularized by John Gray, that 'men are from Mars and women are from Venus'. They make it appear natural and inevitable that men will enjoy watching porn and that women will be coy, embarrassed and passive in the bedroom.

Secondly, the article suggests that relations between the sexes are characterized by antagonism. On men's side there is lust, and on women's there is hostility. It is striking to note that women are recurrently cast as unpleasant and manipulative. For example the problem 'she won't give head' is explained as follows: 'Oral sex is either a device used by females to ensnare a mate, or an occasional treat to keep us docile later in the relationship.' Relations between the sexes are depicted in aggressive, competitive terms. But significantly it is women who are deemed to be responsible for the 'battle of the sexes', thus justifying/excusing the men's bad behaviour.

The ironic tone discussed already pervades this article. The objectification of women – compared to cars, referred to as inanimate objects – is so 'extreme' that one is encouraged not to take it too seriously. The entire article seems to be protected by a knowing wink which makes it difficult to criticize for its offensive depiction of women. The humour here serves as an all-purpose barrier to anyone wanting to engage with its terms to mount an effective critique. It seems, in this way, calculating and motivated.

Another way in which criticism is headed off is through the use of the anti-heroic, self-deprecating discourse discussed above. In the discussion of how to get her to give you a blow job the writer asks: 'how clean are you really?' 'Is the old fella lolling about in piss-drenched pants?' Demonstrating an ability to laugh at men as well, this makes critique of the article's take on women more difficult.

The sheer volume and contradictoriness of the solutions offered also works as a defence. For each 'problem' at least two solutions are offered, such as the cold, heartless: 'Ditch the prude' (because 'she won't let you photograph her in the buff') to the rather more compassionate-sounding advice of an expert: 'Ensure that she understands that she is a loved and desirable person in her own right – a real flesh and blood lover who is infinitely preferable to any celluloid image.' These two differing accounts serve to give the impression that beneath their bravado these lads are truly sensitive and respectful of women – although the advice offered may simply be a more subtle means of getting what you want from a woman. Additionally, expert quotes such as 'over 99% of commercial porn is sexist crap' are designed to show easy familiarity with feminist arguments whilst nevertheless being pressed into service to get her to watch porn and consider acting it out. Discourses of laddism and sexism *together with* feminism and equality are *purposely reconciled* to rebut critique.

This article displays most of the qualities found in lad mags overall – emotional detachment, nostalgia, irony, humour, knowingness, a postfeminist sensibility and a conviction in natural gender differences. I would argue that these different elements work together as part of a motivated whole to offer a particular version of laddish masculinity and to protect the magazine and its readers from feminist and other critiques.

A final, crucial way in which the success of the lad mags should be understood is as a classed and racialized phenomenon. The magazines are constructed around an assumed white, working-class aesthetic and sensibility, centred on football, (beer) drinking, and heterosexual sex. They are explicitly hostile to middle-class articulations of masculinity which are regarded as insipid and inauthentic. The downmarket formula was taken even further by the launch in the UK of two new weekly men's magazines in 2004 – *Zoo* and *Nuts*. These dispense with all pretensions to serious, thoughtful or literary content, and feature a diet of sexy pin-ups, sports news, gadget reports, bizarre true stories, TV listings, hot cars and unashamedly sexist and homophobic jokes. The content is dominated by pictures and the written text is in the populist demotic pioneered in tabloid headlines (e.g. 'Becks, you lucky bugger!').

Not surprisingly, of course, most of the staff who put together the lad mags are – like other journalists – middle-class, and this produces some interesting tensions. Ben Crewe (2003) discusses the ambivalence of *Loaded*'s editors about class. On the one hand they sought to celebrate their working-class credentials and frequently denied or disavowed their impressive higher-education qualifications, but on the other they were quick to fall back on middle-class defences of themselves as intelligent, skilled professionals whenever the magazine was accused of yobbishness or sexism. Beynon (2002) argues that the success of the lad mags was achieved through the exploitation of working-class machismo by a profit-driven industry, populated by ambitious middle-class professionals. He suggests that what emerged in the 1990s was a 'yobocracy' of writers, comedians, football stars, and media people (e.g. Paul Gascoigne, Chris Evans and David Baddiel) who lived/performed the new lad lifestyle, but without any of the costs or consequences it would have for ordinary working-class men.

The whiteness of the new lad is also striking. Carrington (1999) has argued that the rise of new laddism can be interpreted as part of the reassertion of a white English male identity in which football and Britpop played a central role. In softer versions this became the 'Cool Britannia' discourse of the late 1990s. But more chillingly Carrington suggests that new laddism became intertwined with the rise of an 'aggressive, macho, xenophobic form of English nationalism' which then clothed itself in the language of 'heroic working-class resistance' to rebut criticisms of its racism and homophobia (Carrington 1999: 83). Something of the complexity of the relations between gender, race and class is captured in this analysis. What is at stake is not whether men 'really' enjoy the pursuits celebrated by *Loaded, Nuts* and *Zoo*, but whether the commodification of selected aspects of white male working-class culture, along with the appeal to authenticity, has facilitated the growing dominance of racist, homophobic and misogynist scripts.

Conclusion

This chapter has looked at magazines aimed at women, teenage girls and men. Some common themes have emerged from this discussion – for example, the significance of consumer society in understanding the origins of particular magazines, the importance of political economy for understanding the nature and content of magazines, and the ways in which magazines become involved in creating new subjectivities such as 'new lad', or 'sexually desiring, active female subject'.

It should be clear by this point, however, that there are also striking and profound differences between magazines addressed to girls and women and those addressed to men. In teen magazines and those aimed at women, femininity is presented as contingent – something that requires constant vigilance, attention and self-surveillance – to the look and feel of the body, to the performance of (safe and pleasurable) heterosexual intercourse, to the production of the self as a good friend, a good employee, and so on. By contrast, the 'new' men's lifestyle magazines aimed at heterosexual men construct masculinity in terms of playfulness, flight from responsibility, detached and uninhibited pleasure-seeking and the consumption of women's bodies. While men's magazines often use an ironic tone, women's do not – the production of desirable femininity is far too important to be joked about! As Tincknell et al. (2003) have remarked, the sexually assertive, feisty and knowing declarations of girl power sit uneasily next to the constant anxious solicitation of male approval that is found in young women's magazines, and the emphasis upon reading about boys and men to find out what they want and how better to please them. Men are presented in women's magazines as active subjects and holders of social capital, while women are presented in men's equivalents primarily as sexual objects – contained in the plethora of soft porn images – who need to be 'managed' to serve men's interests.

Of course, it is not necessarily the case that all readers will accept the subject positions on offer in women's and men's magazines, and there may be divergent and even subversive readings made of them. What is clear, however, is that the representations on offer are profoundly ideological   designed to naturalize gender difference and male power – even when this is presented in the postfeminist language of choice, freedom, sexual power and pleasing yourself, or in the ironic, self-deprecating tone of the men's magazines.

7

Postfeminist Romance

Iᴛ was once remarked that if a Martian landed in one of the affluent Western countries and turned to the media to find out about life on earth it would probably assume that we all got married at least twice a week – such is the volume of reports, photographs, magazines and fictional genres concerned with weddings. North American and European culture is saturated with wedding imagery in films, sitcoms, news about celebrity marriages, and an entire section of the magazine industry is devoted to bridalwear and wedding etiquette. Secondary wedding markets, such as the toy market, contribute to the cultural preoccupation with getting married – Barbie, alone, possesses no fewer than thirty wedding gowns: 'never married but always prepared' being her motto, and that which is inculcated into the minds of millions of little girls who are exhorted to purchase their own ('My Size Bride Barbie') wedding dresses with sizes that begin at age three (Ingraham 1999).

The 'wedding industrial complex', as Ingraham (1999) calls it, is just the tip of the iceberg of Western culture's obsession with heterosexual romance as a discourse. Romance is one of the key narratives by which we are interpellated or inscribed as subjects. It seems to have shown remarkable resilience in the face of significant cultural and demographic changes, including divorce on a hitherto unprecedented scale, an increase in the number of single-person households, and a diversification of family forms (including stepfamilies, lesbian and gay families, and the notion of 'friends as the new family').

This chapter is concerned with romance as a genre or dominant cultural narrative. It will examine how romance is changing in the light of 'transformations of intimacy' (Giddens 1991) and will focus in particular upon how the influence of feminism has impacted on discourses of romance. The chapter is divided into four parts. In the first, we examine feminist critiques of romance, looking at both early condemnations of the genre as false consciousness or escapist fantasy, and at more recent attempts to grapple with the pleasures of romance. The second section examines the Bridget Jones phenomenon. The Bridget Jones texts are interesting because they are structured by the conventions of the formula romance, but also engage with popular feminism. *Bridget Jones's Diary* is credited with having created a new genre of fiction targeted at women – 'chick lit' – and it is also important for this reason. Constructions of gender, sexuality and 'race' in the Bridget Jones texts are considered, and it is argued that Bridget Jones constitutes a prime example of *postfeminism*. Section three looks at the new genre of chick lit. Drawing on an analysis of twenty recent novels it assesses the extent to which chick lit really marks a departure from traditional romance writing, focusing in particular on the characterizations of the female protagonists. Finally the chapter offers a brief analysis of *Sex and the City* and *Ally McBeal*, asking whether and in what ways they may constitute new representations of gender.

Feminist Approaches to Romance

The Romance Writers of America (2002) define romantic novels as books 'where the love story is the main focus of the novel' and has 'an emotionally satisfying happy ending'. Within this definition there are many different types of romance, including historical romances, bodice rippers, 'sex and shopping' novels and newer sub-genres such as the sci-fi romance, erotic fiction for women and 'chick lit'. In this section I am going to look at feminist approaches to romance and will focus initially upon what Snitow (1986) calls 'hard' romances such as those produced by Harlequin and Mills & Boon.

The basic plot can be summarized as follows: a young, inexperienced, poor woman needs a handsome, wealthy man, ten or fifteen years her senior. The hero is mocking, cynical, contemptuous, hostile and even brutal, and the heroine is confused. By the end he reveals his love for her and misunderstandings are cleared away (Weibel 1977; Modleski 1982). The stories are set in an 'enchanted space' in which the heroine is socially dislocated – perhaps on holiday, having gone away from friends and family to recover from a traumatic event, or even waking from a coma (to find herself staying at the hero's villa or castle). The stories are constructed around a series of obstacles that must be overcome in order for the hero and the heroine to fall in love – these include class, national or racial differences, inhibitions, stubbornness and, last but not least, their mutual loathing! The romance narrative progresses through hostility, separation and reconciliation which brings with it 'the transformation of the man into an emotional being with a heart who declares his love for the heroine' alongside the restoration of a new sense of social identity for the female protagonist (Pearce and Stacey 1995). As Margaret Wetherell has argued:

> In fiction, and in films, romantic discourse often appears as a form of relief from the search for meaning; we move from the image of the couple (usually newly met) locked in a maelstrom of ambiguities, partial disclosures, interpretations and formulations of their relationship to the predictable ending of romance which stifles other interpretations and imposes its authority over other accounts. In the end he loved her. That is the final story and that is all we seem to need to say. (Wetherell 1995: 133)

Given this, it is perhaps not surprising that many commentators have drawn analogies between romances and pornography. Suzanne Moore (1991) suggests that romantic novels 'fetishize' particular emotions in the way that pornography fetishizes particular body parts and positions. In a slightly different vein, Snitow argues that sexual desire is sublimated in romances so that every look and touch signifies its existence and promise; 'pornography for women is different', she contends, because 'sex is bathed in romance' (Snitow 1986: 257). At a broader level, Alison Assiter (1988) suggests that the analogy works because both heterosexual pornography and romantic fiction eroticize the power relations between the sexes, in this way making them both palatable and pleasurable.

This theme, concerned with the ideological nature of romantic fiction, has been common to many feminist accounts of it over the last forty years. In the 1960s and 1970s romance novels were seen variously as a seductive trap which justified women's subordination to men and rendered women complicit in that subordination (Jackson 1995); as a kind of false consciousness – 'a cultural tool of male power to keep women from knowing their real conditions' (Firestone 1971: 139); or as a distraction which diverted women's energies from more worthwhile pursuits. In Germaine Greer's words, romantic fiction is 'dope for dupes' (cited in Jackson 1995) and the unambiguous suspicion and hostility towards it is summed up by the feminist quip: 'You start by sinking into his arms, and end up with your arms in his sink!'

Second-wave feminist antipathy and dismissiveness towards romantic fiction extended to its readers, who were regarded as passive, dependent and addicted to trivial, escapist fantasies. Feminine romance readers were counterposed against heroic feminist figures who had renounced any investment in femininity or romance. This move, and specifically the condemnation of women who were housewives, became such a familiar one that Charlotte Brunsdon (1993) has suggested that it needs to be understood psychoanalytically in terms of the mother–daughter relationship, in which younger feminists were acting out troubled and ambivalent relationships with an older generation of women.

Complicating the story

Two landmark publications disrupted the common sense feminist critique of romance. These were Tania Modleski's *Loving with a Vengeance* (1982) and Janice Radway's (1984) *Reading the Romance*. Both books can be understood as part of a wider attempt to take popular cultural forms seriously, to resist double standards which operated to condemn or dismiss women's genres, and to 'rescue' feminine forms as worthy of attention.

Loving with a Vengeance is a textual analysis of three such forms – soaps, Gothic novels and Harlequin romances. It draws on feminist psychoanalytic theory to speculate about the kinds of pleasures such genres offer to women. Modleski argues that Harlequin romances are not simply escapist fantasies designed to dope women but fictions that engage in complex and contradictory ways with real problems – offering temporary, magical, fantasy or symbolic solutions.

Harlequin romances – whatever their other differences – are invariably built upon the idea that the hero and heroine get off to a Bad Start. He is angry or mocking or contemptuous and she is hurt and confused. Indeed, Modleski argues that the question of why the hero is so hostile constitutes one of two structuring enigmas in these novels. The novels offer many potential ways of understanding this: he is overworked, hurt, emotionally inferior, or using sexuality to degrade or humiliate women. However, one of the pleasures the novels offer to seasoned readers is their superior knowledge as 'experts' familiar with the genre. Because they are positioned as knowing more than the heroine, theirs is not a straightforward identification with her: they know that the hero is behaving so badly because he is unsettled by the heroine and will come to realize that he loves her. Modleski (1982) argues that this superior wisdom can transform for readers even the most problematic aspects of romances – for example the way they draw on ideas about rape. In rape the intention to dominate, humiliate and degrade is often disguised as sexual desire. In romances this is reversed: sexual desire is disguised as hostility and dominance. But readers with privileged knowledge understand this already, and can take pleasure in the way that everything the heroine says and does serves only to increase the hero's desire/hostility towards her.

Another key way in which romantic fiction may offer pleasures to heterosexual women is through the enactment of symbolic revenge. Modleski argues that, contrary to stereotypes, romantic heroines are *not* passive and masochistic, but active protagonists. She points out that the smallest liberty taken by the heroine is described as a real act of resistance – as being performed militantly, rebelliously or defiantly (even if it is only a rebellious upturning of the chin or a defiant flick of the hair). She argues that the so-called masochism of the texts is 'a cover for anxieties, desires and wishes which, if openly expressed, would challenge the psychological and social order of things' (Modleski 1982). Moreover, although the heroine clearly suffers in such novels, the hero is equally tormented by his love for her. Romances might be understood as a kind of revenge fantasy in which the woman obtains power and vengeance from the conviction that she is bringing the hero to his knees; by the end, he is grovelling with her to accept his love and forgiveness. One of the classic strategies of vengeance is for the woman to disappear so that the hero comes to realize how import-ant she is to him and his love for her. In this fantasy, the woman becomes all-powerful, the centre of the man's world.

The third significant pleasure romances may offer women can be understood in relation to the other structuring enigma of such novels – namely how it is that the hero comes to realize that the hero-ine is different from all other women. This is not an abstract fictional dilemma but a real problem for many women who are placed in a double bind: their most important achievement is supposed to be finding a husband, yet their greatest fault is in attempting to do so.

One of the most pernicious aspects of contemporary romantic fiction is the way in which everything the heroine feels is demon-strated to be false – at its base this means that when she says no she really means yes. A classic scene would feature him attempting to kiss her and her struggling and saying 'no, no,' and then melting into his arms knowing all along that this has been right.

> His skin was smooth, more roughly textured than hers, but sleek and flexible beneath her palms, his warmth and maleness enveloping her and making her overwhelmingly aware that only the thin material of the culotte suit separated them. He held her face between his hands, and his hardening mouth was echoed throughout the length and breadth of his body. She felt herself yielding weakly beneath him, and his hand slid from her shoulder across her throat to find the zipper at the front of her suit, impelling it steadily downward. 'No, Logan', she breathed, but he pulled her hands, with which she might have resisted him, around him, arching her body so that he could observe her reac-tion to the thrusting aggression of his with sensual satisfaction. 'No?' He probed with gentle mockery, his mouth, seeking the pointed full-ness of her breasts now exposed to his gaze. 'Why not? It's what we both want, don't deny it.' (Mather 1977)

As readers, we are forced to collude with the idea that the hero knows better than the woman herself what she really wants. Yet Modleski (1982) argues that this is not the whole story and not reason enough to condemn romances outright. Drawing on the work of the feminist psychoanalyst Nancy Chodorow, she proposes that romances promise the kind of transcendent, nurturing love that women may receive in infancy from their mothers, and which they then give to men in later life, but do not receive in return. In romances this inequality of emotional care is resolved in fantasy through the figure of the nurturing male lover who can meet her needs and satisfy them. It is also significant that romantic union usually occurs at precisely the moment when the heroine has taken no care whatsoever with her appearance – the Harlequin equivalent of the chick lit protagonist who, after weeks of trying to engineer the perfect meeting with her dream man, meets him on the one and only occasion that she has gone out of the house with her hair unwashed and no makeup, just to buy milk! This, Modleski argues, gives readers the vicarious pleasure of temporarily transcending the traditional splitting of themselves – where they are both object and subject of the gaze. It offers, in a sense, a chance to symbolically 'let yourself go', secure in the knowledge that he will love you anyway – there is no need to constantly monitor yourself.

Janice Radway's (1984) groundbreaking book *Reading the Romance* combines textual analysis of Harlequin novels with an interview-based ethnographic study of committed romance readers, and a detailed examination of publishing and bookselling as economic enterprises. Her work has been regarded as an exemplary example of media/cultural analysis in its attempt to grapple with different 'moments' of the cultural process – production, distribution, text and audience – in a way that allows romantic fiction to be understood as simultaneously an economic, cultural, ideological and pleasurable phenomenon.

Radway's ethnographic analysis focused on a group of avid romance readers whom she calls the 'Smithton women' all of whom used the services of 'Dot' to advise them on which romance novels to purchase. Using a combination of semi-structured interviews, group discussions and observation, Radway attempted to uncover the meanings the women gave to their romance reading. She found that far from being unintelligent dopes the women were sophisticated readers of romance, able to make subtle differentiations within the genre and to pick up on small nuances and cues from the cover pictures and blurbs in order to determine whether books would meet their particular tastes and needs. Moreover, the women thoroughly rejected the stereotype of them as unintelligent and superficial and placed considerable emphasis on the educational benefits of their romance reading, both in terms of allowing them to learn about different places and historical time periods, and also in 'modelling' reading-behaviour for their children. Many of the women expressed the hope that by showing the pleasure they derived from books they would encourage their children to read more and do better at school.

Radway's work is ambivalently positioned in relation to romantic fiction. On the one hand she is critical of Harlequin novels, arguing that they are profoundly conservative, posing some of the problems of life in a patriarchal society only to resolve them through an idealized depiction of heterosexual love. On the other hand she understands women's use of these novels as – in part – oppositional. Like Modleski she finds that one of the pleasures of romance reading is wish-fulfilment in which, in 'escaping' into the heroine's life, readers vicariously experience what it is to be really loved and nurtured in the way they crave.

The act of reading can also be understood as 'combative' and 'compensatory'; a way of carving out some time or space for themselves: 'In picking up a book . . . they refuse temporarily their family's otherwise constant demands that they tend to the wants of others even as they act deliberately to do something for their own private pleasure . . . Romance reading addresses needs created in them but not met by patriarchal institutions and engendering practices' (Radway 1984: 211). As we saw in chapter 1, Radway's work has become the focus of a number of important debates in media and cultural studies. These are concerned with what feminist cultural criticism should involve (e.g. critique, celebration or affirmation, respect, etc.) and the nature of the relationship between the cultural critic and her respondents.

Romance revisited

In the twenty years or so since Modleski and Radway were writing, discussions of romance have changed. One important factor has been the development of the World Wide Web, which has facilitated many writers and readers of romantic fiction to become involved in debates that were previously the sole province of academics and college students. E-zines, chat rooms and bulletin boards are today the sites of fierce debate on questions such as whether romances can be considered feminist. One posting by the romance writer (and physics PhD) Catherine Asaro on the All About Romance site gives a flavour:

> I have never had the least doubt that romance is feminist. It is the only genre I know where what the heroine values is given priority. It is, in fact, the driving force of the story. She is rewarded for what she values by achieving her goals, as well as winning the hero, who is usually a hunk, among other things . . . Romance acknowledges the 'female gaze'. We hear a lot about the male gaze in literature. What romance does is acknowledge that women also experience sexual feelings. This is far more significant than many critics of the genre realise. Romance says 'hey, it's okay for women to be sexual beings'. It doesn't make heroines pay a price for their sexuality or condemn them for it. (Asaro 1997)

New questions are being asked about romance, connected not simply to gender relations but also to sexuality and 'race'. In what ways are conventional romances *racialized* discourses? How are their constructions of love and desire connected to white fantasies of racial others? (Blackman 1995; Perry 1995; Ingraham 1999; Maddison and Storr 2002). Does romance writing by black women (women of colour) challenge or disrupt traditional generic and normative expectations? (Charles 1995; Nkweto-Simmond 1995; Barr 2000; Squire 2003). Research is also exploring the way that romantic discourse as a Western discourse is being contradictorily taken up and resisted in other postcolonial contexts, complexly negotiated with other traditional discourses of intimacy and kinship (e.g. Kim 2005).

Discussions of lesbian writing also explore the *heterosexism* of romance, and investigate the ways in which erotic discourses in the wake of HIV and AIDS may be challenging or reinscribing conventional narratives (Wilton 1994; Griffin 2000). One of the key questions might be 'can romance be queered?' in the way that other cultural forms (arguably) have been. This would involve not simply replacing heterosexual protagonists with homosexual ones, but, more fundamentally, questioning the very binaries on which conventional romance depends (male/female, gay/straight, virgin/whore, etc.) as well as the premise of fixed identity, and the idea that a declaration of monogamy represents narrative closure. It may be hard to imagine what such texts would look like but there have been a number of notable attempts to experiment with the genre, for example Sally Potter's film *Thriller*, and Jeanette Winterson's novel *Written on the Body*.

Attempts to experiment and innovate with/in the genre have partly come about because of the growing realization of the power of romance as a discourse. What makes it so powerful, Stevi Jackson (1995) has argued, is its narrativity or storied nature – it is one of the most compelling discourses by which Western subjects are inscribed. Its tenacity in the face of social, cultural and demographic changes that include high rates of divorce, the growth of new family forms and broader transformations of intimacy shows that there is no necessary correspondence between changing patterns of sexual relations and romantic desire. In fact, rather than diminishing in importance, the significance of romantic love is undergoing a rapid intensification according to Ulrich Beck and Elizabeth Beck-Gernsheim (1995). They argue that, as the structures of industrial societies break down alongside an increasingly competitive labour market and rising social secularization, traditional sources of security are disappearing fast. In this context 'romantic love is gaining ever greater significance as a "secular" religion' (Beck and Beck-Gernsheim 1995: 173). Ingraham's (1999) research on weddings as a recession-proof industry, alongside many US postings to romance discussion boards in the wake of the World Trade Center attacks would seem to affirm this reading of romance as offering a secure meta-narrative in unsettling times.

The other key to the enduring significance of romance as a discourse lies in its ability to adapt or mutate or evolve (Pearce and Stacey 1995). This can be seen in the changes in romantic fiction over the past two decades: heroines are more independent and assertive, they are more likely to be sexually experienced, increasingly they work outside the home and have satisfying careers, and are seeking more equal partnerships (Jones 1986). In this way romantic fiction has incorporated many of the themes of liberal feminism without having to jettison the central narrative about the search for Mr Right.

In the next section we will look at one direction in which contemporary romantic fiction is evolving: the Bridget Jones effect.

Enter Bridget Jones

Perhaps the most significant and far-reaching adaptation of the romance genre was the publication of Helen Fielding's book *Bridget Jones's Diary* in 1996. Romance buying had begun to dwindle among twenty to thirty-year-olds in the 1990s and a new formula was needed to attract younger readers. *Bridget Jones's Diary* – along with Candace Bushnell's *Sex and the City* – supplied it, and gave birth to the genre of 'chick lit' or 'city girl fiction' as well as to a new prominence for the figure of the thirtysomething single (almost exclusively) white female across a range of cultural forms. Its success impacted on film, advertising and television, where the notion of 'must-she TV' was coined and schedulers created themed weekends and weekly 'girls' nights in' sponsored by advertisers wanting to target affluent women in the twenty to forty age bracket.

Bridget Jones's Diary started life as a column in *The Independent* newspaper, purporting to be an account of the life and preoccupations of a real woman. Although Bridget was a fictional character, the columns achieved a strong sense of realism through a combination of their intimate, confessional style, references to contemporary events and concerns, and the inclusion of a photograph of an attractive thirtysomething woman smoking and holding a wine glass (she was in fact a secretary at the paper). The plausibility of the character is attested to by the number of marriage proposals Bridget is alleged to have received and the instant recognition she generated among many young heterosexual women.

The success of *BJD* was phenomenal. Its stayed on the *New York Times* best-seller list for more than four months, and to date has sold more than 5 million copies in thirty languages. When the film of the book opened in Britain, it took £5.7 million in its first weekend, outstripping both *Four Weddings and a Funeral* and *Notting Hill*, the previous benchmarks of British film success. Ultimately the movie grossed $160 million worldwide (Chambers 2004). The follow-up book and film sequel were also huge successes.

More telling than any of these economic indicators, however, was the veritable explosion of discourses about Bridget Jones. She became an icon, a recognizable emblem of a particular kind of femininity, a constructed point of identification for all women. Newspapers set out to find the 'real' Bridget Jones or sent 'real Bridget Joneses' to review the films. Bridget generated instant recognition among many young heterosexual women; as Imelda Whelehan (2002) has argued, part of the success of the book lay in the 'that's me' phenomenon whereby Bridget became regarded not as a fictional character but a representative of the zeitgeist.

Bridget Jones's Diary (the book) takes place within the space of one year, and opens with Bridget's new year's resolutions which serve to give readers an insight into her character, the themes of the book and the style of the diary. Bridget's aim is to improve her life – find a better job, more exciting leisure activities, and – most importantly – a boyfriend. She also aspires (and this is inextricably connected) to *work on herself* so as to lose weight, give up smoking, cut down on her alcohol consumption and 'develop inner poise'. The humorous style of the book can be seen in the juxtaposition of her new year's resolutions which include the sublime – 'give proportion of earnings to charity' and the ridiculous – 'learn to program video' (Whelehan 2002). As Imelda Whelehan has pointed out, Bridget can be understood as 'chaotically aspirational' – she struggles in every situation to achieve control and do things right yet persists in invariably getting everything wrong.

Much of Bridget's social life is directed towards finding a 'truly functional' relationship with a man. In the spirit of the romantic tradition there are two men to choose from – the hero and the bastard. The hero's name, Mark Darcy, is just one example of the way in which the book signals its debt to *Pride and Prejudice*. True to the genre, Bridget chooses the wrong man, gets hurt and humiliated (on a number of occasions) and fails to notice that the hero is in love with her. In the end, he rescues her, and the book offers the closure of a 'happily ever after'. So far then, so familiar. However, as I have argued elsewhere, there are a number of features of the Bridget Jones texts that mark a rupture with earlier forms of romantic fiction and which locate Bridget Jones as a distinctively postfeminist phenomenon.

How, then, should *Bridget Jones's Diary* be understood? Does it simply update the genre for an audience in the late nineties/early noughties or represent a break with traditional romance? In what ways (if any) does it constitute a *new* depiction of gender relations and how is it situated in relation to feminism? Set in metropolitan London at the turn of the century, how does it engage with issues about class, 'race' and sexuality?

Bridget Jones: postfeminist heroine

Bridget Jones's Diary could not have been written without the impact of second-wave feminism, but this in itself does not make the Bridget Jones texts feminist ones. Bridget takes for granted her right to work, her access to contraception and her entitlement to various kinds of equality. She also has access to many feminist ideas and discourses that have entered common sense in Western democracies. But her relationship to such discourses is deeply ambivalent. Of marriage, for example, she is mistrustful and occasionally critical: 'smug marrieds' are a target for repeated attack and she acknowledges that many of her married friends are unhappy. However, these insights do nothing to disrupt her quest to find the perfect man and marry him. In the film of *Bridget Jones* this is depicted by having Bridget fantasize a wedding, complete with wedding bells, white dress and bridesmaids. As Angela McRobbie (2004a, 2004c) has argued, the humour in these moments is a function of the way in which Bridget signals this is a Bad Thought – she has the fantasy *in spite of feminism*, which is supposed to have eradicated such desires. In this way feminism is set up as censor or 'psychic policewoman', disallowing girls the pleasures of traditional femininity.

Esther Sonnet (2002) notes a similar pattern in contemporary erotic fiction for women. Whilst buying into a feminist notion of women's entitlement to sexual pleasure, the *Black Lace* novels she examines explicitly disavow feminism and indeed suggest that part of the fun of erotic fiction is that it cares nothing for feminist 'political correctness'. Sonnet describes this as the 'naughty but nice effect', where 'disapproval from Big Sister intensifies the secret/guilty pleasures offered to the "postfeminist" consumer of the forbidden pleasures of the unreconstructed "feminine" '(Sonnet 2002: 173).

Bridget's ambivalent feminist sensibility is also displayed in relation to the body and femininity. In (at least) one diary entry, Bridget makes clear that she knows there is nothing 'natural' about femininity – it requires constant work, maintenance and vigilance:

> Being a woman is worse than being a farmer – there is so much harvesting and crop spraying to be done: legs to be waxed, underarms shaved, eyebrows plucked, feet pumiced, skin exfoliated and moisturised, spots cleansed, roots dyed, eyelashes tinted, nails filed, cellulite massaged,

> stomach muscles exercised. The whole performance is so highly tuned you only need to neglect it for a few days for the whole thing to go to seed. Sometimes I wonder what I would be like if left to revert to nature – with a full beard and handlebar moustache on each shin. (Fielding 1996: 30)

Notwithstanding this, the look and shape of the body is presented as the key source of identity for women in a manner that parallels women's magazines and advertising discourses. Bridget may know that 'fat is a feminist issue', but nevertheless she enters obsessively into a programme of self-monitoring in which her weight, calorie count, alcohol intake, etc. are measured and noted each day.

This aspect of the book was greeted by many as a satire on the regimes of bodily control and emotional self-help by which contemporary young women are interpellated. But the satire is not straightforward. Indeed, as Imelda Whelehan (2002) has argued, the body is represented as chaotic and in need of constant discipline; Bridget might just get away with verbal and social gaffes, but neglect of the physical is treated as unforgivable.

The failure of satire in relation to body shape and size can be seen most clearly in the film of Bridget Jones. One of the features of the books is in the acknowledgement that, at somewhere between a British size 10 and size 12, Bridget is far from being fat, and is, in fact, considerably slimmer than the national average. In this way women's distorted and troubled relationship to their own bodies is perhaps made available to readers. However, in the film it is the 'spectacle' of the 'fat' heroine that becomes the focus. Renée Zellweger's body is treated extraordinarily voyeuristically. Her clothes are cut a size too small so that she always seems to be bursting out of them (as spectacle of excess and lack of control) and her body is pawed fetishistically by the camera, particularly in the notorious scene in which she descends down a fire-station pole, her bottom filling the screen.

Reactions to the film were split between those (often feminists) who felt moved to comment on their joy at seeing cellulite on film for the first time (the 'cellulite on celluloid' reaction, as I call it), and those others who devoted their plaudits to the 'bravery' of Renée Zellweger and then her 'achievement' at slimming down to normal Hollywood (i.e. underweight) proportions so quickly. As Stephen Maddison and Merl Storr have pointed out,

> The ecstatic rumblings about Zellweger's 'hello mummy' pants and minusculely rotund tummy do nothing to trouble the underlying discourses of regulation and punishment that often characterized contemporary representations of women's bodies; indeed the level of commentary on Zellweger's non-existent bulges precisely marks the expressiveness of such regulation. (Maddison and Storr 2002: 2)

And, we might add ironically, it is *feminists* who are accused of unfairly policing women!

Writers working in a Foucaultian tradition argue that contemporary neoliberalism offers new forms of constraint that work not by simple top–down domination, but through discourses of self-control, self-discipline and choice (Bartky 1990; Rose 1996; Probyn 1997a); Valerie Walkerdine, Helen Lucey and June Melody (2001) argue that subjects bear 'serious burdens of liberty' in which they are exhorted to render their lives knowable and meaningful through a narrative of free choice and radical autonomy – however constrained they might actually be. What Nikolas Rose (1990) has called the 'aspiration to self-control' can be seen very clearly in the Bridget Jones texts, in Bridget's endless self-surveillance and monitoring of everything from her calorific intake to the number of positive thoughts she has had or how many serious or worthy current affairs articles she has read.

> *Thurs 16 Feb*
> 8 st 12 (weight loss through use of stairs), alcohol units 0 (excellent), cigarettes five (excellent), calories 2452 (not vg), times gone downstairs to check for Valentine-type envelope 18 (bad psychologically but vg exercise wise). (Fielding 1996: 51)

A crucial aspect of the self-surveillance in Bridget Jones's diary is its psychological nature. Whilst the body must be continually worked on and monitored, ultimately what is required is a remodelling of the self. This becomes clear on the one occasion when Bridget reaches her ideal weight. 'Today is an historic and joyous day. After 18 years of trying to get down to 8 st 7 I have finally achieved it. It is no trick of the scales, but confirmed by jeans. I am thin!' (Fielding 1996: 105).

As Louise Chambers (2004) has argued, here body weight and size is presented as a fundamental aspect of Bridget's very *being*, yet – poignantly – achieving 'thinness' does not produce the satisfaction she craves. She goes to a party only to be told she looks tired and seems flat and unlike herself. '18 years of struggle, sacrifice and endeavour – for what? 18 years and the result is "tired and flat". I feel like a scientist who discovers that his life's work has been a total mistake' (Fielding 1996: 106). Chambers argues that this marks a turning point in Bridget's attempt to build self-esteem externally through her body, and the turn, through self-help therapeutics, to reconstruct her *interiority*. She constitutes herself as an object/subject of psychology, who must work on herself to achieve the goals of fulfilment and completion.

One of the interesting features of these texts is the way they make an *articulation* between feminism and femininity. There is a constant to-and-fro movement between feminist discourses and discourses of traditional femininity, but they are not treated on equal terms. Feminist ideas are treated as inauthentic, punitive and disciplining or as hollow and not really speaking women's desires or true selves. This is captured on one occasion when Bridget tells Daniel she is fed up with his fuckwittage – and feels – temporarily – happy and 'empowered' (Fielding 1996: 76–7):

> 5 p.m. feeling v. empowered . . . think might read a bit of Susan Faludi's Backlash
> 5 a.m. Oh God, I'm so unhappy about Daniel. I love him.

In the twelve hours between these diary entries, Bridget realizes that her feeling of confidence and power is illusory, a self-deception, and what she really needs is not feminism, but Daniel.

Sometimes, though, feminism is figured as something which can be used to help Bridget pursue the goals of femininity, as in the example below in which being independent and self-possessed is identified as a strategy for attracting a man: 'Must not sulk about not having a boyfriend, but develop inner poise and authority and sense of self as woman of substance, complete without boyfriend, as best way to obtain boyfriend' (Fielding 1996: 2). This resonates strongly with the discussion of advertising in chapter 3 and also with the discourses of femininity on offer in contemporary women's magazines. In these, self-confidence is a 'technology of the self' required for attracting a man.

The Bridget Jones texts do not, then, ignore or even straightforwardly disavow feminist ideas, but take them into account only to repudiate them – unless they can be articulated in this way to normative femininity. 'Bridget is forever identifying injustices, dissecting them and then endorsing them' (Whelehan 2002: 27). As Maddison and Storr have argued, there is a double movement within the texts which on one hand stresses the 'guilty necessity of being a "feminist" in order to avoid total degradation and humiliation' (Maddison and Storr 2002: 3), while on the other always naturalizes the unattractiveness of feminism. 'There is nothing so unattractive to a man as strident feminism', as Bridget puts it (Fielding 1996: 20). This is reinforced by the book's one 'feminist' character – Shazzer – who is portrayed as unfeminine and dysfunctional, as well as (at times) not *really* a feminist since despite her 'rants' about men she is clearly equally desperate to find heterosexual love, as evidenced, for example, by an occasion on which Bridget catches her dialling last number recall on her phone to see if the man she is after has called (another example of the portrayal of feminism as inauthentic or fake).

The texts' conservatism is also evident in relation to 'race' and sexuality. The whiteness of the texts is 'unmarked, unspoken and all pervasive' (Maddison and Storr 2002: 2). It is naturalized through a combination of Bridget's 'ditzy' character and crude ethnic stereotyping. Maddison and Storr argue that the construction of Bridget's white Englishness owes much to Victorian colonial ideas of white women as anxious and neurotic – in Bridget's case as unable to cope with the demands of her job, her urban living environment or her social obligations.

Bridget and her white friends have no interactions with British members of ethnic minorities at all, despite living in a metropolis (London) where 30 per cent of the population are non-white. Instead, people of colour in the texts are constructed as 'funny foreigners' (Maddison and Storr 2002). In *Bridget Jones's Diary* this role is played by Julio, Bridget's mother's Latin lover who operates as a foil to highlight the superior white masculinity of Mark Darcy – who reveals, at the climax of the book, that Julio is a conman. 'The contrast between Mark and Julio also demonstrates that the exotic Other may be sexually attractive – "wild, drunk, unkempt and, frankly, just the type I fall for", as Bridget writes of this final showdown – but wholly unsuitable for a serious romantic relationship' (Maddison and Storr 2002: 6).

This racialized dynamic is much more apparent in the second novel, *The Edge of Reason*, in which Bridget encounters two kinds of 'funny foreigner': Wellington, the 'wise African' and a number of 'perverted Orientals'. Maddison and Storr argue:

> The failure of Fielding's satire is particularly marked in Wellington: while Bridget slyly contrasts his taste for CD Walkmans and jet skis with his supposedly solemn pronouncements on tribal traditions and ancient cultures, she nevertheless gratefully accepted his 'very still and strong' sympathy over her troubles with Mark and contrasts his 'dignified graciousness' with the twittering white women and drunken white men at her mother's parties. (Maddison and Storr 2002: 6)

The orientalism, by contrast, is highly sexualized and has Bridget and Mark alternately threatened and adored by Southeast Asian characters. The threats, posed by the Filipino 'boy' (*sic*) who is Mark's housekeeper's son and by Bridget's fellow inmates in prison in Thailand both take a homosexual form. In the Thai jail where Bridget ponders such questions as how much weight she will effortlessly lose during her stay, she is awoken by the 'Lesbian Ring' who 'all started kissing and groping bits of me' (Fielding 2000: 311). The threat this poses, however, is quickly abated when Bridget starts teaching her cell mates the words to Madonna's songs. They are thus transformed from sexualized and racialized threats into sexualized and racialized worshippers: 'seemed to be considered some kind of Goddess as knew words to *Immaculate Collection* all the way through' (Fielding 2000: 311). (This also marks an example of the triumph of Bridget's lower middle-class love of popular rather than high culture, a central class theme of the book.)

Like whiteness, heterosexuality is unmarked and naturalized in the novels, and is not challenged by the existence of Tom, Bridget's gay friend, who is one-dimensional, feminized and a self-confessed 'fag hag'. According to Bridget, he has a theory that 'homosexuals and single women in their thirties have natural bonding: both being accustomed to disappointing their parents and being treated as freaks by society' (Fielding 1996: 27). But here, homophobia is enacted rather than analysed. Maddison and Storr show how homosexuality is made 'contingently visible' as either 'pretentious and body fascist (Jerome) or as a misogynistic disavowal of the feminine (Mark going after Rebecca the non-woman), while heterosexuality remains unmarked and naturalised' (Maddison and Storr 2002: 4). They also analyse the double standard by which one married male character's infidelity with another man is treated entirely differently from other instances of men's sexual misdemeanours – as tawdry and disgusting, rather than as a typical example of 'smug married' behaviour.

Moreover, and somewhat contradictorily, the use of a gay male character (Tom) to signal the liberalism and sophistication of Bridget's milieu (in contrast to the suburban homophobia signified by her mother's life) does nothing to challenge the lesophobia which is a striking feature of the Bridget Jones texts. In *Bridget Jones* lesbianism is treated as something disgusting and personally threatening to heterosexual women, whilst a veneer of 'tolerance' and liberalism is simultaneously maintained. When Bridget is being touched by other women in the Thai jail she comments: 'although obviously I felt violated, part of me could not help but feel it was so nice just to be touched. Gaaaah! Maybe I am a lesbian? No. Don't think so' (Fielding 2000: 310).

This dynamic – in which lesbianism is attractive/threatening/disgusting, but 'we are all fine about it' – is found in many other chick lit novels. In *Angels* by Marion Keyes, the main character, Maggie, meets her first 'real, live lesbian' and is made deeply uncomfortable, expending considerable energy speculating about porn films and dildos and 'disgusting' 'lezzer sex', 'like licking a mackerel' (Keyes 2002: 169). A single one night stand with the woman in question, however, miraculously eradicates her lesophobia and she humourously critiques her own 'sexual tourism' whilst (without a shred of irony) accusing her friends of being homophobic. In this way, the novel is able to parade unreflexive lesophobia whilst simultaneously parading its liberal credentials. As with feminism, a knowingness and an easy familiarity with the terminology of sexual-political critique helps to lend credibility to texts that might otherwise be regarded as straightforwardly homophobic, racist and anti-feminist.

Chick Lit: Romance for the Twenty-first Century?

The reverberations of the success of *Bridget Jones's Diary* were felt power-fully in the publishing industry, sections of which had been concerned by the dwindling sales of romance novels amongst twenty to thirty-year-olds in the 1990s and were looking for new formulas to attract younger readers. *Bridget Jones's Diary* supplied this and spawned huge numbers of 'copycat' novels centred on the life a thirtysomething female who was unhappily single, appealingly neurotic, and preoccu-pied with the shape, size and look of her body, and with finding a man.

Louise Chambers (2004) argues that *Bridget Jones's Diary* was so important in establishing chick lit as a genre that one of its defining features might be said to be some kind of bookcover reference to Bridget Jones, for example 'IF YOU LIKED BRIDGET JONES'S DIARY, YOU'LL LOVE THIS' or 'THIS YEAR'S BRIDGET JONES'. Other key factors which helped to create and stabilize chick lit as a new, identifiable category of romance fiction included highly similar cover designs featuring either day-glo or pastel shades and hand-drawn illustrations; the devel-opment of book clubs (e.g. Mango) devoted entirely to selling such fictions to young women; new purchasing strategies in supermarkets which gave prominence to chick lit titles as good reads for women; and the rapid proliferation of chick lit lists on the Amazon and other Internet bookseller sites. Perhaps more explicitly than at any other time in its history, the publishing industry evolved a sexually differ-entiated form of address – a kind of his 'n' hers publishing. By the late 1990s the genre was well established.

In this section I am going to analyse the themes, concerns and characterizations of chick lit novels, drawing on twenty books published between 1997 and 2005 (see list in Box 7.1). The analysis builds on a discussion by Elena Herdieckerhoff and myself (Gill and Herdieckerhoff 2006). The aim is to examine whether the claims made about chick lit as something revolutionary and new hold up, and to explore the constructions of women and gender relations within this genre. I will examine five themes: the construction of sexual experi-ence; depictions of the heroine's intelligence and independence; beauty and appearance; work; and singleness.

Sex in chick lit

In traditional romances the typical heroine is characterized by sexual innocence and passivity. Usually this means that she is a virgin or, as Jane Ussher has argued, she must 'feign innocence and reticence. She lies to hide her desire and always tries to cover up any signs of sexual interest . . . She may want sex, but within the codes of romance, she

---

Box 7.1 Popular publishing after Bridget Jones

V. A. Baglietto, *The Wrong Mr Right*, London: Coronet, 2002.

M. Barrowcliffe, *Infidelity for First Time Fathers*, London: Headline, 2001.

M. Gayle, *My Legendary Girlfriend*, London: Flame, 1998.

M. Gayle, *Mr Commitment*, London: Flame, 1999.

J. Green, *Jemima J.*, London: Penguin, 1998.

J. Green, *Babyville*, London: Penguin, 2002.

W. Holden, *Bad Heir Day*, London: Headline, 2000.

A. Jenkins, *Honey Moon*, London: Flame, 2000.

M. Keyes, *Angels*, London: Penguin, 2002.

S. Kinsella, *The Secret Dreamworld of a Shopaholic*, London: Black Swan, 2000.

I. Knight, *Don't You Want Me?* London: Penguin, 2002.

J. Mansell, *Perfect Timing*, London: Headline, 1997.

J. Moore, *dot.homme*, London: Arrow Books, 2005.

M. Nathan, *Persuading Annie*, London: Piatkus Books, 2001.

F. North, *Polly*, London: Arrow Books, 1999.

A. Parks, *Game Over*, London: Penguin, 2002.

T. Parsons, *Man and Wife*, London: HarperCollins, 2003.

D. Waugh, *The New You Survival Kit*, London: HarperCollins, 2002.

A. Weir, *Does my Bum Look Big in This?* London: Flame, 1997.

A. Weir, *Stupid Cupid*, London: Penguin, 2002.

---

can only have it if she is seduced' (1997: 44). In a world increasingly saturated by sexualized imagery and in which other texts aimed at women (e.g. glossy magazines) are preoccupied with sexual satisfaction, this emphasis on sexual innocence might seem anachronistic. How different, then, are the portrayals of women's sexual identities in chick lit novels? At first glance, they would seem to be entirely different. Far from being virginal, most of the heroines are sexually experienced, describing themselves as 'a great lay' (Waugh 2002: 187) or as able to 'sit here reading about oral, anal, sucking, fucking' (Green, 1998: 60) or casually engaging in one night stands. They no longer need to be seduced and can initiate sexual contact, as Stella in *Don't You Want Me?* does when she says: 'I'm not saying let's get married, Frank. But I am saying, let's go to bed' (Knight 2002: 225).

However, this apparently 'liberated' attitude towards sex is not the whole story. Interestingly, whatever their degree of sexual experience, heroines are frequently 're-virginized' in the narrative when it comes to the encounter with their hero. With him, they return to what we might characterize as an emotionally virginal state, which wipes away previous 'sullying' experiences by making them enjoy sex fully for the very first time, or which allows them to 'admit' their sexual timidity or inexperience after previously having boasted about their sexual expertise. For example, Jo Smiley in *New You Survival Kit* has her very first orgasm with Charlie, and, after years of sex, 'she finally understands what all the fuss was about' (Waugh 2002: 190). Meanwhile,

Kate, in *The Wrong Mr Right* also has a new and totally different experience: 'during her previous sexual encounters she had felt awkward . . . But Tom was a different partner altogether. She had never felt as aroused as this. And she had not expected his touch to wipe away any trace of denial' (Baglietto 2002: 257). Hence, the narrative constructs the heroine as re-virginized and sexually innocent, and only the hero can make her into a real woman. Whilst it is true that the heroines are allowed to 'be capable of desire and even of pursuing men' (Jones 1986: 210), they are nonetheless narratively put into a virginal position when they encounter their hero – their innocence is narratively restored to allow for the reader to relish in the traditional scenario of the 'specialness' of the sexual encounter between hero and heroine.

It would seem, then, that the codes of traditional romance are reinstated 'through the backdoor' with what we call 're-virginization', and further that chick lit, like traditional romance, offers precisely the promise of transcendent love and sexual satisfaction discussed by Modleski (1982). One of the things that makes this important and fascinating is that implicitly it suggests that sexual liberation (here represented by the notion of pursuing sexual pleasure through more than one partner) is not really what women want. Not only does it not speak to women's true desires, but also it is often presented as mere posturing or performance – something that women in a post-*Cosmopolitan* (magazine) world are required to enact, even though it is not what they want. More analysis is needed to examine to what extent feminism is also implicated in this critique, as one of the discourses promoting women's sexual freedom and agency. Certainly from the novels analysed here it appears that (what are coded as) feminist goals in relation to sexuality are presented as inauthentic, in the sense of not speaking to women's deepest desires.

Independent women?

Radway (1984) claims that most of the heroines of romances are 'spirited', 'fiery' and intelligent. Perhaps surprisingly – particularly in the context of claims that heroines are more independent and assertive (Jones 1986) – chick lit heroines seem somewhat less spirited than their Harlequin counterparts. Many heroines are depicted as naive and constantly surprised by events (e.g. Keyes 2002; Green 1998), surpassed by men in terms of career opportunities (Waugh 2002) or tricked by 'evil', 'scheming' female characters who compete for their chosen heroes (Nathan 2001; Waugh 2002; Baglietto 2002). This latter theme draws on the old notion of women as manipulative, particularly in relation to men. Thus, despite a popular belief that chick lit portrays strong female friendships, in fact other women are frequently represented as competitors and therefore not to be trusted. The reason the heroines manage to win the hero's heart in the end is not because they surpass in spirit or intelligence, but because they conform to traditional stereotypes of femininity. Indeed, the downplaying of intelligence sometimes appears to be essential to make the dynamic between the strong hero and needy heroine work. He must save her with the chivalry, wit and expertise she may not have herself.

In *Bridget Jones's Diary* there are three such rescue scenes, the most dramatic of which involves Mark Darcy revealing that Julio, Bridget's mother's lover, is a conman – a rescue which works simultaneously to present Bridget and her mother as naive and gullible and, in a familiar racializing move, to highlight the 'superior white masculinity' of Mark Darcy. In Nathan's *Persuading Annie*, Jake saves Annie and her family from poverty because he discovers a crook within the family company, and Charlie saves Jo in Waugh's *The New You Survival Kit* from going to prison over an illegal business transaction. Being saved from the responsibility of single motherhood is also a common feature of chick lit novels. The heroines seem to need rescuing from independence. *Babyville* by Jane Green is an example – Maeve, a high-powered career woman, gets pregnant from a one-night stand, but eventually Mark comes to the rescue and she no longer has to 'cope' on her own.

Working girls?

In traditional romantic novels, heroines are not normally seen as particularly career-driven, despite their spirited nature and intelligence. Rather, they seek advancement and power through a romantic alliance with a man. In this respect, the female characters in chick lit novels seem markedly different, as they are invariably portrayed as employed and committed to the idea of a career. Most chick lit heroines are, à la Bridget Jones, employed in underpaid positions, typical of the actual situation in which most working women are concentrated in low-paid jobs in the service sector. Often, they are portrayed as dissatisfied and struggling in their jobs. Kate, for example, in *The Wrong Mr Right*, is employed as a secretary after dropping out of university when she became pregnant and was forced to bring her child up alone. Although she does 'protectively' refer to her secretarial work 'as a career . . . it was not what she wanted to do in the long-term' (Baglietto 2002: 117). Similarly, Jemima, in *Jemima J.*, whose work consists of compiling the Top-Tips column at her local newspaper says that: 'sadly my talents are wasted here at the *Kilburn Herald*. I hate this job' (Green 1998: 3).

Interestingly, in both these novels, as soon as they decide to marry their heroes, the heroines magically have the courage to ditch their dead-end jobs and fulfil their dreams. Kate becomes an interior designer and Jemima realizes her ambition to become a magazine journalist. Each explains how the love of a good man gave her the confidence to pursue her goals. Although this type of narrative is perhaps more progressive than the customary return-to-the-home discourse of most traditional romances and contemporary backlash narratives, it is nonetheless striking that the hero is again seen as vital to 'save' the heroine from her dead-end job and to propel her into a 'happy ever after' that in this postfeminist moment now also includes a dazzling career.

The other type of chick lit heroine is professional and successfully employed. Jo in *New You* is a Public Relations executive at a successful company and she 'loved herself. She loved her job, her successful friends' (Waugh 2002: 282). However, her success comes attached with the price tag of being unfeminine, since she is portrayed as cynical, cheating, hard-nosed, snobby and as a frequent drug-user. Jocasta in Parks's *Game Over* is characterized in the same way as cold, manipulative and immoral. She does not believe in love, and unscrupulously exploits people to appear on her reality TV show *Sex with an Ex*. Both Jo and Jocasta are 'saved' by good-natured heroes who see beyond their 'bitchy' and 'hard' facade and melt them with their love, and, in the case of Jocasta's man Darren, with his highly principled belief in love, marriage and fidelity. Jo, in turn, meets Charlie, gives up her job and moves to the countryside to fulfil her destiny as a happy housewife. Positive models of independence and career success are conspicuous by their absence in chick lit, and it would seem that within this genre women are only allowed to be successful at work if this is achieved with the support and endorsement of a loving man. Without that ticket, the successfully employed woman is invariably villainized, as in films like *Fatal Attraction* and *Disclosure*.

Single income, no boyfriend, absolutely desperate (SINBAD)

Closely related to this, the portrayal of singleness in the chick lit is also extremely negative. It might be supposed that at a moment in which demographers tell us that single-person households are the fastest growing group, and in which household forms are diversifying and notions of 'friends as the new family' exert an increasingly powerful hold in popular consciousness, being single might be treated in a positive – or at least neutral – way. But this is decidedly not the case within chick lit novels analysed here. With the exception of the minority of heroines who are in successful careers and are therefore portrayed as cold and unfeminine ('I've turned my heart to steel. In fact even my closest friends ask if I have one at all,' as Jocasta puts it in *Game Over*), most women in chick lit are portrayed as single and unhappy about it. Jemima asks 'what could be worse than being single' and thinks it is entirely understandable that 'women stay in relationships, miserable, horrible, destructive relationships because the alternative is far too horrendous to even consider. Being on their own' (Green 1998: 81). Stella in *Don't You Want Me?* pleads 'I don't want to live the rest of my life on my own, without sex, lonely again' (Knight 2002: 188), and even a 'tough' Jo in *New You* hates spending an evening alone as 'it made her feel like a failure' (Waugh 2002: 7). What they really want is, according to Stella, 'hardcore domestic' (Knight 2002: 17). Or, as Kate puts it in *The Wrong Mr Wright*, 'I do want strings. I want them attached to every part of me. Pulling me down, if that's how you want to see it' (Baglietto 2002: 265).

The terror and misery apparently threatened by being single resonates powerfully with Faludi's (1992) account of backlash trend stories which emphasize the 'man-shortage', the 'infertility epidemic' and the suggestion that a woman over thirty has more chance of being killed by a terrorist than getting married.

Mirror, mirror on the wall . . .

Finally, we turn to the portrayal of beauty and the body within chick lit novels. In traditional romances heroines fall into a category that might be described as 'effortlessly beautiful' – that is, they are blessed by a particularly attractive appearance, but also entirely unselfconscious about this. In chick lit novels, there are broadly two different approaches to beauty taken. In one the heroine is beautiful but, interestingly, is often presented as having been transformed from 'ugly duckling', in order to rebut readers' potential envy or hostility (and also in consonance with the makeover paradigm that dominates contemporary popular culture). *Jemima J.* is a good example of this: she undergoes a dramatic weight loss to become a 'blonde bombshell' who is not only suddenly gorgeous, but also blessed with excellent career prospects, a new circle of friends and the love of her adoring hero. The message is devastatingly simple – as the song says 'be young and beautiful if you want to be loved'. The importance of beauty is emphasized throughout, with Jemima saying things like 'if I had only one wish in all the world I wouldn't wish to win the lottery. Nor would I wish for true love. No, if I had one wish I would wish to have a model's figure' (Green 1998: 2). Chillingly, this echoes the findings of Naomi Wolf's (1990) study of the Beauty Myth, in which she found that young women's single greatest aspiration was to lose 10 lb. It is underpinned in all chick lit novels with a preoccupation with the shape, size and look of the body that borders on the obsessional. What is striking is not only that appearance is such a preoccupation, but that it is depicted as requiring endless self-surveillance, monitoring, dieting, purging and work. It would not be an exaggeration to say that the leitmotif of the *unruly body* that needs constant disciplining is constitutive of the chick lit novel. In this sense, the novels can be read as offering an insight into the disciplinary matrix of neoliberal society, with its emphasis upon policing and remodelling the self. Often a humourous, self-deprecating tone is deployed, as in *Bridget Jones's Diary* but this in no way reduces the palpable anxiety associated with the possibility that heroines might not live up to increasingly narrow normative judgements of female attractiveness.

The second type of chick lit heroine is either less stunning or adamant about being free of the demands of beauty. A postfeminist mantra reverberates through many of the books: 'I choose when to make myself pretty and if I choose to be pretty, then only for myself.' However, such rebelliousness is ironically inverted as soon as a man enters the scene. See Annie's reaction when, to her horror, she finds herself face-to-face with the man she loves in an unwashed and un-preened state: 'Annie's limbs deadened. Her palms dampened. This wasn't how it was meant to be. She hadn't got a scrap of makeup on. Her hair was unwashed. Toxic fumes were escaping from certain regions of her body . . . She wasn't ready for this' (Nathan 2001: 122). The similarity to traditional romances could hardly be overstated and points up the partial nature of the engagement with feminism, and the hollowness of the rhetoric about beauty being all about 'pleasing oneself'.

Must-She TV

In this final section of the chapter my main focus of analysis is the two television shows that have been the subject of most debate about gender representations in recent years – *Sex and the City* and *Ally McBeal*. While, in the first decade of the twenty-first century, there are a number of television shows featuring strong, complex female characters (e.g. Kathryn Janeway in *Star Trek Voyager*, CJ Craig in *The West Wing*, Kerry Weaver in *ER*), it is *Sex and the City* and *Ally McBeal* that have been regarded as emblematic of the shifts in representation being considered here.

Sex and the City focuses on the love lives of four Manhattan-based white middle-class women in their late thirties. Carrie Bradshaw (played by Sarah Jessica Parker) writes a sex column for a New York paper; Samantha Jones (Kim Cattrall) is the owner of a Public Relations firm; Charlotte York (Kristen Davies) is an art dealer; and Miranda Hobbes (Cynthia Nixon) is a successful attorney. Work, however, is largely incidental to the drama – with the exception of Carrie whose column for the fictional *New York Star* provides the 'thoughtful' voice-over for the show, organized around a different question each episode. Questions in the first few seasons have included: is secret sex the ultimate form of intimacy? Are relationships the religion of the Nineties? What are the breakup rules? Is it better to fake it than to be alone? Can you change a man? Can you ever really forgive if you can't forget? Are we the new bachelors?

Through the different characters' lives, the show offers us alternative responses to the issue in question – and in turn the huge volume of intertextual material generated by the show invites us to identify with one (or more) of the characters or 'types': are you 'wicked' Samantha or 'prudish' Charlotte? and so on. *Sex and the City* has an audience of 11 million viewers on HBO in the USA and it has been sold extensively across the world. It was the first cable show to win the Emmy award for an outstanding comedy series (in 2001).

Ally McBeal tells the story of 'a white, middle-class, single, successful professional woman in her late twenties/early thirties making her way in a man's world and looking for love and mental health' (Moseley and Read 2002: 232). The show centres on Ally's attempts to hold together her career as a lawyer with her difficult personal life, and desire for a relationship and a child.

Sex and the City and *Ally McBeal* are both clearly informed by second-wave feminism. They both feature independent, working, mainly single women whose commitment – and sense of entitlement – to equality is evident in a variety of ways throughout the shows (e.g. in *Ally McBeal* with her legal work on sexual harassment cases and struggles around equality in the workplace, and in *Sex and the City* in attempting to forge satisfying sexual relationships with men). Dilemmas in the shows focus upon a familiar feminist terrain: family versus career, female self-presentation, motherhood, difficulties in female friendships, and what sorts of compromises are necessary in heterosexual relationships.

Backlash themes

Backlash themes are most evident in *Ally McBeal*. They do not require sophisticated techniques of textual analysis to 'decode'; the show's ambivalence to feminism is clear. Indeed, *Ally McBeal* was actively promoted as 'politically incorrect' and 'an equal opportunities offender', rejecting the supposed 'orthodoxy' of feminism. As Moseley and Read (2002) have argued, the programme is adept at incorporating the discourses and debates that it generates in the press into individual episodes, and is quite self-conscious in its mobilization of discourses about second-wave feminism.

Like Bridget Jones, Ally often presents herself as a 'failed' feminist who has let 'the sisterhood' down so badly that (as she tells a client in one episode) 'the National Organization of Women has a contract out on my head'. As Alice has argued, this trades on the idea that feminism has pushed women into wanting too much and trying to meet unattainable goals and in this way 'postfeminism is offered as an escape from the imposition of being "superwoman" in order to fulfil a feminist image of success' (Alice 1995: 17).

Ally McBeal is saturated with the elements of backlash discourses: Ally herself is portrayed as unhappy – 'a mess' – and the cause of this is narratively located in her decision to choose her career over her 'True Love' (Billy). She is, as the show's advertising slogan says, 'single, successful and falling apart'. Preoccupied with finding a partner, Ally is also tormented by her desire to have a child, and her repressed maternal instincts produce frequent hallucinations of a dancing baby. She does not reject feminism, but simply cannot live up to it. In one famous scene Ally says that she *does* want to join with other women to 'change the world', but adds 'I just want to get married first.' Feminism is not attacked, but, as in *Bridget Jones's Diary*, it is portrayed as not speaking the truth of women's desires.

In *Sex and the City* the elements of backlash discourses are more complex. What is most striking is the way that the bold, sophisticated and knowing voices of the protagonists mask their very ordinary, traditionally feminine, desires. For all the hype about single fun, 'fabulousness' and sexual freedom, the four women expend most of their energy looking for Mr Right (or in Carrie's case Mr Big). In one episode, having recently broken up with 'Big' for not being able to commit to her, Carrie attempts to make him jealous by dating a player in the New York Yankees. However, she starts crying when he tries to kiss her: 'I'm sorry; this is really embarrassing,' Carrie sobs. 'I just cried in your mouth. I'm not ready!' Later she tells her friends, 'I saw Big and I completely fell apart.'

In a subsequent episode, still yearning for him, she wonders aloud in her column whether she has been true to herself or whether she has been faking more than just her hair colour and her bra size: 'And then I had a frightening thought. Maybe I was the one who was faking it . . . all these years of faking to myself that I was happy being single.'

It is not only Carrie who expresses such views: one episode sees Miranda tormented by having to check the 'single' box on her mortgage application; another has Charlotte buying a puppy to fulfil her need for commitment; and even 'tough', 'promiscuous' Samantha who says she treats sex 'like a man' is found bitterly crying when she has been stood up and left alone in a restaurant without any of her 'armour': 'I can't believe I fell for some guy's line,' she cries to her friends. 'But sometimes you need to hear a "we".'

In a provocative essay for *Urbanities*, Wendy Shalit argues that *Sex and the City* has been fundamentally misunderstood:

> One of the reasons the critics have misunderstood *Sex and the City* is that it features frank sexual banter and women who swear just as much, and are just as crude, as the men. On the surface, this seems like a nod to equality, but not when you appreciate what these girls are all swearing at. To be sure, the girls bitterly deconstruct their ex and current boyfriends' sexual techniques and bodies, but only after their hearts have been broken. Miranda, for instance, refers to her ex-boyfriend as 'that asshole I dated a couple of years ago' but then Carrie's voice over explains, 'Miranda used to call Eric the love of her life, until he left her for another woman.' (Shalit 1999: 4–5)

Notions of choice and entitlement are key themes of postfeminism that are seen in both *Ally McBeal* and *Sex and the City*. As Angela McRobbie has argued, women are endowed with choice so that they can then use their 'feminist' freedom to choose to re-embrace traditional femininity – white weddings, hen nights, the adoption of the male surname on marriage, etc. 'What marks out all these cultural practices is the boldness of this activity and a strong sense of female consent and participation' (McRobbie 2004a: 9). Elspeth Probyn (1997b) has also discussed this pattern as the emergence of a discourse of the *'choiceoisie'* – in which choices are treated as devoid of social and political ramifications. This discourse allows the old and the traditional to be presented as new, so that women can then 'choose' what is deemed natural.

Homosociality and homophobia

One of the pleasures offered by both shows is their feminine address and potential for feminine identification. The use of voice-over to examine dilemmas and give access to inner thoughts and feelings is an innovative aspect of the shows' appeal to women, combined, in *Ally McBeal*, with the use of music and fantasy sequences for emotional realism. In *Sex and the City*, despite the relentless search for the perfect man, the primary relations the women have are those with each other – beautifully captured by Charlotte's joyful announcement to the others of Miranda's decision to go through with her pregnancy: 'we're having a baby!' A female world of safe homosociality is presented, in which, as Jane Arthurs (2003) has argued, the potential dangers of life in New York for a single woman are downplayed or repressed: the City is depicted as 'a place of freedom and safety for women – the worst that can happen is that their clothes might be splashed by a passing car (as happens to Carrie in the title sequence). These women move freely around the cafés and boutiques with a confident sense of possession . . . In this way their dependence on male lovers for emotional and sensual satisfaction is displaced' (Arthurs 2003: 93).

Sex and the City is about being 'one of the girls'; it opens up a world of female bonding. However, the pleasures of homosociality it makes available are not unambiguous. In her excellent analysis of Anne Summers parties, Merl Storr (2003) provides an analysis of female homosociality that has strong resonances for our examination of *Sex and the City*. Storr argues it is constructed around a strongly male-identified notion of femininity and works to promote male interests; it is profoundly racialized and classed; it promotes the idea of openness about sex as a good in its own right (rather than to promote equality) and is highly normative; it is structured around lesophobia.

For all its 'frank' and 'liberated' talk, *Sex and the City* shares these features. Notwithstanding its regular flirtations with lesbianism and bisexuality, it is resolutely heterosexual and phallic, and it is the antithesis of 'queer' in its commitment to normative gender and sexual identities. One episode in season 3 entitled 'Boy Girl Boy Girl' exemplifies this. Carrie's newest boyfriend is bisexual, provoking her to ask the question 'has the opposite sex become obsolete?' At a party she meets her boyfriend's ex-partner who is now involved in a relationship with another man, with whom he is bringing up a baby. The baby is the result of an egg donated by his ex-girlfriend, who has recently been to Hawaii to marry her female partner. While Carrie struggles with her ambivalent feelings about this, Miranda is grappling with her concerns about moving in with Steve, her 'clingy' boyfriend who seeks a more committed relationship with her. During an argument Steve accuses Miranda of being the 'guy' in the relationship – a slur which sends her running to a 'goddess workshop' to rediscover her lost femininity. Meanwhile, Charlotte has met a photographer who wants her to pose for him dressed as a man. She agrees to do so, but subsequently feels uncomfortable about performing masculinity and tries to get out of it with some feeble excuses about being 'bad at math' and unable to 'change a tire' – designed to indicate her lack of masculine qualifications. When the photographer tries to inspire her to feel powerful and dominant, Charlotte responds, 'I think I need a bigger sock' and falls into a passionate embrace with him.

Cindy Royal (2003) has argued that some temporary destabilizing of gender and sexual identities does occur in the show, and it points at least to a far greater diversity of ways of living and loving than is seen in most television drama. However, the normative gender and sexual order is briefly troubled only to be restored in Carrie's final voice-over. Carrie compares herself to Alice in *Alice in Wonderland*, and reflects on falling down the rabbit hole into 'Confused Sexuality Land'. The attribution of confusion, and her evasion of her own discomfort at having kissed another woman by chalking it up to 'youthful dalliances' swiftly reinstates normative heterosexuality.

The show's 'difficulty' (to put it mildly) with bisexuality and lesbianism in particular is further endorsed in the vast amounts of publicity that surround it. In an interview with Barbara Ellen in the British Sunday *Observer Magazine*, Kristen Davis, who plays Charlotte, is asked whether there has been any episode of the show that has shocked her:

> Davis thinks for while and comes up with the one we've seen in Britain recently, where Samantha has sex with a lesbian lover. Davis giggles bashfully, seeming very 'Charlotte' for the first time. 'She's like, oh you know . . .' Goes down on her? 'Yeah, that's it!' Is Davis secretly pleased that she doesn't have to do this kind of scene? 'I'm openly pleased! We are all openly pleased. Kim has to be way, way more shocking than the rest of us. And Kim has been nude, very, very nude. We are like: Kimber, you're so great, you're so brave! I'm so glad I don't have to be.' (*Observer Magazine*, 20 October 2002)

Lynn Comella argues that the show is not just sexually conservative in relation to lesbianism. Discussing the well-known vibrator episode in which Charlotte rejects, but then becomes addicted to her 'rabbit', Comella argues that it flirts with sexual empowerment 'only to uphold the common perception that masturbation isn't real sex' (Comella 2003: 111) and to retreat into the familiar terrain of female sexual shame.

Unruly women? Hedonism, consumption and bodily discipline

One way of thinking about *Sex and the City* is to see it as part of a tradition of showing excessive or unruly women in drama – other contemporary televisual examples are Patsy and Edina in *Absolutely Fabulous* and *Roseanne*. The disruptive power of the unruly female subject – carnivalesque and carnivalized in Bakhtin's sense – contains much potential for feminist appropriation. The parodic excesses of unruly women provide a space to make visible and laughable the tropes of femininity. Kathleen Rowe has discussed how the character Roseanne has been self-consciously created as a spectacle marked by excess and looseness particularly in relation to norms of bodily decorum. The appearance of a 200-plus pound woman in prime time is potentially subversive in itself and this is reinforced by Roseanne's 'appetites' and lack of bodily discipline – as Rowe puts it, 'she sprawls, slouches, flops on furniture and her speech is loose and excessive. She laughs loudly, screams shrilly and speaks in a nasal whine' (Rowe 1997: 79). Just by *being* she violates normative codes of feminine behaviour, and her *ease* with her body, Rowe suggests, triggers much of the *unease* surrounding her. She refuses to take on feminine shame. She celebrates the libidinal pleasures of food and sex and she argues that women should take up more, rather than less, space in the world. Additionally, she offers a critique of white middle-class feminism and its dislocation from many working-class women's lives.

Can the characters in *Sex and the City* be regarded as 'unruly women'? Their dress codes (which often play with the transgressive sexual connotations of leather and bondage) may seem to place them outside traditional bourgeois femininity. Likewise, their assertive sexual behaviour – and Samantha's hedonistic promiscuity in particular – may seem to represent a challenge to how 'nice girls' behave. But rather than flouting the norms of feminine behaviour in the manner that Roseanne does, or drawing mocking attention to them as *Absolutely Fabulous* does, *Sex and the City* works to re-establish and reaffirm precisely the boundaries it appears to threaten. Operating in a context in which, as Myra Macdonald (1995) has argued, the notion of a single template of idealized femininity has given way to much more fragmented representations, *Sex and the City* establishes one kind of 'bourgeois bohemian' femininity as more desirable than other forms (which are castigated as too repressed or unstylish or vulgar). Jane Arthurs argues that an implicit part of *Sex and the City*'s project is to 'work through the problem of establishing the boundaries of respectability in a post feminist culture where women share many of the same freedoms as men, but in which the residual effects of the double standards are still being felt' (Arthurs 2003: 92). This project is one that is deeply inflected by class. The boundaries of the women's behaviour are informed by notions of decorum and respectability that are representative of a new upper middle-class fraction (Skeggs 1997). The particular mix of styles and their codes of sexual behaviour are characterized by an attitude that places emphasis upon sexual freedom but shies away from vulgarity and poor taste – profoundly classed attributions.

Rather than the unruly transgression of boundaries, *Sex and the City* displays a shift from moral boundaries to aesthetic ones, as Jane Arthurs has argued:

> Although Sex and the City rejects the traditional patriarchal dichotomy of virgin and whore, insisting in its explorations of the women's multiple sexual experiences their rights to seek sexual satisfaction without shame, this does not mean that there are no limits. Aesthetic boundaries replace moral boundaries so that men who can't kiss very well, who smell, who are too short, or whose semen tastes peculiar are rejected on those grounds. (Arthurs 2003: 93)

The triumph of the commodified aesthetic over the moral can also be seen in the way that the four protagonists differentiate themselves from other women who dress badly or have poor interior design taste, etc. As in *Bridget Jones*, consumer items are often used as a kind of shorthand to sum up a person who is 'not like us'. In this economy 'white stilettos' or 'a twinset and pearls' convey considerably more information than what a person is wearing. In turn, lapses in consumer taste are used to symbolize emotional turmoil. A pair of yellow flowery flip-flops is, to paraphrase Freud (!), never just a type of footwear.

Overall, consumption is far too important to the show to be treated satirically. As many commentators have remarked, the show is all about consumption. Carrie's shoes and dresses, the women's favourite bars and luncheon haunts, the information on who and what is hot or not (all helpfully detailed on the various *Sex and the City* websites) are presented as a powerful and appealing integrated lifestyle. Without these gorgeous and glamorous accessories and locations – and the money to enjoy them – single fun might look a lot less fabulous.

Conclusion

Finally, I want to return briefly to the place of 'romance' in all this. We have already discussed the way that an apparently liberated sex-talk operates as a cover for much more traditionally feminine desires, such as marriage and monogamy: 'in a city of infinite options, sometimes there is no better feeling than knowing you have only one', as Carrie puts it. Here, I want to consider the relationship of this to the women's status as unruly – or not.

What I want to suggest is that *Sex and the City* constitutes a reinvention of the codes of romance for postfeminist consumer culture. Hilary Radner (1993) first advanced such an argument in her analysis of the film *Pretty Woman*, and it seems particularly apposite for *Sex and the City*. Radner argues that since the late 1960s new technologies of femininity have been developed which place greater stress upon sexual practice, the body and consumerism. Where previously a woman's innocence, inexperience and virtue were what she had to 'offer' in the marriage market, 'her value is now overtly and inextricably tied to the representation of a specific heterosexual practice as sexual knowledge'. Moreover, Radner argues, 'the work of this new femininity must be maintained as he can leave you at any time' (1993: 59). What Radner is interested in is the way that this transformation both changes yet holds in place the traditional romance plot:

> It is the new value of the woman, determined through her mastery of the arts of seduction, sexual gratification and consumer display, that both demands a fundamental reworking of the marriage plot, and yet preserves the story as one in which eroticism and ambition are

inevitably and inextricably linked, in which feminine ambition can only be realised through marriage to the right man. (1993: 60)

Radner's analysis seems to capture the working of romance in *Sex and the City*, in which the women's sexual knowledge, sexual 'skills' and disciplined bodies are depicted as their primary capital. Jane Arthur argues that it is the protagonists' 'adherence to the sleek control of the commodified body' (Arthurs 2003) that most scotches the idea that they are 'unruly' women, and contrasts strongly with the way *Absolutely Fabulous* satirizes consumer culture, the fashion industry and contemporary regimes of self-care (Kirkham and Skeggs 1998). Like – and inextricably linked to – consumption, the work of disciplining the female body is far too serious to joke about. Or rather, in typical postfeminist having-it-both-ways fashion, *it is both joked about and simultaneously reinforced*. This is captured in an episode in series 3 when, after weeks of having sex with her boyfriend, Carrie finally relaxes enough to sleep with him, only for the unthinkable to happen: she farts. The entire episode is spent with her 'replaying' the fart, consumed by fears that her boyfriend will leave her. Her friends' reactions display their usual characteristics. Miranda laughs and says 'you're only human', but Samantha is worried:

> 'Huge mistake,' she says. 'But I'm only human,' says Carrie. 'No, honey, you're a woman,' Samantha replies, 'and men don't like women to be human. We aren't supposed to fart, douche, use tampons, or have hair in places we shouldn't. I mean, hell, a guy once broke up with me because I missed a bikini wax.'

The episode is both *about* women's hangups in a culture that requires that women do not fart, menstruate, snore or even perspire, whilst doing nothing to ridicule or challenge such expectations. In a passionate Web-posting about this, Judith Shulevitz says:

> Here we are at the beginning of the 21st century, and our leading female fictional characters are right back where they were at the beginning of the 20th – tying themselves up in constipated knots in order to make themselves palatable to men. The women's movement might as well never have happened.

Or is it even worse? What makes this episode postfeminist, rather than pre-feminist, is that it *critiques as well as endorses* these strictures. It is to this complex set of entanglements that we turn in the final chapter.

8

Postfeminist Media Culture?

THE notion of postfeminism has surfaced repeatedly in this book. In each chapter questions have been raised about the extent to which media content might be understood as postfeminist. Do the current transformations of journalism herald an era of postfeminist news? Is advertising's focus on choice and sexual subjectification postfeminist? To what extent do contemporary talk shows occupy a postfeminist terrain, marked by confession, individualism and the injunction to work on and transform the self? How and in what ways do magazines aimed at both women and men offer a distinctively postfeminist sensibility? Is postfeminism rewriting romance?

In this final chapter I want to draw the threads of the argument together by engaging in a brief but sustained way with the notion of postfeminism. In the first part of the chapter I will discuss the three key ways in which postfeminism has been understood: as an epistemological shift, as a historical transformation and as a backlash against feminism. Then in the second part I will outline a new way of conceptualizing postfeminism – as a *sensibility* – and will go on to explore the key features which constitute a postfeminist sensibility, and their relationship to contemporary neoliberalism. The chapter will argue that citizens in the West today inhabit a postfeminist media culture in which women rather than men are constituted as the ideal neoliberal subjects.

It is helpful to think about postfeminism as being used in three broad ways. In some accounts it is used to signal an *epistemological break* within feminism – a move to a kind of theorizing influenced by post-structuralism, postmodernism and postcolonial theory. Secondly, it may be used to index a *historical shift*, a move into a new period after feminism and thus characterized by different problems and concerns. Finally, it is deployed by some writers to indicate a political or normative position that is *antithetical* to feminism – in this sense the 'post' suggests a reaction against feminism.

This way of thinking about the different meanings of postfeminism owes a lot to discussions of postmodernism which are similarly characterized by those who emphasize an epistemological shift

(Anderson 1983; Lyotard 1984) a historical shift or a reaction against the project of modernity (e.g. Jameson 1984). In these discussions the different positions are sometimes marked by differences in the way that 'post' is written – with or without a hyphen, capitalized or in lower case, and in some cases (following Derrida) with the word scored through. There is, as yet, no parallel for postfeminism – which perhaps makes the disagreements over its meaning even more difficult to grasp. I will consider each perspective briefly, before moving on to outline an alternative understanding of postfeminism.

Postfeminism as epistemological break

For a number of writers, postfeminism represents an epistemological break with second-wave feminism and marks 'the intersection of feminism with a number of other anti-foundationalist movements including post-modernism, post structuralism and post-colonialism' (Brooks 1997: 4). 'Post', as it is used in this sense, implies transformation and change and signals a critical engagement with earlier/other forms of feminism. It represents a challenge to 'hegemonic' Anglo-American feminism, with its 'dominant and colonising voice' (Alice 1995: 11). It is alleged to have arisen partly as a result of critiques from black and Third World feminists which destabilized dominant feminist theorizing and interrogated the right of (predominantly) white Western (Northern) women to speak on behalf of all others. Combined with this were the critical challenges mounted by postmodernism and post-structuralism, which brought into question the ways in which feminist theory relied on dualistic thinking and upon totalizing concepts (such as 'patriarchy'). Postfeminism in this sense marks a shift away from a focus on equality to a focus on debates about differences, a shift away from structural analysis and meta-theorizing towards a more 'pluralistic conception of the application of feminism' that 'addresses the demands of marginalised, diasporic and colonised cultures for a non-hegemonic feminism capable of giving voice to local, indigenous and postcolonial feminisms' (Brooks 1997). According to Anna Yeatman (1994) postfeminism represents feminism's 'coming-of-age'; able to tolerate difference and to reflect upon its location in relation to other political and intellectual movements.

In cultural and media analysis, postfeminism in this sense is mostly encountered as an analytic perspective, rather than a description of the nature of any particular cultural product. Its value is in stressing the manner in which gender is connected to other forms of marginalization and other axes of power such that it can never be examined separately from 'race', colonialism, sexuality and class – a crucial point. Amanda Lotz (2001), however, suggested a model which can be used to engage with the extent to which texts are postfeminist. She argues that for a text to be considered postfeminist (in this rather positive sense) it should contain the following four features: narratives that explore women's diverse relationships to power; depictions of varied feminist solutions; attempts to deconstruct the binaries of gender and sexuality; and illustrations of contemporary struggles. According to this definition, she would regard *Ally McBeal* as a good example of a postfeminist text – yet it hardly seems to embrace the intersectional analysis advocated above.

Postfeminism as historical shift

In this perspective a historical rather than epistemological or theoretical shift is considered important. This approach attempts to periodize feminism and regards postfeminism as a period after (the height of) second-wave feminism. Sometimes it is used synonymously with third-wave feminism (particularly in the US context, where the notion of a third wave is more fully developed than elsewhere). It seeks to mark a time not after feminism *per se*, but after a particular moment of feminist activity and a particular set of feminist concerns. For Joanne Hollows (2000a) postfeminism is not necessarily anti-feminism, but represents a new kind of feminism for a new context of debate. Hollows is angered by a type of feminist analysis that holds new writing and contemporary cultural texts (whether films or sitcoms or chick lit novels) up against a '1970s version' of feminism – only to find them wanting. The feminism in such popular texts is always said to have been 'neutered' or 'co-opted' or 'emptied of its radical potential', she argues, whereas it may in fact have simply changed – for a new moment. Such critique, Hollows suggests, serves to reify feminism, and works on a 'recruitment' model, rather than thinking of feminism as dynamic, negotiated and in a process of ongoing transformation. (There are some parallels here with the debate between Radway and Ang discussed in chapter 1.)

Similarly, Rachel Moseley and Jacina Read (2002) argue that the polarization in feminist thought between feminism on the one hand and femininity on the other is a product of the thinking of the mid-1970s. Discussing criticisms of *Ally McBeal* that attack the show for wanting to 'have it both ways' (with Ally as a mini-skirted male fantasy *and* a successful, professional woman), they ask: why *shouldn't* she have it all ways? She is, they suggest, a postfeminist heroine, a female protagonist for our times, who wants it all and does not observe (what may seem to her and to her audience) arbitrary boundaries around behaviour, address or aspiration. Here, then, Ally McBeal is invoked as exemplar of a different kind of postfeminism.

This is a powerful argument and the critique of second-wave ideas as the 'one, true way' is an important one. The problem comes in specifying what, if anything, might constitute the *content* of postfeminism. It seems infinitely flexible. Critical observers might note also the way in which a politically sanitized, neoliberal, and highly sexualized version of postfeminism circulates in the media where girl bands like the Spice Girls, female singers like Britney Spears and Christina Aguilera, 'babes' like Ally McBeal, and a silicon-enhanced model turned political candidate (Jordan) are among its most celebrated icons.

A number of feminist media scholars have contributed to analysing the different ways in which feminism has impacted on television programming. Julie D'Acci (1994) and Lauren Rabinovitz (1999) have both analysed the political, economic, social and cultural factors that contributed to making white middle-class women a particularly desirable demographic to advertisers. Advertisers rightly believed that 'career women' had more disposable income than housewives, and more control over how that money was spent. The emergence of a more independent female generation paralleled changes and refinements in marketing and a move away from class-based categories to psychological and lifestyle-informed classifications. Rabinovitz argues that a feminist discourse was important to American television executives in order to target the audiences they aimed to deliver to advertisers.

Early televisual feminisms from the 1970s onwards focused upon the workplace as the key site of feminist characters and narratives. Bonnie Dow (1996) identifies three modes or 'phases' of 'prime time feminism' in the 1970s, 1980s and early 1990s. In the first – the 'working-woman sitcom' (of which *Mary Tyler Moore* is the paradigmatic example) the main conflict for female characters is between career and personal happiness. The second, that began in the mid- to late 1980s, is best represented by *Murphy Brown* and *Designing Women* and is informed by the anti-feminist backlash and by postfeminism. The third phase from the late 1980s to the early 1990s represents the influence of the maternalist feminism (e.g. *Dr Quinn Medicine Woman*). In all three phases Dow points to the media's unremittingly individualistic version of the world which 'implies that most problems can be solved by hard work, goodwill, and a supportive family . . . This logic works well with advertising, which operates on the presumption that an individual's purchasing decision can make an enormous change in his or her life' (Dow 1996: xxi). Ann Kaplan has noted 'television's reliance on constructing numbers of viewers as commodities involves reproducing female images that accommodate prevailing (and dominant) conceptions of "woman" ' (Kaplan 1992: 223). According to Dow, television is similarly restricted in its construction of feminism, preferring only a liberal version, which treats feminism essentially as 'a lifestyle, an attitude, an identity' and 'assiduously avoids reference to feminist politics' (Dow 1996: 210).

Postfeminism and the backlash

The third way in which postfeminism is used is to refer to discourses that constitute part of a backlash against feminist achievements or goals (Faludi 1992). Susan Faludi argues that 'postfeminist' sentiments first surfaced in the 1920s as a reaction against women's activism in the early part of the twentieth century. But the backlash was at its height in the 1980s and 1990s:

> In the Eighties, publications from the *New York Times* to *Vanity Fair* to *The Nation* have issued a steady stream of indictments against the women's movement, with such headlines as 'WHEN FEMINISM FAILED' or 'THE AWFUL TRUTH ABOUT WOMEN'S LIB'. They hold the campaign for women's equality responsible for nearly every woe besetting women, from depression to meagre savings accounts, from teenage suicides to eating disorders to bad complexions . . . But what has made women unhappy in the last decade is not their 'equality' – which they don't yet have – but the rising pressure to halt, and even reverse, women's quest for equality. (Faludi 1992: 3)

Backlash discourses take many contradictory forms. They not only work by attributing all women's unhappiness to feminism, but may also suggest that 'all the battles have been won' or, conversely, that 'you can't have it all – something has to give'; that 'political correctness' has become a new form of tyranny; that (white) men are the new victims, etc., etc. Although postfeminism, in this sense, is somewhat hostile to feminism, postfeminist discourses are much more than simply statements of anti-feminism. This is because of the relationship they claim to/with feminism. As Judith Stacey has argued, postfeminism simultaneously 'incorporates, revises and depoliticises many of the fundamental issues advanced by second wave feminism' (Stacey 1987).

Imelda Whelehan's important discussion of retro-sexism is also closely tied to notions of a backlash against feminism. Exploring the nostalgic quality of much contemporary media, she argues that representations of women, 'from the banal to the downright offensive' are being 'defensively reinvented against cultural changes in women's lives' (Whelehan 2000: 11). For Whelehan, for example, the figure of the 'new lad' is a 'nostalgic revival of old patriarchy, a direct challenge to feminism's call for social transformation, by reaffirming – albeit ironically – the unchanging nature of gender relations and sexual roles' (Whelehan 2000: 5).

Judith Williamson, too, has argued that contemporary sexism is increasingly being couched in period settings, and/or presented with 1960s/1970s typography and graphics. This, she argues, is 'sexism with an alibi: it appears at once past and present, "innocent" and knowing, a conscious reference to another era, rather than an unconsciously driven part of our own' (Williamson 2003: 1). The sense conveyed by both these writers, then, is of pernicious forms of attack on women clothed in nostalgic or retro-chic imagery in order to rebut (potential) accusations of sexism. Such claims have also been made more broadly in arguments about the return of the colour pink and of 1950s imagery in contemporary films (e.g. Glitre, 2004).

These arguments are important and the notion of irony and know-ingness offering a layer of protection against critique is central to understanding the contemporary dynamics of media sexism. However – substantively – I am not convinced that this is always done by 'harking back' to the past. This emphasis may miss what is new about contemporary depictions of women and men. For young people at university, for example, student union club invitations to women to 'come as your favourite porn star' to parties in the bar, or to sign up to (extremely popular) classes in 'pole dancing' are – rightly – not experienced as nostalgic or ironic but as part of an all too current address to women as knowing, active, heterosexually desiring sexual subjects. This address is part of the (post)modernized or postfeminist require-ment for young women to add porn star qualities to their personal CVs – something that is routinely instilled into them by magazine articles on the necessity of acquiring skills such as striptease or putting on a condom with one's mouth – in order to hold men's sexual interest. Much sexism, it seems to me, operates without the alibi of nostalgia for a time when men were men and women were women, but is distinctively *new*. It has to be understood not only as a backlash, a reaction against feminism, but also as a new discursive phenomenon that is closely related to neoliberalism. It is to this articulation that I turn next.

A Postfeminist Sensibility

I want to argue that postfeminism is best understood not as an episte-mological perspective, nor as a historical shift, and not (simply) as a backlash, in which its meanings are pre-specified. Rather, postfemi-nism should be conceived of as a *sensibility*, and postfeminist media culture should be our *critical object*; the phenomenon which analysts must inquire into and interrogate. This approach does not require a static notion of authentic feminism as a comparison point, but instead is informed by postmodernist and constructionist perspectives and seeks to examine what is distinctive about contemporary articulations of gender in the media.

It seems to me that there are a number of recurring and relatively stable themes, tropes and constructions that characterize gender representations in the media in the early twenty-first century. These include the notion that femininity is a bodily property; the shift from objectification to subjectification; the emphasis upon self-surveillance, monitoring and discipline; a focus upon individualism, choice and empowerment; the dominance of a makeover paradigm; the articulation or entanglement of feminist and anti-feminist ideas; a resurgence in ideas of natural sexual difference; a marked sexualization of culture; and an emphasis upon consumerism and the commodification of difference. These themes, I want to suggest, coexist with stark and continuing inequalities and exclusions that relate to 'race' and ethnicity, class, age, sexuality and disability – as well as gender.

Femininity as a bodily property

One of the most striking aspects of postfeminist media culture is its obsessional preoccupation with the body. In a shift from earlier representational practices, it appears that femininity is defined as a bodily property rather than (say) a social structural or psychological one. Instead of caring or nurturing or motherhood being regarded as central to femininity (all, of course, highly problematic and exclusionary) in today's media it is possession of a 'sexy body' that is presented as women's key (if not sole) source of identity. The body is presented simultaneously as women's source of power *and* as always already unruly and requiring constant monitoring, surveillance, discipline and remodelling (and consumer spending) in order to conform to ever narrower judgements of female attractiveness.

Surveillance of women's bodies (but not men's) constitutes perhaps the largest type of media content across all genres and media forms. Women's bodies are evaluated, scrutinized and dissected by women as well as men, and are always at risk of 'failing'. This is most clear in the cultural obsession with celebrity, which plays out almost exclusively over women's bodies. Magazines like *Heat* largely consist of big colour photographs of female celebrities' bodies, with scathing comments about anything from armpit hair to visible panty lines, but focusing in particular upon 'fat'. So excessive and punitive is the regulation of women's bodies through this medium that conventionally attractive women can be indicted for having 'fat ankles' or 'laughter lines'. No transgression is seemingly too small to be picked over and picked apart by paparazzi photographers and writers. The tone of comments is frequently excoriating: for example, 'yes that really is Melanie Griffith's wrinkly skin, not fabric' and 'there's so much fabric in Angelica Huston's dress it looks like it could be used to house small animals on cold nights. Despite that, it's straining over Anje's stomach and fits like a skintight bodysuit' (*Heat*, 19 March 2005).

Ordinary (i.e. non-celebrity) women are not exempt. Shows such as *What Not to Wear* and *10 Years Younger* subject women to hostile scrutiny for their bodies, postures and wardrobes, and evaluations that include the like of 'very saggy boobs' and 'what a minger'. Angela McRobbie notes the following comments from her viewing of *What Not to Wear*:

> 'What a dreary voice', 'look at how she walks', 'she shouldn't put that ketchup on her chips', 'she looks like a mousy librarian', 'her trousers are far too long', 'that jumper looks like something her granny crocheted, it would be better on the table', 'she hasn't washed her clothes', 'your hair looks like an overgrown poodle', 'your teeth are yellow, have you been eating grass?' And 'Oh my God she looks like a German lesbian'. This last insult was considered so hilarious that it was trailed as a promotion for the programme across the junctions of BBC TV for almost 2 weeks before it was broadcast. (McRobbie 2004b: 118)

Importantly the female body in postfeminist media culture is constructed as a window to the individual's interior life: for example, when Bridget Jones smokes forty cigarettes a day or consumes 'excessive' calories we are invited to read this in psychological terms as indicative of her emotional breakdown. A sleek, toned, controlled figure is today normatively essential for portraying success. Yet there is also – contradictorily – an acknowledgement that the body is a canvas that affords an image which may have little to do with how one feels inside. For example, after their break-ups with Brad Pitt and Tom Cruise respectively, Nicole Kidman and Jennifer Aniston were heralded across the media as 'triumphant' when they each first appeared in public – meaning that they successfully *performed* gleaming, commodified beauty and dazzling self-confidence, however hurt or vulnerable they may actually have felt. There was no comparable focus on the men.

The sexualization of culture

Closely related to the intense focus on women's bodies as the site of femininity is the pervasive sexualization of contemporary culture. By sexualization I refer to the extraordinary proliferation of discourses about sex and sexuality across all media forms, as well as to the increasingly frequent erotic presentation of girls', women's and (to a lesser extent) men's bodies in public spaces. This notion has come up repeatedly throughout the book. In chapter 4 the way that newspapers use rape stories as part of a package of titillating material was examined, and the chapter also discussed the way that all women's bodies are available to be coded sexually – whether they are politicians, foreign correspondents or serious news anchors. In relation to talk shows the notion that contemporary 'openness' about sex constitutes 'liberation' was treated sceptically from a Foucaultian perspective which conceives the obligation to confess as a central part of the operation of power. Moreover, the chapter considered the ways in which even apparently anti-normative discourses of sexuality (e.g. from bisexuals or sex workers) were located within a normalizing framework and rendered into psychological issues.

Sexualization was discussed further in chapter 6, which contrasted discourses of sex in men's and women's magazines. Whilst in the 'lad mags' sex is discussed through a vocabulary of youthful, unselfconscious pleasure-seeking, in magazines targeted at teenage girls and young women it is constructed as something requiring constant attention, discipline, self-surveillance and emotional labour. Girls and women are interpellated as the monitors of all sexual and emotional relationships, responsible for producing themselves as desirable heterosexual subjects as well as for pleasing men sexually, protecting against pregnancy and sexually transmitted infections, defending their own sexual reputations, and taking care of men's self-esteem. Men, by contrast, are hailed by the lad mags as hedonists just wanting 'a shag'. The uneven distribution of these discourses of sex, even in a resolutely heterosexual context, is crucial to understanding sexualization. Put simply, in magazines aimed at straight women, men are presented as complex, vulnerable human beings. But in magazines targeted at those same men women only ever discuss their underwear, sexual fantasies, 'filthiest moments' or body parts (Turner 2005).

The lad mags are emblematic of the blurring of the boundaries between pornography and other genres that has occurred in the last decade. 'Porno chic' (as we saw in chapter 3) has become a dominant representational practice in advertising, magazines, Internet sites and cable television. Even children's television has adopted a sexualized address to its audience and between its presenters. The commercially driven nature of this sexualization can be seen in the way that clothing companies target girls as young as five with thongs (G-strings), belly tops and T-shirts bearing sexually provocative slogans, e.g. 'when I'm bad I'm very, very bad, but when I'm in bed I'm better.' The use of the Playboy bunny icon on clothing, stationery and pencils aimed at the preteen market is but one example of the deliberate sexualization of children (girls). The 'girlification' of adult women such as Kylie Minogue and Kate Moss is the flip side of a media culture that promotes female children as its most desirable sexual icons (see Tincknell 2005) for a nuanced discussion of this phenomenon).

From sex object to desiring sexual subject

Where once sexualized representations of women in the media presented them as passive, mute objects of an assumed male gaze, today sexualization works somewhat differently in many domains. Women are not straightforwardly objectified but are presented as active, desiring sexual subjects who choose to present themselves in a seemingly objectified manner because it suits their liberated interests to do so (Goldman 1992). Nowhere is this clearer than in advertising, which has responded to feminist critiques by constructing a new figure to sell to young women: the sexually autonomous heterosexual young woman who plays with her sexual power and is forever 'up for it'.

This shift is crucial to understanding the postfeminist sensibility. It represents a modernization of femininity to include what Hilary Radner has called a new 'technology of sexiness' in which sexual knowledge and sexual practice are central. Furthermore it represents a shift in the way that power operates: a shift from an external, male judging gaze to a self-policing narcissistic gaze. I would argue that it represents a higher or deeper form of exploitation than objectification – one in which the objectifying male gaze is internalized to form a new disciplinary regime. In this regime power is not imposed from above or from the outside, but constructs our very subjectivity. We are invited to become a particular kind of self, and endowed with agency on condition that it is used to construct oneself as a subject closely resembling the heterosexual male fantasy that is found in pornography. As Janice Turner has argued,

> Once porn and real human sexuality were distinguishable. Not even porn's biggest advocates would suggest a porn flick depicted reality, that women were gagging for sex 24/7 and would drop their clothes and submit to rough, anonymous sex at the slightest invitation. But as porn has seeped into mainstream culture, the line has blurred. To speak to men's magazine editors, it is clear they believe that somehow in recent years, porn has come true. The sexually liberated modern woman turns out to resemble – what do you know! – the pneumatic, take-me-now-big-boy fuck-puppet of male fantasy after all. (Turner 2005: 2)

The humorous tone that characterized early examples of this shift – such as the bra adverts discussed in chapter 3, in which billboard models confidently and playfully highlighted their sexual power or traffic-stopping sexiness – should not imply that this shift is not, in fact, profoundly serious and problematic. In the last decade it has gone from being a new and deliberate representational strategy used *on women* (i.e. for depicting young women) to being widely and popularly taken up *by women* as a way of constructing the self: TV presenter Denise van Outen 'confides' in a TV interview, 'I do have a lovely pair. I hope they'll still be photographing my tits when I'm 60'; 'readers wives' write in to lad magazines with their favourite sexual experiences, for example 'he turned me around, bent me over the railings and took me from behind, hard'; and girls and women in the West queue up to buy T-shirts with slogans such as 'porn star', 'fcuk me', 'fit chick unbelievable knockers' or, at my university, 'LSE babe' – presumably designed to promote a combination of brains, beauty and hot sexiness.

To be critical of the shift is not to be somehow 'anti-sex' – though in postfeminist media culture this position (the prude) is the only alternative discursively allowed (itself part of the problem, and eradicating a space for critique). Rather it is to point to the dangers of such representations of women in a culture in which sexual violence is endemic. It is to highlight the exclusions of this representational practice – only *some* women are constructed as active, desiring sexual subjects: women who desire sex with men (except when lesbian women 'perform' for men) and only young, slim and beautiful women. As Myra Macdonald (1995) has pointed out, older women, bigger women, women with wrinkles, etc. are never accorded sexual subjecthood and are still subject to offensive and sometimes vicious representations. Indeed, the figure of the unattractive woman who wants a sexual partner remains one of the most vilified in a range of popular cultural forms. Above all, to critique this is to highlight the pernicious connection of this representational shift to neoliberal subjectivities in which sexual objectification can be (re)presented not as something done to women by some men, but as the freely chosen wish of active, confident, assertive female subjects.

Individualism, choice and empowerment

Notions of choice, of 'being oneself', and 'pleasing oneself' are central to the postfeminist sensibility that I am arguing suffuses contemporary Western media culture. They resonate powerfully with the emphasis upon empowerment and taking control that was discussed in relation to talk shows. A grammar of individualism underpins all these notions – such that even experiences of racism or homophobia or domestic violence are framed in exclusively personal terms in a way that turns the idea of the personal as political on its head. Lois McNay (1992) has called this the deliberate 'reprivatization' of issues that have only relatively recently become politicized.

One aspect of this postfeminist sensibility in media culture is the almost total evacuation of notions of politics or cultural influence. This is seen not only in the relentless personalizing tendencies of news, talk shows and reality TV, but also in the ways in which every aspect of life is refracted through the idea of personal choice and self-determination. For example, phenomena such as the dramatic increase in the number of women having Brazilian waxes (to entirely remove pubic hair and reinstate a prepubescent version of their genitalia) or the uptake of breast augmentation surgery by teenage girls are widely depicted as indicators of women 'pleasing themselves' and 'using beauty' to make themselves feel good. Scant attention is paid to the pressures that might lead a teenager to decide that major surgery will solve her problems, and even less to the commercial interests that are underpinning this staggering trend, such as targeted advertising by cosmetic surgery clinics, and promotional packages that include mother and daughter special deals and discounts for two friends to have their 'boobs' done at the same time.

The notion that all our practices are freely chosen fits well with broader postfeminist discourses which present women as autonomous agents no longer constrained by any inequalities or power imbalances whatsoever. As Fay Weldon has put it, 'Young girls seem to be getting prettier all the time. There is a return to femininity, but it seems to me that most girls don't give two hoots about men. It is about being fit and healthy for *themselves* not for men. (*Observer*, 25 August 1996; emphasis in original). Of course the idea that in the past women dressed in a particular way purely to please men is ridiculous: it suggests a view of power as something both overbearing and obvious, which acted upon entirely docile subjects – as well as implying that all women are heterosexual and preoccupied with male approval. But this pendulum shift to the notion that women just 'please themselves' will not to do as a substitute. It presents women as entirely free agents, and cannot account for why, if women are just pleasing themselves, and following their own autonomously generated desires, the resulting valued 'look' is so similar – hairless body, slim waist, firm buttocks, etc. Moreover, it simply avoids all the interesting and important questions about the relationship between representations and subjectivity, the difficult but crucial questions about how socially constructed, mass-mediated ideals of beauty are internalized and made our own.

What is striking is the degree of fit between the autonomous postfeminist subject and the psychological subject demanded by neoliberalism. At the heart of both is the notion of the 'choice biography' and the contemporary injunction to render one's life knowable and meaningful through a narrative of free choice and autonomy – however constrained one might actually be (Rose 1996; Walkerdine, Lucey et al. 2001).

Take this typical example from *Glamour*'s 'Relationtips' column, October 2005:

> It is possible to make the euphoria of the first date last. In the early weeks, says Balfour, it's best to be the first to end the date. 'It leaves him wanting more.' Then remember the golden rules: don't talk endlessly about your ex, be bitter about men or moan about your awful job/family/life. Most men agree a confident, secure, optimistic and happy woman is easier to fall in love with than a needy, neurotic one. 'It's not about "I need to be more sexy for him and he'll love me more", it's about being confident in yourself.'

Here – as in *Bridget Jones's Diary* and the chick lit we discussed in chapter 7 – achieving desirability in a heterosexual context is explicitly (re-)presented as something to be understood as being done for yourself and *not* in order to please a man. In this modernized, neoliberal version of femininity, it is absolutely imperative that one's sexual and dating practices (however traditional, old-fashioned or inegalitarian they may be – involving strict adherence to rules, rationing oneself and not displaying any needs!) be presented as freely chosen. In this example, some of the strain of this position – the messy suturing of traditional and neoliberal discourses – can be seen very clearly both in the need to explicitly disavow a potential reading that 'you' would be doing this to please a man, and the attempt to gloss 'leaving him wanting more' as – somehow – a modern and powerful position.

Self-surveillance and discipline

Intimately related to the stress upon personal choice is the new emphasis on self-surveillance, self-monitoring and self-discipline in postfeminist media culture. Arguably monitoring and surveilling the self have long been requirements of the performance of successful femininity – with instruction in grooming, attire, posture, elocution and 'manners' being 'offered' to women to allow them to more closely emulate the upper-class white ideal. In women's magazines femininity has always been portrayed as contingent – requiring constant anxious attention, work and vigilance, from touching up your makeup to packing the perfect capsule wardrobe, from hiding 'unsightly' pimples, wrinkles, age spots, or stains to hosting a successful dinner party. What marks out the present moment as distinctive, however, are three features: first, the dramatically increased intensity of self-surveillance, indicating the intensity of the regulation of women (alongside the disavowal of such regulation); secondly the extensiveness of surveillance over entirely new spheres of life and intimate conduct; and thirdly the focus upon the psychological – upon the requirement to transform oneself and remodel one's interior life.

Something of the intensity and extensiveness of the self-surveillance and discipline now normatively required of women was captured in chapter 6, which discussed how bodily shape, size, muscle tone, attire, sexual practice, career, home, finances, etc. are rendered into 'problems' that necessitate ongoing and constant monitoring and labour – which, in an extraordinary ideological sleight of hand, must nevertheless be understood as 'fun' or 'pampering' or 'self-indulgence' and must *never* be disclosed. Magazines offer tips to girls and young women to enable them to continue the work of femininity but still appear as entirely confident, carefree and unconcerned about their self-presentation (as this is now an important aspect of femininity in its own right), for example the solution to continuing a diet whilst at an important business lunch where everyone else is drinking, is to order a spritzer (and surreptitiously to ask the waiter to make it largely mineral water). *J17* includes the following advice to girls texting a 'lad love': 'Do: be flirtatious – no lad can resist an ego massage; text him before he goes to bed – you'll be the last thing on his mind; put in a deliberate mistake to give it that "I'm not so bothered aboutcha" air; wait a minimum of 10 minutes before you reply – yes, 10 minutes!' (*J17*, March 2001). From the sending of a brief text message to the ordering of a drink, no area of a woman's life is immune from the requirement for self-surveillance and work on the self. And more and more aspects of the body come under surveillance: you thought you were comfortable with your body? Well think again! When was the last time you checked your 'upper arm definition'? Have you been neglecting your armpits or the soles of your feet? Do you sometimes have (ahem) unpleasant odours, especially after intercourse?

But it is not only the surface of the body that needs ongoing vigilance – there is also the self: what kind of friend/lover/daughter/colleague are you? Do you laugh enough? How well do you communicate? Have you got emotional intelligence? In a culture saturated by individualistic self-help discourses, the self has become a project to be evaluated, advised, disciplined and improved or brought 'into recovery'. What is so striking, however, is how unevenly distributed these quasi-therapeutic discourses are. In magazines, in contemporary fiction and television, in talk shows, it is women and not men who are addressed and required to work on and transform the self. Again, as we saw earlier, it appears that the ideal disciplinary subject of neoliberalism is feminine: a clear fit between neoliberalism and postfeminist media culture is emerging.

The makeover paradigm

More broadly, we might argue that a makeover paradigm constitutes postfeminist media culture. This requires people (predominantly women) to believe first that they or their life is lacking or flawed in some way, and secondly that it is amenable to reinvention or transformation by following the advice of relationship, design or lifestyle experts, and practising appropriately modified consumption habits. Not only is this the implicit message of many magazines, talk shows and other media content, but it is the explicit focus of the 'makeover takeover' (Hollows 2000b) that dominates contemporary television. It started with food and homes and gardens, but has now extended to clothing, cleanliness, work, dating, cosmetic surgery and raising children.

Such shows start with the production of 'toxic shame' (Peck 1995) in their participants through humiliation – about their inadequacies in the wardrobe/cleanliness/dating/childrearing department, alongside the gleeful and voyeuristic display of their failings to the audience (e.g. 'oh my GOD – what is THAT? No, NO! What's she DOING?!'). Participants are then variously advised, cajoled, bullied or 'educated' into changing their ways and becoming more 'successful' versions of themself (e.g. looking younger, getting past the first date, having a better relationship with their children, etc.). A frequent 'third chapter' of the shows' format allows the hapless victim to be set free to 'go it alone' (e.g. on a date or buying clothes) while, behind the watchful eye of the hidden camera, the 'experts' offer their judgements.

As Helen Wood and Beverly Skeggs (2004) have argued, the ubiquity of such shows produces 'new ethical selves' in which particular forms of modernized and upgraded selfhood are presented as solutions to dilemmas of contemporary life. The scenarios are profoundly classed and gendered – and, as Angela McRobbie (2004b) points out, racialized too, if largely through exclusion, since the kind of hostile judgements routinely made of white working class women would risk being heard as racist if made by white experts about black bodies, practices and lives. The shows reinvigorate class antagonisms which, in this moment of compulsory individuality, no longer work on such 'crude' categories as occupation or social location, but play out on the women's bodies, homes, cooking skills and ability as mothers, through notions of good taste and cultural capital:

> Choice mediates taste, displaying the success and the failure of the self to make itself, for instance in lifestyle programs such as *Changing Rooms* (BBC), *House Dr* (Channel 4) and *Better Homes* (ITV) where the domestic and thus the everyday is transformed through appropriating 'better' taste. (Wood and Skeggs 2004: 206)

McRobbie points to the appalling nastiness and viciousness of the gendered and class animosities enacted, and the sense of people being encouraged to laugh at those less fortunate than themselves. In a programme like *Wife Swap*, however, in which two married women (usually from dramatically different class backgrounds) swap lives, the orchestrated morality is sometimes more complicated, with middle-class 'career women' the target of attack for not devoting enough time or attention to their children (alongside the attacks on working-class women's poor food preparation, incompetence at helping with homework, etc. which McRobbie describes). What is clear from even a cursory viewing of such shows is that women simply *cannot* win; they will always and inevitably 'fail'. But rather than interrogating femininity or social relations or what we as a society expect of women, the shows offer no way of understanding this other than through the dramatized spectacle of conflict between two women.

As I have noted, most of the participants and a large part of the assumed audience for the shows are women. One exception is *Queer Eye for the Straight Guy* in which 'five gay professionals in fashion, grooming, interior design, culture, food and wine come together as a team to help straight men of the world find the job, get the look and get the girl' (executive producer quoted in Allatson 2004: 209). Here, gay men occupy an explicitly feminized position and offer advice based on their cultural capital as wealthy, successful, middle-class and, above all, stylish. There is no space here to reflect on the debates about the show, such as its elision/equation of gayness with stylishness, its eradication of any female 'queer' perspectives, and its role in bolstering and maintaining a heterosexist economy. But it is worth pointing to the difference in tone between this show and similar formats aimed at transforming women – in particular, the ironic distance and lack of a sense of punitive regulation that marks out *Queer Eye*. This is also notable on the occasions in which other shows feature male participants: these are marked in subtle ways as 'less serious', and as offering a kind of symbolic revenge against men. This can be seen most clearly in the now iconic moment in each show (such as *10 Years Younger*) in which male victims are told that they must have their back (or sometimes chest) hair removed. This procedure is lingered over by the camera in a way that seems designed to appeal to female viewers, for whom waxing or electrolysis are assumed to be routine. The 2005 box-office hit *Hitch* in which Will Smith plays life and relationship coach to the sweet but inept Kevin James features a similar scene, whilst also being wrapped in a narrative that reassures male viewers that such self-transformations are not really necessary: being oneself (un-made-over) is all that is required to win the woman's heart, and 'authentic masculinity' wins the day.

The reassertion of sexual difference

If for a short time in the 1970s and 1980s notions of male and female equality and the basic similarity of men and women took hold in popular culture, then this was resolutely dispensed with by the 1990s. A key feature of the postfeminist sensibility has been the resurgence of ideas of natural sexual difference across all media, from newspapers, to advertising, to talk shows and popular fiction. In part, as we saw in chapter 6, this played out in the debates about masculinity in which the figure of the new man was attacked by both women and men as asexual and not manly enough. New man was condemned as inauthentic and fake, and understood by many as an act or a pose that was called into being by the hegemonic dominance of feminism but had little to do with what men were actually like. Against this, the rise of the new lad in the 1990s was widely reported as an assertion of freedom against the stranglehold of feminism and – crucially – as the unashamed celebration of true or authentic masculinity, liberated from the shackles of 'political correctness'. New lad championed and reasserted a version of masculinity as libidinous, powerful and different from femininity. And the cultural power of this articulation was further strengthened by the high visibility accorded to the mythopoetic men's movement in the USA, which sought to reclaim and rebuild male rituals and to celebrate essential masculinity.

Importantly, these discourses of sexual difference were nourished by both the growing interest in evolutionary psychology and developments in genetic science which held out the promise of locating a genetic basis for all human characteristics. Such developments, from concern about the existence of a 'gay gene' to attempts to identify the parts of the brain responsible for risk-taking (and to demonstrate that they were larger in men than in women), were accorded a huge amount of coverage in the press and on television, and it is significant that this interest coincided with a moment in which the lifestyle sections of newspapers were expanding and proliferating, to be filled – in large part – by articles which took as their focus the nature of gender and gender relations.

Notions of sexual difference were also fed by the explosion of self-help literature which addressed – at least as its subtext – the question of why the 'battle of the sexes' continued despite (or in some iterations because of) feminism. One answer rang out loud and clear from many texts: because men and women are fundamentally different. Feminism was deemed to have lost its way when it tried to impose its ideological prescriptions on a nature that did not fit; what was needed, such literature argued, was a frank acknowledgement of difference rather than its denial. Spearheading the movement (or at least the publishing phenomenon) was John Gray, whose Mars and Venus texts soon became a whole industry. Gray's genius was in locating sexual difference as a psychological, rather than essentially biological, matter, and transposing old and clichéd notions through the new and fresh metaphor of interplanetary difference, while (superficially at least) avoiding blame and criticism. (A closer reading tells a different story.)

Gray's work became an important part of postfeminist media culture in its own right, as well as in its citations in other popular cultural texts from magazines to chick lit, and its inauguration of the notion of (interplanetary) 'translation'. The idea (also found in more expressly feminist texts such as Deborah Tannen's (1992) work on language) is that men and women just do not understand each other. A large role for the popular media, then, is translating or mediating men's and women's communication, customs and 'funny ways' to each other (in a manner, I would argue, that still systematically privileges male power).

Sexual difference discourses also serve to (re-)eroticize power relations between men and women. At one level this simply means that difference is constructed as sexy. At another, as we saw in chapter 3, discourses of natural gender difference can be used to freeze in place existing inequalities by representing them as inevitable and – if read correctly – as pleasurable.

Irony and knowingness

No discussion of the postfeminist sensibility in the media would be complete without considering irony and knowingness. Irony can serve many functions. In chapter 3 I discussed how it is used in advertising to address what Goldman called 'sign fatigue', by hailing audiences as knowing and sophisticated consumers, flattering them with their awareness of intertextual references and the notion that they can really 'see through' attempts to manipulate them. Irony is also used as a way of establishing a safe distance between oneself and particular sentiments or beliefs, at a time when being passionate about anything or appearing to care too much seems to be 'uncool'. As Ian Parker has noted in relation to declarations of love, the postmodern and ironic version of 'I love you' might be 'as Barbara Cartland would say, "I love you madly"' (Parker 1989). Here the quotation or reference sets up a protective distance between the speaker and the expression of love. Jackson, Stevenson and Brooks (2001) have argued that irony may also offer an internal defence against ambivalent feelings – as well as outwardly rebutting charges of taking something – or worse, oneself – too seriously.

Most significantly, however, in postfeminist media culture irony has become a way of 'having it both ways', of expressing sexist or homophobic or otherwise unpalatable sentiments in an ironized form, while claiming this was not actually 'meant'.

It works in various ways. As Whelehan (2000) and Williamson (2003) have argued, the use of retro-imagery and nostalgia is a key device in the construction of contemporary sexism. Referencing a previous era becomes an important way of suggesting that the sexism is safely sealed in the past, whilst constructing scenarios that would garner criticism if they were represented as contemporary. In the recent Happy Days advert for Citroën C3 cars, for example, the first frame shows a young woman having her dress entirely ripped off her body to reveal her bright red underwear (which matches the car). She screams but the action soon moves on, as the interest is in her body not her distress. The 1950s iconography and soundtrack from the *Happy Days* TV show works to protect it from potential criticism: it is as if the whole thing is in ironic and humorous quotation marks.

The return and rehabilitation of the word 'totty' in popular culture marks another example of this, allowing middle-class television presenters to refer to women in an entirely dehumanizing and objectifying manner, while suggesting that the sexism is not meant seriously. The word has a nostalgic quality, redolent of 'naughty' seaside postcards.

Irony can also operate through 'silly' neologisms. This happens routinely in the lad magazines. *FHM*, for example, in evaluating photographs of readers' girlfriends' breasts, makes such comments as 'if we're being fussy, right chesticle is a tad larger than the left' – the sheer silliness of the term 'chesticle' raising a smile so that one might almost overlook the fact that this is a competition ('breast quest') to find the 'best pair of tits' in Britain!

As we saw in chapter 6, irony also functions through the very extremeness of the sexism expressed: as though the mere fact that women are compared to 'rusty old bangers' or posed against each other in the 'dumbest girlfriend' competition is (perversely) evidence that there is no sexism. (That is, the extremeness of the sexism is evidence that there is no sexism!) Magazine editors routinely trot out the line that it is all 'harmless fun'. (When did harmless and fun become yoked together so powerfully?) And some academic commentators agree: David Gauntlett argues that the sexism in such magazines is 'knowingly ridiculous, based on the assumption that it's silly to be sexist (and therefore is funny in a silly way)' (2002: 168).

Yet if we suspend our disbelief in the notion that it's 'just a laugh', we are left with a fast-growing area of media content (itself profoundly influencing other media) that is chillingly misogynist, inviting men to evaluate women only as sexual objects. A recent issue of *FHM* asks men: 'how much are you paying for sex?' Readers are invited to calculate their 'outgoings' on items such as drinks, cinema tickets and bunches of flowers, and then to divide the total by the number of 'shags' they've had that month in order to calculate their 'pay per lay'. Under a fiver per shag is 'too cheap – she is about the same price as the Cambodian whore'; around £11 to £20 is 'about the going rate for a Cypriot tart' and each shag should now be compared with the value and pleasure to be obtained from purchasing a new CD. Any more expensive than this and you should expect a performance worthy of a highly trained, sexy showgirl.

It's hard to imagine any other group in society being so systematically objectified, attacked and vilified, with so little opposition – and this tells us something about the power of irony. Any attempt to offer a critique of such articles is dismissed by references to the critic's presumed ugliness, stupidity or membership of the 'feminist thought police'. Frequently, criticisms are pre-empted by comments which suggest that the article's writer is expecting 'blundering rants' from the 'council of women', etc. In this context, critique becomes much more difficult – and this, it would seem, is precisely what is intended.

Feminism and anti-feminism

Finally I want to turn to constructions of feminism which are an integral feature of the postfeminist sensibility considered here. As I argued at the start of this book, one of things that makes the media today very different from the television, magazines, radio or press of the 1960s, 1970s and early 1980s is that feminism is now part of the cultural field. That is, feminist discourses are expressed within the media rather than simply being external, independent, critical voices. Feminist-inspired ideas burst forth from our radios, television screens and print media in TV discussions about date rape and sexualized imagery, in newspaper articles about women's experiences of war or the increasing beauty pressures on young girls, in talk shows about domestic violence or anorexia. Indeed, it might be argued that much of what counts as feminist debate in Western countries today takes place in the media rather than outside it.

However, it would be entirely false to suggest that the media have somehow become feminist, have unproblematically adopted a feminist perspective. Instead it seems more accurate to argue that the media offer contradictory, but nevertheless patterned, constructions. In this postfeminist moment, as Judith Stacey (1987) has put it, feminist ideas are simultaneously 'incorporated, revised and depoliticised', and, I would add, attacked. Angela McRobbie (2004c) has referred to this as the contemporary 'double entanglement' of neoliberal values in relation to gender, sexuality and family life and a feminism that is at once part of common sense, yet also feared, hated and fiercely repudiated.

What makes contemporary media culture distinctively postfeminist, rather than pre-feminist or anti-feminist, is precisely this entanglement of feminist and anti-feminist ideas. This has been discussed throughout the book in relation to advertising, talk shows and magazines. But it was perhaps most evident in the discussion of contemporary screen and paperback romances in chapter 7. In these, feminism is not ignored or even attacked (as some backlash theorists might have it) but is simultaneously taken for granted and repudiated. A certain kind of liberal feminist perspective is treated as common sense, whilst at the same time feminism and feminists are constructed as harsh, punitive, inauthentic and as not articulating women's true desires (Tasker and Negra 2005). In a recent interview, Marian Keyes, author of a series of successful chick lit novels (one of which was included in the analysis in chapter 7) refers to herself as part of a 'postfeminist generation' that grew up in fear of being 'told off' by feminists and 'having everything pink taken out of my house' (*Start the Week*, BBC Radio 4, 7 June 2004). This caricature captures well what Esther Sonnet has called the 'naughty but nice' effect where 'disapproval from Big Sister intensifies the secret/guilty pleasures offered to the "postfeminist" consumer of the forbidden pleasures of the unreconstructed "feminine"' (Sonnet 2002).

Perhaps this also relates to the pleasures of the sexism in lad mags – targeted as they are at men 'who should know better' (to use *Loaded's* strapline). It is precisely the knowingness of the 'transgression', alongside the deliberate articulation of feminist and anti-feminist ideas, that signifies a postfeminist sensibility. Indeed, as we saw in chapter 6, discourses of laddish sexism are purposely reconciled with discourses of liberal feminism in order to rebut critique.

As we have seen, postfeminist heroines are often much more active protagonists than their counterparts in popular culture from the 1970s and 1980s. They value autonomy and bodily integrity and the freedom to make individual choices. What is interesting, however, is the way in which they seem compelled to use their empowered postfeminist position to make choices that would be regarded by many feminists as problematic, located as they are in normative notions of femininity. They choose, for example, white weddings, downsizing, giving up work or taking their husband's name on marriage (McRobbie 2004c). One reading of this may highlight the exclusions of second-wave feminism and suggest that it represents the 'return of the repressed', such as the pleasures of domesticity or traditional femininity (Hollows 2003). Another – not necessarily contradictory – reading might want to stress the ways in which pre-feminist ideals are being (seductively) repackaged as postfeminist freedoms (Probyn 1997) in ways that do nothing to question normative heterosexual femininity. Two things are clear, however: first that postfeminism constructs an articulation or suture between femininist and anti-feminist ideas, and secondly that this is effected entirely through a grammar of individualism that fits perfectly with neoliberalism.

Conclusion

What I have tried to do in this chapter is to pull together the arguments of the book by setting out some of the distinctive elements of the postfeminist sensibility that seems to me to characterize contemporary media culture. It has been of necessity brief and schematic and has paid insufficient attention to the ways in which this sensibility operates in relation to differences besides gender, in particular class, race and ethnicity, sexuality and age. But I hope that I have offered enough discussion of this elsewhere in the book to compensate for the inattention here. As I indicated in chapter 1, I believe that feminist media studies today requires an intersectional approach which recognizes the ways in which various axes of oppression and difference always and inevitably work together.

To conclude, however, I want to return to another of the issues raised at the start of this book: namely what kind of cultural politics is appropriate for engaging with postfeminist media culture? In chapter 1 I considered many of the strategies of resistance and activism deployed by feminists in the 1970s and 1980s: calls for positive images, sticker campaigns, demonstrations, demands for more women working within the media, calls for women-only spaces, the development of alternative media, and attempts to use existing regulatory bodies to challenge and change representations of women. Some of the strengths and weaknesses, successes and failures of the strategies were examined.

How appropriate would these strategies be for critiquing contemporary media representations? How effective would they be at engaging with a postfeminist sensibility? It seems to me that these are open yet urgent questions. What I have tried to do in this book is to take one step back – to rewind, pause and refresh. The aim has been to ask a prior – but in my view absolutely crucial – question about the nature of representations of women, men and gender relations in the media today. It has been my argument that only by understanding the dynamics of contemporary sexism will we know which political tools might be necessary or useful to engage in this cultural field.

It seemed to me when I started writing this book that, compared with the confidence and certainty of early media critique, today's feminist media scholars were more tentative and less certain. They had a much more secure institutional base than in the recent past and a rich vocabulary of theoretical languages, but were much less sure of what – if anything – should be the target of critique. The growing sophistication of media studies, Katherine Viner (1999) argued, seemed to make it harder and harder to actually object to any kind of representational practice. Indeed, as Judith Williamson (2003) pointed out, the very term 'sexism' was starting to have a 'quaint ' ring to it; a concept from an earlier era.

> Sexism isn't just a phenomenon, it's an idea – and once the word stops being used, the idea goes out of fashion. What then becomes passé isn't actually sexism, which is doing just fine, but the concept of sexism in advertising or anything else. (Williamson 2003: 1)

Like Williamson, I believe that the notion of sexism needs to be held on to and revitalized (however old-fashioned it might sound). This book has begun the task of identifying how sexism operates in the contemporary media. It has argued that there have been huge shifts in representational practices in the last two decades, partly in response to feminist critique. Today's media culture has a distinctive postfeminist sensibility organized around notions of choice, empowerment, self-surveillance, and sexual difference, and articulated in an ironic and knowing register in which feminism is simultaneously taken for granted and repudiated. The challenge now is to articulate the politics that can engage effectively with this new sensibility, and move forward to more open, equal, hopeful and generous gender relations.

References

Acland, C. R. (1995). *Youth, Murder, Spectacle: the cultural politics of youth in crisis.* Boulder, Colo., Westview.

Alice, L. (1995). What is postfeminism? Or, having it both ways. In *Postmodernism, Postfeminism: Conference Proceedings.* New Zealand, Massey University.

Allatson, P. (2004). Queer eye's primping and pimping for empire et al. *Feminist Media Studies* 4(2): 208–11.

Althusser, L. (1984). *Essays on Ideology.* London, Verso.

Amos, V. and P. Parmar (1984). Challenging Imperial Feminism. In H. Mirza, ed., *Black British Feminism.* London, Routledge.

Amy-Chinn, D. (2006). This is just for me(n): lingerie advertising for the post-feminist woman. *Journal of Consumer Culture* 6(2).

Anderson, P. (1983). *In the Tracks of Historical Materialism.* London, Verso.

Ang, I. (1985). *Watching Dallas: soap opera and the melodramatic imagination.* London, Methuen.

Ang, I. (1990). Melodramatic identifications: television fiction and women's fantasy. In M. E. Brown, ed., *Television and Women's Culture.* London, Sage.

Ang, I. (1996). *Living Room Wars: rethinking media audiences for a postmodern age.* London, Routledge.

Ang, I. (2001). *On not Speaking Chinese: living between Asia and the West.* London, Routledge.

Anzaldúa, G. (1999). *Borderlands = La frontera.* San Francisco, Aunt Lute Books.

Arthurs, J. (2003). Sex and the City and consumer culture: re-mediating post-modernist drama. *Feminist Media Studies* 3(1).

Arthurs, J. (2004). *Television and Sexuality: regulation and the politics of taste.* Maidenhead, Open University Press.

Arthurs, J. and J. Grimshaw (1999). *Women's Bodies: discipline and transgression.* London, Cassell.

Asaro, C. (1997). A quickie with Catherine Asaro – on feminism and romance. At Likesbooks.com.

Ashcroft, B., G. Griffiths and H. Tiffin (1995). *The Post Colonial Studies Reader.* London, Routledge.

Assiter, A. (1988). Romance fiction: porn for women? In G. Day and C. Bloom, eds, *Perspectives on Pornography: Sexuality in Film and Literature.* Basingstoke, Macmillan.

Attwood, F. (2004). Pornography and objectification: re-reading 'the picture that divided Britain'. *Feminist Media Studies* 4(1): 7–19.

Baehr, H., ed. (1980). *Women and Media.* Oxford, Pergamon.

Baehr, H. (1996). A woman's place? *Broadcast* 7 June.

Baglietto, V. A. (2002). *The Wrong Mr Right*. London, Coronet.

Ballaster, R., M. Beetham et al. (1991). *Women's Worlds: ideology, femininity and the women's magazine*. London, Macmillan Education.

Bardin, L. (1977). *L' Analyse de contenu*. Paris, PUF.

Barile, P. and G. Rao (1992). Trends in Italian media law. *European Journal of Communication* 7: 261–81.

Barker, M. (1981). *The New Racism: Conservatives and the ideology of the tribe*. London, Junction Books.

Barnard, S. (1989). *On the Radio: music radio in Britain*. Milton Keynes, Open University Press.

Barnes, C. (1992). *Disabling Imagery and the Media: an exploration of the principles for media representations of disabled people*. London: British Council of Organizations of Disabled People.

Barr, M. S. (2000). Biology is not destiny; biology is fantasy: Cinderella, or to dream Disney's 'impossible'/possible race relations dream. In E. R. Helford, ed., *Fantasy Girls: Gender in the New Universe of Science Fiction and Fantasy Television*. Oxford, Rowman & Littlefield.

Barrowcliffe, M. (2001). *Infidelity for First Time Fathers*. London, Headline.

Barthes, R. (1973). *Mythologies*. London, Paladin.

Bartky, S. L. (1990). *Femininity and Domination: studies in the phenomenology of oppression*. New York/London, Routledge.

Bausinger, II. (1984). Media, Technology and Daily Life. *Media Culture & Society* 6(4): 343–51.

BBC (2003). Men Cringe as Adverts Show 'Girl Power', http://news.bbc.co.uk.

Beasley, M. H. (1992). *Newspapers: Is there a new majority defining the news?* Thousand Oaks, Calif., Sage.

Beck, U. and E. Beck-Gernsheim (1995). *The Normal Chaos of Love*. Cambridge, Polity.

Benedict, H. (1992). *Virgin or Vamp: how the press covers sex crimes*. New York, Oxford University Press.

Bennett, T., G. Martin et al., eds. (1981). *Culture, Ideology and Social Process*. Milton Keynes, Open University Press.

Benwell, B. (2003). Ambiguous Masculinities: heroism and anti-heroism in the men's lifestyle magazines. In Benwell, ed., *Masculinity and Men's Lifestyle Magazines*. Oxford, Blackwell.

Berger, J. (1972). *Ways of Seeing: based on the BBC television series with John S Berger*. London, British Broadcasting Corporation and Penguin Books.

Berger, W. (2001). *Advertising Today*. London, Phaidon.

Betterton, R., ed. (1987). *Looking On: images of feminity in the visual arts and media*. London, Pandora.

Beynon, J. (2002). *Masculinities and Culture*. Philadelphia, Open University.

Bhabha, H. K. (1990). *Nation and Narration*. London, Routledge.

Bhabha, H. K. (1994). *The Location of Culture*. London, Routledge.

Bhavnani, K.-K. (2001). *Feminism and 'Race'*. Oxford, Oxford University Press.

Bhavnani, K.-K. and A. Phoenix, eds, (1994). *Shifting Identities, Shifting Racisms: a feminism & psychology reader*. London, Sage.

Biddulph, S. (1995). *Manhood: an action plan for changing men's lives*. Sydney, Finch.

Billig, M. (1987). *Arguing and Thinking: a rhetorical approach to social psychology*. Cambridge, Cambridge University Press.

Billig, M. (1991). *Ideology and Opinions: studies in rhetorical psychology*. London, Sage.

Blackman, I. (1995). White Girls are Easy, Black Girls are Studs. In L. Pearce and J. Stacey, eds, *Romance Revisited*. London, Lawrence & Wishart.

Blackman, L. and V. Walkerdine (1996). *Mass Hysteria: critical psychology and media studies*. London, Palgrave.

Blum-Kulka, S. (2001). The Many Faces of *With Meni*: the history and stories of the Israeli talk show. In A. Tolson, ed., *Television Talk Shows*. Hillsdale, NJ, Erlbaum Associates.

Bly, R. (1990). *Iron John: a book about men*. Reading, Mass., Addison-Wesley.

Bogdan, R. (1988). *Freak Show: presenting human oddities for amusement and profit*. Chicago, University of Chicago Press.

Boggs, C. and T. Dirmann (1999). The myth of electronic populism: talk radio and the decline of the public sphere. *Democracy and Nature* 5: 65–94.

Bordo, S. (1993). *Unbearable Weight: feminism, Western culture, and the body*. Berkeley, University of California Press.

Bordo, S. (1999). *The Male Body: a new look at men in public and in private*. New York, Farrar, Straus and Giroux.

Bourdieu, P. (1984). *Distinction: a social critique of the judgement of taste*. London, Routledge.

Brah, A. (1996). *Cartographies of Diaspora: contesting identities*. London, Routledge.

Branston, G. (2002). September 11th, as we now call them. *Feminist Media Studies* 2(1): 129–31.

Brooks, A. (1997). *Postfeminisms: feminism, cultural theory and cultural forms*. London, Routledge.

Brown, B., N. Green, et al., eds (2005). *Wireless World: social and interactional aspects of the mobile age*. London, Springer-Verlag.

Brown, M. E., ed. (1990). *Television and Women's Culture: The Politics of the Popular*. London, Sage.

Brown, M. E. and D. Gardetto (2000). Representing Hillary Rodham Clinton: - gender, meaning and news media. In A. Sreberny and L. Van Zoonen, eds, *Gender, Politics and Communication*. Cresskill, NJ, Hampton Press.

Brunsdon, C. (1987). Feminism and soap opera. In K. Davies, J. Dickey and T. Stratford, eds, *Out of Focus: writings on women and the media*. London, Women's Press.

Brunsdon, C. (1993). Identity in feminist TV criticism. *Media, Culture and Society*, 15: 309–20.

Brunsdon, C. (2000). *The Feminist, the Housewife and the Soap Opera*. Oxford, Clarendon Press.

Brunsdon, C. (2005). Feminism, Postfeminism, Martha, Martha and Nigella. *Cinema Journal* 44(2): 110–16.

Brunsdon, C. and D. Morley (1978). *Everyday Television: Nationwide*. London, British Film Institute.

Buchbinder, D. (1998). *Performance Anxieties: re-producing masculinity*. St Leonards, NSW, Allen & Unwin.

Bull, M. (2000). *Sounding out the City: personal stereos and the management of everyday life*. Oxford, Berg.

Bull, M. and L. Back (2003). *The Auditory Culture Reader*. Oxford/New York, Berg.

Butler, J. P. (1990). *Gender Trouble: feminism and the subversion of identity*. New York/London, Routledge.

Butler, J. P. (2004). *Undoing Gender*. New York/London, Routledge.

Caputi, J. (1987). *The Age of Sex Crime*. Bowling Green, Ohio, Bowling Green State University Popular Press.

Carby, H. (1982). White Woman Listen! Black feminism and the boundaries of sisterhood. In CCCS, *The Empire Strikes Back: race and racism in 1970s Britain*. London, Hutchinson.

Carpignano, P., R. Anderson et al. (1990). Chatter in the age of electronic reproduction: talk television and the 'public mind'. *Social Text* 25: 33–5.

Carrington, B. (1999). Too many St George's crosses to bear. In M. Perryman, ed., *The Ingerland Factor: Home Truths from Football*. Edinburgh, Mainstream Publishing.

Carter, C. (1998). When the 'extraordinary' becomes 'ordinary': everyday news of sexual violence. In C. Carter, G. Branston and G. Allen, eds, *News, Gender and Power*. London, Routledge.

Carter, C. and C. K. Weaver (2003). *Violence and the Media*. Buckingham, Open University Press.

Carty, V. (1997) Ideologies and forms of domination in the organization of the global production and consumption of goods in the emerging postmodern era: a case study of Nike Corporation and the implications of gender. *Gender, Work and Organization* 4.

CCCS Women's group (1978). *Women Take Issue*. London, Hutchinson.

Chambers, D., L. Steiner et al. (2004). *Women and Journalism*. London, Routledge.

Chambers, L. (2004). Bridget Jones and the postfeminist condition: towards a genealogy of thirtysomething femininities, PhD thesis, Goldsmiths College, University of London.

Chapman, R. and J. Rutherford (1988). *Male Order: unwrapping masculinity*. London, Lawrence & Wishart.

Charles, H. (1995). (Not) compromising: inter-skin colour relations. In L. Pearce and J. Stacey, eds, *Romance Revisited*. London, Lawrence & Wishart.

Christmas, L. (1997). *Chaps of Both Sexes? Women Decision Makers in Newspapers: do they make a difference?*, Women in Journalism/British Telecom.

Cockburn, C. and S. Ormrod (1993). *Gender and Technology in the Making*. London, Sage.

Cohan, S. and I. R. Hark (1993). *Screening the Male: exploring masculinities in Hollywood cinema*. London/New York, Routledge.

Cohen, S. and J. Young, eds. (1973). *The Manufacture of News, Deviance and Social Problems in the Mass Media*. London, MacGibbon & Kee.

Coles, J. (1997). Boy zone story. *Guardian*, 28 April.

Comella, L. (2003). (Safe) sex and the City: on vibrators, masturbation and the myth of 'real' sex. *Feminist Media Studies* 3(1): 109–12.

Connell, R. W. (1987). *Gender and Power: society, the person and sexual politics*. Cambridge, Polity.

Connell, R. W. (2000). *The Men and the Boys*. Cambridge, Polity.

Corber, R. J. and S. Valocchi, eds. (2003). *Queer Studies: an interdisciplinary reader*. Oxford, Blackwell.

Cortese, A. J. P. (1999). *Provocateur: images of women and minorities in advertising*. Lanham, Md., Rowman & Littlefield.

Coward, R. (1984). *Female Desire*. London, Paladin.

Cowie, E. (1978). Woman as sign. *M/f* 1: 49–73.

Creedon, P. J., ed. (1993). *Women in Mass Communication*. Newbury Park, Calif., Sage.

Crewe, B. (2003). Masculinity and editorial identity in the reformation of the UK men's press. In B. Benwell, ed., *Masculinity and Men's Lifestyle Magazines*. Oxford, Blackwell.

Crisci, R. (1997). Italian neo-TV and the private in public: romance, family and melodrama in container programmes and people shows. PhD thesis, Goldsmiths College, University of London.

Cuklanz, L. M. (1996). *Rape on Trial: how the mass media construct legal reform and social change*. Philadelphia, University of Pennsylvania Press.

Cuklanz, L. M. (2000). *Rape on Prime Time: television, masculinity, and sexual violence*. Philadelphia, University of Pennsylvania Press.

Cumberbatch, G. and R. M. Negrine (1991). *Images of Disability on Television*. London/New York, Routledge.

Curran, J. (1997). Television journalism: theory and practice. In P. Holland, ed., *The Television Handbook*. London, Routledge.

Curran, J. and J. Seaton (1981). *Power without Responsibility: the press and broadcasting in Britain*. London, Fontana.

Currie, D. H. (1999). *Girl Talk: adolescent magazines and their readers*. Toronto, University of Toronto Press.

D'Acci, J. (1994). *Defining Women: television and the case of Cagney & Lacey*. Chapel Hill, University of North Carolina Press.

De Lauretis, T. (1984). *Alice Doesn't: feminism, semiotics, cinema*. Bloomington, Indiana University Press.

De Lauretis, T. (1989). *Technologies of Gender: essays on theory, film, and fiction*. Basingstoke, Macmillan.

Dent, G., M. Wallace et al. (1992). *Black Popular Culture*. Seattle, Bay Press.

Dines, G. and J. M. Humez (2003). *Gender, Race and Class in Media: a text reader*, 2nd edn. Thousand Oaks, Calif., Sage.

Doty, A. and B. Gove (1997). Queer representation in the mass media. In A. Medhurst and S. Munt, eds, *Lesbian and Gay Studies Reader*. London, Cassell.

Dovey, J. (2000). *Freak Show: first person media and factual television*. London, Pluto.

Dow, B. J. (1996). *Prime-time Feminism: television, media culture, and the women's movement since 1970*. Philadelphia, University of Pennsylvania Press.

Dowd Hall, J. (1983). 'The mind that burns in each body': women, rape and racial violence. In A. Snitow, A. Stansell and S. Thompson, eds, *Powers of Desire: the politics of sexuality*. New York, Monthly Review Press.

Du Gay, P. (1997). *Doing Cultural Studies: the story of the Sony Walkman*. London/Thousand Oaks, Calif., Sage in association with the Open University.

Dyer, G. (1982). *Advertising as Communication*. London, Methuen.

Dyer, R. (1982). Don't look now: the male pin-up. *Screen* 23(3–4): 61–73.

Edwards, T. (1997). *Men in the Mirror: men's fashion, masculinity and consumer society*. London, Cassell.

Edwards, T. (2003). Sex, booze and fags: masculinity, style and men's magazines. In B. Benwell, ed., *Masculinity and Men's Lifestyle Magazines*. Oxford, Blackwell.

Ehrenreich, B. (1983). *The Hearts of Men: American dreams and the flight from commitment*. London, Pluto.

Ehrenreich, B. (1995). In defence of talk shows. *Time* magazine, 4 December.

Eie, B. (1998). *Who Speaks on Television? A European comparative study of female participation in TV programmes*. Oslo, NRk.

Epstein, D. and D. Steinberg (1996). 'All het up': rescuing heterosexuality on the Oprah Winfrey show. *Feminist Review*, no. 57.

Epstein, S. (1996). A queer encounter: sociology and the study of sexuality. In S. Seidman, ed., *Queer/Sociology*. Oxford, Blackwell.

Fairclough, N. (1989). *Language and Power*. Harlow, Longman.

Fairclough, N. (1995). *Media Discourse*. London/New York, E. Arnold.

Faludi, S. (1992). *Backlash: the undeclared war against women*. London, Chatto & Windus.

Featherstone, M. (1991). *Consumer Culture and Postmodernism*. London, Sage.

Feldman, S. (2000). Twin Peaks: the staying power of BBC Radio 4's Woman's Hour. In C. Mitchell, ed., *Women and Radio: airing differences*. London, Routledge.

Fielding, H. (1996). *Bridget Jones's Diary*. London, Picador.

Fielding, H. (2000). *The Edge of Reason*. London, Picador.

Fine, M. (1996). *Off White: readings on race, power and society*. New York, Routledge.

Fine, M. (2004). *Off White: readings on power, privilege, and resistance*. New York, Routledge.

Firestone, S. (1971). *The Dialectic of Sex: the case for a feminist revolution*. London, Jonathan Cape.

Fiske, J. (1987). *Television Culture*. London, Routledge.

Fiske, J. (1990). Television and women's culture: the politics of the popular. In M. E. Brown, *Television and Women's Culture*. London, Sage.

Fleming, J. (1996). *Hello Boys*. London, Penguin.

Foster, H., ed. (1985). *Postmodern Culture*. London, Pluto.

Foucault, M. (1978). *The History of Sexuality*. New York, Pantheon.

Foucault, M. (1980). *Power/Knowledge: selected interviews and other writings, 1972–1977*, ed. C. Gordon. New York, Pantheon.

Frankenberg, R. (1993). *White Women, Race Matters: the social construction of whiteness*. Minneapolis, University of Minnesota Press.

Franklin, B. (1997). *Newzak and News Media*. London, Arnold.

Franks, S. (1999). *Having None of It: women, men and the future of work*. London, Granta.

Fraser, N. (1989). *Unruly Practices: power, discourse and gender in contemporary social theory*. Minneapolis, University of Minnesota Press/Cambridge, Polity.

Frazer, E. (1987). Teenage girls reading Jackie. *Media, Culture and Society* 9: 407–25.

Friedan, B. (1963). *The Feminine Mystique*. London, Gollancz.

Frosh, S., A. Phoenix and R. Pattman (2000). 'But it's racism I really hate': young masculinities, racism and psychoanalysis. *Psychoanalytic Psychology* 17: 225–42.

Frosh, S., A. Phoenix and R. Pattman (2002). *Young Masculinities: understanding boys in contemporary society*. Basingstoke, Palgrave.

Furnham, A. and N. Bitar (1993). The stereotyped portrayal of men and women in British television advertisements. *Sex Roles* 29(3/4): 297–310.

Furnham, A. and E. Skae (1997). Changes in stereotyped portrayal of men and women in British advertisements. *Sex Roles* 29: 297–310.

Gallagher, M. (2001). *Gender Setting: new media agendas for monitoring and advocacy*. New York, Zed Books.

Galtung, J. and M. Ruge (1973). Structuring and selecting news. In S. C. and J. Young, eds, *The Manufacture of News, Deviance, Social Problems and Mass Media*. London, Sage/Constable.

Gamson, J. (1998). *Freaks Talk Back: tabloid talk shows and sexual nonconformity*. Chicago, University of Chicago Press.

Gauntlett, D. (2002). *Media, Gender and Identity: an introduction*. London, Routledge.

Gayle, M. (1998). *My Legendary Girlfriend*. London, Flame.

Gayle, M. (1999). *Mr Commitment*. London, Flame.

Geraghty, C. (1991). *Women and Soap Opera: a study of prime time soaps*. Cambridge, Polity.

Giddens, A. (1991). *Modernity and Self-Identity: self and society in the late modern age*. Cambridge, Polity.

Gilkes, M., A. Kaloski-Naylor et al. (1999). *White? Women: critical perspectives on race and gender*. York, Raw Nerve Books.

Gill, R. (1993). Justifying Injustice: broadcasters' accounts of inequality in radio. In E. Burman and I. Parker, eds, *Discourse Analytic Research: Readings and Repertoires of Texts in Action*. London, Routledge.

Gill, R. (2003). Power and the production of subjects: a genealogy of the new man and the new lad. In B. Benwell, ed., *Masculinity and Men's Lifestyle Magazines*. Oxford, Blackwell.

Gill, R. and E. Herdieckerhoff (2006). Rewriting the romance? New femininities in chicklit. *Feminist Media Studies* 6.

Gill, R., K. Henwood and C. McLean (2000). The tyranny of the six pack? In C. Squire, ed., *Culture in Psychology*. London, Routledge.

Gill, R., K. Henwood and C. McLean (2005). Body projects: the normative regulation of masculinity. *Body and Society* 11(1): 37–63.

Gillespie, M. (1995). *Television, Ethnicity and Social Change*. London, Routledge.

Gledhill, C. (1978). Recent developments in feminist criticism. *Quarterly Review of Film Studies* 3(4): 457–93.

Glynn, K. (2000). *Tabloid Culture: trash taste, popular power, and the transformation of American television*. Durham, NC, Duke University Press.

Goffman, E. (1979). *Gender Advertisements*. London, Macmillan.

Goldman, R. (1992). *Reading Ads Socially*. London/New York, Routledge.

Gray, A. (1987). Behind closed doors: video recorders in the home. In H. Baehr and A. Dyer, eds, *Boxed in: women and television*. London, Pandora.

Gray, A. (1992). *Video Playtime: the gendering of a leisure technology*. London/New York, Routledge.

Gray, J. (2002). *Men are from Mars, Women are from Venus: how to get what you want in your relationships*. London, HarperCollins.

Green, J. (1998). *Jemima J*. London, Penguin.

Green, J. (2002). *Babyville*. London, Penguin.

Greer, G. (1999). *The Whole Woman*. London, Doubleday.

Griffin, G., ed. (2001). *Visibility Blues: representations of HIV and AIDS*. Manchester, Manchester University Press.

Grimshaw, J. (1999). Working out with Merleau Ponty. In J. Arthurs and J. Grimshaw, eds, *Women's Bodies: discipline and transgression*. London, Cassell.

Grindstaff, L. (2002). *The Money Shot: trash, class, and the making of TV talk shows*. Chicago, University of Chicago Press.

Grint, K. and R. Gill, eds (1995). *The Gender Technology Relation: contemporary theory and research*. London, Taylor & Francis.

Gunter, B. (1995). *Television and Gender Representation*. London, John Libbey.

Haarman, J. (2001). Performing talk. In A. Tolson, ed., *Television Talk Shows*. Hillsdale, NJ, Lawrence Erlbaum.

Habermas, J. (1992). *The Structural Transformation of the Public Sphere: an inquiry into a category of bourgeois society*. Cambridge, Polity.

Hakkala, U. (2001). Masculinity in Advertising: a semiotic analyisis of Finnish and US print advertising. Turku, School of Economics and Business Administration.

Hall, S. (1973). A world at one with itself. In S. Cohen and J. Young, eds, *The Manufacture of News, Deviance and Social Problems*. London, Hutchinson.

Hall, S. (1980). Recent developments in theories of language and ideology: a critical note. In S. Hall, D. Hobson, P. Lowe and P. Willis, eds, *Culture Media Language: working papers in cultural studies 1972–9*. London, Hutchinson.

Hall, S. (1982). The rediscovery of 'ideology': return of the repressed in media studies. In M. Gurevitch, T. Bennett, J. Curran and J. Woollacott, eds, *Culture, Society and the Media*. London, Methuen.

Hall, S. (1986). Cultural studies: two paradigms. In J. Curran, M. Gurevitch and J. Woollacott, eds, *Media, Knowledge and Power*. Milton Keynes, Open University Press.

Hall, S. (1988a). New ethnicities. In K. Mercer, ed., *Black Film, British Cinema*. London, BFI/ICA Documents 7.

Hall, S. (1988b). The toad in the garden: Thatcherism among the theorists. In C. Nelson and L. Grossberg, eds, *Marxism and the Interpretation of Culture*. Basingstoke, Macmillan.

Hall, S. (1996). When was 'the post-colonial'? Thinking at the limit. In I. Chambers and L. Curti, eds, *The Post-colonial Question: common skies, divided horizons*. New York, Routledge.

Hamill, L. and A. Lasen (2005). *Mobile World: past, present and future*. London, Springer Verlag.

Harding, S. (1993). Rethinking standpoint epistemology: what is 'strong objectivity'? In L. Alcoff and E. Potter, eds, *Feminist Epistemologies*. London, Routledge.

Hare, D. (1992). The Late Show, BBC2, 15 October.

Harvey, D. (1990). *The Condition of Postmodernity: an enquiry into the origins of cultural change*. Oxford, Blackwell.

Hebdige, D. (1988). *Hiding in the Light: on images and things*. London/New York, Routledge.

Hemmings, C. (2002). *Bisexual Spaces: a geography of sexuality and gender*. New York, Routledge.

Henley, J. (2003). Ads with arrogance. *Guardian*, 8 October.

Hennessee, J. and J. Nicholson (1972). NOW says: TV commercials insult women. *New York Times Magazine* 13: 48–51.

Hermes, J. (1995). *Reading Women's Magazines: an analysis of everyday media use*. Cambridge, Polity.

Hevey, D. (1992). *The Creatures Time Forgot: photography and disability imagery*. London, Routledge.

Hill, D. (1997). *The Future of Men*. London, Phoenix.

Hill Collins, P. (1989). The Social Construction of Black Feminist Thought. *Signs* 4(4): 745–73.

Hill-Collins, P. (1991). *Black Feminist Thought: knowledge, consciousness and the politics of empowerment*. New York, Routledge.

Hodges, I. (2001). A problem aired: radiotherapeutic discourse and modes of subjection. In J. Morss, N. Stephenson and H. Van Rappard, eds, *Theoretical Issues in Psychology*. Massachusetts, Kluwer.

Hodges, I. (2003). Broadcasting the audience: radiotherapeutic discourse and its implied listeners. *International Journal of Critical Psychology* 7: 74–101.

Holden, W. (2000). *Bad Heir Day*. London, Headline.

Hollows, J. (2000a). *Feminism, Femininity, and Popular Culture*. New York, Manchester University Press.

Hollows, J. (2000b). Makeover takeover on British TV. *Screen* 41(3): 299–314.

Hollows, J. (2003). Feeling like a domestic goddess: postfeminism and cooking. *European Journal of Cultural Studies* 6(2): 179–202.

hooks, b. (1982). *Ain't I a Woman: black women and feminism*. London, Pluto Press.

hooks, b. (1984). *Feminist Theory from Margin to Centre*, Boston, South End Press.

hooks, b. (1990). *Yearning: race, gender, and cultural politics*. Toronto, Between the Lines.

Hrzenjak, M., K. H. Vidmar, Z. Drglin, V. Vendramin, J. Legan and U. Skumarc (2002). *Making Her Up: women's magazines in Slovenia*. Ljubljana, Mediawatch.

Hutchby, I. (2001). Confrontation as spectacle: argumentative frame of the Ricki Lake Show. In A. Tolson, ed., *Television Talk Shows*. Hillsdale, NJ, Lawrence Erlbaum Associates.

Ingraham, C. (1999). *White Weddings: romancing heterosexuality in popular culture*. New York, Routledge.

Jackson, P. (1994). Blackmale: advertising and the cultural politics of masculinity. *Gender, Place and Culture* 1: 49–60.

Jackson, P., N. Stevenson and K. Brooks (2001). *Making Sense of Men's Magazines*. Malden, Mass., Polity.

Jackson, S. (1995). Women and Heterosexual Love: complicity, resistance and change. In L. Pearce and J. Stacey, eds, *Romance Revisited*. London, Lawrence & Wishart.

Jaddou, L. and J. Williams (1981). A theoretical contribution to the struggle against the domination representations of women. *Media, Culture and Society* 3(2): 105–24.

Jameson, F. (1984). Postmodernism, or the cultural logic of late capitalism. *New Left Review* 146: 53–92.

Jeffords, S. (1994). *Hard Bodies: Hollywood masculinity in the Reagan years*. New Brunswick, NJ, Rutgers University Press.

Jenkins, A. (2000). *Honey Moon*. London, Flame.

Jhally, S. (1987). *The Codes of Advertising: fetishism and the political economy of meaning in the consumer society*. London, Pinter.

Johnson, L. and J. Lloyd (2004). *Sentenced to Everyday Life: feminism and the housewife*. Oxford, Berg.

Jones, A. R. (1986). Mills & Boon meets feminism. In J. Radford, ed., *The Progress of Romance: the politics of popular fiction*. London, Routledge.

Kaplan, E. A. (1992). Feminist criticism and television. In R. C. Allen, *Channels of Discourse, Re-assembled*. London, Routledge.

Keen, S. (1991). *Fire in the Belly: on being a man*. New York, Bantam.

Kennedy, H. (1992). *Eve was Framed: women and British justice*. London, Chatto & Windus.

Keyes, M. (2002). *Angels*. London, Penguin.

Kilbourne, J. (1995). Beauty and the beast of advertising. In G. Dines and J. Humez, eds, *Gender, Race and Class in Media*. Thousand Oaks, Calif., Sage.

Kilbourne, J. (1999). *Deadly Persuasion: why women and girls must fight the addictive power of advertising*. New York, Free Press.

Kilbourne, J. (2000). *Can't Buy my Love: how advertising changes the way we think and feel*. New York/London, Touchstone.

Kim, J. (2005). Global media, audience and transformative identities: femininities and consumption in South Korea. PhD thesis, London School of Economics.

Kimmel, M. (2001). Masculinity as homophobia: fear, shame and silence in the constitution of gender identity. In S. Whitehead and F. J. Barrett, eds, *The Masculinities Reader*. Cambridge, Polity.

Kinsella, S. (2000). *The Secret Dreamworld of a Shopaholic*. London, Black Swan.

Kirkham, P. and B. Skeggs (1998). Absolutely fabulous: absolutely feminist? In C. Geraghty and D. Lusted, eds, *The Television Studies Book*. London, Sage.

Kitzinger, J. (1998). The gender politics of news production: silenced voices and false memories. In C. Carter, G. Branston and S. Allan, eds, *News Gender and Power*. London, Routledge.

Kivikuru, U. (1997). Women in the Media: Report on existing research in the European Union (available from author).

Klein, N. (1999). *No Logo: taking aim at the brand bullies*. New York, Picador USA.

Klobas, L. E. (1988). *Disability Drama in Television and Film*. Jefferson, NC, McFarland.

Knight, I. (2002). *Don't You Want Me?* London, Penguin.

Laclau, E. (1977). *Politics and Ideology in Marxist Theory: capitalism, fascism, populism*. London, New Left Books.

Laclau, E. and C. Mouffe (1985). *Hegemony and Socialist Strategy: towards a radical democratic politics*. London, Verso.

Lafky, S. A. (1989). The progress of women and people of color in the US journalistic workforce: a long, slow journey. In P. J. Creedon, ed., *Women in Mass Communication*. Thousand Oaks, Calif., Sage.

Lafky, S. A. (1991). Women Journalists. In D. H. Weaver and G. Cleveland Wilhoit, eds, *The American Journalist: a portrait of US news people and their work*. Bloomington, Indiana University Press.

Langer, J. (1997). *Tabloid Television: popular journalism and the 'other news'*. London/New York, Routledge.

Lazar, M. (2004). (Post-) feminism in contemporary advertising: a global discourse in a local context. Paper presented at Globalisation, Media, Gender Workshop. Cardiff University.

Lazar, M. (2006). 'Discover the power of femininity!': analysing global 'power femininity' in local advertising. *Feminist Media Studies* 6.

Lazier-Smith (1989). A new 'generation' of images to women. In P. J. Creedon, ed., *Women in Mass Communication: challenging gender values*. London, Sage.

Lee, V. (1996). Knickers in a twist. *Guardian*, 14 May.

Lees, S. (1996). *Ruling Passions: sexual violence, reputation, and the law*. Philadelphia, Open University Press.

Leiss, W., S. Kline and S. Jhally (1986). *Social Communication in Advertising: persons, products & images of well-being: William Leiss, Stephen Kline, Sut Jhally*. Toronto/London, Methuen.

Levine, L. (1988). *High Brow Lowbrow: the experience of cultural hierarchy in America*. Cambridge, Mass., Harvard University Press.

Light, A. (1989). Putting on the style: feminist criticism in the 1990s. In H. Carr, ed., *From my Guy to SciFi: genre and women's writing in the postmodern world*. London, Pandora.

Livingstone, S. and G. Green (1986). Television advertisements and the portrayal of gender. *British Journal of Social Psychology* 25: 149–54.

Livingstone, S. M. and P. K. Lunt (1994). *Talk on Television: audience participation and public debate*. London/New York, Routledge.

Lorde, A. (1984). *Sister Outsider: essays and speeches*. Trumansburg, NY, Crossing Press.

Lotz, A. (2001). Postfeminist television criticism: rehabilitating critical terms and identifying postfeminist attributes. *Feminist Media Studies* 1(1): 105–21.

Lovdal, L. T. (1989). Sex role messages in television commercials: an update. *Sex Roles* 21: 715–24.

Lupton, D. (1994). Talking about sex: sexology, sexual difference and confessional talk shows. *Gender* 20: 45–65.

Lyotard, J.-F. (1984). *The Postmodern Condition: a report on knowledge*. Manchester, Manchester University Press.

McClintock, A. (1995). *Imperial Leather: race, gender and sexuality in the colonial conquest*. New York/London, Routledge.

McCracken, E. (1993). *Decoding Women's Magazines*. Basingstoke, Macmillan.

Macdonald, M. (1995). *Representing Women: myths of femininity in the popular media*. London, E. Arnold.

Machin, D. and J. Thornborrow (2003). Branding and discourse: the case of Cosmopolitan. *Discourse & Society* 14: 453–71.

Mackinnon, K. (2003). *Representing Men: maleness and masculinity in the media*. London, E. Arnold.

Mclaughin, L. (1993). Chastity criminals in the age of electronic reproduction: reviewing talk television and the public sphere. *Journal of Communication Inquiry* 17(1): 41–55.

McNair, B. (2002). *Striptease Culture: sex, media and the democratization of desire*. London, Routledge.

McNay, L. (1992). *Foucault and Feminism: power, gender and the self*. Cambridge, Polity.

McRobbie, A. (1977). Jackie: an ideology of adolescent femininity. CCCS occasional paper, Birmingham, University of Birmingham.

McRobbie, A. (1978). Working class girls and the culture of femininity. In CCCS Women's Studies Group, *Women Take Issue*. London, Hutchinson.

McRobbie, A. (1991). *Feminism and Youth Culture: from 'Jackie' to 'Just Seventeen'*. Basingstoke, Macmillan Education.

McRobbie, A. (1999). *In the Culture Society: art, fashion, and popular music*. London/New York, Routledge.

McRobbie, A. (2004a). Notes on postfeminism and popular culture: Bridget Jones and the new gender regime. In A. Harris, ed., *All about the Girl: culture, power and identity*. New York, Routledge.

McRobbie, A. (2004b). Notes on 'What Not to Wear' and post-feminist symbolic violence. In L. Adkins and B. Skeggs, eds, *Feminism after Bourdieu*. Oxford, Blackwell/*Sociological Review*.

McRobbie, A. (2004c). Post feminism and popular culture. *Feminist Media Studies* 4(3): 255–64.

McRobbie, A. (2004d). 'The rise and rise of porn chic'. *Times Higher Education Supplement*, 2 January.

Maddison, S. and M. Storr (2002). The edge of reason: the myth of Bridget Jones. Paper presented at Transformation in Politics, Culture and Society Conference, Brussels.

Magor, M. (2002). News terrorism: misogyny exposed and the easy journalism of conflict. *Feminist Media Studies* 2(1): 141–4.

Majors, R. and J. Billson (1992). *Cool Pose: the dilemmas of black manhood in America*. New York, Lexington.

Mansell, J. (1997). *Perfect Timing*. London, Headline.

Marinescu (1995). Does indeed Angela walk along? Women and media in the Romanian case. Paper at IAMCR Conference, Communication Beyond Nation State, Portoroz, Slovenia.

Marx, K. and F. Engels (1970). *The German Ideology*. London, Lawrence & Wishart.

Mascariotte, G. J. (1991). C'mon Girl: Oprah Winfrey and the discourse of feminine talk. *Gender* 11: 81–110.

Mather, A. (1977). *Born Out of Love*. London, Mills & Boon.

Mayes, T. (2000). Submerging in 'therapy news'. *British Journalism Review 430–5* 1(4): 30–5.

Media Watch (1995). *Women's Participation in the News: global media monitoring project*. Toronto, Media Watch.

Mercer, K. (1994). *Welcome to the Jungle: new positions in black cultural studies*. New York, Routledge.

Merskin, D. (2003). Fashioning foreplay: fashion advertising and the pornographic imagination. *Feminist Media Studies* 3(1): 106–9.

Meyers, M. (1997). *News Coverage of Violence against Women: engendering blame*. Thousand Oaks, Calif., Sage.

Miller, P. and N. Rose (1997). Mobilizing the consumer: assembling the subject of consumption. *Theory, Culture and Society* 14(1): 1–36.

Minh-ha, T. (1991). *When the Moon Waxes Red*. New York, Routledge.

Mirza, H. S. (1997). *Black British Feminism: a reader*. London, Routledge.

Mitchell, C. (2001). *Women and Radio*. London/New York, Routledge.

Modleski, T. (1982). *Loving with a Vengeance: mass produced fantasies for women*. New York, Routledge.

Modleski, T. (1991). *Feminism without Women*. New York, Routledge.

Mohanty, C. (1988). Under Western eyes: feminist scholarship and colonial discourses. *Feminist Review* 30: 51–79.

Montgomery, M. (1986). DJ Talk. *Media, Culture and Society* 8: 421–40.

Moore, J. (2005). *dot.homme*. London, Arrow Books.

Moore, S. (1988). Here's looking at you kid! In L. Gamman and M. Marshment, eds, *The Female Gaze: women as viewers of popular culture*. London, Women's Press.

Moore, S. (1991). *Looking for Trouble: on shopping, gender and the cinema*. London, Serpent's Tail.

Moores, S. (1988). 'The box on the dresser': memories of early radio and everyday life. *Media, Culture and Society* 10: 23–40.

Moorti, S. (2002). *Color of Rape: gender and race in television's public spheres*. Albany, State University of New York Press.

Morley, D. (1980). *The Nationwide Audience*. London, British Film Institute.

Morley, D. (1986). *Family Television: cultural power and domestic leisure*. London, Comedia.

Morley, D. (1992). *Television, Audiences and Cultural Studies*. London, Routledge.

Morley, D. and K. Robins (1995). *Spaces of Identity: global media, electronic landscapes and cultural boundaries*. London/New York, Routledge.

Mort, F. (1996). *Cultures of Consumption: commerce, masculinities and social space*. London/New York, Routledge.

Moseley, R. and J. Read (2002). Have it Ally: popular television and postfeminism. *Feminist Media Studies* 2(2): 231–50.

Mulvey, L. (1975). Visual pleasure and narrative cinema. *Screen* 16(3): 6–18.

Munson, W. (1993). *All Talk: the talkshow in media culture*. Philadelphia, Temple University Press.

Munson, W. (1995). Constellation of voices: how talk shows work. In G. Dines and J. M. Humez, eds, *Gender, Race and Class Media*. London, Sage.

Myers, G. (2001). 'I'm out of it; you guys argue': making an issue of the Jerry Springer show. In A. Tolson, ed., *Television Talk Shows*. Hillsdale, NJ, Lawrence Erlbaum Associates.

Myers, K. (1987). Towards a feminist erotica. In R. Betterton, ed., *Looking On: Images of Femininity in the Visual Arts and Media*. London & New York, Pandora.

Nathan, M. (2001). *Persuading Annie*. London, Piatkus Books.

Nixon, S. (1996). *Hard Looks: masculinities, spectatorship and contemporary consumption*. London, UCL Press.

Nixon, S. (2001). Re-signifying masculinity: from 'new man' to 'new lad'. In D. Morley and K. Robins, eds, *British Cultural Studies*. Oxford, Oxford University Press.

Nkweto-Simmond, F. (1995). Love in black and white. In L. Pearce and J. Stacey, eds, *Romance Revisited*. London, Lawrence & Wishart.

North, F. (1999). *Polly*. London, Arrow Books.

O'Hagan, S. (1991). Here comes the new lad. *Arena*, spring/summer.

Ong, A. (1988). Colonialism and modernity: feminist re-presentations of women in non-western societies. *Inscriptions* 3(4): 79–93.

Onwurah, C. (1987). Sexist, racist and above all capitalist: how women's magazines create media apartheid. In K. Davies, J. Dickey and T. Stratford, eds, *Out of Focus: writings on women and the Media*. London, Women's Press.

Osgerby, B. (2001). *Playboys in Paradise: masculinity, youth and leisure-style in modern America*. Oxford, Berg.

Osgerby, B. (2003). A pedigree of the consuming male: masculinity, consumption and the American 'leisure class'. In B. Benwell, ed., *Masculinity and Men's Lifestyle Magazines*. Oxford, Blackwell.

Parker, I. (1989). *The Crisis in Modern Social Psychology and How to End it*. London, Routledge.

Parkin, F. (1972). *Class Inequality and Political Order: social stratification in capitalist and communist societies*. London, Paladin.

Parks, A. (2001). *Game Over*. London, Penguin.

Parry-Giles, S. J. (2000). Mediating Hillary Rodham Clinton: television news practices and image-making in the postmodern age. *Critial Studies in Media Communication* 15(2): 171–207.

Parsons, T. (2003). *Man and Wife*. London, HarperCollins.

Pearce, L. and J. Stacey (1995). *Romance Revisited*. New York, New York University Press.

Peck, J. (1995). TV talk shows as therapeutic discourse: the ideological labour of the televised talk cure. *Communication Theory* 5(1): 58–81.

Pendergast, T. (2000). *Creating the Modern Man: American magazines and consumer culture, 1900–1950*. New York, Columbia University Press.

Perry, K. (1995). The Heart of Whiteness: white subjectivity and interracial relationship. In L. Pearce and J. Stacey, eds, *Romance Revisited*. London, Lawrence & Wishart.

Petley, J. and G. Romano (1993). After the deluge: public service television in western Europe. In T. Dowmunt, ed., *Channels of Resistance*. London, British Film Institute.

Phoenix, A. (1997). Theories of gender and black families. In H. S. Mirza, ed., *Black British Feminism: a reader*. London, Routledge.

Postman, N. (1986). *Amusing Ourselves to Death: public discourse in the age of show business*. London, Heinemann.

Potter, J. and M. Wetherell (1987). *Discourse and Social Psychology: beyond attitudes and behaviour*. London, Sage.

Press, A. (1990). Class, gender and the female viewer: women's responses to Dynasty. In M. E. Brown, ed., *Television and women's culture*. London and Newbury Park, Calif., Sage.

Press, A. L. (1991). *Women Watching Television: gender, class, and generation in the American television experience*. Philadelphia, University of Pennsylvania Press.

Press, A. L. and E. R. Cole (1999). *Speaking of Abortion: television and authority in the lives of women*. Chicago, University of Chicago Press.

Priest, P. J. (1995). *Public Intimacies: talk show participants and tell-all TV*. Cresskill, NJ, Hampton Press.

Pring-Ellis, J. (2001). Harmless fun or cause for concern? The reputation of women in FHM magazine. London, Masters dissertation, LSE.

Probyn, E. (1993). *Sexing the Self: gendered positions in cultural studies*. New York, Routledge.

Probyn, E. (1997a). Michel Foucault and the uses of sexuality. In A. Medhurst and S. Munt, eds, *Lesbian and Gay Studies: a critical introduction*. London, Cassell.

Probyn, E. (1997b). New traditionalism and post-feminism: TV does the home. In C. Brunsdon, J. D'Acci and L. Spigel, eds, *Feminist Television Criticism: a reader*. Oxford, Blackwell.

Quinonez, N. and A. Aldama, eds (2002). *Decolonial Voices: chicana and chicanocultural studies in the 21st century*. Bloomington: Indiana University Press.

Rabinovitz, L. (1999). Ms-representation: the politics of feminist sitcoms. In M. B. Haralovitch and L. Rabinovitz, eds, *Television, History and American Culture*. Durham, NC, Duke University Press.

Radner, H. (1993). Pretty is as pretty does: free enterprise and the marriage plot. In J. Collins, H. Radner and A. Preacher Collins, eds, *Film Theory Goes to the Movies*. London, Routledge.

Radner, H. (1999). Queering the girl. In H. Radner and M. Luckett, eds, *Swinging Single: representing sexuality in the 1960s*. Minnesota, Minnesota Press.

Radway, J. (1984). *Reading the Romance: women, patriarchy and popular literature*. New York, Verso.

Rakow, L. (1992). *Gender on the Line: women, the telephone and community life*. Chicago, University of Illinois Press.

Ramazanoglu, C. (1989). *Feminism and the Contradictions of Oppression*. London, Routledge.

Rapping, E. (1995). Daytime inquiries. In G. Dines and J. M. Humez, eds, *Gender, Race and Class in Media*. Thousand Oaks, Calif., Sage. London, Sage.

Rapping, E. (1996). *The Culture of Recovery: making sense of the self-help movement in women's lives*. Boston, Beacon Press.

Rattansi, A. (1992). Changing the subject? Racism, culture and education. In J. Donald and A. Rattansi, eds, *'Race', Culture and Difference*. London, Sage.

Robb, J. (1999). *The Nineties: what the fuck was all that about?* London, Ebury Press.

Roiphe, K. (1993). *The Morning After: sex, fear, and feminism on campus*. Boston, Little Brown.

Romance Writers of America (2002). RWA defines the romance novel. At www.rwanational.org.

Rose, N. (1989). *Governing the Soul: technologies of human subjectivity*. London, Routledge.

Rose, N. (1990). *Governing the Soul: the shaping of the private self*. London/New York, Routledge.

Rose, N. (1996). *Inventing Our Selves: psychology, power and personhood*. New York, Cambridge University Press.

Ross, K. (2002). *Women, Politics, Media: uneasy relations in comparative perspective*. Cresskill, NJ, Hampton Press.

Roventa-Frumusani, D. (1995). Images of women in the postcommunist society and media: Romania's case. A Paper at IAMCR conference, Communication Beyond Nation State, Potoroz, Slovenia.

Rowe, K. (1997). Roseanne: unruly woman as domestic goddess. In C. Brunsdon, J. D'Acci and L. Spigel, eds, *Feminist Television Criticism*. Oxford, Oxford University Press.

Royal, C. (2003). Narrative structure in *Sex and the City*: I couldn't help but wonder. Unpublished article available at www.cindyroyal.com/ronal_sex_ paper.

Said, E. W. (1985). *Orientalism*. Harmondsworth, Penguin.

Sandoval, C. (1991). 'Us Third World Feminism': The Theory and Method of Oppositional Consciousness in the Postmodern world. *Genders* 10: 1–23.

Saussure, F. de., ed. R. Harris et al. (1974). *A Course in General Linguistics*. London, Duckworth.

Sawicki, J. (1991). *Disciplining Foucault: feminism, power and the body*. New York, Routledge.

Scannell, P. (1989). Public service broadcasting and modern public life. *Media, Culture and Society* 11: 135–66.

Scannell, P., ed. (1991). *Broadcast Talk*. London, Sage.

Sebba, A. (1994). *Battling for News: the rise of the woman reporter*. London, Sceptre.

Sedgwick, E. K. (1991). *Epistemology of the Closet*. London, Harvester Wheatsheaf.

Segal, L. (1990). *Slow Motion: changing masculinity, changing men*. London, Virago.

Seighart, M. and G. Henry (1998). *The Cheaper Sex: how women lose out in journalism*. London: Women in Journalism.

Shakespeare, T. and M. Corker, eds (2002). *Disability/postmodernity: embodying disability theory*. London, Continuum.

Shalit, W. (1999). Sex, Sadness and the City. *Urbanities* 9(4): 1–6.

Shattuc, J. (1997). *The Talking Cure: TV talk shows and women*. New York/London, Routledge.

Silverstone, R. and E. Hirsch (1992). *Consuming Technologies: media and information in domestic spaces*. London/New York, Routledge.

Simpson, M. (1994). *Male Impersonators: men performing masculinity*. London, Cassell.

Sinfield, A. (1994). *Cultural Politics: queer reading*. London, Routledge.

Skeggs, B. (1997). *Formations of Class and the Gender: becoming respectable*. London, Sage.

Snitow, A. (1986). Mass market romance: pornography for women is different. In A. Snitow, C. Stansell and S. Thompson, eds, *Desire: the politics of sexuality*. London, Virago.

Sonnet, E. (2002). Erotic fiction by women for women: the pleasures of post-feminist heterosexuality. *Sexualities* 2(2): 167–87.

Soothill, K. and S. Walby (1991). *Sex Crimes in the News*. London, Routledge.

Speer, S. (2005). *Gender Talk: feminism, discourse and conversation analysis*. London, Routledge.

Spender, D. (1985). *Man Made Language*. London, Routledge & Kegan Paul.

Spivak, G. C. (1988). Can the subaltern speak? In C. Nelson and L. Grossberg, eds, *Marxism and the Interpretation of Culture*. London, Macmillan.

Springer, K. (2002). Third wave black feminsim? *Signs: Journal of Women in Culture and Society* 27(4).

Squire, C. (1997). Empowering women? The Oprah Winfrey Show. In C. Brunsdon, J. D'Acci and L. Spigel, eds, *Feminist Television Criticism: A Reader*. Oxford, Oxford University Press.

Squire, C. (2003). Can an HIV positive woman find True Love? Romance in the stories of women living with HIV. *Feminism and Psychology* 13(1): 73–100.

Sreberny-Mohammadi, A. and L. Van Zoonen (2000). *Gender, Politics and Communication*. Cresskill, NJ, Hampton Press.

Stacey, J. (1987). Sexism by a subtler name: postindustrial conditions and postfeminist consciousness in the Silicon Valley. *Socialist Review* 17(6): 7–28.

Stenner, P. and P. Lunt (2005). The Jerry Springer Show and the emotional public shere. *Media, Culture and Society* 27(1): 59–81.

Stevenson, N., P. Jackson and K. Brooks (2000). The politics of 'new' men's lifestyle magazines. *European Journal of Cultural Studies* 3(3): 366–85.

Stevenson, N., P. Jackson and K. Brooks (2003). Reading men's lifestyle magazines: cultural power and the information society. In B. Benwell, ed., *Masculinity and Men's Lifestyle Magazines*. Oxford, Blackwell.

Storr, M. (2003). *Latex and Lingerie: shopping for pleasure at Ann Summers parties*. Oxford, Berg.

Swanson, G. and P. Wise (1998). *Going for Broke: women's participation in the arts and cultural industries.*, Australian Key Centre for Cultural and Media Policies.

Tannen, D. (1992). *You Just Don't Understand: women and men in conversation*. London, Virago.

Tasker, Y. (1991). Having it all: feminism and the pleasures of the popular. In C. Lury, S. Franklin and J. Stacey, eds, *Off-centre: feminism and the cultural studies*. London, Routledge.

Tasker, Y. (1993). *Spectacular Bodies: gender, genre, and the action cinema*. London/New York, Routledge.

Tasker, Y. and D. Negra (2005). 'In focus' postfeminism and contemporary media studies. *Cinema Journal* 44(2): 107–10.

Taylor, K. (2006). Today's ultimate feminists are the chicks in crop tops. *Guardian*, 23 March.

Thompson, J. (1984). *Studies in the Theory of Ideology*. Cambridge, Polity.

Thornborrow, J. (2001). 'Has it ever happened to you?' Talk show stories as mediated performance. In A. Tolson, ed., *Television Talk Shows*. Hillsdale, NJ, Erlbaum Associates.

Tincknell, E. (2005). *Mediating the Family: gender, culture and representation*. London, Hodder Arnold.

Tincknell, E., D. Chambers, J. Van Loon and N. Hudson (2003). 'Begging for it': new femininities, social agency and moral discourse in contemporary teenage and men's magazines. *Feminist Media Studies* 3(1): 27–46.

Tsagarousianou, R. (2001). Diasporic audiences' media uses and constructions of 'community': the case of London's South Asian and Greek Cypriot communities. In K. Ross, ed., *Black Marks: research studies with minority ethnic audiences*. London, Ashgate.

Tuchman, G. (1978). The symbolic annihilation of women in the media. In G. Tuchman, A. Daniels and J. Benet, eds, *Health and Home: images of women in the mass media*. Oxford, Oxford University Press.

Turkle, S. (1984). *The Second Self: computers and the human spirit*. London, Granada.

Turner, J. (2005). Dirty Young Men. *Guardian Weekend*, 22 October.

Tweedie, J. (1984). *Letters from the Fainthearted Feminist*, London, Picador.

Ussher, J. M. (1997). *Fantasies of Femininity: reframing the boundaries of sex*. London/New York, Penguin Books.

Van Zoonen, L. (1994). *Feminist Media Studies*. London, Sage.

Van Zoonen, L. (1998). One of the girls? The changing gender of journalism. In C. Carter, G. Branston and S. Allan, eds, *News, Gender and Power*. London, Routledge.

Viner, K. (1999). The personal is still political. In N. Walter, ed., *On the Move: feminism for a new generation*. London, Virago.

Wajcman, J. (1991). *Feminism Confronts Technology*. Cambridge, Polity.

Walby, S. (1990). *Theorizing Patriarchy*. Oxford, Blackwell.

Walkerdine, V. (1997). *Daddy's Girl: young girls and popular culture*. London, Macmillan.

Walkerdine, V., H. Lucey and J. Melody (2001). *Growing up Girl: psychosocial explorations of gender and class*. Basingstoke, Palgrave.

Walklate, S. (2001). *Gender, Crime, and Criminal Justice*. Cullompton, Devon Portland, Oreg., Willan.

Walkosz, B. J. and H. C. Kenski (1995). The year of the woman: how the national media portrayed women in the 1992 election year. Paper presented at *Consoling Passions: television, video and feminism conference*. Tuscon, Ariz., April.

Ware, V. and L. Back (2002). *Out of Whiteness: color, politics, and culture*. Chicago, University of Chicago Press.

Waugh, D. (2002). *The New You Survival Kit*. London, HarperCollins.

Weed, E. and N. Schor, eds (1997). *Feminism Meets Queer Theory*. Bloomington, Indiana University Press.

Weedon, C. (1987). *Feminist Practice and Poststructuralist Theory*. Oxford, Basil Blackwell.

Weibel, K. (1977). *Mirror, Mirror: images of women reflected in popular culture*. New York, Anchor Books.

Weir, A. (1997). *Does my Bum Look Big in This?* London, Flame.

Weir, A. (2002). *Stupid Cupid.* London, Penguin.

Werkmeister, M. (2003). Men's magazines in Germany. At http://theoryhead. com/gender/germany.htm.

Wernick, A. (1991). *Promotional Culture: advertising, ideology and symbolic expression.* London, Sage.

Wetherell, M. (1995). Romantic discourse and feminist analysis: interrogating investment, power and desire. In S. Wilkinson and C. Kitzinger, eds, *Feminism and Discourse.* London, Sage.

Wetherell, M. and J. Potter (1992). *Mapping the Language of Racism: discourse and the legitimation of exploitation.* Hemel Hempstead, Harvester-Wheatsheaf.

Whelehan, I. (2000). *Overloaded: popular culture and the future of feminism.* London, Women's Press.

Whelehan, I. (2002). *Bridget Jones's Diary: a reader's guide.* London, Continuum.

Whelehan, I. (2004). Having it all (again?) Paper presented at ESRC Seminar on New Feminities, LSE November.

Whitaker, B. (1981). *News Limited: why you can't read all about it.* London, Minority Press Group.

White, S. and M. Wetherell (1987). Fear of fat: a study of discourses concerning eating patterns and body shape. Paper presented at the British Psychological Society annual Social Section conference, Canterbury.

Wicke, J. (1998). Celebrity material: materialist feminism and the culture of celebrity. In J. B. Landes, ed., *Feminism, the Public and the Private.* Oxford, Oxford University Press.

Williams, P. J. (1997). *Seeing a Color-blind Future: the paradox of race.* London, Virago.

Williamson, J. (1978). *Decoding Advertisements: ideology and meaning in advertisements.* London, Marion Boyars.

Williamson, J. (1986a). *Consuming Passions: the dynamics of popular culture.* London, Marion Boyars.

Williamson, J. (1986b). The problem being popular. *New Socialist* 4: 14–15.

Williamson, J. (1986c). Woman is an island: feminity and colonization. In T. Modleski, ed., *Studies in Entertainment: Critical Approaches to Mass Culture.* Bloomington, University of Indiana Press.

Williamson, J. (2003). Sexism with an alibi. *Guardian*, 31 May.

Wilton, T. (1994). Feminism and the erotics of health promotion. In L. Doyal, J. Naidoo and T. Wilton, eds, *AIDS: Setting a Feminist Agenda.* London, Taylor & Francis.

Wing, A. K., ed. (1997). *Critical Race Feminism: a reader.* New York, NYU Press.

Winship, J. (1978). A woman's world: women and ideology of feminism. In CCCS Women's Studies Group, *Women Take Issue.* Birmingham, Hutchinson.

Winship, J. (1981). Handling Sex. *Media, Culture and Society* 3(1): 25–41.

Winship, J. (1987). *Inside Women's Magazines.* London, Pandora.

Winship, J. (1991). The impossibility of *Best*: enterprise meets domesticity in the practical magazines of the 1980s. *Cultural Studies* 5(2): 131–55.

Winship, J. (2000). Women and outdoors: advertising, controversy and disputing feminism in the 1990s. *International Journal of Cultural Studies* 31(1): 27–55.

Wolf, N. (1990). *The Beauty Myth.* London, Chatto & Windus.

Wood, H. (2001). 'No, you rioted!' The pursuit of conflict in the management of 'lay' and 'expert' discourse on Kilroy. In A. Tolson, ed., *Television Talk Shows*. Hillsdale, NJ, Erlbaum Associates.

Wood, H. and B. Skeggs (2004). Notes on ethical scenarios of self on British reality TV. *Feminist Media Studies* 4(2): 205–8.

Yeatman, A. (1994). *Postmodern Revisionings of the Political*. New York, Routledge.

Young, L. (1996). *Fear of the Dark: 'race', gender and sexuality in the cinema*. London/New York, Routledge.

Yuan, F. (1999). A resource for rights: women and media in China. Paper presented at Women's World 99 International Interdisciplinary Congress on Women, Tromso, Norway.

Yuval-Davies, N., ed. (1989). *Woman-Nation-State*. London, Palgrave/Macmillan.

Index

Figures and boxes are indicated by italic type.